A Progress of Sentiments

David Hume, from an unsigned portrait, reproduced with the
kind permission of its owner, Ian Ross, W.S., Edinburgh.
Photo by Malcolm Liddell.

A Progress of Sentiments

Reflections on Hume's *Treatise*

Annette C. Baier

Harvard University Press
Cambridge, Massachusetts
London, England
1991

Library of Congress Cataloging-in-Publication Data

Baier, Annette.
A progress of sentiments: reflections on Hume's Treatise /
Annette C. Baier.
p.   cm.
Includes bibliographical references and index.
ISBN 0–674–71385–0
1. Knowledge, Theory of.   2. Reason.   3. Skepticism.
4. Philosophical anthropology.   I. Hume, David, 1711–1776.
Treatise of human nature.   II. Title.
B1489.B35   1991
128—dc20   90–47103
                                                  CIP

Contents

	Abbreviations	*vi*
	Preface	*vii*
1	Philosophy in This Careless Manner	*1*
2	Other Relations: The Account of Association	*28*
3	Customary Transitions from Causes to Effects	*54*
4	Necessity, Nature, Norms	*78*
5	The Simple Supposition of Continued Existence	*101*
6	Persons and the Wheel of Their Passions	*129*
7	The Direction of Our Conduct	*152*
8	The Contemplation of Character	*174*
9	A Catalogue of Virtues	*198*
10	The Laws of Nature	*220*
11	The Shelter of Governors	*255*
12	Reason and Reflection	*277*
	Chronology	*291*
	Notes	*295*
	Index	*325*

Abbreviations

T. David Hume, *A Treatise of Human Nature,* edited by
L. A. Selby-Bigge and P. H. Nidditch (Oxford: Clarendon
Press, 1978).

E. David Hume, *Enquiries,* edited by L. A. Selby-Bigge and
P. H. Nidditch (Oxford: Clarendon Press, 1975).

Essays David Hume, *Essays: Moral, Political and Literary,* edited by
Eugene F. Miller (Indianapolis: Liberty Classics, 1985).

Preface

As it has recently become the custom to ask: Why another book on Hume? Because he is a philosopher who invited "the latest posterity" to reinterpret him, because my own interpretations differ in some ways from others, including those to which I am very much indebted, and because my own interpretations of the *Treatise* would "loosen and fall of themselves, when unsupported by the approbation of others" (T. 264–265) or at least by the concurrence of some readers. To say this is to be a little disingenuous, since many colleagues, students, and friends and fellow Hume enthusiasts (if we may call ourselves that) have read and reacted to earlier versions of what this book says. Indeed it is largely because of their encouragement that I persevered with this book, which has been long in the making.

More than most of Hume's readers, I take his *Treatise* to be one work. It appeared serially, first two of its books, then the third, and in my view we understand none of them properly unless we understand all of them, and the progression of thought within the work as a whole. Like Descartes in his *Meditations,* so Hume in his *Treatise* stages a thinker's dramatic development from inadequate and doubt-inviting approaches to more satisfactory reflections. Hume's *Treatise* is "of human nature," and that is his topic throughout. One cannot say that epistemology is done, and finished with, within Book One, that passions are reserved for Book Two, and that Book Three is an appendix of interest only to moral philosophers. On the contrary, Hume tells us at the beginning of Book Three that his work is intended to acquire more force as it proceeds. In my treatment of it, I begin more or less in the middle, in the famous conclusion of Book One, return to the book that it concluded, then proceed to the subsequent books, for which it prepared the way. But even in later chapters, when I roughly follow Hume's order of treatment, I raid later and earlier discussions in the *Treatise* for insights on the topic under discussion.

I do not pretend to treat all the topics Hume discusses. Since I am not a mathematician I merely allude to his discussions in Part II of Book One, except where their themes prepare the way for his treatment of the identity of continuants. I refer to, but do not try to evaluate, his original and remarkable analysis of probability estimates. I merely touch on his treatment of other philosophers, ancient and modern. My main purpose is evident in my title: it is to present Hume's work as exhibiting a progress of thought and sentiment, and acquiring "new force as it advances" (T. 455). I attempt to restate Hume's positive theses about our efforts to determine truth and falsity, reason and folly. Hume's family's motto, which appears on his book plate, was "True to the End," and I think Hume was, in his literary career, true to the end to the program he evolved and laid out in the *Treatise*. But it is only at the end of the *Treatise* that we can fully grasp what Hume has shown us there about "truth and falshood, reason and folly," and about the connection between the truth of beliefs and being "true to the end". It is only from the vantage point of the end of the journey that we can appreciate the nature of the journey and the steadfastness of the traveller. I believe that the quest that was begun in the *Treatise* was continued in Hume's later works, so that, to see the *Treatise* properly, it helps to have the vantage point of the *Enquiries, Essays* and *Histories*. The unity of Hume's thought not merely in the *Treatise* but in all his writings is increasingly recognized, so that there is nothing very novel in my assumption that, to understand any of it, we have to form some hypothesis about its unifying goal, about the purpose to which Hume was true to the end. Hume scholars can be expected to disagree about the best characterization of this goal, and about the extent of the corrections of method, direction, and conclusions that Hume made in works after the *Treatise*. In principle the sort of interpretation I advance here should be continued beyond the *Treatise* to the later works, and so I hope it will be, if not by me then by some sympathetic Hume interpreter, or group of us. For the moral of the story, as I am telling it, is that *all* our interpretations will "loosen and fall of themselves" until they become cooperative and mutually corrective.

My own retracing of Hume's path has been anything but steadfast. There have been many shoals and near shipwrecks, many temptations to abandon ship and sit it out on some not so barren rock. But rescuers always turned up. My debts are almost too many to try to list. My first philosophy teacher at Otago University, David Daiches Raphael, passed on to me his contagious interest in Hume's ethics. From my later teacher there, John Passmore, I caught puzzlement about the overall intent of the author of the *Treatise*. From my colleague at the University of Auckland, Richard P. Anshutz, I received a farewell gift of a first edition of Hume's most extraordinary work, *My Own Life,* and so began to try to connect the life to the works. John Mackie was my colleague at the University of Sydney, and conversations with him there, as well as reading his subsequent books on Hume's account of causation, and on his moral theory, have helped me in my attempts to connect these Humean themes. Conversations with John Bricke, David Falk, Robert Fogelin, Peter Jones, Donald Livingston, Alasdair MacIntyre, Barry Stroud and Fred Whelan, as well as reading what they wrote, have enlightened me, and also stimulated me to try to correct some of what I saw as their overemphases. I am of course in debt to the classics by John Laird, H. H. Price and Kemp Smith, to Páll Árdal's more recent classic, and to many others who have written about Hume. Members of the Hume Society have over many years provided good discussion and good fellowship, as have my colleagues and former colleagues Bob Brandom, Joe Camp, Richard Gale, David Gauthier, Adolf Grünbaum, Paul Guyer, John Haugeland, Louis Loeb, Jerry Massey, John McDowell, Mickey Perloff, Wes Salmon and Jerry Schneewind, with all of whom I have discussed Hume's views. From Duncan Forbes's writings, from Robert and Carolyn Birmingham, Neil MacCormick and Gerald Postema, I have been helped to see the influence of Hume's law studies. From fellows with me at the University of Edinburgh "Institute Project Scottish

Enlightenment," in 1986, I learned a lot about Hume's Scottish cultural environment. From a host of graduate students who shared or patiently indulged my Hume enthusiasms, I have had helpful reactions and encouragement. Among the fellow enthusiasts were Walter Brand, Alisa Carse, Deb deBruin, Richard Dees, Ken Gemes, Patrick Maher, Arthur Ripstein, Rob Shaver, Saul Traiger, Bill Vitek and Chris Williams. They and other sympathetic readers of earlier drafts have kept alive my occasionally flagging resolve to get this book written. Chris Williams also checked the endnotes and many of the quotations from Hume in the text, and corrected numberless infirmities. (He found me to have displayed a truly eighteenth-century insouciance regarding accuracy of quotation.) Remaining errors, of this and other sorts, are of course my own.

I am grateful to a descendant of Hume's family, Ian Dalrymple Ross, W.S., of Edinburgh, for his kind permission to let his little-known portrait of Hume be photographed and reproduced in this book. The portrait is probably an adaptation by Donaldson of the more famous Ramsay portrait. Formerly, and probably originally, it was in the possession of the Earls of Stair (that is, in the Dalrymple family), and hung in Oxenfoord Castle until sold in this century to the Ross family. I thank Robin Crole for taking me to Oxenfoord Castle on a fruitless but interesting search for the portrait, and for trespassing with me on the Ninewells banks of the Whitadder river. I am grateful to Malcolm Liddell, of Edinburgh University Library, for his willingness to photograph the portrait *in situ,* once I had discovered its true location.

The penultimate draft of this book was written in the agreeable surroundings of the Wissenschaftskolleg zu Berlin, whose support, like that of the National Endowment for the Humanities and the American Council of Learned Societies, I gratefully acknowledge. The final draft was prepared in Pittsburgh while I had the support of a Guggenheim fellowship. Once again, I have had the invaluable help of Collie Henderson in preparing the final manuscript. Maria Ascher, of Harvard University Press, eliminated some infelicities of style. Robert Haraldsson, Hibi Pendelton, Laura Ruetsche and Lisa Shapiro were coopted from my 1990 Hume seminar to help with proofreading, and I am very grateful to them. My colleague Nuel Belnap generously provided expert advice and assistance with the indexing. The greatest support, sympathy and critical encouragement came from my husband, Kurt Baier. His sceptical doubts about my Humean enthusiasms got this book started, and without his encouragement to me to continue with it when my spirits were faint and languid, it would in all likelihood never have been completed. This book is for him.

Nexilis ante fuit vestis quam textile tegmen.
(Garments of piecework come before garments of woven cloth.)

Lucretius, *De Rerum Natura*, V, 1350,
translated by W. H. D. Rouse

1

Philosophy in This
Careless Manner

For my part, my only hope is, that I may contribute a
little to the advancement of knowledge, by giving in
some particulars a different turn to the speculations of
philosophers, and pointing out to them more distinctly
those subjects, where alone they can expect assurance
and conviction.   (T. 273)

In this chapter I shall attend in fairly close detail to the section of
the *Treatise* from which the quotation above is taken, that is,
Hume's conclusion to its first book. This section is of very great
importance for understanding what precedes it, as well as what
follows it. It both brings the line of thought in Book One to its
preordained conclusion, and moves us on to the themes of Book
Two. In its pages, Hume enacts for us the turn he wants us to
imitate, a turn from a one-sided reliance on intellect and its methods of proceeding to an attempt to use, in our philosophy, *all* the
capacities of the human mind: memory, passion and sentiment as
well as a chastened intellect. That is what Hume attempts from
Book Two onwards—not only are passions his topic there, but his
approach to them is to be guided by experience-informed passion,
and he recommends that his readers indulge their sentiments when
they join him in his pursuit of philosophy "in this careless manner" (T. 273). The new approach is to be careless in the older
sense, carefree rather than negligent. (The O.E.D. gives us the
biblical reference of *Judges* 18.7, "They dwell careless after the
manner of the Zidonians, quiet and secure.") The new philosopher
is to dwell careless after the manner of the Zidonians, quiet and

secure after casting off the anxieties and tyranny of obsessive theorizing. Hume and his followers are to be carefree and liberated
from all compulsions, including the compulsion to pursue the theoretical details of their own philosophy: "If the reader finds himself in the same easy disposition, let him follow me in my future
speculations. If not, let him follow his inclination, and wait the
returns of application and good humour" (ibid.). Hume has had
to wait long enough to find readers who will apply themselves in
following him from Book One to Book Two,[1] or relating both
those books to Book Three. My aim is to follow Hume, and to
see how his speculations beyond Book One relate to those within
it, and to see in what particulars his philosophical turn is different,
before and after the conclusion of Book One.

The carefree philosophy whose inauguration Hume announces
at the end of Book One is to provide assurance and conviction for
those converted ex-rationalists who will follow him in his turn
away from intellect's "cold and general speculation," into his new
investigation of the whole mind by the whole mind. If this philosophy is successful, its adherents will have that "power to take
or leave it" (T. 314) which Wittgenstein, two centuries later, saw
to be the highest achievement of any philosophical enterprise, the
gaining of the ability to stop doing philosophy. If Hume's philosophy of reflection-assisted passions succeeds in its aims, its followers will have easy compliance with Hume's injunction, "Be a
philosopher; but, amidst all your philosophy, be still a man"
(E. 9).[2] In this chapter I shall not discuss Hume's eventual verdict
on the success of his enterprise within the *Treatise,* or the justice
of that verdict, but simply look in detail at the inauguration of the
program, the section of the *Treatise* where a turn is announced and
effected. This is the most dramatic moment in Hume's *Treatise,*
which itself enacts the "total alteration in philosophy" which is its
intended enduring effect.

The turn itself occurs at T. 269 when Hume joins the diners and
backgammon players. It is both preceded and followed by a quite
intricate series of dialectical moves and countermoves.[3]

He begins with two striking images of his state of mind, after
his preceding attempts in Part IV to give intellectual analyses of
the way intellect works, in particular analyses of its use of the

concepts of external object and personal identity. He is, he says, like a sailor on a barren rock, about to set out in a leaky weather-beaten vessel to encompass the globe, but pausing to consider the wretched condition of his craft, and aware of the dangers of "that boundless ocean, which runs out into immensity" (T. 264). Apprehension sets in. The second image takes up one feature of the first, namely that the sailor is alone, setting out on a solo voyage, without assistance from any fellows. So the philosophical voyager speaks of "that forelorn solitude, in which I am plac'd in my philosophy, and fancy myself some strange uncouth monster, who not being able to mingle and unite in society, has been expell'd all human commerce, and left utterly abandon'd and disconsolate" (ibid.). This philosophically induced solitude has, I think, two levels. First is the fact that most of Part IV has been a solo attempt of a single thinker, distrustful of education and testimony, and confined to the ideas he can get for himself. Despite many references to other persons, and occasional rhetorical appeals to the reader to confirm the first-person singular findings, no appeals were made at any point to any pooling of data or to any really cooperative procedures for error detection or error correction. The porter who appeared when the protagonist was thinking about how to synthesize broken appearances into the concept of a lasting object was not asked for visual data to supplement the auditory fragments he had, from his solitary experience. Hume had indeed, throughout Part IV of Book One, sailed a one-person ship, albeit in an ocean where other manned ships were clearly visible.

But, given his near Cartesian solitude, he had *not* reached typically Cartesian conclusions about the seaworthiness of his singly manned and singly maintained vessel. "I have expos'd myself to the enmity of all metaphysicians, logicians, mathematicians, and even theologians" (ibid.). Solitary intellects do tend to expect other solitary intellects to agree with them, but Hume's single-handed excursion had turned up discoveries both about the lay of the land and the nature of the vessel which invited "dispute, contradiction, anger, calumny and detraction." His discoveries set him against established intellectualist findings. Yet it is an anomaly for a Cartesian solitary intellect to care about the "approbation of others" (T. 265), and the protagonist finds this incoherence in his solitary defiance. Can he afford to disdain the opinions of others? Why should his findings about intellect be thought correct, and the pretensions of other solitary intellect-users be thought mistaken? How can he, or any of his intellectualist opponents, even expect to recognize error, were it present in their own thinking? The incoherence of setting oneself up in arrogant monstrous isolation, denouncing the errors of others, yet without any protection against one's own errors, drives the protagonist to seek some common ground, some position in which, against the background of the infirmities that all share, he may recognize "those numberless infirmities peculiar to myself." "Can I be sure, that in leaving all establish'd opinions I am following truth?" (T. 265).

This question of why departure from the established course of thinking should be thought a safe route to truth provides the opportunity for the "monster" to find some affinities, if not in doctrine at least in capacities, with those who will not join him. The solitary stance is given up, for a humbler position of some solidarity with fallible fellow persons. Whether or not they agree with him, they all are guided by the same principles, by experience, habit and the same general customs of belief formation. All have their ideas enlivened into beliefs by the same sorts of causes. "The memory, senses, and understanding are, therefore, all of them founded on the imagination, or the vivacity of our ideas" (ibid.). The imagination[4] varies the vivacity of ideas, and in its regular workings increases the vivacity of those ideas that are the conclusions of causal inferences, and supplies us with the ideas of the continuously and independently existing things that we take to be around us. It may also be responsible for the vivacity of that idea of self, as identical enduring person, owner of one's own passing perceptions, since vivacity is the only credential that has so far been found for that idea. In this passage at T. 265–266, that particular belief is not mentioned. The anxieties that soon appear are restricted to belief in causation and belief in the continued existence of external objects. The question of the continuing identity of the one who begins the conclusion with brave ambition that quickly turns to diffidence and fear, goes through many moods in the course of a few pages, and ends in a hopeful and carefree frame of mind, cannot be really addressed until that very fluctuation of moods and sentiments has been studied in Book Two, until "our identity with regard to the passions serves to corroborate that with regard to the imagination" (T. 261). At the very nadir of the despair, the cry arises, "Where am I, or what?" (T. 269) as if the very difference between personal identity and the identity of external objects[5] is slipping away, but the findings of the preceding sceptical section, "Of personal identity," are not explicitly brought to bear on the "Conclusion of this book."

What occasions instability in the attempted reunion with mankind in common servitude to habit and imagination is the contradiction which is found within that joint authority. It is an unsatisfactory master, since "'tis this principle, which makes us reason from causes and effects; and 'tis the same principle, which convinces us of the continu'd existence of external objects, when absent from the senses. But tho' these operations be equally natural and necessary in the human mind, yet in some circumstances they are directly contrary, nor is it possible for us to reason justly and regularly from causes and effects, and at the same time believe the continu'd existence of matter" (T. 266). Hume here adverts to his demonstration, in the section "Of the modern philosophy," that if causal analysis shows secondary qualities to be mere effects on the observers of primary qualities, it also seems to destroy the primary qualities. "When we reason from cause and effect, we conclude, that neither colour, sound, taste, nor smell have a continu'd and independent existence. When we exclude these sensible qualities, there remains nothing in the universe, which has such an existence" (T. 231). The latter conclusion followed from resolving all primary qualities into ones dependent on solidity, and resolving solidity into impenetrability. But *what* is it which cannot penetrate what? "Two non-entities cannot exclude each other from their places . . . Now I ask, what idea do we form of those bodies or objects, to which we suppose solidity to belong? To say, that we conceive them merely as solid, is to run on *in infinitum*" (T. 229).

This disappearance into non-entity of all the supposed defining qualities of lasting objects is occasioned by certain philosophical uses of causal analysis, which themselves require the supposition of more regularity than we have in fact witnessed. The "broken appearances" within our limited experience have to be supplemented by the hypothesis of unperceived perceptions, and of external continuously existing objects as "homes" for these postulated possibilities of perception. Hearing the door opening, without seeing its movement, could otherwise count as a breach of a regularity. "These observations are contrary, unless I suppose that the door still remains, and that it was open'd without my perceiving it" (T. 196–197). Unless we postulate enduring objects, "these phaenomena of the porter and letter . . . are contradictions to common experience, and may be regarded as objections to those maxims, which we form concerning the connexions of causes and effects" (T. 196). Thus belief in causal regularities is *saved* by the postulation of external objects, yet destroys its saviour. Imagination's workings, as examined in Part IV of Book One, alternately support and subvert one another.

This realization, that in seeing oneself (like one's opponents) as a slave to the imagination, one must see oneself as a fellow *victim* of an internally incoherent master, makes this position unstable, and prepares us for the next. Just as the first position, the "rock" of isolation, was rent by the contradiction between arrogant self-sufficiency and that "weakness" whereby "I feel all my opinions loosen and fall of themselves, when unsupported by the approbation of others" (T. 264–265), so the second position, the common ground of reliance on imagination's workings, also turns out to be no secure ground, but the site of mutually conflicting principles, undermining each other.

One response would be to hop from side to side, as the shifts in ground demand, to rely on causal inference to expected phenomena for predictive purposes, and switch to material object realism when need arises. But "in case we . . . successively assent to both, as is usual among philosophers, with what confidence can we afterwards usurp that glorious title, when we thus knowingly embrace a manifest contradiction?" (T. 266). We would embrace only half a contradiction at a time, but even if we were successful in that delicate bigamous dance, we would scarcely, Hume claims, deserve the title "philosopher." This is an interesting claim, in the light of Hume's endorsement, later in the "Conclusion," of a policy of letting contrary moods succeed one another. A "careless" attitude to apparent contradiction in attitudes is eventually to be presented as the true philosophy. Can opposed moods decently share time in the soul, while opposed purely intellectual beliefs cannot?

At this point, before vacating the shifting ground of common-sense fallibilism, Hume adds an interesting note on what might have shored up that position. The rift between causal analysis and object synthesis might have been compensated "by any degree of solidity and satisfaction in the other parts of our reasoning" (T. 266). Which other parts? The part that fails to provide this hoped-for consolation is described as the attempt to know "the causes of every phaenomenon," to discover not merely interme-diate causes but "the original and ultimate principle. We wou'd not willingly stop before we are acquainted with the energy in the cause, by which it operates on its effect; that tie, which connects them together; and that efficacious quality, on which the tie de-pends" (ibid.). Our discovery that "this connexion, tie, or energy lies merely in ourselves" cuts off all hope of finding any external source of efficacious energy. Hume here seems to treat the tracing back of causes as a different enterprise from that causal analysis that destroyed the concept of physical atom. How does it differ? Is it the fact that the moves in the attempt to trace the phenomena back to some original explanatory principle are not from cause to effect but from effects to causes?[6] That, surely, was precisely what the modern philosophers did with secondary qualities, and what Hume himself continued to do with primary qualities, until they vanished into nothingness. Is it the fact that the *necessity* of the connection is the focus of attention in these "other parts" of our reasoning? Hume's Book One, Part III treatment of causal infer-ence and of necessity had seemed solid and satisfactory enough, at the end of Part III, despite the fact that no "ultimate principle," internal or external, had been found.[7] It does, however, seem here to be the search not just for prior causes for later effects but for "the ultimate principle" which "connects them together" which has proved unsatisfactory, at least to those who want it to lie "in the external object" rather than "merely in ourselves." If we make this demand, then we will, in our discourse about necessity and causal necessitation, "contradict ourselves, or talk without a meaning" (T. 267).

The most obvious case where this demand comes into play is in theological searches for the world's cause, in "unusual and extraordinary" causal investigations, so it is our cosmological and theological reasonings that may appear least solid and satisfactory, once Part III's conclusions about causal necessity are accepted. The religious world-explanation does collapse rather dramatically if we are convinced by Hume that the energy lies only in ourselves. It is as if Hume were here referring to parts of his own reasoning which he put not into the *Treatise* but into the *Dialogues on Natural Religion,* not published in his lifetime. The best sense I can make of this paragraph at T. 266–267 is that Hume is referring to some implications of his account of cause which he had not dared include in the *Treatise,* but put aside for the *Dialogues.* The *Treatise* section "Why a cause is always necessary?" is the only one which hints at these implications of Hume's position. This interpretation is supported by the opening of the next paragraph, T. 267, when Hume says that in common life we are not sensible of these deficiencies in our ideas. He may have refrained from trying to make his contemporaries sensible of all the implications of his views, and been persuaded to let common life go on its normal religious way a little longer.[8]

The mutually destructive tendencies of the concepts of cause and physical object lead the protagonist to move to a higher level, to an attempt to distinguish between successful and troublesome workings of the human imagination responsible for these concepts. If we fall into incoherence when we use the imagination's usual products in an unrestrained way, perhaps the proper policy is to put some proto-Kantian restraints into effect, to try to separate the reliable workings of the imagination from its troublesome workings. But how are we to draw the line? *Which* workings are productive of illusion and contradiction, and which are free of these defects? What has just been shown is, unfortunately, that it is precisely when we attempt to avoid the *illusions* of imagination, by seeing clearly what our concept of cause and of physical atom amount to, that we find contradictions cropping up. So perhaps our concepts are best left unclarified, and their implications not too punctiliously traced? Should we be content to be taken in by illusions? "The question is, how far we ought to yield to these illusions" (T. 267).

A dangerous dilemma now presents itself, Hume says. Either we say that we should yield to *all* the illusions of the imagination, in which case we become totally undiscriminating and let ourselves be led into "such errors, absurdities, and obscurities, that we must at last become asham'd of our credulity," or we continue to try to discriminate between the acceptable and the unacceptable inventions of the human imagination. One way to do that is to distinguish "the trivial suggestions of the fancy," totally undisciplined flights of imagination, from its "general and more establish'd properties," calling the latter "reason" or "understanding." But to reject the imagination's trivial suggestions, while accepting its regular or disciplined suggestions, "wou'd be most dangerous, and attended with the most fatal consequences" (T. 267).

These fatal consequences are not those already noted, the mutual subversion of the concepts of matter and cause. The concept of physical object, after all, depended on some "trivial" (T. 217) workings of the fancy for its construction, and the concept of causal regularity needed help from this "fanciful" concept. However common and ineradicable the concept of physical object may be, it is not a paradigm product of what Hume here calls the understanding. The most "general and establish'd" workings of imagination turn out to be those shown in deductive argument, causal inference and probability estimation, the subject matter of Part III and the first section of Part IV, rather than of its later sections. Here, even if we avoid all fictions and illusions, we face grave problems. When we turn our ability to recognize causes, to measure frequency and to estimate probability onto our deductive reasoning, and raise the question of the likelihood of error, then "I have already shewn, that the understanding, when it acts alone, and according to its most general principles, entirely subverts itself, and leaves not the lowest degree of evidence in any proposition, either in philosophy or common life" (T. 267–268). Here the reference is to the section "Of scepticism with regard to reason," where probability of error had been turned on demonstration, and higher-level probability of error turned on lower-level probability.

The effect of this operation was claimed to be the removal of all trace of evidence.[9] This section began with the remark that reason was a sort of cause, of which, provided things work properly, truth is the result. But since we know that its calculations quite often are incorrect, on any given occasion the odds that we get truth are less than overwhelming. Whatever estimate we give of those odds, there is again a non-negligible probability that we erred in making it, and so on. "Let our first belief be never so strong, it must infallibly perish by passing thro' so many new examinations" (T. 182–183). Hume writes that this "reflex act of the mind" (T. 182), of turning one's critical scrutiny on one's own critical powers themselves, produces "a total extinction of belief and evidence" (T. 183). This is the fatal consequence which follows from placing one's trust in the most regular workings of that form of the imagination that we call the understanding, or reason. So again, the ground that we took to be firm ground gives beneath our feet.

Before deserting this position, of trust in reasoning, we need to ask whether the reasoning in question includes causal inference. The reason which subverted itself in the section "Of scepticism with regard to reason" was deductive reason, combined with probability estimation. Causal inference was not explicitly involved, except in providing a frame for the whole argument, by the assumption that reason is itself a cause with whose truth-producing workings other factors can interfere. To answer the question of whether causal inference is subverted by this argument we must consider what its relation is to those probability estimates which are involved in reason's self-subversion.

Causal reasoning, for Hume, is reasoning which projects past uniformities into the future, whereas probability estimation projects past frequencies into the future. One might have expected him therefore to treat causal uniformities as a limit case of frequency, but he does not do this. On the contrary, he treats anything less than a perfect uniformity in our past as a case of "conflict" in experience. Complete uniformity gives us "proofs," on which causal inference and "knowledge" is based, whereas all other cases, in which the evidence is mixed, give us "probabilities," and uncertainty about the next case (T. 124). Hume also considers a "species of probability"[10] which is based not on mixed evidence but on uniform but meagre evidence, and he supposes that we all build up our causal beliefs by "slow steps" from this species of probability to proof and "full assurance" (T. 130). But "no one, who is arriv'd at the age of maturity, can any longer be acquainted with it" (T. 131) since, once we get assurance that there are exceptionless uniformities, we seize on this concept and use it in all cases, including those where our evidence is only a single experiment, as well as those where our evidence is not uniform. We treat these last cases (probability in its normal guise) as cases where there is "a secret and conceal'd cause" (T. 130). We interpret the mixed evidence as evidence of *complication* of not yet revealed causes, as "the secret opposition of contrary causes" (T. 132). At least the philosophers, if not the vulgar, expect an eventual causal explanation of the variation in the observed phenomena. "A peasant can give no better reason for the stopping of any clock or watch than to say, that commonly it does not go right: But an artizan easily perceives, that the same force in the spring or pendulum has always the same influence on the wheels; but fails of its usual effect, perhaps by reason of a grain of dust, which puts a stop to the whole movement" (ibid.). Where there is, on the peasant's part, a habit of expectation of "inferior force, proportion'd to the inferior degree of steadiness" in experience, Hume treats this as an exception to "the principle that most commonly influences the mind in this species of reasoning" (T. 133). This principle is an "oblique" working of a strong and uniform habit to expect the future to resemble the past, and to insist (in Kantian fashion) on expecting exceptionless uniformities at some level in the apparently conflicting data. Indeed, Hume's reference to the data as "contrary" enbodies this Kantian demand. That rhubarb purged last week and did not purge this week presents us with "a contrariety in our experience" only if each case is taken as a representative of all similar cases, *as* a case, not a single unique event. Hume thus treats all experience of less than a uniformity as evidence for complication or opposition of causes, and claims that it is natural for the human mind to do so, to expect all "probabilities" to resolve into "proofs," once the analysis becomes sufficiently fine grained. Or perhaps it is natural for human nature to do this only in the guise it assumes in Book One—for *intellect* and for intellectuals, for reason and for rationalists.

When Hume in Part IV, Section I, called reason a kind of cause and truth its natural effect, he treated its malfunctioning, and the "contrariety" between correct and incorrect calculations, as evidence of "the irruption of other causes," as well as of "the inconstancy of our mental powers" (T. 180). If the *a priori* determinism of the earlier sections on probability is to be applied here, the "inconstancy" of our mental powers should be only apparent, the appearance of it always explicable by "the irruption of other causes." One might, like Kant, exempt the human mind from the demand for causal constancy which is made of everything else, but Hume does not do this. I think that at T. 180 he intended the "inconstancy," like all contrariety, to be taken as evidence of opposed forces working in perfectly constant ways. So causal inference will then be indirectly implicated in the subversion of reason, since all probability estimates are interim conclusions, conclusions about "the probability of causes." Causal inference, however, is not just part of the subverted; it is the chief subversive agent—it is the attempt at formulating a causal regularity covering reason's workings that leads to reason's downfall. Cause was also a subversive member of the uneasy coalition of the concepts of cause and external object. Causation, however, is never called a "fiction," and within Part III it was used reflexively on causal inference with quite positive results. In Part IV, when it is turned on a coalition of itself plus other sorts of inferences, it seems to subvert itself along with its fellows. It is the Samson of Hume's version of the categories of the understanding; it is a powerful concept which, in the wrong conditions or in the wrong relation to its fellows within the understanding, brings down the temple of reason on itself and its intellectual fellows. What it might do in better conditions is a topic I will return to later.[11]

The attempt to separate out and repose trust in the more established workings of the imagination, namely our powers of inference, as distinct from its more frivolous workings, has had fatal consequences. A new foothold must be found. "We save ourselves from this total scepticism only by means of that singular and seemingly trivial property of the fancy, by which we enter with difficulty into remote views" (T. 268). It was only by somewhat abstruse arguments that reason had been subverted. One response would be simply to forbid such elaborated uses of our intellect's tools—to stick with commonsense objects rather than refined views of matter, to argue and reason only on practical matters, and to prevent such "reflex" turns of the mind as Hume effected in "Of scepticism with regard to reason." Could we limit the application of the troublesome categories and operations to a narrow realm, and avoid the areas where we now know trouble to lie, reason might be salvaged, in a somewhat humbler guise. "Shall we, then, establish it for a general maxim that no refin'd or elaborate reasoning is ever to be receiv'd?" (ibid.).

At this point in Hume's "conclusion," the dialectic quickens its pace. The positive suggestion is no sooner made than it is rejected, for three progressively stronger reasons. "Consider well the consequences of such a principle. By this means you cut off entirely all science and philosophy" (ibid.). Newton's books would have to be burned, along with Clarke's and Warburton's, Descartes' scientific writings along with the *Meditations*. And why exactly should we cut down science? To elevate to authority one trivial preference of the fancy, that for sensible easy impressions over refined thoughts. But why this trivial feature rather than any other? The second reason for rejecting this suggestion is its arbitrariness. "You proceed upon one singular quality of the imagination, and by a parity of reason must embrace all of them" (ibid.). What are the others that clamour for equality of treatment? Presumably among them are those trivial features of imagination on which the concept of a physical object was found to be based. Summing up his conclusions in the section "Of scepticism with regard to the senses," Hume said that, although he had begun with the conviction that "'tis in vain to ask, *Whether there be body or not?*" (T. 187) since nature gives us no choice but to believe in such bodies, by the end of the section "I feel myself *at present* of a quite contrary sentiment, and am more inclin'd to repose no faith at all in my senses, or rather imagination, than to place in it such an implicit confidence. I cannot conceive how such trivial qualities of the fancy, conducted by such false suppositions, can ever lead to any solid and rational system" (T. 217). If these trivial qualities have been denied authority, why should we choose another equally trivial quality, namely our intolerance for elaborate arguments, to be judge of the limits of the understanding?

This second objection is followed by an even more decisive reason not to opt for giving arbitrary power to any one trivial propensity. This, the third objection, is that to let such a propensity rule would be to expressly contradict oneself, "since this maxim [banishing refined and elaborate reasoning] must be built on the preceding reasoning, which will be allow'd to be sufficiently refin'd and metaphysical" (T. 268). Here Hume faces the problem which led Wittgenstein at the end of the *Tractatus* to recommend that we discard that book once we had got its message, the problem which Kant seemed not to see as also facing his own elaborate attempt to draw the limits of the understanding. Hume faces the issue without any double talk: "What party, then, shall we choose among these difficulties? If we embrace this principle, and condemn all refin'd reasoning, we run into the most manifest absurdities. If we reject it in favour of these reasonings, we subvert entirely the human understanding. We have, therefore, no choice left but betwixt a false reason and none at all" (ibid.).

Which option gives us a false reason, and which gives us no reason at all? I take it that the reason subverted by its own unrestrained and reflexive application is ultimately "no reason at all," whereas the false reason is the prophetically Kantian understanding which uses forbidden reasoning to arrive at that very prohibition, which thinks beyond the limits of the understanding to discern those limits. It is false to itself—it expressly and manifestly disobeys its own ruling.[12] What is to be done, when the choice is reduced to this? There is no rational solution to the problem which now faces the unhappy would-be rational person. "For my part, I know not what ought to be commonly done in the present case. I can only observe what is done; which is, that this difficulty is seldom or never thought of; and even where it has once been present to the mind, is quickly forgot, and leaves but a small impression behind it" (ibid.). Certainly Hume's presentation of this difficulty seems to have made small impression on Kant, or even on Wittgenstein[13] and later intellect-restraining intellectuals. The natural reaction, Hume notes, is simply to ignore the problem. The one who aspires to the glorious title of lover of wisdom, however, cannot so easily give in to this natural escapist move, if that wisdom is supposed to come from the use of a divine self-luminous self-approving reason. "Very refin'd reflections have little or no influence on us; and yet we do not, and cannot establish it for a rule, that they ought not to have any influence; which implies a manifest contradiction" (ibid.). If we rest in this position, we renounce all claim to endorse our own habits, to be able to bear our own survey once we become reflective recognizers of our rules rather than blind creatures of our habits.[14] This would be the defeat not only of reason but of any pretension to norm-recognition and to reflection. Significantly, Hume's protagonist does not rest here.

Whatever success other people commonly have in ignoring these problems of bad faith in their intellectual life, the thinker at this stage of the *Treatise* cannot ignore or forget them, cannot resign himself to unreflective thoughtless ease. "But what have I here said, that reflections very refin'd and metaphysical have little or no influence upon us? This opinion I can scarce forbear retracting, and condemning from my present feeling and experience. The *intense* view of these manifold contradictions and imperfections in human reason has so wrought upon me, and heated my brain, that I am ready to reject all belief and reasoning, and can look on no opinion even as more probable or likely than another. Where am I, or what? From what causes do I derive my existence, and to what condition shall I return? Whose favour shall I court, and whose anger must I dread? What beings surround me? and on whom have I any influence, or who have any influence on me? I am confounded with all these questions, and begin to fancy myself in the most deplorable condition imaginable, inviron'd with the deepest darkness, and utterly depriv'd of the use of every member and faculty" (T. 268–269).

BEFORE MOVING ON to the alternation of moods by which Hume's thinker escapes this deepest darkness, it is worth pausing a little, to note some features of the dialectic down to this nadir. The features I wish to stress are, first, the role played by "express contradictions" that are not formal contradictions; second, the

choice offered at several points between the "illusions" produced
by the imagination's trivial properties and the "contradictions"
produced by the attempt to use the more established operations of
the understanding to expose and avoid these illusions; and, third,
the repeated alternation of attempts to join up with others, to accept established views, with swings back into idiosyncratic solitude.

The "manifest contradiction" at T. 268, end of paragraph, lay
in admitting that refined reflections do not influence us, while also
admitting that we cannot say that they ought not to influence us.
What contradiction is there in the Pyrrhonian sceptic's exercising
and acknowledging his own habits, while refusing to give them
normative endorsement?[15] Certainly it is not manifest in the way
a contradiction "in terms" is manifest. Nor was the "express contradiction" a half paragraph before a contradiction in terms. That
contradiction lay in adopting a maxim which must be disobeyed
to get the reason for its own adoption. The maxim "contradicted"
its own ancestry, as it were. Hume calls these two cases "express"
and "manifest" contradictions, and he uses the latter expression
earlier at T. 266, for the attempt to let the contrary categories of
physical object and cause gain our successive assent. In this last
case, of vacillation, one phase of our thinking involves a rejection
of both its predecessors and its successors—the incoherence is one
which shows over a period of time, when today's commitments
are compared with yesterday's, or this hour's with the previous
hour's. It is consistency in sustained belief which is Hume's concern, not merely consistency in the body of "beliefs" that one can
embrace at one moment, only to disown them the next.

This is the first important point about what Hume means by
contradiction—it is unresolved conflict for one's fairly *sustained*
commitment. The contradiction may be present even when only
one of the contenders gets explicit acceptance in today's words.
The second point is that the sort of "express contradiction" that
Hume is concerned with is like that present in "I am not thinking,"
the sort of contradiction that prevented Descartes from doubting
his existence as a thinker. If one says "I am not speaking," the
speech act belies its own words. In a similar way the rationalist
sceptic's attempt to reach and formulate a maxim outlawing re-

fined reasoning would defeat the claim expressed in that maxim. In it, as in "I am not a thinker," the words deny what the saying of them shows. The "building" of the maxim to restrict reason's scope itself extends that scope beyond the formulated restrictions. Such a contradiction is "express" in that the act of expression defeats the expressed resolve.

The "manifest contradiction" of renouncing pretensions to norms of reason or reflectiveness is "express" in this sense. Since the buildup to this renunciation has itself been a process of reasoned or norm-guided reflection, this contradiction is of the same expression-dependent or pragmatic type. Those who fall into it will be those purporting to find reasons for casting off norms. Do thoughtless persons also contradict themselves, when they accept their thoughtless habits without turning them into normative rules? Hume seems here to be implying that any mode of human life, whether or not philosophical and intellectual, commits us to turning some habits into normative rules. Once we are fully self-conscious, any attempt to be free of all norms will reveal our possibly once hidden commitment to some norms or other. At this point in the text this is merely hinted, not developed. We will return later to Hume's views on this matter, once the *Treatise* gathers more force as it proceeds.

Contradictions and "falsity" of this pragmatic sort were one recurrent pitfall for our voyager. The other main danger was "illusion." The series of moves so far charted can be seen as alternate optings for what proves to be illusion, followed by optings for what proves to imply a contradiction. In escaping from illusion we encounter contradiction, and to escape contradiction we seem to have to yield to illusion. The transitions so far discussed can be summed up as a sequence of changes in self-conception, each driven by the realization that there was either illusion or self-contradiction involved in the previous version of the introspective protagonist. The "conversions" were:

1. From bold original independent thinker to solitary shunned monster (T. 263–264);
2. From solitary thinker to typical fallible thinker (T. 264–265);

3. From typical thinker, subject to the human imagination's distinctive habits, to typical victim of its self-destructive workings (T. 265–266);
4. From victim of imagination to willing adherent of "the understanding," namely the imagination in its most regular and established workings (T. 267);
5. From one who discriminates between imagination's established workings (intellect) and its trivial workings (the fancy), to agent and witness of the vanishing of evidence, the total destruction of reason through subversion from within (T. 268);
6. From total sceptic to one willing to be ruled by a "trivial property of the fancy," namely intolerance of long and elaborate reasonings, such as the preceding (T. 268);
7. From banisher of elaborate reasoning to science-rejector, and breaker of one's own rules, since the path from conversion 1 to conversion 6 has been even longer than that from 1 to 5 (T. 268);
8. From breaker of one's own rules to renouncer of all rules, advocate of forgetting difficulties (T. 268);
9. From liberator from norms and their difficulties to failed liberator, unable to forget that it was by reasoning that one came to banish the norms of reason (T. 268);
10. From manifestly self-contradicting thinker to despairing self-doubter, "in the most deplorable condition imaginable" (T. 268–269).

These transformations of self-description are fired by an internal dialectic, the urge to expose illusion and contradiction, to get an honest version of the thinker. Temerity and independence of thought turn out to be illusory—the thinker needs others, if only to impress them with his originality (conversions 1 and 2). But once he strips off the illusion of independence and sees himself under the rule of shared habits of thought, he finds self-contradiction within basic products of that common thinking, the ideas of physical object and of causal dependency, themselves now described as "illusions." From this point on, he seems involved only in a choice between illusions, and he escapes self-contradiction at one point only to have it recur at a higher level. The difference between coherent illusion and manifest self-contradiction becomes harder to draw, when the illusions concern one's own thought habits, and when the contradictions concern one's claims to be able to live free of illusion.

These moves in the dialectic show roughly alternating realizations of illusion and of self-contradiction, and also alternating swings to and from orthodoxy or establishment, of various forms. The first such swing comes with the realization that the thinker cares how others see him, and that the superiority of the confident independent would-be innovator over his fellows may be illusion and self-deception (1 and 2). He may need others to get any criterion of truth. He therefore tries to find common ground with them, and finds it in his reliance on the same propensities of the imagination. But these very propensities, whose recognition freed him from arrogant illusion, turn out to produce contrary and conflicting principles (3). From this point on, there are ever more rapid alternations of illusion and contradiction, and there are also swings from independent unorthodox positions to acceptance of some orthodoxy. From orthodoxy of belief content, rejected at the start, we move to orthodox trust in human thought, and on to a more elitist trust only in its own *most* "orthodox" workings—that is, to trust in reasoning (4). Then, when that is undermined, there are moves to and from various more or less orthodox responses to the ensuing scepticism—an attempted limitation of reason's province (5 and 6), or the "common" reaction of refusing to think about such matters (7 and 8). At the point of despair, the protagonist has, by the very intensity of his feelings about the bad faith and false consciousness that have been revealed as endemic to rational man, once again separated himself from orthodoxy, whether sceptic or rationalist.

Two things are important about this most despairing stage. One is its utter solitude, amounting to autism. This is an accentuation of the solitude with which the progression began, and an ironic outcome of the Cartesian assumptions of self-sufficiency present throughout Part IV of Book One. The second important thing to note is that by now, when reason is subverted, there no longer are "reasons" for the present position, or non-position. The predicament at this stage is described as an intense feeling, and an over-heating of the brain. We are already making the crucial Humean turn, from intellect to feeling.

AFTER THESE COMMENTS on the charges of contradiction, illusion, and false self-sufficiency in the downward path of Hume's dialectic, I now return to the dialectic itself, and now in its "upward" path. I have already abandoned the metaphor of shifting positions, the search for solid ground, by describing the transitions as changes in the narrator's self-conception, rather than in the ground he thinks he stands on. Now we can follow Hume in describing them as changes not just in self-description but also in the way he really is, as changes in him. Now he has plunged into that boundless ocean, abandoning altogether both the leaky vessel and the shifting rocks and sands, and, after going briefly under, he is swimming free, gathering new strength.

The first upturn comes when paralyzed despair is relaxed by "nature herself." The very distraction that was offered and refused earlier, thoughtless amusement which enables a forgetting of the difficulties, now takes over and "cures me of this philosophical melancholy and delirium" (T. 269). Why can distraction work now, whereas a half page earlier it could not? Nature herself, in the form of exhaustion leading to relaxation of "this bent of mind," or in the form of readiness for the distraction of a "lively impression of the senses, which obliterate all these chimeras" (ibid.), can dispel the dark clouds that reason had produced, but only when they have intensified to their deepest pitch, when total despair has set in, and is recognized *as* a state of feeling, an over-heating of the brain. For only then is there an acceptance of natural sentiment not as mere distraction but as the *replacer* of reason. Reason must be worked through, taken to the end of its tether, before sentiment can take over the guiding role. Sentiment and preference have been present throughout the earlier dialectic, which indeed began with ambitious temerity turning to apprehension and melancholy, but they had been presented as reason-grounded, and were subjected primarily to an intellectual testing and examination. From this point on, the moves are dictated by feeling, are swings in moods, not zigzags of argument. The transitions are motivated not by a realization of intellectual incoherence in the earlier phase, but merely by the incompleteness of the initial mood, its natural fate of supplementation by a successor mood. As mood succeeds mood, the ability of any one mood to sustain itself increases, but only at the end of the *Treatise* will a self-sufficient and self-sustaining state of mind be achieved. Here, at this transitional point between Book One's *reductio ad absurdum* of Cartesian intellect[16] and the rest of the *Treatise's* development of its more passionate and sociable successor, Hume gives us a short sequence of moods as a sort of preview of the dialectic of the passions which is to be more fully developed in Books Two and Three.

The first mood, accepted as such, without any attempt to intellectualize about it, is the sociable cheerful mood of the dinner-table companion and backgammon player, to whom the preceding speculations and intellectual agonizing appear cold, strained and ridiculous. In this mood, one cannot sustain sceptical doubts, but finds in oneself an "indolent belief in the general maxims of the world" (ibid.), along with an impatience for philosophical reasonings. There is a natural alliance with ordinary people and their ordinary beliefs, whatever the philosophical credentials of those beliefs. It is a return not to any *philosophical orthodoxy,* but to a wholly "blind submission" (ibid.) to natural belief, a renunciation of all philosophy, both orthodox and heterodox. In this mood, there is no willingness to "torture my brain with subtilities and sophistries" (T. 270), be they the "subtilities" of the sceptics or of the rationalists. "If I must be a fool, as all those who reason or believe any thing *certainly* are, my follies shall at least be natural and agreeable" (ibid.). The emphasized certainty distinguishes this position from any extreme scepticism, as well as from any other philosophical position. Belief in ordinary certainties, that fire warms and water refreshes, and commonsense reasoning of a practical sort, are taken to be harmless and unavoidable, but philosophical beliefs and refined reasonings are "painful" and avoidable. It is their painfulness, not their internal incoherence, that now counts decisively against them. The "spleen" in this first mood is reserved entirely for philosophers.

But neither the spleen nor the indolence of this mood can sus-

tain itself. One tires of the company of the indolent natural believers, and one's anti-philosophy spleen exhausts itself, to be followed by a return of philosophical curiosity. But this "return" to
philosophy is not a reversion to the earlier obsessive intellectual
theorizing. Now it is not intellect but "my mind all collected
within itself" (ibid.) which takes up "those subjects, about which
I have met with so many disputes in the course of my reading and
conversation" (ibid.). Even the dinner-table conversation may
touch on the disputes between Hutcheson and Clarke, or between
Locke and Harrington. To think about these matters, "the principles of moral good and evil, the nature and foundation of government" (T. 271), the protagonist withdraws from company to
indulge in "a *reverie* in my chamber, or a solitary walk by a river
side" (T. 270).

The philosophical enterprise in this new phase is and knows
itself to be an indulgence of sentiments, a relief from uneasiness.
"I am uneasy to think that I approve of one object, and disapprove
of another; call one thing beautiful, and another deform'd; decide
concerning truth and falshood, reason and folly, without knowing
upon what principles I proceed" (T. 271). The aim now is self-
consciousness without uneasiness, knowledge and acceptance of
what one is doing and feeling. And the ambition to achieve this
sort of self-consciousness, as well as the aim of "acquiring a name
by my inventions and discoveries" in this pursuit, are themselves
sentiments. "These sentiments spring up naturally in my present
disposition; and shou'd I endeavour to banish them, by attaching
myself to any other business or diversion, I *feel* I shou'd be a loser
in point of pleasure; and this is the origin of my philosophy"
(ibid.). Philosophy is now recognized as the self-indulgence of
self-conscious animals, their discovery and cultivation of the pleasures peculiar to such animals.

In the list of topics given for the new reformed self-avowedly
sentiment-based philosophy, metaphysics is a significant absentee.
We are still to do some epistemology, to become aware of how we
decide concerning truth and falsehood, but the question of what
ultimately exists is not on the revised agenda. Even earlier, at the
darkest phase, the question "What beings surround me?" seemed
to be limited in its intention to the sort of being whose favor

might be courted, or whose support might be won. Now, when philosophy in a new key is resumed, ontology is subordinate to moral and practical questions.[17] Some occasional excursions into ontology may still be needed, however, and Hume adds a paragraph explaining why metaphysics cannot yet be totally banished. The natural propensity of the human mind to be curious about principles and origins has led it into superstition, and the new philosopher will be led into "speculations without the sphere of common life" in order to deal with these superstitions. Religions spring up because "'tis almost impossible for the mind of man to rest, like those of beasts, in that narrow circle of objects, which are the subject of daily conversation and action" (ibid.). Once we indulge our human wish to know causes, the danger is that we are receptive to some religious system which "opens a world of its own, and presents us with scenes, and beings, and objects, which are altogether new" (ibid.). Unless it is carefully watched, the reverie in the chamber can turn into creed recital in the chapel. The moves of the human heart towards superstition, and away again, are ones taken to be natural to humans, but the former are taken to be easier than the latter. The justification of what metaphysics the new philosopher will continue to practice is that it tries to "discover" or reveal the sources of religious impulses, and the alternative satisfactions that true philosophy can afford. "For as superstition arises naturally and easily from the popular opinions of mankind, it seizes more strongly on the mind, and is often able to disturb us in the conduct of our lives and actions. Philosophy on the contrary, if just, can present us only with mild and moderate sentiments; and if false and extravagant, its opinions are merely the objects of a cold and general speculation, and seldom go so far as to interrupt the course of our natural propensities" (T. 271–272). The "just" philosophy will correct religious superstition without itself overheating the brain with either enthusiasms or cynical extravagances of despair, extravagances of the sort that Hume has just enacted. As if in comment on that despair, and on Book One, Part IV itself, Hume adds, "Generally speaking, the errors in religion are dangerous; those in philosophy only ridiculous" (T. 272). In the first *Enquiry,* where Hume gives us not a reenactment of scepticism but some comments on it, he refers to the deep despair as "momentary amazement and confusion" which the first trivial event of real life will banish (E. 160). Ridiculous indeed.

We have now arrived at a mental state stable enough to serve to launch Books Two and Three. The thoughtless sociability of the backgammon table has been followed by a return to the study. Although it is portrayed as a return to solitude, it is only a temporary solitude, and is to be devoted to a calm attempt to "instruct mankind," to assist its attempts at critical self-consciousness of its procedures, and to plead the cause of a just philosophy in "preference to superstition of every kind or denomination." All that remains to be done, before beginning the new reformed philosophy, is to announce its program and method as clearly as possible. In doing that, in the final pages of the conclusion, Hume recognizes that those outside the study, the "many honest gentlemen" who will never read the *Treatise,* have a crucial role to play in the grounding of any inventions or discoveries that the new philosophy may advance.

The new philosophical enterprise, whether thought out in solitude or in conversation, will aim to "establish a system or set of opinions, which if not true (for that, perhaps, is too much to be hop'd for) might at least be satisfactory to the human mind, and might stand the test of the most critical examination" (T. 272). To be satisfactory, it will have to "suit with common practice and experience" and so it will need to have a share of "this gross earthy mixture" of the general public to whom the *Treatise* is not addressed. There is here a touch of paradox. Of these men of the world Hume says, "I pretend not to make philosophers, nor do I expect them either to be associates in these researches or auditors of these discoveries" (ibid.). It is philosophy which must become worldly, not the world which must become philosophical. Men (and women?) of the world, and their attitudes, are to inform the new philosophy, but not, it seems, to do its critical examining. The new philosopher is not to ignore the men and women of the world, but neither is he to submit to their judgment. Their earthy mixture is to temper the philosophers' "fiery particles," yet the test of philosophers' systems is not current popularity or general acceptance but "the examination of the latest posterity" (T. 273), a posterity, perhaps, who are themselves produced by the worldly philosophers, and so have in them the right proportions of philosopher and honest burgher. Hume's own philosophy is to be judged outside the study, in the world, but not by his own unphilosophical contemporaries. (At this point in the *Treatise,* Hume seems to have predicted, and in advance discounted, the *Treatise's* own initial reception.)

The new philosophy will be a "science" (a deliberate attempt to get knowledge) of human nature. By turning philosophical studies towards human persons, instead of towards God and the universe, Hume took himself to be giving "a different turn" to philosophical activities, and to be turning them towards "those subjects where alone they can expect assurance and conviction." This "science," Hume had told us in the "Introduction" to the *Treatise,* will not be able to experiment, in our contemporary sense of the term, upon the thing it studies, as Newton could experiment on bodies. "When I am at a loss to know the effects of one body upon another in any situation, I need only put them in that situation, and observe what results from it. But should I endeavour to clear up after the same manner any doubt in moral philosophy, by placing myself in the same case with that which I consider, 'tis evident this reflection and premeditation would so disturb the operation of my natural principles, as must render it impossible to form any just conclusion from the phaenomenon" (T. xix). Hume was initiating not the science (in our sense) of psychology, either introspective or experimental, but a broader discipline of reflection on human nature, into which Charles Darwin and Michel Foucault, as much as William James and Sigmund Freud, can be seen to belong.[18] It is the uselessness of attempts at *self*-experimentation that he speaks of here, but the same "disturbance" by deliberate contrivance also affects the phenomena when deliberate experimenter and experimented-upon are different persons, as in the controlled experiments done in psychology laboratories. Hume is quite explicit about the sort of study of human life that he intended to inaugurate; it was to be one in which "we must therefore glean up our experiments in this science from a cautious observation of human life, and take them as they appear in the common course of the world by men's behaviour in company, in affairs, and in their pleasures" (ibid.). This inexact human science of self-conscious human nature, engaged in by those aiming to further increase human self-consciousness, without disturbing it by too much premeditation, is a delicate enterprise, and Hume may be right to warn us that, although assurance and conviction are possible in this field, "two thousand years with such long interruptions, and under such mighty discouragements are a small space of time to give any tolerable perfection to the sciences; and perhaps we are still in too early an age of the world to discover any principles, which will bear the examination of the latest posterity" (T. 273). All he hopes is to make a contribution, and "acquire a name" for bringing the new philosophy, or science of human nature, "a little more into fashion" (ibid.). This "science" certainly has flourished in the nineteenth and twentieth centuries, and in the case of Darwin, at least, the influence of Hume is amply documented.[19]

The new philosophy is to be "careless," despite the test of "the most critical examination" which it is to undergo. Its practitioners will be free of tyrannizing obsessions, including an overdedication to the new philosophy itself. Hume invites the reader, if he (or she?) finds himself (or herself) of like mind, to follow him into Books Two and Three. "If not, let him follow his inclination, and wait the returns of application and good humour" (ibid.). Hume, too, will expect his own application to be intermittent, and will not be worried by that fact. Nor will he be worried by vacillation in respect of certainty "*in particular points, according to the light, in which we survey them in any particular instant*" (ibid.). The reformed philosopher makes no bogey out of contradiction, but expects to change her mind and be corrected. What Hume hopes is to "contribute a little to the advancement of knowledge," and that may be done more by an instructive series of mutually contradicting self-correcting theses than by a polished but static consistent system. What Hume is preparing us for, at this point, is obviously his exploration in Book Two of "those several passions and inclinations, which actuate and govern me" (T. 271), and his tracing, in Book Three, of the principles of moral good and evil. Less obvious may be the reference to his rethinking, in those books, of what had already in Book One been said about the principles on which we "decide concerning truth and falshood, reason and folly" (ibid.). There will, in the nature of the enterprise, be contradictions between various parts of the *Treatise* on these points. That will not worry the one who is really following Hume through from the intellectual hang-ups of Book One to the delicate dialectical satisfactions of the study of "philosophy in this careless manner."[20] The reformed philosopher will have a reformed epistemology, a new cooperative method for deciding not only good and evil, but also truth and falsehood, reason and folly. Once the monsters and chimeras of Part IV of Book One are behind us, and we have fellow fallibilists and good-humoured fellow philosophers as company, the prospects for epistemology are quite transformed.

The *Treatise* is a dramatic work which presents and does not merely describe a new turn in philosophy. I have tried to bring out the dialectic within the conclusion of Book One, because I believe that it serves as a microcosm of the work as a whole. The test of this treatment of this one section will be the plausibility of that total interpretation, given in the following chapters.

2

Other Relations:
The Account of Association

For as it is by means of thought only that any thing
operates upon our passions, and as these are the only ties
of our thoughts, they really are *to us* the cement of the
universe, and all the operations of the mind must, in a
great measure, depend on them.   (T. 662)

Thus the relation of blood produces the strongest tie the
mind is capable of in the love of parents to their children.   (T. 352)

Here is a kind of ATTRACTION, which in the mental
world will be found to have as extraordinary effects as
in the natural, and to shew itself in as many and as various forms.   (T. 12–13)

In Book One of the *Treatise,* "natural relations," the outcome of
association, are what tie ideas together. They tie simple ideas
within any one complex idea; they tie sequences of ideas in trains
of thought, as one idea "naturally introduces" another in the
course of our thinking; and they somehow give us the ideas of the
more numerous and more abstract "philosophical relations" that
we discern between ideas (T. 11–13). In Book Two, Hume relates
these spontaneous relations of ideas to "one *relation* of a different
kind, *viz.* betwixt ourselves and the object" (T. 352), where the
"object" of attention here is a living person who is, and who is
taken to be, a blood relative. Relations between thinking persons
and relations between thought contents turn out not to be independent of each other. Hume's naturalism in epistemology takes
human nature as the nature closest to hand, and takes our nature

to be social and passionate, before it is cognitive. "Before" is dangerous, since our cognitive capacities, both in the species and in each human infant, develop along with our social and emotional capacities. But for understanding our understanding, Hume's preferred metaphors are ones taken from our social and passionate life. Here he follows the mode of speech of John Locke, in his brief pregnant chapter "Of the Association of Ideas" at the end of Book II of his *Essay Concerning Human Understanding*. There, in Section V, Locke writes, "Ideas that in themselves are not at all of kin, come to be so united in some mens Minds, that 'tis very hard to separate them, they always keep in Company, and the one no sooner at any time comes into the Understanding but its Associate appears with it; and if they are more than two which are thus united, the whole Gang always inseparable shew themselves together." Like Locke's idea-associates, so Hume's "perceptions" behave like people. They "make their way into our thought or consciousness" (T. 1), they "introduce" each other, as one "follows" others. They "attract" each other, and the Newtonian metaphor in Hume's hands returns to its human source.[1] "Liveliness" (or "vivacity") and "force" are the dimensions along which perceptions are assessed. The more lively perceptions are fertile; they can pass on their life, can produce resembling "copies" of themselves in ideas, so that "all the perceptions of the mind are double, and appear both as impressions and as ideas" (T. 2–3). Our ideas copy our impressions not merely in their "simple" content, but in their perceived relationships, in their keeping company, and their ganging up. It is perceived relations and associations between persons that provide the models for Humean mental relationships, and his idea-associates *can* be "kin." Our social relationships are the outcome of our biological mammalian nature, of our friendships, and of the social artifices and inventions we have made, and all three affect Locke's, Hume's and our perception of our mental and feeling states, and their relationships. Poetical enthusiasm can "counterfeit" (T. 123) the belief-feeling. Ideas of pleasures and pains "are always wandering in the mind" (T. 119). Passions "attend" one another, give life to their resembling successors, or deal death to opposing rivals. A pervasive personification, inspired perhaps by Locke's metaphors, but much more persistent, runs throughout

Hume's treatment of the contents of the human mind, and throughout his account of perceptions' behaviour in relation to each other. The person as a bundle of perceptions is balanced by the personification of each perception in the bundle. The ties between perceptions seem to be biological and social ties, writ small in the soul.

Hume argues that the "constant conjunction of our resembling perceptions, is a convincing proof, that the one are the causes of the other; and this priority of the impressions is an equal proof, that our impressions are the causes of our ideas, not our ideas of our impressions" (T. 5). This causal thesis might be taken as evidence that at least the biological metaphor has its limits—an idea is seen to "copy" or "correspond with" a single generative perception, not a pair of parent impressions. An idea is "in a manner the reflexion" of the impression it is derived from. Cartesian metaphors of light, and the propagation of images, as well as of life, and derivative life, persist throughout the *Treatise*. This is undeniable, so we should not push the liveliness talk too hard. Still, it is persistent, and as much as anything else gives Hume's philosophy its distinctive tone, its freshness, and one is almost tempted to say its innocence. (Hume is the philosopher of both innocence and experience.) Whereas earlier philosophers such as Descartes suppressed the deep source of their philosophical conviction that an effect must derive its reality from its cause, avoided acknowledging the obvious paradigm of their version of cause-effect, namely mother and child (indeed, Descartes tried to reduce away the category of life, to exorcise it from his thought), Hume gives parenthood as his first example of causation in the section on the natural relations (T. 11), and uses the language of life transmission right from the start of his discussion of our minds. It really is our mental "*life*" that Hume is analyzing, and he does it with a lot less than the usual repression of its debt to our preoccupation with ourselves as living persons, generated by other "prior" or "preceding" living persons, associating with or "attending" our parents and other loved ones, "conjoining" with some (occasionally constantly conjoining), able to generate more or less resembling successors. All this familiar "life world" is on the surface of Book One, in its language, and is in the subject matter as well as the language of Books Two and Three. In this chapter I shall look at Hume's version of the "correlatives" between which natural relations hold, at some odd features of his account of the varying variety of these relations, and at some related features of Hume's treatment of one of our most puzzling and powerful ideas, that of time. Temporal contiguity is essential to the idea of cause, as Hume analyzes it, and this will be my topic in Chapters 3 and 4. Our complex ideas of substances, of physical bodies and of minds, will be the topic of Chapter 5, and those ideas presuppose that of temporal duration. Since this relation, that between "before and after" (see T. 14), is, as Donald Livingston[2] has emphasized, basic to almost everything else that Hume discusses, it is proper to attend to it before we look at his treatment of ideas that presuppose it, as it is proper to look at mental association before looking at that special form of it that Hume takes inference to be.

Hume's official story about the "correlatives" or relata between which relations hold is the Lockean one, that we acquire simple ideas when a "copy" is taken by the mind of the simple sense impressions and impressions of reflection (passions) that it undergoes, and that our subsequent recombinings of these simples in our thoughts, both free imaginings and constrained beliefs, are guided by the "natural relations" that we have perceived between those simples—relations of resemblance, of spatial and temporal contiguity, and of causation, "if I may be allowed to use that term" (T. 11).[3] We may separate and reunite simple ideas as we please, but "the gentle force" of already formed associations guides even our freest flights of fancy, and selects the complexes for which we have words in our language. Hume cites the inter-translatability or "near correspondence" of different languages as evidence that the gentle force of mental association operates fairly uniformly— "nature in a manner pointing out to every one those simple ideas, which are most proper to be united into a complex one" (T. 10– 11). The reference to a language and languages here paves the way for the role words are to play in Hume's Berkeleyan account, a few sections later, of how particular ideas become general and abstract. Fully determinate ideas become "general in their representation" (T. 20) when we have learned one name for some respect in which the object of that particular idea resembles other encountered and encounterable objects. We then let any determinate idea substitute for any other to which that word applies, so ideas of determinate particulars become "general in their representation." Words are general in their meaning, and we learn to use words, thus to let our thought be guided by linguistic universals. "A particular idea becomes general by being annex'd to a general term; that is, to a term, which from a customary conjunction has a relation to many other particular ideas, and readily recalls them in the imagination" (T. 22). The first human customs that Hume needs to invoke, to carry out his philosophical program that is to make custom play a central role, are the customs of language users. Customs of classifying and labelling give us competency at abstraction and generalization. Our habit of thought, in particular our grasp of necessary relations between our ideas, "follows the words" (T. 23). Customs of thinking follow customs of speaking.

There is no individualist bias to Hume's epistemology within most of Book One—membership in a linguistic community, itself one of several such communities whose languages "nearly correspond" to each other, is essential for the sort of mental activity that he is analyzing in Part I of Book One, indeed in the whole of the *Treatise*. Only in Part IV of Book One, when scepticism and solipsism are worked through, is there any experiment made of separating the thinker from the normal human world. The person whose thought is being thought about at the beginning of the *Treatise* is no solitary abandoned outcast, but a confident member of a language community, where children are given oranges to teach them the idea and the word "orange" (T. 5), where the role and special features of memory are linked with the task of and special demands made on historians (T. 9), where beliefs are formed from the testimony and on the authority of others, including historians (T. 83, 117), as well as from one's own experience of things other than the reliability of what one's fellows tell one, where ideas about time presuppose recourse to timepieces (T. 65). The retreat into a presocial or a postsocial self does not occur until Part IV, and even then is only intermittent. The world in which the thinkers of most of Book One do their thinking is one containing clocks, calendars, schools, globes; one where fellow thinkers talk to us, where there are translators, mathematicians, anatomists, historians, poets, all recognized as such and taken to have special social roles, involving special permissions (poets may lie) and special duties (good, "exact" historians relate events in the order in which they are believed to have occurred). Except in Part IV, there is no pretense of building up a public world from subjective pre-social certainties of the sort Descartes seemed to be searching for in the first two of his *Meditations.* Living human persons, their voices, eyes, brains, hands, pens, desks, clocks, calendars, dictionaries, printing presses, and copies of Caesar's *De Bello Gallico,* are as fully present as the thinker. And indeed, for most of the time, the meta-thought is about *us* and how *we* proceed "in the course of our thinking" (T. 11).

Persons and their works are primary; one is tempted to say that for Hume *they* are the "original existences." Perceptions seem to be modelled on persons, and this is not surprising if, for the generality of mankind, "those very sensations, which enter by the eye or ear, are . . . the true objects" (T. 202) and if our most lively and enlivening sensations are of our companions, whose appearance awake us "as it were, from a dream," presenting us with "the liveliest of all objects" (T. 353). It will be flesh and blood persons, not hats, shoes, or stones (T. 202), that are our paradigm perception-objects. And since what we expect of such a fellow person, when he is an intimate, is unguarded disclosure of "all the actions of his mind . . . his inmost sentiments and affections . . . all the emotions, which are caus'd by any object" (T. 353), it will be expressive passionate fellow persons, rather than, say, persons insofar as they exhibit particular sizes, shapes and shades of color, that provide our most lively perceptions, and it will be perceived relations between passionate persons that give us our paradigm relations. Of course, any expressive face that makes us privy to its owner's "inmost sentiments" will also exhibit size, shape, movement and color, but these impressions will not be the crucial ones for recognizing the sentiments that are expressed. (Patterns of movement and alterations in it, voice, tone and alterations in them, will, however, become very important.)

If our most lively and enlivening perceptions are indeed of companions who candidly express their sentiments, then we could get a version of which ideas are basic or "simple," which derivative, which are concrete and which abstract, that is quite different from Locke's official[4] account. Hume does not give us this reversal, in his claims about simples and complexes. "Her smile" is for him officially a very complex idea, a "mode," while the simpler ideas will be of her face color, her mouth size, shape and so on. "We cannot form to ourselves a just idea of the taste of a pine-apple, without having actually tasted it" (T. 5).[5] And no more can we form a just idea of a welcoming smile or of rejoicing company without having savored that. Although in theory Hume's empiricism requires him to distinguish simple from complex perceptions, since it is only simple ideas that must be traced back to simple impressions (T. 3), he rarely bothers to analyze out any simples, and the distinction does little real work for him. As he is aware, the idea of a simple idea is a highly abstract meta-idea (T. 637). The "simplicity" in which all simple ideas resemble each other is never very clearly explicated either by Hume or by his empiricist predecessors.

"Simple perceptions or impressions and ideas are such as admit of no distinction nor separation. The complex are the contrary to these, and may be distinguished into parts" (T. 2). The parts of a smile may perhaps be distinguished, but does what it expresses have any parts? "For can any one conceive a passion of a yard in length, a foot in breadth, and an inch in thickness?" (T. 234). The ideas of divisibility and indivisibility into spatial parts get no grip on those things that *"may exist, and yet be no where"* (T. 235), and Hume has great fun, in "Of the immateriality of the soul," with the absurdities of talk of indivisible thinking substances and their perceptions. "Is the indivisible subject, or immaterial substance if you will, on the left or on the right hand of the perception?" (T. 240). "A moral reflection cannot be plac'd on the right or on the left hand of a passion" (T. 236). He had not earlier asked if the taste of the pineapple was on the right or the left hand of its texture, but now that he has established the non-extended nature of passions, smells, tastes and sounds, he does try to explain our habit of allocating spatial position to sounds, tastes and smells. (The bitter taste of the olive at one end of the table and the sweet taste of the fig at the other are perceived as "separated from each other by the whole length of the table"—T. 236.) It is because we take the taste to be caused by what can be unproblematically located that we allow the effect to share in the locatability of its cause. We add to causation a sort of honorary conjunction in place, we "feign . . . conjunction in place, in order to strengthen the connexion" (T. 238). Since we do not similarly see our passions to be directly caused by unproblematically locatable, tangible or visible points or arrays of points, we are not so tempted to feign a spatial location for them, although we might indeed also see the fig eater's cloying delight as separated from the olive fancier's saltier satisfaction by the whole length of the table. At any rate the "simplicity" of the fig's taste, the olive's and the pineapple's cannot be a simple matter of their spatial separability from other perceived qualities of fig, olive or pineapple. Hume simply does not bother to tell us what sort of separability it is, so we are left free to relativize simplicity to the particular concerns at hand.

Simplicity is non-analyzability by a given method of analysis, relative to a given set of abstract ideas, and so of linguistic customs, as tools of analysis. As there are "distinctions of reason" between what are not conceivably separable in space, namely between color and visible shape (T. 25), and as there are what we could call courtesy conjunctions of reason between what has position and what strictly does not, so there may be distinctions of reason, or of reflective passion, between smiles and smiling mouths, smiles and lit up eyes, smiles and faces. The distinction between the left half and the right half of the face that smiles may license a "separation of reason" between the right and the left half of the smile, but scarcely between the right and the left halves of the pleasure (or the villainy) that the smile expresses. Although the smile is the extended effect of an unextended mental cause, we do not confer honorary extension on the feeling-cause; Hume is right that "a moral reflection cannot be plac'd on the right or on the left hand of a passion" (T. 236).

Passions cannot be subjected to the mode of analysis into simples on which Hume usually relies when he is analyzing those things that must be somewhere in order to exist. In Book Two he separates out the different pleasures, pains and ideas involved in the various passions for which we have names, like "pride" and "malice." He says that these claimed components of our familiar passions are often "confounded" (T. 331) by the persons in whose hearts and minds they are compounded. In particular, the hedonic components, although theoretically distinguishable, "like colours, may be blended so perfectly together, that each of them may lose itself, and contribute only to vary that uniform impression, which arises from the whole" (T. 366). On Hume's theory, pride proper is a "simple and uniform" impression (T. 277), a pleasurable glow of self-satisfaction, always accompanied or introduced by the "separate pleasure" (T. 285) of admiration of some good thing, which in this case is taken to be one's own. But the proud person typically confounds the two pleasures, which "lose themselves" in each other. The similarities and variations in our pleasures, and the similarities and variations in all our "uneasy" feelings or dis-pleasures, are bedrock facts for Hume, the foundation of his system. "There is something very inexplicable in this variation of our feelings; but 'tis what we have experience of with regard to all our passions and sentiments" (T. 617). When we "survey" moral beauty of character, we get a slightly different-feeling pleasure from that which we get from looking at a beautiful human face, and it is noticeably different from the pleasure a splendid sunset gives us. Our pleasure in human character shifts in quality as we shift attention from good motives to good judgment, or from good will to good humor. Hume takes both the variations and the similarities as his "given," and this given surely is no myth. "For 'tis what we have experience of with regard to all our passions and sentiments," as it is also with regard to colors, tastes and sounds. He takes it as his business as a philosopher not to explain the spectrum of our pleasures, but to "save" these phenomena in his "system." Anatomists proper may explain why our capacity for pleasure has as much "flexibility" as Hume finds it to have (T. 617), why some pleasures "pass easily" into slightly different ones, provided they get some "assistance" from easy transitions between the ideas of what they are pleasures in, but Hume as philosopher-anatomist of human nature takes it to be his business to let his "system" do justice to the variety, to characterize it perspicuously, and to point up significant resemblances, differences and correlations, not just in the array of our passions spread out statically in the philosopher's mind, but in the shifts, slides, passages, transitions—in the dynamics of our emotional life.

In the account he gives us in Books Two and Three, pleasures and pains are in theory simple impressions of sense, that into which more complex chunks of our passionate life are analyzed. In fact they turn out, like colors, to be determinate versions of flexible determinables, and to be able to blend perfectly, and "lose themselves" in each other. The separation out of simple components from the perfect blends is done by attention to the recognized variations, covariations, independent variations, just as Hume "separated" the presence of color from the presence of shape in the section "Of abstract ideas." Figure and color are always copresent, but we can separate them by considering the different "resemblances, of which they are susceptible" (T. 25). We "tacitly carry our eye" to one set of resemblances and differences when we consider the color of the white globe, to a different set when we consider its spherical form. The word "color," and the names we have for different colors, guide us in this tacit mental operation. In precisely the same way, the word "pleasure," and the plurality of names we have for the variety of takings of pleasure (joy, admiration, pride, love, approval) guide the anatomist of human nature in Book Two. The "experiments to confirm this system," in Part II of Book Two, are explicit rather than tacit carryings of the reader's mental eye to these hedonic variations, to their partial correlation with variations in beliefs, and with shifts in thought or mental associations. "The double relation of impressions and ideas," the system Hume is confirming, can be seen as involving a "distinction of reason" between the various hedonic components and between them and the thought components of our passions. To confirm his system he must separate the hedonic dimension and attend to its distinctive variations.

In Book One, Hume confidently asserts that our ideas of conquest, negotiation, government, are complex (T. 23). What sort of "separability" is to be found between "all the simple ideas" we might "spread out in our minds" (T. 23) were we to break any of them down into simple components? He himself later (in Book Three, Part II) subjects government to an acute analysis, but does not tell us exactly what his method is. It involves the sort of attention to what does and does not covary that the analysis of passions involved. Natural-historical analysis, as well as linguistic or conceptual analysis, goes into it. In Book One it is "absurdity" that he appeals to, in order to show the involvement of the idea of superior force in that of conquest: "Thus if instead of saying, *that in war the weaker have always recourse to negotiation,* we shou'd say, *that they have always recourse to conquest,* the custom, which we have acquir'd of attributing certain relations to ideas, still follows the words, and makes us immediately perceive the absurdity of that proposition" (T. 23). Relations of abstract ideas are involved, and so "knowledge" of them can be taken for granted in any person familiar with the linguistic customs that give stability to these word-anchored ideas. We *know* that conquest is taken as proof of superior not inferior fighting power, and we know this without needing to study military history. But in order to be convinced that government is the sort of humanly created thing, authority to command, that Hume is to tell us that it is, knowing our verbal customs will not be enough—we will need to be convinced of the presence of other customs as well, the human customs giving rise to more primitive social "artifices" than that of government, the ones that he takes government itself to presuppose.

Once Hume gives his full attention to concepts such as government, justice, obligation, obedience, military commander, he does not try to show them to be "complex" in the sense that implies "able to be analyzed into simples that we can spread out in our minds." We would be hard put to list the simple ideas in Hume's social philosophy. What he seems to find when he explores these concepts are webs of interrelated concepts. Some perhaps are less complicated than others, but even the "simpler" ones are mutually involving, as mutually involving, indeed, as our ideas of differing pleasures, or of differing shades of blue, or even of colors more generally. Theoretically the color of an orange orange and a scarlet scarlet tanager are, like the taste of a pineapple, and of a fig, "simple" perceptions. Actually they involve their relations to at least some of their fellow colors and fellow tastes. The idea of a single-color perceiver, or of a single-taste taster, would be as "absurd" as that of a militarily weak conqueror, or a one-perception perceiver, the fancied sub-oyster that suffers monotonous uninterrupted hunger-cum-thirst (T. 634). Not only must there be some variety of perceptions for us to keep a grip on the concept of a perceiver, but these perceptions must not be found unrelated to one another, must not degenerate into "a monstrous heap" (T. 282). Our perceptions of pleasures, colors and tastes *do* come as related—resemblances between colors "strike the eye, *or rather the mind*" (T. 70, my emphasis). We "intuit" the connection between scarlet and orange, once we have sense-derived ideas of them, and, given the idea of either, we can "raise up" the idea of the other, so long as we have enough experience of other colors such as yellow or crimson. The instance of the missing shade of blue is far from being "particular and singular" (T. 6). It is quite typical of ideas of particular sense qualities within a given sense modality. Hume continues to treat particular pleasures and colors as "simples," even when he has granted that we can sometimes derive one from others, and can "intuit" their resemblances and differences from each other. This shows the perfunctoriness of his use of the simple / complex distinction,[6] and the relativity of that very complex concept, the simple.

In Book Two, where passions and their interrelationships are his subject matter, and where his theory of "the double relation of impressions and ideas" is proudly advanced, Hume claims that association between passions is explicable by just one of his three earlier principles of association, resemblance. Association by contiguity and causation need not be invoked to explain why a given type of passion brings passions of other types in its train, why hatred is attended by anger, or love by benevolence. Hume supposes that hedonic resemblance between the "uneasiness" of hate and anger, and the "agreeability" of love and benevolence, will be enough to explain the spontaneous association of these passions. "Grief and disappointment give rise to anger, anger to envy, envy to malice, and malice to grief again, till the whole circle be compleated. In like manner our temper, when elevated with joy naturally, throws itself into love, generosity, pity, courage, pride, and the other resembling affections . . . 'Tis evident, then, there is an attraction or association among impressions, as well as among ideas; tho' with this remarkable difference, that ideas are associated

by resemblance, contiguity, and causation; and impressions only
by resemblance" (T. 283). This contraction of Hume's explanatory
principles itself calls for remark.

Why does Hume think that impressions (pleasures and pains)
are associated only by resemblance? Resemblance, unlike contiguity and causation, is one of the relations of ideas that "depend
entirely on the ideas," whereas contiguity and causation are relations that "may be chang'd without any change in the ideas"
(T. 69). Experience gives us and corrects or updates our versions
of the latter "independent" relations between particular relata,
whereas we can "intuit" the "dependent" relation[7] of resemblance
between two things once we have had impressions of each of
them. A person I have never seen before may so resemble a portrait I have seen that I immediately connect the one with the other,
and thereafter associate the portrait with that person. This custom
of thought-moves will not itself be dependent, for its formation,
on constant conjunctions or indeed on any conjunctions in sense
experience. In order to associate ideas by contiguity, I must have
experienced the two associates together, conjoined in space or
time. To associate ideas by causation, I must normally have experienced some constancy in their objects' temporal conjunction.
But to associate by resemblance I need merely be reminded by one
thing of something else that I recall, and that it resembles. Association by resemblance, of ideas as much as of impressions, is not
dependent upon facts about what pairings there have already been
in one's past impressions. It is not experience-dependent in the
way association by contiguity and by causation are. It "depends
entirely upon the perceptions" that are associated, be they ideas or
impressions. As "our imagination runs easily from one idea to any
other that *resembles* it" (T. 11),[8] whether or not the two resembling
things of which we have ideas were ever observed together, so
our heart will run easily from a given passion to a resembling passion, whether or not this particular sequence of passions has been
enacted in us before. We do not need to be *reenacting* a passion-
sequence for it to exhibit association by resemblance. When "grief
and disappointment give rise to anger," the explanation need not
be that these passions have kept company before, that we are reenacting an infantile scenario.[9] For the same explanation will be

given of the first as of the subsequent occurrences of this sort of passion-sequence, namely the hedonic resemblance, the "agreement" (see T. 283) between these passions, their intrinsic "suitability" to each other.

Hume invokes the association of impressions by hedonic resemblance, along with the association of ideas by resemblance, contiguity or causation, to explain, in the first instance, why the "separate pleasure" that a fine cloak is taken to give anyone who sees or recalls it will lead to the more special pleasure of a glow of pride, when the cloak is one's own. Whereas the idea of the cloak, which is the "object" of the former pleasure, leads to the thought of its owner by some mix of associative relations that link the two ideas in a person's mind, the two impressions of pleasure or joy, whose resemblance leads one to follow the other, seem to have a quite different sort of association. Association of ideas, one might have thought, presupposes some *perceived* resemblance, some noted contiguity, some believed causation. That sort of association, one might reasonably think, requires a conscious associator. But it is not because of *noted* resemblances of past pleasures of admiration with past glows of pride that the one now introduces the other. These passion-associations are not learned responses. It is not that we feel admiration and then, even unconsciously, think, "I might as well slide into pride, since I have learned that it is similar in its pleasant feel." No sort of recognition by the passionate person of the likenesses of her sequential passions is needed for the sequence to occur, on Hume's theory, any more than we need to recognize the resemblance between ourselves and those we sympathize with, in order to feel sympathy.

Most of Hume's readers have found his claim that *two* pleasures are involved in pride (and in love) somewhat surprising. They really were "perfectly blended," before Hume separated them. If there really are *two* hedonic states associated by resemblance here, the plurality of states and their association may well have been covert before Hume exposed it. Could the associative relations between thoughts be similarly covert, unconscious relations between unrecognized relata, relata whose very separateness from each other may also have gone unrecognized by the person in whose mind the association is claimed to occur? Hume's first ex-

amples of association of ideas do not encourage readers to think
that he is talking about unconscious association, but neither does
his discussion of association rule that out. There is plenty of talk
(T. 60–61) of animal spirits moving along channels in the brain,
and the "smooth slides" and "easy transitions" of the sort of thinking that he wants association of ideas to explain are often ones that
it would be most implausible to suppose were consciously guided
by recognition of the relations he finds. This is most obviously so
in his accounts in Book One, Part IV, of how we form and retain
our ideas of lasting bodies and lasting persons. So the association
of ideas that explains our complex ideas of lasting "substances"
may well have to be taken to be often unconscious. "A relation of
ideas operates secretly and calmly on the mind" (T. 334). The secret can, but need not, become common knowledge. Could the
relata be secret too? Could it be a secret that in a given case there
are numerous ideas, candidates for association? Although Hume
says in Book Two that "Ideas never admit of a total union, but are
endow'd with a kind of impenetrability, by which they exclude
each another, and are capable of forming a compound by their
conjunction, not by their mixture" (T. 366), neither their plurality
nor their conjunctions were self-evident in Book One. Especially
in his account, in "Of the sceptical and other systems of philosophy," of why we take it that persons and bodies have identity over
time, Hume is willing to speak of our "error and deception" in
this very matter. "Nothing is more apt to make us mistake one
idea for another, than any relation betwixt them, which associates
them together in the imagination, and makes it pass with facility
from one to the other" (T. 202). This "mistaking" is a matter of
"confounding" ideas, of "not perceiving the change" from one
sense impression or idea to the next. When we confound "succession with the identity" (T. 204), we are supposed by Hume to
miscount our distinguishable perceptions. A kind of inverse of
pressing our eye with our finger makes our mind's eye see one
where there really are two or more perceptions. In these passages,
Hume has to press our mind's eye a bit, to get us to see the plurality he wants us to recognize. Whatever else they show, I think
they show that he is willing to postulate that we might have more

separable "ideas" and sense impressions, more candidate mental associates, than we may have realized. The existence of the associates, as well as their association, can be "secret."

Association of impressions is a psychological mechanism that by-passes awareness more radically than does even unconscious or subconscious association of ideas, including the latter's association by resemblance. Of course, once Hume (or one's psychiatrist) directs one's attention to the hedonic resemblances to be found among one's sequential passions, one may well recognize them, and afterwards be affected by that "raised consciousness" of hedonic relations. But no greater preceding consciousness of them than our speech habits imply is necessary, in order for Hume to be right about the psychological dynamics. Our use of the word "pleasurable," to describe a variety of feelings, implies implicit recognition of their resemblance, but it may take Hume's help before we *do* apply it to love, generosity and pity. Certainly he needs to persuade us that hatred and anger are as "painful" or "uneasy" as grief, and that *two* pains are involved in hate. He gives us what amounts to a theoretical redescription of the range of human passions for which we have names, a redescription designed to enable him to classify them all as either pleasurable or painful, or mixtures of pleasurable and painful elements. So to recognize the resemblances that on his theory guide the "association of impressions," we have first to grasp and accept his "new and extraordinary" opinions (T. 659) about the sort of association operative in our emotional lives. He knows that his psychological "system" is not self-evident, especially as concerns the association of impressions. "'Tis not so evident at first sight, that a relation of impressions is requisite to these [i.e., the indirect] passions, and that because in the transition the one impression is so much comfounded with the other, that they become in a manner undistinguishable" (T. 331). We need Hume's help to "make the separation" (ibid.) and so to intuit the resemblance and discern the association.

"It is by means of thought only that any thing operates upon our passions" (T. 662). Hume treats passions, or impressions of reflection, as pleasurable or painful feelings that are introduced by some idea or sense impression. What makes them passions, as distinct from mere sensations of pleasure or pain, is precisely this temporal contiguity and causal dependence on the thought that introduces them. A letter or a newspaper article refers to a place where the reader passed pleasant days, and so bittersweet nostalgia for those vanished joys is a predictable follow-up to the recalled memories of that place. The idea of past pleasures "returns upon the soul" and produces "the new impressions of desire and aversion, hope and fear, which may properly be called impressions of reflexion, because derived from it" (T. 8). The very concept of a passion is for Hume a causal, indeed a meta-causal, concept—it is a pleasure or pain caused by the thought of former pleasures or pains, and of their believed causes and recalled contexts. Causation and contiguity drop out of the association of impressions, but they remain built into the nature of these particular sorts of associates, and indeed into the nature of mental association as such. Association in its very nature is the selection of what, given a particular present perception, the next (contiguous) perception will be, and it is treated by Hume as a matter of the earlier perception's *causing* its successor perception. The mind is "convey'd from one idea to another" (T. 11) and is also conveyed from impression of reflection to impression of reflection. Such impressions are essentially associative transitions from ideas of past pleasures (along with their occasions) to "new" derivative pleasures, desires, hopes, loves, pride. The associations that their transitions exhibit are, then, strictly associations of associations. This meta-association, like any mental association, will be a case of mental causation, so Hume's claim that only resemblance is needed to explain association of this sort becomes the claim that, at this level, mental effects *resemble* their mental causes, resemble them in hedonic quality.

I have given no adequate answer to my question of why Hume is (perhaps wrongly) confident that passions are associated only by resemblance. I have merely noted that in any case resemblance is the odd one out, the *necessary* (as distinct from contingent) natural relation. Passions of a feather flock together; ideas of a feather flock together; and Hume takes both flockings, as it were, to stand to reason. When he is explaining how sympathy operates, he appeals to the "great resemblance among all human creatures," and supposes that the greater the resemblance, the easier the "communication of passions." "This resemblance *must* very much contribute to make us enter into the sentiments of others, and embrace them with facility and pleasure" (T. 318, my emphasis). Like sympathizes with like. The association of impressions can be seen as a sort of psychological sympathy between passions, their ability to convert themselves into their resembling successors.

Passion effects, when explained by "association of impressions," resemble their passion causes. This amounts to an interesting concession to the Cartesians. Ideas too, as mental effects, are supposed to resemble their causes, indeed to be true copies or images of impressions of sensation, images not necessarily of their "feel," or "vivacity," but of their cognitive content. In the section of Book One, Part III entitled "Of the effects of other relations, and other habits" (from which I have borrowed my chapter title), Hume, when he is discussing credulity, speaks of the passed-along belief of a human person as "an image as well as an effect" of its causes in the testifier's experience (T. 113). It is taken as an "image" of the facts that caused it. Some effects, especially mental effects, really can be what the rationalists took all effects to be, transmitters of the reality or quality of their causes. "Resemblance, when conjoin'd with causation, fortifies our reasonings" (ibid.). Hume warns us against overrating the extent to which idea effects, in the form of beliefs, do reliably image the facts that they purport both to represent and to be caused by. Between the facts and the sincere claim about them come the impressions of sensation that the believer relies on, and also her interpretation and verbal formulation of what they amount to. "Rash inference" from effects to resembling causes is the occupational disease of thinkers and speakers, and this is not surprising if at the root of all their reasonings is reliance on ideas as true copies of the impressions from which they are "taken."

Faith in *some* perception-effects as imaging their perception-causes is needed for any belief at all, even if it were restricted to belief about our own perceptions.[10] And faith it will be, whenever an already vanished lively perception is taken to be "copied" in an idea that occurs a bit later, whether it is an idea of imagination or of memory. Hume raises the germs of a sceptical worry about the reliability of our memory of witnessed events. "I think, I remember such an event, says one; but am not sure. A long tract of time has almost worn it out of my memory" (T. 85–86). But even when it appears fresh and vivacious we should not be too sure, since it is "impossible to recal the past impressions, in order to compare them with our present ideas" (T. 85). This fact did not deter Hume earlier when he claimed that our ideas "correspond" with impressions from which they are derived, that idea "*copies*" will be taken of the child's impressions of the color and taste of an orange or a pineapple. All that we can check to determine match or mismatch is our expectation of how the next orange (or the same orange) will taste, an expectation formed by our past orange-tastings, compared with what our next tasting turns out to be like. Does it meet or disappoint our expectations? But if it should disappoint our expectations, that could be either because the next orange is really different (or the original one has changed), or else because the original idea copy was sloppily taken, or sloppily replicated in replacement copies (since perceptions are "temporary and perishing"), so that the current idea-copy is not just faint, but inaccurate. No later fleeting perception can be put, as it were, side by side with the earlier fleeting perception that it is taken to re-present, so no estimates of accuracy or justness of mental representations to their vanished originals are ever possible, if this is the only way in which they could properly be made.

Were mental representations our only representations, their accuracy could not be investigated. Fortunately they are not our only representations. We also have portraits of our absent and present friends, and in the latter case we have little trouble judging whether or not they bear a resemblance to their subject (see T. 99). We have mirror images, and other natural reflections; we have printing presses and can judge "the fidelity of Printers" (T. 146). We acquire our ideas of accuracy from these external representations that *can* be compared with their enduring originals, and we can compare our expectations of them with our current impressions of them. We learn what lasts relatively well, what fades quickly, what rate of change to expect in originals and in their copies. All our talk of true images, and of relative accuracy, derives from our social interpersonal world, where an orange is taken not to change in taste in a matter of seconds, and almost certainly to change in a matter of weeks, where contemporary written reports by witnesses to an event are given a different authority from the memoirs of those same witnesses, where different witnesses' reports are collated and checked for coherence, where motivations for deception and self-deception are recognized and investigated. Hume *is* supposing that we know roughly how long a ripe pineapple will stay ripe and pineapple-tasting, not rotten and foul-tasting, that we *do* manage to detect defects and imperfections in one another's memories (T. 9), even though none of us can "recall," in the sense of make present again, the remembered or reported sequence of past events. Not just the vividness of the memory, but also the coherence of the memory report with all the other evidence we together take ourselves to have, goes into our judgment of whether this is a remembering or a misremembering. Idea-copies, taken more or less at the time of occurrence of the copied impression, are limit cases of such fallible memory traces. A little help from our fellow copiers will always be needed to judge the truth or accuracy of copies, whether of the fleeting or of the lasting, since without that help we will not know what can reasonably be expected to last, and what not to last.

We need each other's help in judging the fidelity or "truth" of representations, and we have that help. Persons among persons are the liveliest objects of our mental attention, in part because we depend in so many ways upon those persons. The associations and relations between persons give us, in a parallel way, the liveliest of all our conceptions of relations. For Hume, the strongest of these perceived relations is "the love of parents to their children" (T. 352). Which of Hume's official "natural" associative relations are perceived by parents between themselves and their loved children? "All the relations of blood depend upon cause and effect" (T. 11–12). Human adults perceive a causal tie to their children, and there is usually also a perceptible relation of prolonged spatial contiguity, and of resemblance. All three natural relations of ideas are united in "one *relation* of a different kind" (T. 352), that between parent and child. Locke again is Hume's philosophical father[11] here. He reserves the term "natural relations" (in Chapter

28 of the *Essay Concerning Human Understanding,* Book Two, a
chapter entitled "Of Other Relations") for relations having to do
with "circumstances of their (the *relata's*) origin or beginning;
which being not afterwards alter'd, make the relations depending
on them as lasting as the subjects to which they depend; e.g. Father and son, brothers, cousins-german, which have their relations
by one community of blood wherein they partake in several degrees . . . These I call *natural relations.*" Locke also notes how "the
use of common life" affects our recognition of such relations. "For
'tis certain, that in reality the relation is the same between the begetter and the begotten, in the several races of other animals as
well as men, but yet 'tis seldom said, this bull is the grandfather
of such a calf, or that two pigeons are cousins-german." (He also
notes how in some societies men take greater interest in their
horses' pedigrees than in their own.) So Hume's special treatment
of "the tie of blood," among the "natural" relations, has Lockean
precedent. For Locke, however, these natural relations were
merely among the "other relations" that are thought to deserve a
chapter after the philosophically important relations, such as identity and diversity, cause and effect, have already been discussed.
But for Hume, I am suggesting, all other relations are "cousins-
german" of "the relation of blood," aspects of it, variants of such
aspects, or abstract descendants of them. The three Humean "natural relations" come together in it, and his philosophical relations
are "remarkable effects" of the natural relations at work in our
thought.[12]

In "the relation of blood," as Locke's remarks emphasize, temporal relations are an essential element. It is a relation that concerns
origins or beginnings, a relation "not afterwards altered," even if
forgotten or ignored. Temporal "contiguity" between begetter
and begotten is contained in the begetting relation—indeed we
could say that for Hume our understanding of the temporal relation is begotten of our most primitive "natural" sense of the par-
ent-child relation. Hume's treatment of time in Book Two presents it as a dimension that can be abstracted from our version of
history, and of family history as represented on a genealogical
chart.[13] We represent "our ancestors to be, in a manner, mounted
above us, and our posterity to lie below us" (T. 437). Taking our-

selves as reference point, since "ourself is intimately present to us" (T. 427), our thought can "proceed" or make a "progression" forward to imagine the lifetime of our children, beyond our own projected lifetime, and can turn back to consider times in the recalled youth of parents, before our own birth, and so construct a conception of a progression of overlapping generations. The past is that into which the memories of older persons, our parents and grandparents, reach further than our own memories. The future is that into which our children and grandchildren will live and live to remember further than we will. "Contiguous" or rather overlapping generations, and our consciousness of their succession, give us a lively idea of historical time, from which we abstract a fainter idea of a sequence of contiguous moments, the sort of refined and abstract concept of time that Hume analyzes in Book One. With a bit of exaggeration we could say that the idea of the succession of momentary "points," impersonally considered, is derivative from the perceived succession of persons, whose existence is more durable and of whom our perceptions are liveliest.

Hume's concerns in Book Two are with those conceptions that are involved in our passions and our will—the sections on time and temporal distance follow directly after the section devoted to "the influence of the imagination on the passions," and they apply the theses advanced there to the special case of interest in the past and the future. In Book One, Part II, "Of the ideas of space and time," time took a back seat to space, and it was the ideas of mathematicians that Hume was primarily aiming to analyze. These more abstract notions influence at most the special passions of mathematicians, and so are not what Book Two is concerned about; and it is temporal rather than spatial contiguity and distance that there take pride of place. Spatial metaphors still abound, but "tho' distance both in space and time has a considerable effect on the imagination, and by that means on the will and passions, yet the consequence of a removal in *space* are much inferior to those of a removal in *time*. Twenty years are certainly but a small distance of time in comparison of what history and even the memory of some may inform them of, and yet I doubt if a thousand leagues, or even the greatest distance of place this globe can admit of, will so remarkably weaken our ideas, and diminish our passions. A *West-India* merchant will tell you, that he is not without concern about what passes in *Jamaica;* tho' few extend their views so far into futurity, as to dread very remote accidents" (T. 429). Why twenty years is compared with a thousand leagues is not at all clear, and surely the merchant will also be concerned with next month and next year. Hume's main point is that it is easier for us to take what is now happening anywhere on earth into our current concern than to extend it to, say, the entire earthly past and projected future of one city, such as Edinburgh, or even of one family line. Once his concern is with what spatio-temporal relations are emotionally salient, it is the asymmetries that interest him, asymmetries between removal in space and in time, between distance in the past and distance in the future, between attitudes to ancestors and attitudes to posterity. This contrasts with Book One, where divisibility was the main concern, and where conclusions about spatial intervals were simply carried over to temporal ones. ("The infinite divisibility of space implies that of time, as is evident from the nature of motion. If the latter, therefore, be impossible, the former must be equally so"—T. 31.) Even when Hume there moves to the "other qualities" of space and time, those other than divisibility, the claims about time are adaptations of the parallel claims about space—that our idea of each is of "the manner of appearance" of a plurality of perceptions, abstracted from perceivable arrays of colors, and from "some *perceivable* succession of changeable objects" (T. 35) into a "disposition of points." Hume's brief account of "those appearances, which make us fancy we have that idea" of duration without change (T. 65) are a fairly perfunctory adaptation of his longer explanation of the errors that lead us to fancy we can form the idea of a vacuum, of a space without any perceptible points arrayed in that space. In Book Two, however, conceptions of time are given more serious attention, and their distinctive asymmetries are the focus of attention.

There is no incompatibility between Book One and Book Two on these topics, simply a different level or kind of abstraction. In Book One, Hume had distinguished the idea of space from that of time in the way Kant later would: the idea of time is the idea of the manner of appearance of *all* our perceptions, "ideas as well as impressions, and impressions of reflection as well as of sensation"

(T. 35). All go into the succession from the experience of which the Book One idea of time is derived. The idea of spatial extension is derived from a more restricted phenomenological base. "Our internal impressions are our passions, emotions, desires and aversions; none of which, I believe, will ever be asserted to be the model, from which the idea of space is deriv'd" (T. 33). But our passions do feed into the succession from which the idea of time is derived. Our passions and our conception of time are mutually dependent. Hume is willing to claim that "no object is presented to the senses, nor image form'd in the fancy, but what is accompany'd with some emotion or movement of spirits proportion'd to it" (T. 373), some emotion such as admiration at the sheer perceived size of "an army, a fleet, a crowd" (ibid.). This means that the succession of our emotions and passions can be seen not just as feeding into that succession of changing perceptions that clock subjective time for us, but as themselves enough to constitute that clock. The idea of time can be derived either from the successive "manner of appearance" of the main objects of our passions, living persons and especially family members, or from the succession of our passions themselves. (In both cases, Hume takes members of the succession to exhibit causation as well as temporal contiguity—ancestors cause their descendants' existence, and "our passions are found by experience to have a mutual connexion with and dependance on each other"—T. 195.)

Our beliefs and our images of temporal distance influence the intensity of our passions, and the passage of time itself affects passions. When discussing long possession as one title to property, Hume pronounces "as 'tis certain, that, however every thing be produc'd in time, there is nothing real, that is produc'd by time; it follows, that property being produc'd by time, is not any thing real in the objects, but is the offspring of the sentiments, on which alone time is found to have any influence" (T. 508–509). This is a deep pronouncement, whose full implications for phenomena such as fading memories I leave aside, noting here simply the very intimate interrelationship Hume finds between our idea of time and of temporal distance on the one hand, and the dynamics of our passions and sentiments on the other. The sentiments at issue in the above passage are directed at persons as proprietors and would-be proprietors, and Hume's whole treatment of our passions makes them fundamentally person-directed. Although it is only what he calls the "indirect" passions that have persons as their official or proper "object," even the examples he gives of "direct" passions like joy and grief are person-involving—joy at the birth of a son, grief at the loss of a lawsuit (T. 441), anxiety about a friend's health (T. 446), the bride's embarrassment of mind on her wedding night (T. 447). Even attitudes to landscapes are taken to be mediated by sympathy for the human inhabitants—delight in fertile plains, dislike of a "barren or desolate country" (T. 388). Coloring all our passions, if Hume is right about us, is a vivid awareness of our fellow persons, and a concern for them (that varies with their degree of various sorts of "closeness" to us) and also for their awareness of us. Unlike Hobbes and Rousseau, for whom other persons figure as obstacles or as aids to the satisfaction of desires such as the desire to survive, to avoid pain, to possess power, to enjoy "the sentiment of existence," to think well of oneself, to be free, which make no necessary reference to other persons, Humean passions, even pride and curiosity,[14] are fellow-person-permeated.

There are three sorts of association that Hume is concerned with in the *Treatise*—in reverse order of treatment, these are associations of persons, associations of passions or reflexive impressions, associations of ideas. I have suggested that the last should be understood in the light of Hume's claims about the other two. This is not to underplay Hume's claim in the first quotation at the head of this chapter, that association of ideas is the cement of our universe since it is by means of our thought that anything operates upon our passions. The association of ideas is a part-determinant of our passions, including our person-directed passions. But they in their turn, and our reflective awareness of them, also influence our ideas about our ideas, and about their relations. Hume's philosophical awareness of idea-relationships seems to be contentedly dependent upon his version of associations of passions and on his version of associations between passionate persons. Person-directed passions are guided by ideas and their association; self-consciousness of these ideas and their association is guided by self-consciousness about interpersonal associations, and about the dynamics of the passions of sociable persons.

I have in this chapter moved to and fro in Hume's *Treatise,* collecting various theses about various sorts of association, and trying to show the links between the philosophy of mind of Book One, and that of Books Two and Three—between the investigation of "our thought or imagination," and "our passions or the concern we take in ourselves" (T. 253). In the following two chapters my concern will be with what for Hume is the most vital of all the operations of our disciplined thought, causal inference. He construes this as a special case of the association of ideas, one where vivacity is transferred from associate to associate in such a way as to enliven the "younger" associate enough to make it a belief, able itself to generate successor beliefs. This remarkable and revolutionary account of causal reasoning is given within Part III of Book One, and I will not need to ask the reader to leap with me from one end of Hume's philosophical creation to the other, to the extent that I have done in this chapter, but can remain pretty much within Part III of Book One, and not deviate so much from the order in which the text proceeds. Should it seem that my preliminary foray into Hume's phenomenology of mind, in this chapter, has not only involved leaps from Book One to Book Two and back, but has been "without any certain method or order" (T. 92), I beg the reader's indulgence, and make the specious plea that one may be permitted some fairly free association of ideas in treating of Hume's treatment of association. My interpretation has been gently constrained by Hume's text, but not by its order of treatment. Inference is, on Hume's account, a much less gentle mental operation, and temporal order is of its essence. In the interests of reflexive consistency, as well as to understand Hume's strategy in Book One, Part III, I shall in the following chapter, after some general remarks about scepticism, proceed pretty much in the order that Hume proceeded.

3

Customary Transitions
from Causes to Effects

Through experience . . . I hope I shall be saved.
(William Langland, *Piers Plowman*)

Common experience and the ordinary course of things
have justly a mighty influence on the minds of men.
(John Locke, *Essay Concerning Human Understanding,* IV, ch. 16)

'Tis easy to observe, that in tracing this relation, the inference we draw from cause to effect, is not deriv'd
merely from a survey of these particular objects, and
from such a penetration into their essences as may discover the dependance of the one upon the other. (T. 86)

Hume's account of causal inference has been written about so
much[1] that it takes a rash person to add another word, let alone
two chapters. My aim in this chapter is to be true to Hume's actual
account of causal inference in the *Treatise,*[2] and to avoid what
Fogelin calls the common fault of "displacing" the *Treatise's* claims
into the context of the rather different treatment of the topic that
Hume gives in the first *Enquiry,*[3] and even into the context of later
thinkers' assaults on "the problem of induction." As Fogelin says,
"the danger, of course, is that Hume's own contribution, especially that in the *Treatise,* may come to have, at best, only an *an-
cestral* relaton to what comes to be known as the *Humean* position
on some topic."[4] This certainly has actually happened, most egre-
giously with Hume's views on causal inference, and with his version of practical deliberation. Nor does Fogelin, alert as he is to
the danger, himself avoid some retrospective "displacement" of
Hume's *Treatise* views, which he is content to refer to as "his skep-

tical attack on induction," despite the pretty obvious fact that Hume does not include this discussion in the part of the *Treatise* labelled "Sceptical systems" (Part IV) and does not himself talk at all, within Part III, of any "sceptical doubts," only of sceptical smiles (T. 150). Any self-proclaimed doubts about causal investigations, within the *Treatise,* arise only after the problems that are encountered in Part IV are confronted, before being banished, within the conclusion of Book One. Those problems, significantly, do not concern induction; rather, they concern the effects of causal analysis on the idea of a physical atom, and the disappointment that some feel when it is concluded that "this connexion, tie, or energy lies merely in ourselves" (T. 266).

Fogelin is of course not alone in assuming that what is of lasting interest in Hume's analysis of causal inference in the *Treatise* is "his attack upon induction and his attempted regularity definition of causation."[5] It is because of the widespread acceptance of this version of what Hume offers us in the *Treatise* that I am rash enough to enter the fray, and present my rereading of Part III of Book One. I shall try to observe Fogelin's rule, of looking and seeing rather than reading in the preoccupations of later philosophers, or even of the Hume of the first *Enquiry*. If I have a prejudice, it is against any sceptical reading except the one that attributes "true" meta-scepticism.[6] For if Hume really *distrusts* causal inference, and the inductions on which, if he is right, it rests, then he must distrust his own *Treatise.*

The *Treatise,* from start to finish, traces what appear to be causal dependencies. Hume began with the dependency of our ideas on our impressions, and he ends Book Three with worries about the effects of his own "abstruse" moral philosophy on his readers' conception of morality. This last turn of thought is a typically Humean one—he turns his moral reflections on themselves. This is the very essence of "reflection," to turn a mental operation back onto itself and its source, and I shall argue that Hume does this with causal inference in Book One, Part III. He had relied on causal inference before that point in the *Treatise;* he relies on it during it; and he will rely on it after it. The last scarcely deniable fact might, however, be considered by those who take Hume to distrust causal inference as showing no more than that "Nature, by an absolute and uncontroulable necessity has determin'd us to judge as well as to breathe and feel" (T. 183), so that "the sceptic still continues to reason and believe, even tho' he asserts, that he cannot defend his reason by reason" (T. 187).

As Fogelin emphasizes, the central argument of Book One, Part III is not any problem about induction, but rather the positive thesis that experience[7] saves us, when deductive[8] reason lets us down. It is observation and experience, not the rationalists' reason, that can underwrite our causal inferences. The terms "infer" and "inference" are used by Hume in a broad way, to cover any confident transition from existent convictions to a new belief, any "induction" of a new belief out of the evidence at hand. The term "infer" has a nicely naturalistic root meaning,[9] convenient for Hume's philosophical purposes in this part of the *Treatise*. It will be my purpose in this and the following chapter to infer from Hume's text when he believes inferences, and in particular causal inferences, to be well grounded, and so trustworthy. For unless some are well grounded, most of the claims of the *Treatise* itself will be groundless.

Hume's causal examination of causal inference in Part III leads, in Section XV, to the formulation of the "Rules by which to judge of causes and effects." Hume here in this penultimate section repeats his earlier finding, from Section VI, that "by the mere survey, without consulting experience" (T. 173), all we can say is that "any thing may produce any thing". He goes on to spell out *how best we can consult experience* in order to come to "know" what "really" causes a particular thing.[10] He calls these rules a "Logic." Can this be scepticism? Only if the whole of Section XV can be treated as a piece of particularly sustained and heavy irony. Can it? Is there a Humean sceptic secretly smiling here, as some sceptics smiled earlier, when, in Section XIII, Hume gave us notice that he would later be formulating rules that guide "wise men" (T. 150)? These "rules, by which we ought to regulate our judgment concerning causes and effects" (T. 149) are to be general rules which will oppose other, more "rashly formed" general rules, those that we call "prejudices." The sceptics may smile, Hume writes, at the spectacle of "all philosophy ready to be subverted by a principle of human nature, and again sav'd by a new direction

of the very same principle" (T. 150). If this is what pleases sceptics, then they may well smile at Hume's rules for judging causes
and effects, and smile for just the same reason at his later rules of
justice, or "laws of nature." To arrive at any just conclusions about
the extent and type of Hume's scepticism, we need to fix a meaning for that slippery term "sceptic."

The true sceptic, Hume tells us in the conclusion of Book One,
is not the one who feels despair at discovered "contradictions" in
our pretensions to knowledge, but the one who is "diffident of his
philosophical doubts, as well as of his philosophical conviction;
and will never refuse any innocent satisfaction, which offers itself,
upon account of either" (T. 273). To the true sceptic, satisfactions
taken in "elaborate philosophical researches" need not be guilty
ones so long as there is this proper diffidence, and "a due deference
to the public"(T. 274). Hume's own work may indeed be the work
of a *true* sceptic, but it is not this higher meta-scepticism which is
usually attributed to him by those who find his account of causal
inference sceptical. Fogelin distinguishes what he calls "theoretical
scepticism" from "prescriptive scepticism," and attributes only the
former to Hume, so far as causal inferences goes. The theoretical
sceptic takes all causal inferences to be without warrant, but, unlike the prescriptive sceptic, continues to make them. This sounds
like the hypocritical rather than the true sceptic, and I do not see
Hume as having any toleration for such a split between habits and
acknowledged norms. Like Arnauld and Nicole, he thinks that
would amount to bad faith.[11] He sees it as a "manifest contradiction" to live by self-acknowledged habits when we cannot "establish it for a rule" that we ought so to live (T. 268). The sorts of
scepticism that Hume himself distinguishes within the *Treatise*
seem merely to be the "true" from the false, and the "smiling"
from the despairing. If he is a sceptic, he is a true and smiling one,
not a false or a despairing one. He himself at T. 183 refers to sceptics in general[12] as "that fantastic sect," and says that he is displaying their arguments only to persuade the reader of the truth of his
claims about the role of custom and experience. It is "superfluous"
to disavow "total scepticism," since no one could be a total sceptic,
and to avow any other sort of scepticism, short of "true scepticism," is to join a "fantastic sect." I shall use the term "true scep-

ticism" to refer to Hume's own meta-scepticism, and otherwise refer to "fantastic scepticism," which may come in two main varieties, the smiling and the despairing. The ancient sceptics, both Pyrrhonian and Academic, aimed at peace of mind, and so were committed to smiling, but we have seen in the previous chapter that Hume's protagonist, in the conclusion of Book One, found nothing to smile about when all warrants seemed to be undermined. One version of false scepticism is that which purports to smile when it cannot endorse its own habits, whose smile, we might say, is the hypocrite's villainous smile. Hume's eventual true "sceptic" is certainly a smiling sceptic, but one who is attempting to bear his own survey, to find habits that are endorsable. Theory and practice must come together, in order for him to smile.

Hume's "true sceptic," like his "true theist," is the one who sees, clearly and without self-deception, what drives a person to fantastic and to despairing scepticism, and how unstable they ultimately are. In seeing them so clearly, one sees through them. True scepticism collapses into mere openmindedness, as "true theism" becomes indistinguishable from "attenuated deism,"[13] agnosticism or undogmatic atheism. The sceptics who see a "signal contradiction in our reason" (T. 150) when we rely on general rules to correct more rashly formed rules have particularly good reason to be diffident. As Fogelin remarks, the "contradiction" is rather lame.[14] Pleasure in the spectacle of the human addiction to general rules correcting itself by giving itself "a new direction" seems to be an innocent sceptical pleasure and one that a true sceptic could take. It is, after all, pleasure in the "saving" of the whole of philosophy, and the true sceptic permits herself to be a philosopher. Hume's "true sceptic" allows himself the use of "such terms as these, *'tis evident, 'tis certain, 'tis undeniable*" (T. 274), so long as these temporary convictions are punctuated by moments of diffidence, and willingness to be corrected. Is the penultimate section of Book One, Part III, which gives us rules to tell what really causes what,[15] such a merely temporary burst of positive thinking, coming from one who is not just remembering his own sceptical smiles at his "contradictions," but anticipating the unsmiling scepticism that occurs in the conclusion of Book One? We should not, while reading that section, forget Section XIII's references forward to it, and it may be significant that Hume goes on in Section XIII to raise the question of whether "conceal'd strokes of satire" are less hurtful than open abuse. Is Section XV concealed satire on any project of telling us how we ought to judge of causes and effects? If so, the satire there is well concealed. On the face of it Hume is, for the moment at least, endorsing eight rules and telling us that by using them we can find out what really causes what. To decide how to take these "rules," whether Hume himself is among the sceptics smiling at their endorsement and (if he is) whether his smiling scepticism is fantastic and sectarian, we need to look at Part III as a whole, and at what leads up to and what follows the formulation of the rules.

I proceed on the assumption that, at least out of one side of his smiling mouth, Hume is giving us an account of how custom, and the "accustom'd unions" it forms in our imaginations, can have "equal weight and *authority*" (E. 41, my emphasis) with the "arguments" of "reason." What Fogelin calls the "triumph of the imagination" in Part III, which is also the triumph of experience, is the triumph of another source of norms, not the defeat of all normative discourse. After all, Hume is giving us a causal account of our causal inferences, and so is continuing to "reason" about causes after he has, in Section VI, presented the "argument" that many have taken to deny any warrant to any causal inference. The true sceptic must wonder what sort of reasoning it might be that can continue without implicit deference to norms of reasoning, without any inference warrants. Hume seems to take himself to be able, in good faith, to continue. He ends Section VI telling us how we are "able to reason" (T. 94) on causation as a natural relation, and tells us that all our (and his) causal reasonings are reasonings based on that associative relation. Hume's bold and interesting question is what a warrant is like when it comes from sources other than the human intellect. Only those fantastic sceptics who shelter under the throne of rationalist reason will dismiss all the apparent evidence of Hume's constructive normative enterprise, his "rules," his claims about the "authority" of custom, the "foundation" of our causal inferences, of our ability to find "real causes," as ironical. If this all is irony, all tongue in cheek, then the tongue and the cheek "are of gigantic proportions," to borrow a phrase from Passmore (in a passage with which Fogelin begins his book).[16]

Before addressing the question of how these few famous pages of Section VI (T. 88–91), where Fogelin and others find an unsolved "problem of induction" and so "skepticism about induction," really fit into the whole plan of Part III, I first need to say something about "reason" and its authority, in Hume's treatment of it, and about "truth." In Part IV he tells us that "our reason must be consider'd as a kind of cause, of which truth is the natural effect; but such-a-one as by the irruption of other causes, and by the inconstancy of our natural powers, may frequently be prevented" (T. 180). The "reason" at issue here is reason in "the demonstrative sciences". It is the faculty which can give us "knowledge" as it had been treated in Section I of Part III, as it had been contrasted with "probability" in Section II, as it had been defined and contrasted with both experimental "proof" and with "probability" in the narrower sense at T. 124. "Reason" for Hume is often restricted to the faculty of intellectual intuition and demonstration, that which can discern "intelligible" connections. The O.E.D. gives the third and philosophical sense of "intelligible" as "Capable of being apprehended only by the understanding (not by the senses); objective to intellect. (Opp. to *sensible*.)" Reason in Hume's narrowest sense is this discerner of "intelligible" relations of ideas. He tends to restrict "argument" to what this sort of reason produces and to the inferences it makes, but eventually uses "reasoning" in a much broader way, to cover any sort of inference, or confident transition to a new belief. Animals are said by Hume to reason and to infer (T. 177, 178), but they cannot argue or run through arguments. They can form beliefs, and make transitions to new beliefs. It is unlikely, Hume thinks, that very young children do their causal inference "by any process of argument or ratiocination" (E. 39). Argument is "ratiocination," the activity of *ratio*. But since Hume wants to use the verbs "to reason" and "to infer" to cover all sorts of endorsable thought transitions, he extends the term "reason," within Part III, to whatever it is that enables any thinker or "reasoner" to make transitions from belief to belief. This means that he can speak of animal inference and of "the reason of animals." "Reason" comes to cover both the "cog-

itative" and the "sensitive" parts of our curious truth-seeking natures. It is reason in this larger sense that he later, in Book Two,
says is and ought to be the slave of the passions. By then "reason"
has become whatever may be at work in us when we indulge our
"curiosity or the love of truth," when we add to our collection of
what we take to be truths.

Hume claims explicitly that his Part IV section titled "Of scepticism with regard to reason" is directed at reason as ratiocination
or cogitation. He writes that his intention in displaying so carefully the arguments of the "fantastic sect" of sceptics who try to
destroy ratiocination with their ratiocination "is only to make the
reader sensible of the truth of my hypothesis, *that all our reasonings
concerning causes and effects are deriv'd from nothing but custom; and that
belief is more properly an act of the sensitive, than of the cogitative part
of our natures*" (T. 183). Hume's uses of "sensible" and "sensitive"
here are carefully calculated, as is also, I think, his use of "reasoning." It has already been shown that causal reasoning need not be
pure cogitation, but can be sensitive and sensible. The sort of abstract calculations of probabilities on probabilities that his "fantastic" sceptic went in for in this section were only minimally expe-
rienced-informed, and not at all experience-corrected. They were
mere "cogitations," not the sort of self-revising experienced-based
probability estimations that Hume had carefully (if not without
some elements of fantasy) described in Section XII of Part III. As
with "reason," so with "probability"; there are both purely cogitative and more empirical versions of each. Hume's own doubts,
as well as his sceptical character's arguments, are directed at
overinflated claims concerning "pure" intellect and what it can
make "intelligible." If we read Section VI of Part III carefully, we
will find that the negative conclusions concern "intelligibility" in
the narrow sense in which it means what we would call interded-
ucibility. The "reason" whose limits Hume draws in Section VI is
the tracer of "intelligible" connections. He balances his account,
at the end of Part III, by claiming that the animal reason that he
has tried to make comprehensible to us, by his sustained reflexive
use of it, is "wonderful and unintelligible" (T. 179). It is indeed
"unintelligible," but Hume's use of it in Part III leaves it less incomprehensible to itself than before. Hume says, after giving his

definition of cause, that the influence of constant conjunction on our minds is "perfectly extraordinary and incomprehensible; nor can we be certain of its reality, but from experience and observation" (T. 172). Here he underreaches himself, for his display of various experiential certainties, and their causal and meta-causal relations, surely make them at least partially comprehensible. It all depends on what we are trying to grasp them with: our pure intellect, our experienced senses and seasoned imagination, or our mind "all collected within itself" (T. 270).

And what do we, if we are following Hume, take truths to be? Hume notoriously tells us little, except that truth is reason's natural effect, and that it consists in agreement "either to the *real* relations of ideas, or to *real* existence and matter of fact" (T. 458). He certainly is no ancestor of those engaged in the currently flourishing industry elaborating theories of truth. To call a belief true, for Hume, is to say that it is correct, that it needs no revision, that it will not be found to be false, since it "agrees" with the reality it purports to represent. Since "to reflect on anything simply, and to reflect on it as existent, are nothing different from each other" (T. 66), Hume needs the emphatic "*real* existence" and "*real* relations" in the above one-sentence non-theory of truth. Since "real" and "true" are virtual synonyms to Hume and to most of his philosophical predecessors, what the emphatic "real" does, in Hume's non-theory, is to introduce circularity. I postpone (to Chapter 12) the question of whether Hume has a theory of agreement, whether more about truth can be got out of "agreement," and whether what can be got has virtuous or vicious circularity. For present purposes it would not hurt to take him to hold something like the prosentential theory[17]—to call some claim true is simply to reaffirm it, to agree with it.

How then should we read Hume's famous argument about the principle *"that the course of nature continues always uniformly the same"* (T. 89)? We should read it just as Fogelin says we should, in context. That context goes back at least to Hume's Part I treatment of the association of ideas, and goes forward at least to the very end of Part III. But even its immediate context, within Section VI, should be a corrective to interpreting it simply as "Hume's skepticism concerning induction."[18]

By the time Hume gets to this sixth section of his Part III exploration "Of knowledge and probability," he is already well along on the roundabout path he is taking to find the source of our idea of the causal relation, and in particular of the necessity that we take to be such an important component of it (T. 77). He had begun Part III distinguishing our "knowledge" of such relations of ideas as "depend entirely on the ideas" (T. 69) from the merely "probable" conclusions of our reasoning when it traces relations that "may be chang'd without any change in the ideas." The "demonstrative sciences" of mathematics trace quantitative relations, and contrariety, which are relations of the former kind. Our judgments about identity, about when and where something happened, and about causes, all depend upon our attempts to trace the latter relations, which do not depend solely upon our ideas of their relata. "Of those three relations, which depend not upon the mere ideas, the only one, that can be trac'd beyond our senses, and informs us of existences and objects, which we do not see or feel, is *causation*" (T. 74). Here, right at the beginning of the long road to his definitions of cause, we get Hume's central governing insight: cause is the relation we reason on, when we make confident judgments about non-present realities. Confident though we may be, such judgments do not have the same status as those obtained from our demonstrative mathematical reasonings, so Section II is titled "Of probability; and of the idea of cause and effect." He will later distinguish probability in this wide sense, where although we cannot have "knowledge" we can have convincing "proof," from probability in a narrower sense, his topic in Sections XI, XII, and XIII, where what we have is "evidence, which is still attended with uncertainty" (T. 124). Right at the start of his investigation of the causal relation, he has *contrasted* causal inference with "demonstration." "Probability" judgments, however certain they may be, do not give "knowledge." This does not commit him from the start to scepticism about causal inference, since in Section XI he can speak of the conclusions of at least some of our causal inferences as "entirely free from doubt and uncertainty" (T. 124), but it does prejudge the question of whether causal inference can be recast as sound deductive argument. Hence he can say, at the start of Section VI, that it is "easy to observe" that causes do not imply their effects. "There is no object, which implies the existence of any other if we consider these objects in themselves . . . Such an inference wou'd amount to knowledge, and wou'd imply the absolute contradiction and impossibility of conceiving any thing different" (T. 86–87).

In Section II, as Kemp Smith emphasized,[19] Hume is very clear that more than merely spatio-temporal relations are involved in causal relations. "An object may be contiguous and prior to another, without being consider'd as its cause. There is a NECESSARY CONNEXION to be taken into consideration; and that relation is of much greater importance, than any of the other two above-mention'd" (T. 77). So his task is to investigate that necessary connection, and it takes him another ten sections to do so, by the chosen indirect route of examining "other questions, the examination of which will perhaps afford a hint" (T. 78). These other questions shift the necessity. They are "Why a cause is always necessary?" and "Why we conclude, that such particular causes must *necessarily* have such particular effects; and what is the nature of that *inference* we draw from one to the other, and of the *belief* we repose in it?" (T. 78).

The particular stretch of the indirect path that Hume is traversing in Section VI is that which comes after he turned from the first question, and from looking for an explanation of *how* "experience" produces in us the belief that everything must have a cause, since it has become clear that neither intuition nor demonstration was able to legitimate this belief, to considering *"Why we conclude, that such particular causes must necessarily have such particular effects"* (T. 82). He comments on his move here that perhaps "the same answer will serve for both questions" (ibid.). We will be able to understand how experience can produce the conviction that "a cause is always necessary" when we have understood how experience produces our convictions about *particular* causes necessarily producing *particular* effects. So as early as Section III we find Hume implicitly anticipating his claim, made explicitly in Section VI, that it is only experience, not deductive reason even when that is helped by experience, that is responsible for our conviction that fire will continue to bring painful burns to human flesh coming in contact with it, that water in human lungs will continue to bring death. What Fogelin sees as Hume's "reversal of his field"[20] after the supposedly sceptical argument about induction in Section VI, is in fact a continuation of the same game plan that he had been following since Section II, the plan of contrasting "probability" with "knowledge" and of showing how "experience" can produce the probability judgments that "reason" is impotent to produce.[21] The pattern of Section VI repeats that of Section III—first a negative argument to show something "reason" cannot do, then a conclusion that experience must do it, and an advance on the way to understanding *how* experience does it. Hume had displaced necessity from causes onto our thoughts about causes as early as Section III, and his own analysis has been transparently causal from the very beginning of the *Treatise*.

Fogelin writes that "what we now call Hume's skepticism concerning induction, for all its independent importance, occurs as a step leading to the conclusion that causal inferences (so-called) are the products of the imagination."[22] This is surely right. Hume's main line of reasoning about causal inference was sketched before Section VI, when in Section IV he had laid out the three component parts of our causal reasoning that he would go on to explain: an impression of sense or memory from which our reasoning starts (the topic of Section V), the transition of the mind which is his topic in Section VI, and, third, the vivacious idea we move to, the inferred belief, which he will consider in Section VII, before he generalizes and tests his "extraordinary" principles (T. 106–107) in Sections VIII and IX. The whole account is causal and naturalistic, before and after the few pages showing that deductive reason cannot be the source of our confidence *"that the course of nature continues always uniformly the same"* (T. 89).

Section V gave us a naturalistic account of the assent that we give to sense and memory, to what provides the starting points of our causal inferences. Hume there analyses the belief-inducing character of our premises in causal inference as a matter of their superior vivacity, and introduces us to the causal role of custom and repetition, whose vivacity-increasing or vivacity-accumulating power is to be so be important in his account. Frequent repetition of lies can turn what at first was not believed into a "counterfeit" memory, mere repetition having "the same influence on the mind as nature, and infixing the idea with equal force and vigour" (T. 86). We have here, at the end of Section V, a look forward at the line of thought that Hume will pursue in the next four sections. At T. 117 he refers back again to this passage, when he likens the eventual assent of pupils to what they are indoctrinated with to the eventual belief of the liar in his often-repeated lies. If anything is a reversal of Hume's field, it is the break in his causal story that comes when he looks to see if deductive reason could deduce, from certainties available to it from any source, that nature will continue uniformly the same. But even this is not really a break; it is a part of the causal investigation of just what is "produced" by deductive reason, and what by experience-sensitive "imagination."

When Hume has shown that we cannot "satisfy ourselves by our reason" that past constancies of conjunction will remain constant in the future, he turns from "reason" as the rationalists construe it to the other belief source that he has already recognized—association and, in particular, the influence of repetition on our minds. "We have already taken notice of certain relations, which make us pass from one object to another, even tho' there be no reason to determine us to that transition" (T. 92). This reminds us not just of Part I's account of association, but of Part III Section III's appeal to "experience" as the determiner of what reason fails to determine, and of Section V's claim about the influence of any sort of repetition, even of words, on our sensitive minds. Hume's use of "no reason" in this passage need not, indeed must not, be taken to mean "no warrant." That he says "no reason to determine us" should be taken to show that reason here is being treated as one causal force, one possible determiner among others.[23] He is here answering the question raised at T. 88–89 of whether it is reason or association-prone imagination that determines our causal inferences. Just which psychological causal force has highest authority still remains an open question.

The steps taken in Section VI are quite straightforward. First Hume asks where we get our confidence that this flame will burn our hands, and gives us the same answer he gave in Section III about the necessity of causes—not from intuition or demonstration, but from "experience only." Then he looks at the nature of experience, and takes it to be a matter of remembered (or some-how retained) repeated similar sequences, what he calls "constant conjunctions." Then the question arises whether these experienced constancies might be a source of the idea of necessity, which is what the whole hunt since Section II has been after. To this ques-tion Hume answers coyly that "there are hopes, that by this means we may at last arrive at our propos'd end" (T. 87–88), hopes that he sustains despite doubts about how mere repetition can give us a new idea (or an idea of anything except repetition). But "as it wou'd be folly to despair too soon," he encourages us, and so the causal investigation is to continue, with an unquenched hope that a cause for our idea of necessity will be found, and that constant conjunction will be somehow implicated.

It is at this point, a point in the middle of a cause-tracking dis-course, that the supposedly sceptical analysis of induction occurs. It is introduced by the causal question, "Whether experience pro-duces the idea by means of the understanding or of the imagina-tion; whether we are determin'd by reason to make the transition, or by a certain association and relation of perceptions" (T. 88–89). "The idea" here is the lively idea that is the conclusion of the causal inference. It is already established that the transition to this idea is "founded on past experience" and on some sort of memory of the constant conjunctions we have experienced. Now the question is how this memory influences or determines our inference. Is it by some explicitly formulated generalization, along with deductive inference from that to a conclusion about the current case? It is to this question that Hume gives us a negative answer. It is no more sceptical an answer than that given to the parallel question of Sec-tion III, namely whether we can get a sound deductive inference to the conclusion that every event has some cause. The negative answer he gives to his question, here at T. 89, is no surprise, nor is it expected to be a surprise. "Our foregoing method of reason-ing will easily convince us, that there can be no *demonstrative* ar-guments to prove, *that those instances, of which we have had no ex-perience, resemble those, of which we have had experience*" (T. 89). The only point on which we need to spend a little time is to see whether "reason" can get assurance of the principle of induc-tion by other means. If it is not a case of "knowledge," is it a case of "probability"? By reason's own rules, that would be to beg the question, to assume the principle of induction in order to give the wanted grounding. It is reason that needs a "principle," spelled out and ready to serve as part of a demonstration. "If reason determin'd us, it wou'd proceed upon that principle" (T. 89). It is reason that demands non-circular justifications, so rationalists cannot appeal to higher-level inductions at this point. Hume, the one who is pushing the rationalist into this corner, puts the impossibility in an interesting mixture of the causal theorist's terminology combined with appeal to "reason's" certainties: "The same principle cannot be both the cause and effect of another; and this is, perhaps, the only proposition concerning that relation, which is either intuitively or demonstratively certain" (T. 90).[24] Hume is after the "causes" and the "effects" of our confidence that nature will continue as before, and he wants to show that the rationalists cannot cite known principles that can serve as rational causes of the relevant beliefs. His investigations have been into the causal powers of the rationalists' "reason," when it uses such evidence as memory of constant conjunctions can yield. His conclusion is negative. Reason, using reason's rules of evidence and proof, cannot establish the "principle" that reason needs, to provide a reason-cause of the conclusions of our causal inferences.

A question facing my interpretation[25] is whether the experience-based thought which is here contrasted with "reason" also needs that certain principle. Can we think in a circle, and take causes to be mutual causes, so long as we are not purporting to be doing demonstrations? Is that intuitively or demonstratively certain proposition, that the same principle cannot be both the cause and the effect of another, one which causal and meta-causal theorists of human nature can ignore or deny? My answer to that must wait until I have given my version of Hume's own final claims about causal inference. For the moment I note merely that the argument here concerns the evidence, or rather the lack of evidence, for an explicit principle that is needed, or thought to be needed, for a valid demonstrative argument whose conclusion would be, "This fire will burn my hand painfully, if I put it in the fire." It is not an argument about the presuppositions of inferences not purporting to be demonstrative. (I also note that Hume later seems to ignore the supposedly sole "rational" certainty about causes and effects, when in his account of "the true idea of the human mind" he writes that "our distant perceptions influence *each other* . . . giving us a present concern for our past or future pains or pleasures" [T. 261, my emphasis]. Mutual causal influence seems to become almost the norm for the human phenomena that Hume, as scientist of human nature, is most concerned with. Just how this can work, if causes must be temporally prior to their effects, and just when reason-causes and conclusion-effects can be mutual causes and mutual effects, is unclear. But "as it wou'd be folly to despair too soon, we shall continue the thread of our discourse.")

Sections VII and VIII examine the second component of causal reasoning, the belief to which a mental transition is made. Hume in Section IV listed the components, in Section V analyzed the first component, in Section VI analyzed the transition, and now comes to analyze the second component, the conclusion. His earlier stress on the vivacity of the perceptions that provide the points of departure for a mental transition or inference has prepared us for the line he takes in these sections. In Section VII belief is defined as "A LIVELY IDEA RELATED TO OR ASSOCIATED WITH A PRESENT IMPRESSION" (T. 96), and he is here obviously recalling the previous section's title, "Of the inference from the impression to the idea." Predictably enough, the sort of association that "the idea or belief" is found to involve is inference, a special form of association that communicates the high vivacity of an impression or of a memory.

Hume makes inference a special case of a more general phenomenon of vivacity communication by natural association. In Section VIII, he cites the enlivening power of association by resemblance and contiguity, as well as by causal association. Religious "mummeries" and superstitions exploit this power, by associating intellectual views of "distant and immaterial objects" with postures and ceremonies, and with relics that "inliven" devotion and quicken fervor. Association by cause and effect, it should be noted, is not *always* inference to a new belief. The believer whose fervor is quickened by being in the presence of some "handy work of a saint" need arrive neither at the belief in the saint, nor at belief that this is her handiwork, by the current causal associations. Both beliefs may already be fixed by other, earlier causal inferences. A causal association, for Hume, always provides a basis for a possible causal inference, once we have some certainty about the real existence of one of the two associated objects. Many beliefs, however, will be overdetermined. Inferences that could have taken place need not always take place. *What is special about causal association is that it can take us from an impression to an idea that gets our assent from that very association.* Not merely does this sort of association, like the other two sorts, communicate liveliness; it communicates enough liveliness to transform a hitherto fairly inert idea into a firm belief, to bring it over that somewhat mysterious vivacity-threshold that separates impressions, memories and firm beliefs from mere speculative hypotheses, from bets or estimates of high probability, from hopes and from idle fancies.

The power of one impression to confer this "belief-feeling" on its causal associate comes, Hume suggests, from the background constant conjunction, which is retained in memory. He asks how an impression can produce "so extraordinary an effect" as belief in, or assent to,[26] its mental associate, and "then I observe, that the present impression has not this effect by its own proper power and efficacy, and when consider'd alone, as a single perception, limited to the present moment . . . We must in every case have observ'd the same impression in past instances, and have found it to be constantly conjoin'd with some other impression" (T. 102). Hume here toys with a sort of conservation theory: repetition of events, and of sequences of events, does make a difference. It affects not the content but the vivacity and communicable vivacity of a perception, what it has available to communicate to its associates. Hume here begins to do what he had at T. 88 hinted that he would do, namely show us how, on second or third viewing, "multiplication" of instances does make a difference to an idea, or pair of ideas. It gives each the power to raise its associate to its own belief level. This passage is a bridge between T. 88 and T. 155, where Hume returns to the question of what repetition does to the perceptions repeated. Indeed, the whole intervening stretch of discourse is largely concerned to complete that bridge—Hume has now got to the point where he advances his thesis that custom is what determines the mind in inference. His treatment of probability in the narrow sense, in Sections XI–XIII, is attention to habits or customs that are not "full and perfect," to cases where there is loss as well as gain of accumulated communicable vivacity, loss through disappointment of earlier expectations. These are the cases when there are "contrary experiments," and these "produce an imperfect belief" (T. 135).

"When by any clear experiment we have discover'd the causes or effects of any phaenomenon, we immediately extend our observation to every phaenomenon of the same kind" (T. 173–174). In Section IX, Hume continues to develop and test the associationist causal theses that he has advanced, both the general theses about the vivacity-transmitting power of all the natural relations, and the specific thesis about the role of causal association in producing belief. He announces his intention of "turning the subject on every side, in order to find some new points of view, from which we may illustrate and confirm such extraordinary, and such fundamental principles" (T. 106–107). The restatement that he gives us of these extraordinary principles is itself rather extraordinary. It develops his root metaphor of the derived life of a perception: "I have also observ'd, that when of two objects connected together by any of these relations, one is immediately present to the memory or senses, not only the mind is convey'd to its corelative by means of the associating principle; but likewise conceives it with an additional force and vigour, by the united operation of that principle, and of the present impression. All this I have observ'd, in order to confirm by analogy, my explication of our judgments concerning cause and effect" (T. 107). Hume's own analogies in this passage between the force and vigor of a belief's somewhat incestuous "conception," and other conceptions transmitting life to "a relation of another sort" (T. 352), strike with their own force and vigor. (See T. 615 for his discussion of force and vigor "of another sort.") His theses are extraordinary both in matter and in manner of presentation.

Now he asks if he can explain why only causal association brings enough transferred vivacity to make the difference between what is thought possible or probable and what is accepted as true, between mere association and inference. Here he is in effect applying his own later-formulated rules for verifying causal claims, checking to find not just the common cause of common effects, but also the differently proportional effects, and the special cause of that special effect, firm belief. First he describes the empirically known facts about human webs of beliefs in the terms provided by his own theory. We have one "system" of what we take as facts, provided by current impressions and our vivid memories of our own pasts. To this we attach, by causal inferences, another "system," of derived beliefs about "such existences, as by their removal in time and place, lie beyond the reach of the senses and memory. By means of it I paint the universe in my imagination" (T. 108). Causal inference from sensed or remembered facts "peoples the world" and furnishes the universe. Hume here uses "imagination" for the faculty that paints the universe for us, but almost immediately he goes on to say that the ideas in this derived "system" are such that "by their force and settled order, arising from custom and the relation of cause and effect, they distinguish themselves from the other ideas, which are merely the offspring of the imagination" (T. 108). This quick switch from "imagination" in a sense that includes causal inference to one that excludes it is confusing, and it is only later in this section, at T. 117 in a note, that he warns us of the double use he has "been oblig'd to fall into." Imagination, when contrasted with memory, can include all inferred beliefs, as well as "whimsies," "prejudices," and the work of "the fancy." When contrasted with reason, however, it excludes all inferred beliefs, demonstrative or causal. The imagination that paints the universe as we believe it to be is imagination in the wide inference-including sense, helped out perhaps by a few prejudices and contributions from the fancy, ones that Hume will explore in Part IV.

Already at this point, at T. 108, Hume is introducing us to his claim about how causal association differs from other sorts of mental association, and differs in a way that explains its belief-selecting power, that explains how it can be inference. It produces ideas with "force *and settled order*" (my emphasis), arising from that cause of causal inference, custom. Custom itself is settled order in our experience, and from this settled order comes the relative fixity of the ideas we get by causal association. Hume links this fixity with superior vivacity, and so with belief-feeling. The special "advantages" of causal association, which Hume contrasts with the "imperfections" of the vivacity-communication of the other forms of association, come from this fixity. Like the impressions of memory to which causal association is anchored, the ideas to which we make transitions by causal inference are "fixt and unalterable . . . each impression draws along with it a precise idea, which takes its place in the imagination, as something solid and real, certain and invariable" (T. 110). From these customary transitions to what experience has accustomed us to expect, we get full assurance, not "those momentary glimpses of light" (T. 110) which "fluctuating and uncertain" association by resemblance and contiguity may bring (T. 109). Hume links force, or vivacity-communicating power, with constancy. A belief is a vivacious idea, and it is a *constant* answer given to the question it answers. Causal association depends on constancy in past experience, and produces constancy in our mind-set. With the other associative principles, where any one given "object" may have a great many "co-relatives," no one correlative idea will be fixed. "The mind forsees and anticipates the change; and even from the very first instant feels the looseness of its actions, and the weak hold it has of its objects" (T. 109–110). But cause and effect (which presumably enable the mind to foresee its own changes of idea in the non-causal associations) has all the "opposite advantages . . . The thought is always determin'd to pass from the impression to the idea, and from that particular impression to that particular idea, without any choice or hesitation" (T. 110).

It is as if Hume sees each lively impression of sense or memory as having a fixed legacy to pass on. When only one candidate comes forward, then the inheritance is settled on that one. When many equally close relatives come forward, no settlement is reached; there are only capricious and temporary favorites. No would-be heir can have assurance that it will not soon be displaced. But the causal relation fixes one heir for the vivacity legacy, and can do that because it preserves past fixities or constancies. As a product of constancy, it has constancy to exhibit and bestow. It is in this way that it can produce or induce those steady ideas that are our beliefs.

Now if Hume is really arguing like this, and so finding some psychological effects in some respects to be images of their causes, then it would be proper for him to examine his apparently Cartesian finding. These effects seem to inherit the reality of their causes (vivacity, constancy and fixity). We find him doing just this—he moves on to consider how, in cases where effects are found to resemble their causes, we find the causal relationship "consistent and natural" (T. 111), and see the resemblance as binding cause and effect "in the closest and most intimate manner to each other, so as to make us imagine them to be absolutely inseparable" (T. 112). We find the causes of motion by motion "natural and consistent," because association by resemblance here reinforces the causal association that experience has forged in our minds.

Hume does not take back his claim that there is no "rationally intelligible" connection between these causes and effects, that there are no cases where some reality can really be seen to be "communicated" by the causal relation. He demotes such apparent "intelligiblity" into natural association by resemblance, and then he allows it to add its force to causal association. In this way he can explain not just the errors and half-truths of the rationalists, but the more ordinary error of "a too easy faith in the testimony of others" (T. 112). When what I say to you is not merely caused by but also repeats what I say in my soul, and when that belief is both caused by and also reflects the facts it concerns, then "the testimony of men . . . is to be consider'd as an image as well as an effect" (T. 113). So influenced are we by the expectation that effects will have causes resembling them, that we rashly take others' testimony to communicate their sincere beliefs, and take those beliefs to reflect the facts that they purport to reflect. Hume, right from the start of the *Treatise,* has focused on cases where effects do seem to preserve something apparently communicated by their causes—for he focused on ideas as effects, as image-copies of impressions. Here in Part III, Section IX, he is allowing for the influence of perceived resemblance on our thought, and on his own thought, but restricting it to the role of "fortifying" already perceived causal relations.

When resemblance fails to "compleat the union" that has been forged in our minds by other associative principles, careless and stupid persons with "slow imaginations" (T. 114), Hume ironically notes, may fail to give real credence to distant effects. When these are portrayed as having little resemblance to the familiar present realities on which they are supposed to depend, there may be "obstinate . . . incredulity" (T. 113) in them. Those of slow imaginations do not believe in the eternal damnation of a non-bodily self, a damnation that is portrayed as the non-resembling result of present loose living. Whatever people say they believe on this matter, their behavior shows that "they are really infidels in their hearts" (T. 114). Hume gets obvious satisfaction from noting that his theory can explain this obstinate incredulity in a future condition "so far remov'd from our comprehension" (ibid.). Such incredulity, he tells us, will be a matter "of wonder to the studious, and of regret to the pious man" (T. 113).

Causal association always depends on the force of association of resembling *sequences* of events—the constancy of a conjunction is a matter of the resemblance between a given conjunction and the other past conjoinings of objects resembling the first conjunct, with objects resembling the second. Causal association is always a special case of association by resemblance, and also of association by contiguity. The special feature is repetition, which is itself a matter of resemblance of pairings. "Custom" presupposes perceived resemblance. "As belief is an act of the mind arising from custom, 'tis not strange the want of resemblance shou'd overthrow what custom has establish'd, and diminish the force of the idea, as much as that latter principle encreases it"(T. 114). Hume here assimilates custom and constant conjunction to association by resemblance, so he can explain in one fell swoop both the errors of the obstinate infidels and those of the rationalists. He has indeed turned objections to his own theory against the objectors! (See T. 110.)

In this section he examines the effects on our minds not just of "other relations" besides the natural relation of cause and effect, but also of "other habits" besides that custom to which causal inference has been reduced. Habit and custom operate by repetition of resembling sequences. The habit of repeating the verbal formulation of an article of faith or dogma has some vivacity-increasing power, and repeating the formulation of an already formed belief tends to "establish" it. Hume looks at the effects of "education" and "inculcation," and looks again at that process by which even "liars, by the frequent repetition of their lies, come at last to remember them" (T. 117). Here, mere "artificial" repetition simulates the effect of the repetitions that nature arranges without our aid, whenever she trains us, by Locke's "normal course of things," to make causal inferences. Hume allows that "more than one half of those opinions, that prevail upon mankind, to be owing to education" (T. 117). This seems to be a contradiction to what up till now in Part III has been one of his main theses, that our beliefs about non-present objects are caused by causal inference. He cheerfully claims, however, that his own "present hypothesis will receive additional confirmation, if we examine the effects of other kinds of custom, as well as of other relations" (T. 115). What is confirmed is the general thesis that repetition can make a difference to the mental force of what is repeated. But what of the earlier thesis that it is repetition of sequences *in nature* that produces our beliefs? Hume here contrasts "natural" causes of belief with education, which is "an artificial and not a natural cause," and whose maxims "are frequently contrary to reason" (T. 117). In the following section he also invokes the power of indoctrination and entrenched opinion to explain away the expected rejection of his own theory. "I expect not to make many proselytes to my opinion" (T. 118). The confirmation of his theory comes from the power of his general hypothesis about what causes our beliefs to explain those beliefs that he regards as contrary to reason, as well as to explain our more reasonable beliefs. But the earlier claim that cause, as a natural relation, is *the* relation that "we" can reason on, when we form new beliefs, must now be restricted to those of us who are not stupidly credulous, or corrupted by indoctrination. We sensible people form our beliefs by causal inference. "Experience" saves us from silly credulity and from believing everything we are taught, as well as saving us from the ignorance in which deductive reason leaves us.

Does Hume think that "artifice" always produces maxims that are contrary to reason? When is belief in testimony not silly credulity, but a proper experience-based "assurance of the veracity of men" (T. 113)? These important questions must be left aside if we are to follow the thread of Part III's discourse to its end. I began by emphasizing that the account would lead to an endorsement of a "logic" of causal inference. We have now traced the path through nine of the fifteen sections it takes Hume to arrive at that endorsement. The remaining sections will be the topic of the following chapter, where I will also take a closer look at the less customary transitions from cause to psychological effect, and from effect back to cause, that he has himself been making, in his attempt to account for our idea of causal necessity, and for our more customary causal transitions. To understand his eventual definition of the causal relation, and the way he ends Part III, we must look closely at Hume's own meta-causal transitions, and their import for his evaluation of the human understanding. Only then can we see just how, and to what extent, we can trust experience to save us after false reason has betrayed us.

4

Necessity, Nature, Norms

Upon the whole, necessity is something, that exists in the mind, not in objects.   (T. 165)

There is but one kind of *necessity*.   (T. 171)

There must be a constant union betwixt the cause and effect.   (T. 173)

At the end of his account of the causal relation, Hume moves from natural necessity, including psychological necessities, to normative necessities, when he tells us what we must do if we are to discover what really causes what. Since "there is but one kind of necessity," either all musts are ultimately normative musts, or else the normative ones reduce to non-normative ones. I shall argue that the former alternative is closer to what Hume is saying, although it has to be admitted that he says it somewhat enigmatically and indirectly. This chapter will do some reconstructing as well as retelling of what Hume wrote in Part III of Book One.

The quarry in Part III has been the source of our idea of causal necessity. Once the catch is in hand (in Section XIV), it turns out to be bigger game than anticipated, for what we have is an account of necessity as such. Not merely is it reaffirmed that psychological causal necessitation is no different from other natural causation, but the account is also generalized to cover deductive necessities: "Thus as the necessity, which makes two times two equal to four, or three angles of a triangle equal to two right ones, lies only in the act of the understanding, by which we consider and compare these ideas; in like manner the necessity or power, which unites causes and effects, lies in the determination of the mind to pass from the one to the other" (T. 166). Earlier, in Sections I, II, VI, and XI, Hume had separated "demonstration" fairly sharply from causal inference; now he unites them, in that both are cases where necessity is projected from the inferrer to the subject matter of the inference.

He will unite them again in Section XVI, when both capacities get included under the general heading of "wonderful and unintelligible" epistemic instincts, differing only in that demonstration, like migration or nest-building, is minimally dependent on past experience, whereas causal inference is a manifestation of our instinct to learn from experience. Both are to be wondered at, and neither can be made comprehensible by "pure" intellect, by reason as intuition or demonstration. Hume writes that his own hypothesis about the great effect on our minds of repetitions in our experience, about the epistemic force of custom or habit, gets confirmation from the fact that, when we turn our minds onto their own operations, familiarity breeds a false sense of self-explanatoriness: "men are not astonish'd at the operations of their own reason, at the same time, that they admire the *instinct* of animals, and find a difficulty in explaining it, merely because it cannot be reduc'd to the very same principles" (T. 178–179). To see matters aright, in Hume's view, we must assimilate our cognitive capacities to animal reason and animal instinct, not take our own special mathematical and language-dependent capacities as self-luminous, as the norm for comprehension and comprehensibility. (Hume really does try to effect what amounts to a total reversal in epistemology.)

In order to see how he can and does move from constant conjunctions in nature, through mental determination, to normative necessities for human truth-seeking, we need to grasp why he took so long to be ready to give the account of necessity, and the relation of the account to Hume's infamous double definition of causation. For both these purposes it is vital that we learn what Hume means by "the determination of the mind," since the feeling of that determination is found to be the long-sought source of the idea of necessity, and this determination is referred to in Hume's definition of cause as a natural relation.

Part III's references to what determines the mind grow in frequency as Hume, from Section XI on, approaches the climax of

the hunt. But as early as Section VI we have him writing of the
mind in causal inference being "not determin'd by reason, but by
certain principles, which associate together the ideas of these objects, and unite them in the imagination" (T. 92). This tells us that
"demonstrative" reason determines the mind in some of its inferences, but not in causal ones. What is special about inference, as
distinct from mere suggestion or association? As we have seen in
the previous chapter, Hume tells us in Section IX what is special
about the association guiding causal inference, and the same feature is present in all inference, namely that "the thought is always
determ'd to pass" to a particular "fixt" idea as conclusion, "without any choice or hesitation" (T. 110). Inference is the determination, fixing, or unique selection of a new belief by older beliefs
or sense certainties. Hume's use of "determine" and "determination" is that standard one, the first sense that Samuel Johnson lists,
in which it means to fix or to settle. The O.E.D., to illustrate this
use, cites Hobbes's famous claim in *Leviathan,* Chapter X: "As in
other things, . . . not the seller, but the buyer determines the
Price." The determination of the mind, at a given time, is the fixing of what perception (idea or impression) it has at that time,
perhaps also the fixing of how lively that perception is and how
much life it has to bestow on associated perceptions. Some determiner fixes it, and for Hume, the causal theorist, the determiner
will always be a determining cause, be it deductive reason with its
principles, or the principles of association, or the force of custom,
or nature herself, when she determines us to judge as well as
breathe and feel, and determines also our current sense perceptions, our receivings of the "perishing" impressions that we are
naturally determined to trans-substantiate[1] into in the real presence
of lasting bodies.

Determination requires both a determiner and a determined,
and Hume's chief interest in Book One is in the cases where the
conscious mind is determined rather than determiner, effect not
cause. Even in Books Two and Three, when he gets to the will
and to voluntary action, he usually emphasizes the determiners
and influences lying behind the conscious mental determiners and
influences, and he defines the will as our consciousness of some
new mentally caused perception, one presumably ultimately

caused by something other than will. This is why he can dismiss
as of very limited importance the question of which virtues are
voluntary. He tries to get behind will to the passions doing the
more ultimate determining, as he wants to get behind "reason" to
the instincts, natural forces, and human passions whose agent can
be recognized as reason in its various forms. Almost never does
Hume use "determine" or its cognates in such a way as to imply
a mental determiner rather than a mental determined. (One nicely
ambiguous use occurs in his "Advertisement" to the *Treatise*
[T. xii], where he writes that he is determined to regard the judgment of the public as his best instruction. A resolve? An acknowl-
edgement of his ruling passion? Both?)

Hume in Section IX makes it very clear how determination differs from mere "influence," and in subsequent sections he is careful
to use the weaker term, "influence," for causal factors that do not
fix the effects in question, for causes that are not "compleat" or
determining causes. Association by resemblance or by contiguity
influences but does not uniquely select the next thought a person
will have. When these forces are at work, "their influence is very
feeble and uncertain . . . There is no manner of necessity for the
mind to feign any resembling and contiguous objects; and if it
feigns such, there is as little necessity for it always to confine itself
to the same, without any difference or variation . . . The mind
foresees and anticipates the change; and even from the very first
instant feels the looseness of its actions, and the weak hold it has
of its objects" (T. 109–110). The famous references to the impression of reflection that is a feeling of determination, five sections
later, should be understood as picking up the phenomenology of
free and constrained association, begun here and picked up again
in Book Two's discussion of liberty and necessity, where Hume
again refers to this feeling of a "certain looseness" in the transitions
that our mental life displays (T. 408). It is, he tells us there, a *"false
sensation or experience . . .* of the liberty of indifference" (ibid.),
false because it confuses ignorance of determining causes with absence of them; that is, with absence of grounds from which, if we
knew them, we could and would infer the effect. The most that
we are aware of, when we are subject to association by contiguity
or by "free fancy" resemblance, or when we freely "make up our

minds," are the influences on us, not what determines our mind. But in inference we *feel* that we are determined. We may make mistakes about the "compleat cause" of our inference, but we realize that we are determined; we take the evidence to force the conclusion upon us, without looseness and fluctuation.

In Section X, Hume discusses the "influence" of belief on the will and on action, as well as on our enjoyment of conversation and reading. This is not "determination" of the will (or of our pleasure) by our beliefs, any more than passions are later said to determine the will. Both belief and passion must "concur" before we have a complete cause of intention and action—each alone is mere "influence." (This section of Book One is an essential but usually neglected companion to Book Two's "Of the influencing motives of the will," to which it makes forward reference at T. 118.) Influences are partial but not complete or determining causes, or, perhaps better, they become part-causes when there is concurrence with some other completing partial cause. (Hume does not say this in so many words, but it seems a reasonable gloss on his use of "influence," "determination," "concurrence" and "compleat cause.")

In Section XI, the first of three sections dealing with probability in the narrow sense that he switches to at T. 124 ("evidence, which is still attended with uncertainty"), he gives us a helpful restatement of the determination of the mind by experienced constant conjunctions, and the weaker "influence" of anything less than constancy. "A cause traces the way to our thought, and in a manner forces us to survey such certain objects, in such certain relations. Chance can only destroy this determination of the thought" (T. 125). Hume assimilates negation to "destruction" of the negated. Any disconfirming instance that "destroys" a former constancy destroys our full confidence in inferring what will be conjoined with a given event, when it next occurs. It makes "the way to our thought" a little rougher, a little less of a smooth groove, but it need not completely counteract the influence of the earlier firm habit. It leaves us with "evidence . . . attended with uncertainty." I have spoken here of what Hume supposes to happen when what was earlier deemed a causal relation, a constancy of conjunction, gets demoted to a mere "probability of cause"—not what it takes for "full assurance," belief in a causal relation, to be initially acquired "by these slow steps" (T. 130), as we perfect a particular habit of firm expectation and get a gradually confirmed "proof" of a causal connection. Hume thinks that uncertainty attends both the child whose experience is still too brief for any significant constancies to have been experienced or tested, and the more experienced person who has suffered disappointments to earlier formed expectations, or who all along had "mixed" experience—say, that when twenty ships set out across the Atlantic, only nineteen return (T. 134). The child has not had time to perform enough "experiments"; the disillusioned adult has "contrary experiments"; and "contrary experiments produce an imperfect belief, either by weakening the habit, or by dividing and afterwards joining in different parts, that *perfect* habit, which makes us conclude in general, that instances, of which we have no experience, must necessarily resemble those of which we have" (T. 135). (Here, that imperfection of reason, the so-called problem of induction, gets promoted into the "perfection" of habit. See also T. 134.)

In these pathbreaking sections on probability, which Hume in the *Abstract* singles out for mention, for the way in which they remedy the defects of those earlier theories of knowledge that were "too concise when they treat of probabilities" (T. 647), and also for their confirmation of the "new and remarkable" (or even "curious") arguments adduced in Part III's main claims about belief formation, there is frequent discussion of the determination of the mind (T. 125, 132, 133, 134, 154). I shall discuss the contributions these sections make to Hume's main arguments, and to his hunt for the causes of our idea of necessity; the discussion of their contribution to that new part of the "science of man" that is probability theory, I shall leave to those in a better position to estimate it.[2] These sections clearly were intended by Hume to take up Leibniz's challenge, as well as to provide confirmation for the claims he had already made about the role of experience of constant conjunctions in grounding causal inference and so in forming belief. They tell us how the "wise man proportions his belief to the evidence" (E. 110) when the evidence is less than perfect.

The seventh rule endorsed in Section XV requires that "when

any object encreases or diminishes with the encrease or diminution of its cause, 'tis to be regarded as a compounded effect, deriv'd from the union of the several different effects, which arise from the several different parts of the cause" (T. 174). We find this rule or maxim anticipated in Section XII, where it is applied to the search for the cause of our imperfect assurance of some merely probable future event. Such less than perfect assurance arises from "imperfect habit." "As the belief, which we have of any event, encreases or diminishes according to the number of chances or past experiments, 'tis to be considered as a compounded effect, of which each part arises from a proportionable number of chances or experiments" (T. 136). The "perfect habit," the determination of the mind to infer the event in question, is not treated similarly by Hume, not treated as compound. Only when its perfection is shattered, by "experiments of a contrary nature," do we need to recognize "parts." "Proof" is not a limiting case of probability; probability is the outcome of destruction or degradation of a "proof." In the passage already quoted Hume says that contrariety leads us to divide, and afterwards to join in different parts, the originally perfect pre-contrariety habit (T. 135). We divide it into as many units as are needed to capture the proportion of positive to negative results of our experiments. If our data show that for every twenty ships that set out, nineteen return, then we will need twenty units. If the data show that only fifteen of every twenty return, we will need only four units, to express the three-to-one proportion. The nineteen-to-one proportion, after the needed "division," will undergo a "joining" of the nineteen, which will be "melted together" (T. 140) to produce the fairly confident but less than certain expectation that a given ship will return. Hume spends some time on the mechanism of the dividing of perfect habits, and the rejoining of their fragments into imperfect habits, the making of second-best probabilities out of the remains of ruined "proofs." The account is, as the *Abstract* says, remarkable and curious. For my purposes, its most surprising feature is its resolute adherence to faith in that familiar maxim that a cause is always necessary. Hume here gives us a causal, not a probabilistic, account of probability estimates, and he treats them as estimates of "the probability *of causes*." Chance is treated not as absence but as

ignorance of cause. Those who are "artizans" rather than "peasants" are never content with anything less than "proofs," interpreting "probabilities" always as indicators not of "the uncertainty
of nature" (T. 131), but of "the secret opposition of contrary
causes" (T. 132). Hume is Kantian in his faith that probabilities are
interim findings, ultimately replaceable, once we refine our "experiments," by proofs. Probability is not turned on itself here. The
dubious meta-probabilities that Hume gives us later, in Section I
of Part IV, are neither designed to explain themselves, nor formed,
tested and reformed in the way the empiricist of Part III would
progressively revise estimates of the chances of a ship being lost
at sea. Hume here in Part III exhibits the "artizan's" approach to
the human understanding; he is determined to find "proofs" of
secret causes, to know the causes of our uncertainty, not content
simply to shrug and say that "commonly our reasoning is imperfect."

A cause is always necessary, it seems, because our minds (or
those of artisans) are bent on forming perfect not just imperfect
habits.[3] They come instinctively equipped with the "full and perfect" habit (T. 134) or "determination" (ibid.) to expect uniformity and to "make the past a standard for the future" (T. 133), both
in general and in particular matters. This is why the same explanation can serve to explain both why a particular cause is thought
to necessitate its effect, and why we believe there must always be
a cause (T. 82). In both cases the explanation is habit, in the latter
case a meta-habit, the habit of forming more specific epistemic
habits. In both cases the necessity is displaced from "the determination" of the mind, in the latter case from a meta-determination,
the general determination (by instinct) of one's mind to be determined by particular experienced constancies, and to be discon-
tented until its epistemic habits are perfect ones. Probabilities are
mere placeholders for later-to-be-discovered causes. It becomes
very clear, in this section, titled "Of the probability of causes,"
that Hume is tracing the idea of necessity to mental determination,
as displayed in "perfect" epistemic habit, so that the way is prepared for Section XIV. At T. 133 he speaks of the "habitual determination" of our minds in unreflective causal inference; at T. 134,
of the "habit or determination to transfer the past to the future,"

a habit that gets "broke into pieces" when the past comes to contain disappointment of expectations, "experiments . . . of a contrary nature." At T. 135 he links the "perfection" of inductive habit to the general conclusion "that *instances,* of which we have no experience, must necessarily resemble those of which we have" (my emphasis). Events are treated as instances of some regularity, reinforcers of some habit of expectation. Necessity goes with "proof," with certainty, with perfect habit. Possibility, the negation of necessity, goes with "probability," uncertainty, broken habits (see T. 135–136). With good reason Hume can write that the principles we found convincing with regard to "our most certain reasonings from causation" acquire "a new degree of evidence" from his findings concerning "conjectural or probable reasonings" (T. 139). His seventh rule (T. 174), including his caution about abrupt qualitative changes, is carefully kept here, as are others of its companion rules, such as the fifth and the sixth. Hume's search for the causes of all our "imperfect habits" of inference, analogical reasoning as well as probability estimation, "unphilosophical" as well as "philosophical" probability estimates, and for the special causes and distinctive effects of each, as well as for their common causes and common effects, is, by the standards if his own later-espoused logic, exemplary.

Section XIII gives confirmation to Hume's general thesis, and to the particular claim that, until contrariety breaks it, we do have an initially perfect habit to "transfer past to future," one that is cued into operation simply by acquiring a past showing some uniformities. Hume in Section XIII shows the costs of this unwillingness to tolerate lack of uniformity. Our "mighty addiction to general rules" explains our prejudices as well as our reflective causal insights. Hume lists several other varying forms of the factors involved in our habits of causal inference and reasoned reflective probability estimation (see T. 135), forms that "have not had the good fortune to obtain the same sanction" (T. 143). Besides "prejudices," that is to say, rashly formed generalities that are resistant to revision by counter-instances, there is also the exaggerated influence of temporal contiguity, which leads us give more weight to an argument based on a recently observed fact than to one based on a fact in the more remote past. The relative vividness of our

memory of a fact "secretly changes the authority of the same argument" (T. 143), "not withstanding the opposition of philosophy" (ibid.). In this section, for once, the philosophers are wiser
than the vulgar, so that all species of "unphilosophical probability," except its own negative feedback in tentative rules for correcting more rashly formed rules, are here subjected to gentle disapproval.

Long chains of reasoning, and long chains of testimony, produce less assurance than short ones, "however infallible the connexion of each link be esteem'd" (T. 144). Hume raises and answers a question about whether successive editions of a published
book also weaken assurance in the factual information it gives,
whether our trust in "the fidelity of Printers" (T. 146) is on the
same footing with our trust in general human veracity or in human calculation. He answers that, since it is the same operation
that is reliably repeated, many editions do not weaken assurance
in the way a long line of informants do. So he is reassured that,
thanks to the invention of the faithful printing press, "our posterity, even after a thousand ages," need not "ever doubt if there has
been such a man as JULIUS CAESAR" (T. 145). Hume is at his quirk-
ish best in this section, which is stuffed both with acute psychological observations, and with ideas he will later develop more
fully. We get a preview of the argument to be given in Part IV
Section I against "reason," the argument which turns probability
of error on deduction and on the probability of error in calculating
those probabilities. Reiterating meta-probabilities of error until
the original convinction dwindles towards zero is here said to be
an adaption of a "very celebrated argument against the *Christian
Religion*" (T. 145) which Hume will borrow to use against that
ally of theology, rationalism.

After an ambiguous discussion of the effect of veils in height-
ening the impact of what is veiled, Hume ends the section with a
summary of the whole argument of Part III thus far, a summary
intended to point up "what principally gives authority to this system" (T. 154), the way the different independently supported parts
of it give each other mutual support. This summary takes the
main topic to have been human belief, its varieties and its sources.
"The belief, which attends our memory, is of the same nature with

that, which is deriv'd from our judgments: Nor is there any difference betwixt that judgment, which is deriv'd from a constant
and uniform connexion of causes and effects, and that which depends upon an interrupted and uncertain" (T. 154). Any system
which fails to acknowledge that belief is a matter of superior vivacity, and that our judgments are "the effect of custom on the
imagination," will lose itself, he says, "in perpetual contradiction
and absurdity" (T. 155). This is either heavy irony or one of the
smuggest and least sceptical passages in the *Treatise,* devoid for the
moment not just of despairing scepticism, but even of true scepticism, of proper diffidence. In these sections Hume has not turned
empirically self-correcting probability estimates on themselves, or
even yet turned unphilosophical probability on itself, as he has
promised us he eventually will (in Section XV). He has turned
causal, not probabilistic, thinking onto various sorts of probability
estimations, and in Section XIV he is ready for the fully reflexive
turn of causal inference onto causal inference.

LET US, LIKE HUME, "return upon our footsteps" (T. 155) and see
just what we have found him to have done in Part III as a whole.
He set out to hunt down the causal origin of our idea of cause,
and in particular the element of necessity in it that we see as licensing our causal inferences, and so as giving us most of our beliefs
about matters of non-present fact. He has found, as he promised
us early on that he would, that "the necessary connexion depends
on the inference, instead of the inference's depending on the necessary connexion" (T. 88). He now tells us exactly how, from the
impression of mental determination that we have during inference, we derive the idea of necessity, which we then project back
beyond the mental determination itself onto its cause, namely an
experienced constant conjunction in nature, and onto the subject
matter of the inference which produces the impression, namely a
particular instance of this conjunction. The foregoing sections
have accustomed us to associate necessity with the determination
of the mind, and the latter with experienced constant conjunctions. Now we are in a position to see that the relation is causal,
not just association by temporal contiguity. Hume first states his
thesis about how the idea of necessity is derived from the impres-

sion we have when our minds are caused to infer an effect from a cause, and how that determination arises from experienced repetition; then he moves on to give his claims about our projection of this idea beyond its immediate source, and so explains erroneous views about necessity. Only then is he ready to "collect all the different parts of this reasoning, and by joining them together form an exact definition of the relation of cause and effect" (T. 169). The definition does collect and join all the preceding reasoning, but does so in a somewhat understated way, so that its full subtlety has often been missed. Even its reflexivity has frequently been denied, ignored, or dismissed as vicious circularity,[4] although Hume has made no secret of the fact that his understanding of cause is causal, and no secret about the causal sense he intends "determination" to be taken to have.

He defines "cause" both as a philosophical and as a natural relation, and so we need to understand how these two types of perceived relation are inter-related. (Reflexivity seems as irresistible in Hume interpretation as it clearly was irresistible to Hume.) Hume told us that clearly enough at the end of the early section "Of the connexion or association of ideas," when he wrote that our ideas of relations, including philosophical relations, are among the most remarkable effects of association or the natural relations of ideas (T. 13). Only cause as a natural relation can guide our non-deductive inferential moves (T. 94), so it is cause as a natural relation that helps lead us to our idea of cause as a philosophical relation, once, like Hume, we "think proper" to probe behind the natural relation to its preconditions, both in ourselves and in the world of which we are part. Thus we are led to notice constancies in nature, and our own reaction to experience of them, and so led to see the ground for Hume's definition of cause as a philosophical relation in terms of constant conjunction. But remembering the role of cause as a natural relation in producing our idea of cause as a philosophical relation, we will not be surprised if there is causal interdependence between the terms of the two alternative definitions.

I say interdependence, since the double definition continues and encapsulates the careful balance Hume has preserved throughout his long preparation for the definition, a balance between the empiricist emphasis on the determination of our minds by nature's constancies, and the idealist emphasis on what only mind can contribute, the modal element, the "must," the "'tis necessary." The "most violent" paradox that "the efficacy or energy of causes is neither plac'd in the causes themselves, nor in the deity, nor in the concurrence of these two principles; but belongs entirely to the soul" (T. 166) is balanced by the thesis that it is only when the soul has experienced the constant "union of two or more objects" (ibid.), and only because it is naturally constituted so as to respond to such involuntary repetition in the way it does, by developing its own "perfect habit" of inference, that the soul can come up with the idea of causal necessity. Hume's double thesis is that thought depends upon causes for its operation, and that our interpretation of causes, including mental causes, depends upon features of our thought. He has not so much "reversed the order of nature" (see T. 167) by making human thought the source of the ideas of necessity and law, as reversed the order of theology, and it is no accident that he notes he is displacing necessity from the deity as well as from non-human nature. But since it is empiricist thought which is to be the source of norms and of necessity, nature retains her rights.

The whole account has advanced two theses of equal importance: that we and our thought are causally determined by the nature of which we are part, and that it is our thought that produces necessity. The idea of necessity is an inference-mediated effect of natural constant conjunctions, an effect which, like almost all effects, does not accurately image its ultimate causes. Hume has spent a lot of time arguing that effects need not copy their causes, while conceding that it pleases us when they do, when resemblance "compleats the union" made by the causal relation. The idea of necessity, like all ideas, resembles its impression cause, the feeling of determination, but the impression of determination, and its cause, inference or the determination of the mind, do not resemble the constancies that cause them, any more than a burning pain resembles the fire that causes it. Hume has traced the idea of necessity to a very special impression, one that is "of reflexion," a reflex reaction of the mind to what no other part of nature can do, namely make inferences. He has balanced this idealist thesis with his investigation of our mind's dependency, in its causal inferences, on experience of repetition in the rest of nature. It would have been inappropriate to have any definition other than a double one as the climax of this carefully balanced long preparation for the definition.[5]

To see how the double definition does capture Hume's empiricist thesis about causal inference, we need to attend not just to the part that defines cause as a philosophical relation, but to the "foreign objects" in each alternative version of the definition. The foreign objects in the first version are the other earlier instances of the causal constancy. The foreign object in the second version is the "union" of ideas in the human imagination, leading to the determination of the mind in inference. It is these that display the causal relations on which Hume has dwelt so long and so carefully in the foregoing account. The repetition of previous event sequences like the current one is what determines the mind in this inference. Causal inferences are what enable us to trace and recognize constant conjunctions, and their effect on us. Hume's double definition of the causal relation itself displays a meta-causal relation, and that is what gives it its authority.

Hume can be confident that his definition does present the truth about our concept of cause, precisely because the definition displays how the concept, under this analysis, can successfully be turned on itself. It is a self-demonstrating and self-verifying real definition, arrived at by a causal investigation into our concept of cause, and itself joining together the various results of that long complex exercise in reflexivity. Empirical thinking is here thinking itself. And as successful reflexivity gives the definition its authority, so the same reflexivity is what enables Hume to promote the habits of causal thinking that were used in arriving at it into "rules" for finding out what "really" causes what.[6] This occurs in the immediately following section, and to understand the definition is to understand its relation to its follow-ups, as well as its long (fourteen sections long) introduction.

Among its follow-ups or "corrollaries" within Section XIV, is the claim I have placed at the beginning of this chapter, the claim that "there is but one kind of *necessity*" (T. 171). Hume's discussion of this claim makes it quite clear that he does regard his definition as capturing not denying the "necessary connexion" of cause and effect, that element in causation whose great importance he had begun his account by emphasizing (T. 77). Commentators like Antony Flew have complained that the definition leaves out this supposedly vital element,[7] but clearly Hume expected us to see the implied reference to it, or he would not so blithely have drawn his corollary about necessity. What he says to support the conclusion that there is one kind of necessity makes it very clear that constant conjunction, along with the determination of the mind (the foreign object of the definition of cause as a natural relation) are taken by him to include the needed necessity in the definition. " 'Tis the constant conjunction of objects, along with the determination of the mind, which constitutes a physical necessity" (T. 171). Hume puts this point with typical reflexivity in Book Two's discussion of liberty and necessity: "Here then are two particulars, which we are to consider as essential to necessity, *viz.* the constant *union,* and the *inference* of the mind" (T. 400). Both these statements about what necessity necessitates conjoin rather than disjoin the foreign objects of the two supposedly alternative versions of his double definition. This is, I think, because the two "views" of cause are each non-eliminable alternatives. To understand either is to see that it brings the other "along with" it. We can get at cause from either view, since each leads us by causal inference to its attendant view. As both constant conjunction and the inference of the mind are essential to necessity, and necessity is essential to causation, so both of Hume's two views of cause must be grasped, and the double or mutual causal dependency between their foreign objects properly appreciated, before we see what precisely his definition says and shows.

How then does Hume define a cause? A cause-effect pair is the subject matter of causal inference, or an instance of the constant conjunction, experience of which causes such an inference. We could it also put it thus:

> The relation between a constant conjunction (an experienced one, along with the not yet experienced constant conjunctions that our minds' and brains' workings exhibit) of events of type P and events of type Q, and a causal inference from P to Q, is that of *cause and effect.* Any other pair is a cause-effect pair if it is either an instance

of such a conjunction, or an instance of the subject matter of such
an inference.

This is a more "abstruse" restatement[8] of what Hume put less
pompously. My formulation highlights what Hume's only implied: the crucial role of the higher-level cause-effect pair. There
may of course be further higher-level cause-effect pairs to be discovered, such as those explaining our instinct for causal inference,
our sensitivity to certain sorts of repetitions. Hume ends Part III
by highlighting these instincts, while disclaiming any full causal
understanding of them. Until the time of Darwin and his followers, they did remain not just "unintelligible" but, what is more
important, not yet comprehensible to experience-grounded and
experience-corrected reasoning. Hume has Philo, in the *Dialogues,*
hazard a few prophetic hypotheses about natural selection, but of
course he is not in a position to verify such hypotheses. The *Dialogues* as a whole, however, do much to advance our understanding of how and why our thoughts "have . . . gone on in the same
train with the other works of nature" (E. 54–55). One might give
the following very free paraphrase of their main message, to show
how it is an extension of the balanced claims of the *Treatise* in
Book One, Part III: order is projected from the contemplating
mind back onto the contemplated world, and, since the mind is
part of that world and sensitive to it, it is no accident that what it
has to project "fits" as well as it does the facts that stimulate the
projection. How else could a thinking animal persist unless its
thinking were adapted to the world it thinks about?

The acceptability of the definition of cause depends upon its
reflexivity, and that encapsulates the reflexivity of the reasoning
leading up to it. The rules that Hume enunciates and endorses in
the following section also get their normative force from the fact
that reasoning conforming to them has just been demonstrated to
be capable of being turned successfully on itself. They are not just
the rules that Hume will observe in most of the rest of the *Treatise*
to conduct his causal investigation into our nature as passionate
and moral beings; they are the rules he has been using to arrive at,
and confirm, his hypotheses concerning what causes our ideas,
our inferences, and our degrees of belief and disbelief. The first

four rules, requiring that a cause be contiguous and prior in time, and constantly conjoined with its effect, are easily seen to have been kept. The requirement of temporal priority and contiguity was given some discussion in Section II, and Hume has been careful in his own account to locate the causes of causal inference both in the past (past experience of constancies) and in the past closest in time to the inference—in a "present impression" which reactivates an already formed association. What the fourth rule, "The same cause always produces the same effect, and the same effect never arises but from the same cause," adds to the third, requiring their "constant union," is a little mysterious (T. 173). (It may indicate that "constant conjunction" strictly makes a cause a sufficient but not a necessary condition of its effect, so that it takes the fourth rule to require that "the same effect never arises but from the same cause," thus making "compleat" causes both sufficient and necessary conditions of their effects.) It is the last four rules that are not so automatically kept in ordinary causal inference, and that most often distinguish the epistemic habits of "wise men" from those of the less wise. The fifth rule stipulates that "where several different objects produce the same effect, it must be by means of some quality, which we discover to be common amongst them" (T. 174). Hume employed this rule in searching for a common factor in the various apparent causes of firm human conviction—in memory, sense perception, belief in inferred matters of fact. His hypothesis about vivacity-transfer among perceptions is a hypothesis designed to provide a common cause for all occurrences of human certainty about matters of fact. His claim in Section XVI that induction is an "instinct" in us assimilates the cause of our expectations about non-present facts to the supposed causes of similar expectations of other animals. The sixth rule makes a parallel requirement that variation of effects of resembling causes "proceed from that particular, in which they differ" (ibid.). Hume's own hypothesis in Section IX about what explains the variation in the effects of the different varieties of mental association, what explains why causal association not merely enlivens an idea but "persuades us of any real existence" (T. 109), employs his sixth rule, as well as the fifth. Hume employs it to explain the varying effects not just of causal and non-causal association, but also of experience of nature's repetitions and experience of "other habits," of humanly contrived repetitions such as indoctrination. The whole section is a self-conscious employment of Hume's fifth and sixth rules—or, if you prefer, the rules articulate the norms observed in that part of the account leading up to that articulation.

The seventh rule (more or less equivalent to J. S. Mill's method of concomitant variation) applies where we have a range of causes and effects exhibiting discernible quantitative variation, where we can talk of diminution and increase. Hume stipulates that these quantities be treated as compounded out of their unit elements, so that we have "compounded" causes and effects. "The absence or presence of one part of the cause is here suppos'd to be always attended with the absence or presence of a proportionable part of the effect" (T. 174). The parts of his own preceding reasoning that most obviously employed this rule were, as we have seen, the sections on probability.[9] The discontinuity between even very high probability and what Hume calls "proof" is like the discontinuity he mentions in his commentary on his seventh rule, between increase of pleasure as warmth increases, and the pain of a burn. (He mentions this case to warn us against unrestrained extrapolation of the causal dependencies that were learned by noting concomitant variation in restricted conditions.) It is in part because of this discontinuity in the effects of repetition that "there is but one kind of *necessity*." There is no "moral necessity" that is a weaker sort of necessity.

The eighth rule tells us "that an object, which exists for any time in its full perfection without any effect, is not the sole cause of that effect, but requires to be assisted by some other principle, which may forward its influence and operation" (ibid.). Where has Hume employed this rule in the preceding account? He had stated it as "an establish'd maxim both in natural and moral philosophy" at T. 76, and he used it there to argue that if any cause were contemporary with its effect, all would be, and we would have "no less than the destruction of that succession of causes, which we observe in the world; and indeed, the utter annihilation of time" (ibid.). This Kantian claim about the mutual dependency of our experience of a succession of causes and the temporal character of our experience is casually offered to us by Hume, and he advises the reader not to worry if the argument fails to "appear satisfactory," since "the affair is of no great importance" (ibid.). So much for transcendental deductions! What is of importance to Hume is that, given that we do experience a succession of events, our causal explanations try to explain the precise time of occurrence of the explanadum. Time lapse alone is not, for Hume, a causal factor in the mind-external world: "however every thing be produc'd in time, there is nothing real that is produc'd by time" (T. 508–509).[10] In his own causal account of our causal inferences, and our idea of necessity, there are many cases of joint causes. To explain the time of the acquisition of a new belief in a matter of non-present fact, Hume, in Sections IV–VIII, cites both a standing associative union of ideas and also a "present impression." Only the present impression, from which we infer, explains why our tendency to make causal inferences of a given kind is presently activated. The eighth principle is both stated and observed in Hume's own causal reasoning leading up to the endorsement of this rule. Perhaps another unstated but gently hinted application of it can be found in Hume's claims for his own causal role in the discovery of the causes of our ideas of cause and causal necessity. Causal inference, and the ideas of cause and of necessity, had existed for a long time in their "full perfection" without generating the idea of their origin that Hume comes up with.

I have given this partial account of Hume's own observance of his eight rules in the reasoning leading up to their endorsement to support my claim that, in Part III, he thinks he has found mental causes that do not "shoulder aside reasons,"[11] indeed that he has discovered which mental causes are good reasons. *They are those which exhibit the workings of habits of belief-formation which can "bear their own survey"* (see T. 620). It took Hume to turn causal inference fully and thoroughly onto causal inference, and the result of this adventure in reflection is dramatically different from that which befalls rationalist or intellectualist reason in the first section of Book One, Part IV. Hume begins that section with a confident causal claim that "our reason must be consider'd as a kind of cause" (T. 180). After showing there how calculative (non-causal) reasoning appears to destroy itself, when made reflexive, he tells us that his intention in going through these intellectualist and sceptical reflexive moves is to "make the reader sensible of the truth of my hypothesis, *that all our reasonings concerning causes and effects are deriv'd from nothing but custom; and that belief is more properly an act of the sensitive, than of the cogitative part of our natures*" (T. 183). This, as I emphasized in the previous chapter, is said to disown any ultimately sceptical intentions, not to embrace them. Hume after all has just concluded Part III's successful turn of self-consciously sensitive and custom-dependent causal reasoning on itself, a reflexive turn that leads to endorsement, as rules, of those habits that had survived the test of reflexive employment. The whole of the *Treatise* searches for mental operations that can bear their own survey, sorting those that can (causal reasoning in its naturalistic and non-metaphysical employment, virtues and the moral sentiment which discerns them) from those that get into "manifest contradictions" or self-destructive conflict when turned on themselves. The whole enterprise is a search for norms with the sort of grounding that a reflective naturalist can accept.

When we reason as Hume's rules advise us to reason, not only can our thoughts about nature go "on in the same train with the other works of nature" (E. 54–55), but we can begin to understand how they can do that, and so endorse both their self-corrective natural working, and their more philosophical self-conscious working.

The causal account of necessity, the double definition of cause in which it is embedded, the endorsed rules, the final generalizations about epistemic habits and instincts, are the outcome of Hume's reflexive causal inferences. The causal sequence that we are intended by the end of Part III to discern, and discern as fairly well confirmed, is one which doubles back onto consciousness of itself. We could represent it thus (where each vertical arrow indicates a causal relation):

A. Nature, with her own habits (her constancies of conjunction of events);

$\downarrow$

B. Human minds, experiencing some of nature's constancies, and sensitive to them;

$\downarrow$

C. A union in the human imagination of the ideas of such events as have been experienced as constantly conjoined;

↓

D. An irresistible human tendency to infer the later of any such event pair, given a belief that the earlier has occurred, and a feeling of having no choice but to thus infer;

↓

E. An idea of causal determination or necessity, and a (resistible) tendency to project this back both into the subject matter of the inference that caused it, and into the experienced natural constancy causing that;

↓

F. Puzzlement, in reflective minds, about the sources and truth-presenting power of this idea of causal necessity;

↓

G. Formulation of the causal hypotheses contained in the chain A–E, as genealogy of the idea of causal necessity, and concern about the truth of these hypotheses;

↓

H. Confirmation of these causal hypotheses, by finding no decisive counter-examples, and by finding analogous confirming examples (repetition-sensitivity in other living things, other cases of vivacity-communicating human associative thinking, and other cases of human thinkers projecting the feeling of determination);

↓

I. Renewed attention to the natural constant conjunctions that affect both what we are and what we experience, and special attention to their perceptible effects on our habits of thought;

↓

J. New causal inferences (about our causal inferences), based on newly noticed constant conjunctions, and their newly noticed effects;

↓

K. Increasing self-consciousness of the causal conditions of human causal inferences, and of human awareness of nature's constancies;

↓

L. Increased self-confidence in endorsing, as rules of causal inference, the habits of inference that have proved not just self-correcting (since experience-determined), but able to be turned without incoherence on themselves, thus giving us self-knowledge, and promising us new possibilities of knowledge and of reliable inference.

This version of Hume's reasoning in Part III acknowledges, indeed highlights, Hume's use of causal terms in his definition of cause,[12] and treats that not as a defect but as a part of the self-referential subtlety of the whole account. Hume's reasoning to the existence of the causal sequence A–L is not a closed circle, but an open-ended spiral,[13] one that Darwin and his followers continue. (One is tempted to say that the double definition is part of an account whose structure is that of a double helix.) The definition of cause fixes explicitly upon two members of this causal and meta-causal sequence, A and D, each of which refers to event pairs. *A cause is either an instance of a special cause (constant conjunction) or the subject matter of a special effect (causal inference).* We can take our pick, since, once we are conscious of their meta-causal relation, each pair leads us to the other attendant pair. It is only because the chain goes on to consciousness of A and D, and of their causal connection, that the definition can be given, and once given, understood and accepted. It is only because the habits of causal inference referred to in this causal sequence are also used in recognizing it as a causal sequence, only because they have successfully surveyed themselves, that they are endorsed as rules.[14]

Just as we must use the language of good reasons to reason about good reasons, so, if reasons are a special sort of self-conscious mental cause, we must make special sorts of causal inference to reason causally about causal inference. Hume, the causal theorist, would have failed in his project had his account of cause not been couched in causal terms. He has made causal reasoning transparent, or at least translucent, to itself. He has shown how the idea of causal necessity derives from inference, namely from the causal determination of the mind by its repeated exposure to its subject matter, and he has shown which inferences or mental transitions we can endorse. The ones we endorse are the ones that can become successfully reflexive. *Successful reflexivity is normativ-*

ity. In the ultimate analysis, then, not only is there only one kind of necessity, but the one kind is that of reflexivity-tested human norms. The account of moral norms which Book Three will give us will later be found to confirm this general claim, but its confirmation for "demonstration" can be briefly given here, since its support comes from Book One as well as Book Three.

In Book Three, Hume gives natural language as an example of a set of conventions, or human agreements (T. 490). Linguistic conventions, once accepted and established, become linguistic norms. I noted in Chapter 2 how, in Book One, Part I, Hume followed Berkeley in claiming that the fixity of our general abstract ideas depends upon their being "annex'd to" a given general term (T. 22). Without language, then, there would be no generality, no abstraction, no ideas of the sort that have *a priori* knowable "relations." When Hume discusses our idea of space, he makes it clear that he believes that our linguistic conventions, such as our use of the term "circle," are natural fictions in the sense that the ideas annexed to even our most abstract general terms are suggested by the sorts of qualities and complexes of which we have impressions. Our idea of a perfect circle is reached by idealization from a series of progressively less imperfect circles (T. 48–49). Experience, idealization and convention combine to give us the ideas of whose relations we can be certain by demonstration. Thus, the determination of the mind that is projected into the subject matter of a demonstrative inference (T. 166) is collective self-determination. Hume has the makings of a conventionalist account of mathematical and logical necessity. Our norms, our linguistic self-imposed (but nature-suggested) necessities, are what get "spread . . . on" (T. 167) the mind's objects, in mathematical reasoning. Thus, Hume really does have reason to claim both that "there is but one kind of *necessity*" (T. 171) and that it "belongs entirely to the soul" (T. 166). All necessity derives from normative necessity, and all the norms available to us are our human norms, the products of our reflection.

5

The Simple Supposition of
Continued Existence

Since therefore 'tis almost impossible for the mind of
man to rest, like those of beasts, in that narrow circle of
objects, which are the subject of daily conversation and
action, we ought only to deliberate concerning the
choice of our guide, and ought to prefer that which is
safest and most agreeable.   (T. 271)[1]

The identity, which we ascribe to the mind of man, is
only a fictitious one, and of a like kind with that which
we ascribe to vegetables and animal bodies.   (T. 259)

Thus we feign the continu'd existence of the perceptions
of our senses, to remove the interruption; and run into
the notion of a *soul,* and *self,* and *substance,* to disguise
the variation.   (T. 254)

In Part IV of Book One, especially in its treatment of our assumptions about bodies and minds, and their identity over time,
Hume's sceptical persons (or one of his several sceptical personae)
makes the narrow range of ordinary objects of our conversation
as strange as any theologian's extraordinary objects, and makes the
old familiar world "altogether new." Hume's reader must deliberate concerning the choice of a guide through this metaphysical
transfiguration of the commonplace, for Hume's own guidance is
gnomic. Part IV, Book One of the *Treatise* is where those commentators who read Hume simply as a sceptic, a member of "that
fantastic sect" (T. 183), have their easiest triumph, at least until
they get to the second half of Part IV's conclusion, when not just
ordinary beliefs but also some theoretical ambitions seem to be
revived. What interpretation is safest and most agreeable? What is

a "fiction," and what is the "fictitious identity" of rocks, vegetables, animals and human minds?

Causal inference, Hume told us in Section IX, Part III of Book One, peoples our world, enlarging it beyond the reach of current impressions and personal memory. But in Part IV, problems arise about how exactly we perform this particular inferential operation. Our beliefs about the world and the vegetables, animals and persons in it are found to go beyond what causal inference from sensation and memory strictly could warrant. It is the "simple supposition" (T. 198) of the continued existence of lasting things and identical persons that poses the problem. Most of these things and persons are granted to be changing, and particularly with persons change seems to be a problem. A person's perceptions "succeed each other with an inconceivable rapidity, and are in a perpetual flux and movement" (T. 252). Vegetables and animals show change at a more conceivable rate—"in a very few years both vegetables and animals endure a *total* change, yet we still attribute identity to them, while their form, size, and substance are entirely alter'd" (T. 257). What enables the imagination to make "easy transitions" from one time slice of a vegetable to later ones, Hume writes in "Of personal identity," is "a *sympathy* of parts to their *common end*" and "the reciprocal relation of cause and effect in all their actions and operations" (T. 257). These facilitators of mental transitions had not been cited earlier, when, in "Of scepticism with regard to the senses," Hume looked at the "fiction" of "the continued existence of bodies." The bodies mentioned in that earlier section were mostly non-living bodies (mountains, stones, doors, hats, shoes), and the problems with our attribution of identity over time to them were found to lie not so much in their change, so long as that was "coherent," but more in our assumption that they have an uninterrupted existence, that they are there, more or less where we left them, whenever we or our attention are somewhere else. Change was not a special worry; indeed, change in something in our perceptual field was decreed a prerequisite of the applicability of the concepts of temporal duration and identity over time. In "Of personal identity," Hume discusses change in inanimate things, and finds that what makes "the passage of the thought" about the changing things "smooth and easy"

(T. 256) is the gradualness and coherence of the changes they show, or some constancy of relation they exhibit in even abrupt change (the rebuilt church at T. 258). But in his first discussion of their "fictitious identity" it was mainly interruption that had to be "removed," rather than variation "disguised" (see T. 254).

The "fictions" he is concerned about are, first, the assumption that when our attention is interrupted, what we were attending to, the "objects" of our attention, are not *ipso facto* interrupted in their existence, and, second, the assumption that when some sequence, such as our own states of mind, varies in a reasonably coherent way (whatever that means), the variation can be taken to be variation in some one persisting thing—that each of us has one lasting mind, and it is merely its *states* that change, or that there is one lasting mountain, whose appearance varies from season to season. In calling these assumptions "fictions," Hume is saying not that they are false,[2] but rather that they are unverifiable, and so unverified. In the nature of the case, we cannot directly check to find out if the perceptible world is still there when all human observers are asleep or dead. Neither can we peel off the changing states and appearances of minds and mountains to reveal unchanging "owners" of the changes. If we treat whatever we find, even if it is some constancy, as just another perception, then of course we will never get behind perceptions or appearances to their hypothetical real owners. Yet the postulates of the independence of the world from our observations, and of the background presence of something that is invariant in all our mind's variations, seem to make factual claims, albeit about rather large matters of fact. They are indeed precisely the sort of beliefs that Kant was to dub "synthetic *a priori*." They are neither assured nor ruled out by the definitions of the terms combined in them. They do not assert merely what Hume called "relations of ideas," so they are "synthetic." They are not empirically verifiable or falsifiable, so they are "*a priori*." Hume calls them "fictions," and this is quite different from calling them false. What is provably false is to deny that they are fictions, and Hume does think that we are prone to such falsehoods. Fictions are plausible stories we tell ourselves to organize our experience, to "bestow on the objects a greater regularity than what is observ'd in our mere perceptions" (T. 197). Fictions structure our version of ourselves and our environment, making both us and it "real and durable" (ibid.). Like the poets Hume discusses at T. 121–122, we start from what is familiar to us, our perceptions, and build from that a "system" that goes beyond what we strictly know to be true. Its anchors in the known facts "procure a more easy reception for the whole" (T. 122). In return for the greater regularity and systematicity bestowed on the non-fictitious parts of the whole, they "bestow a force and vivacity on the others" (ibid.), that is to say, on the strictly fictitious parts of the story. In our intense sceptical moments we will decree them to be "groundless and extraordinary opinions" (T. 218). In our more pragmatic moments we will take them to be quite ordinary and sensible postulates—some versions of them, indeed, ones needed for sanity and survival, "so that upon their removal human nature must immediately perish and go to ruin" (T. 225).

The fictional components in our beliefs about stones, trees and animals include both some interruption-removals and some disguises of variations, but it is mainly the former that are Hume's topic in "Of scepticism with regard to the senses." Why were these postulates not a problem when causal inference was examined in Part III? The causal inferences that Hume had looked at in Part III were ones that proceeded from an impression of, say, a river (T. 103) to what would happen if one walked into it. That the river would last a while, and remain there while one's back was turned, and that one would be the same person after as before one's encounter with the river, seemed to be taken for granted. Indeed, Hume's whole story about the effect on human minds of repetitions of sequences required that the same mind last and also be changed by its experience. That people did last, and communicate their beliefs to one another, was not questioned in, for example, the discussions of credulity, and our causal inferences about one another's reliability as reporters (T. 113).

At the start of Part IV Section II, Hume writes, "We may well ask, *What causes induce us to believe in the existence of body?* but 'tis in vain to ask, *Whether there be body or not?* That is a point, which we must take for granted in all our reasonings" (T. 187). He had certainly taken it for granted in his reasonings about causal inference, and also taken personal identity over time for granted both there in Part III and in the first section of Part IV, where a person's mind had to last at least long enough for the meta-probabilities of its own errors to be worked out and to bring about the supposed "total extinction of belief and evidence" (T. 183). In Section II, however, Hume is to "observe, that what we call a *mind,* is nothing but a heap or collection of different perceptions, united together by certain relations, and suppos'd, tho' falsely, to be endow'd with a perfect simplicity and identity" (T. 207). By the end of the section he finds himself "of a quite contrary sentiment" in comparison to his views at the start of the section, and finds that he is "more inclin'd to repose no faith at all in my senses, or rather imagination" (T. 217). The "implicit confidence" in the existence of lasting bodies is said to rest on a "gross illusion," namely "that our resembling perceptions are numerically the same, which leads us into the opinion, that these perceptions are uninterrupted, and still existent, even when they are not present to the senses" (T. 217). The lasting world, and persons we can trust out of our sight, seem to have thinned out into episodic phenomenal wraiths. How serious is Hume here? Did we ever make the false supposition that minds are "perfectly simple," when we surely always realized that they change ("change of mind"), can be divided (people are commonly of "divided mind," or "of two minds"), and can be the scene of the sorts of conflict and contradiction that Hume is busy enacting for us? Surely any "disguise" of variation we perform on ourselves is one of those harmless ones, which do not take us in.

What Hume says after his exposure of our ordinary assumptions about our world as resting on a "confusion of groundless and extraordinary opinions" (T. 218) is that although inattention may, indeed certainly will, restore our faith in "both an external and internal world," "profound and intense reflection" (ibid.) will always revive our sceptical doubts. Is the reflection that has brought him to this at least temporary certainty about the dependable return of fairly unsmiling sceptical doubt about the familiar world a different type of reflection, more intense perhaps, than that which had left him apparently smiling at the end of Part III? There he seemed fairly satisfied with his system's story about how we can tell what really causes what, but now he writes, "'Tis impossible upon any system to defend either our understanding or senses; and we but expose them farther when we endeavour to justify them in that manner" (ibid.). In what manner exactly? Has the manner of reflection and justification changed since Part III? Or does Part IV correct the confidence of Part III, and wipe the smile—at least for a while—from the earlier sceptic's face? (The true sceptic is smiling again, and smiling after reflecting on all these matters, by the end of Book One.)

What sort of sceptic is it who is insisting on showing the limited success of hypothetical attempts to infer the existence of lasting objects from phenomenal data? Can customary causal inference have causal inference turned on itself with self-congratulatory results, but not have it turned on belief in the sort of object and inferrer it takes for granted? Is it the true sceptic's scepticism that is being expressed in Part IV's "sceptical systems"? I have already suggested that the sort of reflection on the understanding and on the senses that dependably leads to unsmiling sceptical doubts is that highly intellectual reflection of intellect on intellect and on its sensory data that Hume enacts within Part IV, which sets out to look at sceptical (and other) systems. It is not that turn of empirically informed and empirically tested inference on itself which Hume enacted in Part III, the part of the *Treatise* officially dealing with knowledge and probability. Hume does not observe his own rules for judging causes and effects very well in Part IV, in this "intense" thought about what makes us assume that things and persons do not play hooky from existence while our backs are turned. It is Cartesian-style justification that is sought, and found missing, and the search is conducted entirely in one person's (temporarily continued) armchair. So "intense" is the thought that the thinker does not even turn to greet the porter who brings a letter during it, and certainly does not pool information about the world with him. Had he got the porter's assurance that there had indeed been an observable door movement to cause the observed sound, then the world with its causally ordered things might not have seemed so threatened with a loss of a great measure of "the regularity of their operation" (T. 196). The thinker in this section is as resolutely a single unaided thinker as Descartes in his meditations. Of course, even if this thinker had availed himself of other human observations and memories, he would not have gotten verification for all his pre-reflective assumptions about the world. But neither would he have gotten any disconfirmation. Only excessively world-distrusting persons, or Berkeleyans excessively confident of their own world-making, world-sustaining and world-destroying mental powers, will be seriously worried by the extraordinary opinions reached in this section about the belief in bodies that "we must take for granted in all our reasonings". It takes a special delusion of power to suppose that the stairs might be "annihilated by my absence" (T. 196). That really *would* be "an extraordinary and groundless opinion."

I will here seem guilty of picking and choosing which parts of Hume's text to take as seriously meant, and which as irony or reductios ad sceptical absurdum, in a way that begs controversial interpretative questions. Every reader of Hume, however, has somehow to select which bits are ironic, and which moments in such an obviously dramatic development as Hume presents in Part IV of Book One are the moments when a conclusion is drawn that is not later to be withdrawn. At the end of his intense reflection on our belief in an external world, Hume says that we must expect vacillation, not correction, of views, as we and he proceed. Do we also get vacillation in his views about mental vacillation? Or are these conclusions to remain calm and steady? Is it only intense sceptics who will vacillate between despairing scepticism and escapist inattention as restorative light relief? Such questions can only be tentatively answered, and the better answer will be that which makes the whole text more interesting, without ignoring either what is there or the order in which Hume put it there. What interests some, however, bores others, so Hume readers will continue to disagree. I take the sentiments expressed at T. 218 about sceptical doubt to be part of a lengthy, controlled, and dialectical stretch of thought about sceptical thought, one that reaches a reasonably steady conclusion only on the last pages of Book One. There has been a fairly dramatic reversal between the beginning and the end of Section II, a reversal that is first paraded as a correction, then demoted into a case of vacillation, as despairing scepticism gets turned on itself. But the last word (or rather the unrevised and not later contradicted Humean word) on such vacillations is yet to come. (Only dogmatists would claim last words on this as much as any other matter.)

Now to the fantastic sceptical worries expressed in the body of Section II. This is territory that has been admirably surveyed by others.[3] Fogelin finds the title, "Of scepticism with regard to the senses," perplexing, "since for the most part Hume does not forward sceptical arguments against our perceptual faculties."[4] But if we remember that Hume has just transfigured our faculty of causal inference and the beliefs it yields into an achievement of "the sensitive part" of our natures, we will more easily see why an attack on the concepts in which we couch our ordinary beliefs about ordinary causes and effects, the concepts of water, bread and so on, when these occur as terms in our causal inferences, will count as an attack on the sensitive part of our natures. Fogelin begins his discussion of this section by finding its title perplexing, and ends wondering why the "false belief" in an external world was esteemed by Hume (as well as by nature) to be an affair of great importance. It was important at least to Hume's own previous non–phenomenalist account of causal inference and how that takes place. If there are no lasting human brains to store our memories of constant conjunctions during our dreamless sleep, and during the times when we are not attending to them, then it becomes very hard to see how exactly past experience can causally "operate on our mind in such an insensible manner as never to be taken notice of" (T. 103). Belief in unnoticed or secret causes will be ruled out if all we believe in is what we, whether individually or collectively, have kept strictly under our notice. So it is important for the earlier parts of the *Treatise* that there be "both an external and internal world" (T. 218). Hume has felt free to appeal to animal spirits which "rummage that cell, which belongs to the idea" (T. 61) in unobserved brains, even while leaving anatomy largely to the anatomists (T. 8). He had taken lasting human bodies and other human believers very much for granted, and, as he says at T. 191, our own bodies present the same problem about mind-independence and continued existence as the paper we write on or the desk that supports it. Hume's own "system" needs the supposition of an external world, and one that is peopled.

What exactly is found wrong with this supposition? In Section II it is the supposed mind–independency and continuity of existence of worldly objects that is found without discoverable "justification," if it does not count as a justification that we need these suppositions if we are to keep our belief in causal regularities, and continue to make our customary transitions from causes to effects. Our only basis for the supposition is found in the "constancy and coherence" of our sense impressions, or rather in those of them that we take to give us information about the current state of "something real and durable" external to minds.

Hume finds this constancy and coherence to be less evident in the impressions that we take to inform us about an external world than in those comprising our internal world. He makes a Lockean distinction between three sorts of sense impressions: first those of "the figure, bulk, motion and solidity of bodies" (T. 192), then colors, tastes, smells, sounds, heat and cold, which "the vulgar" regard as on the same footing as the first group, and, third, pains and pleasures, which no one takes to be anything but "interrupted and dependent beings," "merely perceptions" (ibid.). Pleasures, pains and also passions (which always involve pleasures or pains, on Hume's analysis) are paradigm inhabitants of the internal world. Even when passions are "fleeting and perishing," or taken as such, they have "a certain coherence or regularity in their appearances" (T. 195). They are "found by experience to have a mutual connexion with and dependance on each other; but on no occasion is it necessary to suppose, that they have existed and operated, when they were not perceiv'd, in order to preserve the same dependance and connexion, of which we have had experience" (ibid.). It is these same passions which later can count as virtues of which we might be proud, and as vices of which we might be ashamed. So they had better not be too fleeting, or, if they are fleeting, they had better be fleeting appearances of durable character traits, since "what is casual and inconstant gives but little joy, and less pride . . . We compare it to ourselves, whose existence is more durable; by which means its inconstancy appears still greater" (T. 293). Are constancy and coherence of manifestation enough to constitute the durability both of persons and of their passions? Constancy and coherence as observed by whom? By the person in question? Few of us note the regularities of our own passions, without help from observant friends, enemies and psychologists. Throughout this whole section it is unclear, and I think deliberately unclear, whether the mind-distinctness at issue is to be construed as "distinct from my mind as I know it without help from anyone else," or "distinct from all our minds, as we together know them." My passions are not believed to be distinct from my mind as we and as I construe it, but awareness of the regularity of their operation takes more than my observation. Colors are not taken, even by philosophers who try to correct vulgar errors, to be dependent on any *one* mind. If I stop looking at the blue of the sky, someone else is fairly dependently still looking in that direction, and can reassure me that it is still blue. The passions that I feel do depend on my mind; the colors I see, if they *are* mind-dependent, are dependent on *our* minds. They will not, like my passions, go out of existence with me. Should shapes and positions, and the stones, hats and shoes whose shape and position they are, be deemed to have the same status as colors, so far as mind-distinctness goes, then they will be dependent on the human mind, but not on mine personally. If, however, the thought in this section is solipsistic, and is as sceptical about other minds as about bodies, then these distinctions will collapse. But then I surely will need to postulate as many unobserved passions as colors and shapes, in order to find regularity and constancy in my passions.

Hume claims that passions display a "mutual connexion," "a certain coherence or regularity in their appearance." What exactly does he mean here, and elsewhere, by "coherence," and how does its "regularity" differ from that he calls "constancy"? We earlier encountered constancy as an attribute of a "conjunction" of "objects," like fire and painful burns.[5] There it seemed to refer to the exceptionlessness of some perceived regularity of co-occurrence, or rather of close temporal sequence. Whenever we can truly say, "Whenever we perceive X we also perceive Y, always in the same relation to X," there we have constancy. In that discussion in Part III, Hume allowed that we do depend heavily on the testimony of others for acquiring our factual beliefs and making our causal generalizations, and he claimed that causal inference itself could establish, and where necessary correct, such reliance. Was it that

solitary minds used their restricted data to come to learn to trust
what some other voices say? The child who acquired the idea and
the word "orange" by being given an orange and told its name
must already trust the giver, if language is to be learned from her.
As we have seen, the Humean world seems to have been peopled
from the start, or at any rate from the start of a thinker's language-
dependent use of general ideas. Without these, causal inference
could not occur, so it is hard to see how anyone who can perform
causal inference could have any doubt that there are other people,
and that they sometimes can be believed. What they *can* do with
their socially acquired inferential skills is what Hume himself does
in the essay on miracles: investigate differential human reliability.
Without reliable constancies in speech customs, there would be no
recognition of causal constancies. Once we have such recognition,
we can see that speech itself involves causal dependencies of the
sort that Hume discusses at T. 113.

The problems that Hume finds in Section II of Part IV concern
the belief in constancies of simultaneous rather than of sequential
conjunction. (Our attention to them will usually take some time,
and so will exhibit sequences of the sort Kant discusses,[6] sequences
that we take to be reversible.) "These mountains, and houses, and
trees, which lie at present under my eye, have always appear'd to
me in the same order; and when I lose sight of them by shutting
my eyes on turning my head, I soon after find them return upon
me without the least alteration" (T. 194). The order in question
here is spatial, implying no particular temporal sequence. The
trees and mountains, if not the houses, presumably do show some
alteration after long (season-long) "interruptions" in the thinker's
gazing from his study window. Will they then exhibit less perfect
constancy? Is constancy always a matter of the invariance of some
order, spatial or temporal? Seasonal change itself will show rough
constancy, if this is taken as invariance of temporal order, as spring
regularly follows winter, the trees dependably come into bud as
the snows on the mountains thaw and vanish.

What Hume calls "coherence" in change is "imperfect" constancy whether of temporal or spatial conjunction. There is lack
of constancy, when bodies "change their positions and qualities,
and after a little absence or interruption may become hardly

knowable" (T. 195). They may change, however, in a "regular" way. Hume's example is the fire that has burned low partly in his presence and partly in his absence from the room. Here there will be changes not just in, say, color of logs and coals, as winter may bring color changes to trees and mountains, but changes in the "order" of burning coals when the observer returns after an hour's absence. Hume says that this coherence, or "regular dependence" of changes that we have only partly observed, "is the foundation of a kind of reasoning from causation" (T. 195). The "constant conjunction" that regular causal reasoning depends on is constancy in temporal sequence, and since Hume has previously claimed that to perceive sequence is to perceive change (T. 65), it is constancy in a perceptual field that must exhibit some change. Hume is to tell us a couple of pages later that coherence-grounded "reasoning from causation" is "considerably different" from regular custom-based causal reasoning, and arises from custom "in an indirect and oblique manner" (T. 197). The differences are said to lie in our postulation of unobserved changes in currently unwatched objects, such as the logs that burned in our absence. The example now given is of the unseen door movement taken to cause the heard familiar squeak. "I never have observ'd, that this noise cou'd proceed from anything but the motion of a door; and therefore conclude, that the present phaenomenon is a contradiction to all past experience, unless the door, which I remember on t'other side the chamber, be still in being" (T. 196). Here we are tempted to imagine the terribly neurotic past experience this thinker must have had, keeping unblinking watch on that untrustworthy door, and on all other partners in causal relations that he wants to reason on, desperately trying to keep his whole world under his vigilant gaze. A more normal thinker would have enough experience of her own regularly incomplete observations of causal sequences to see no contradiction threatening if once again she takes her current non-verification of an earlier-confirmed causal relation as not amounting to a disconfirmation, nor to any kind of threat to her epistemic security. The past experience that forms her expectations here will show "coherence" between the few conclusions she has based on fully verified constancies (where "fully" means neurotically fully, missing no opportunity for verification) and those other more usual conclusions based on constancies that she has only "imperfectly" observed and only occasionally verified. For a custom of causal inference to be set up, by Hume's account, we need to experience "frequent" cases of the conjunction in question, and no counter-examples (for they would turn our "proof" of the dependency into a mere "probability"). On Hume's version of competent causal inference, there was no requirement that, even where we do not work together but are solitary inferrers, we forgo "little absences," that we seize every opportunity to test whatever we currently presume to be a causal constancy. To keep Hume's rules for discovering what really causes what, we did not have to give up blinking and sleeping. Admittedly he does in those rules say that, when experience has once suggested a causal connection, "we *immediately extend our observation to every phaenomenon of the same kind,* without waiting for that constant repetition, from which the first idea of this relation is deriv'd" (T. 173–174, my emphasis). But even such impatience to extend and further verify our causal hypotheses allows blinks, even if it does rule out too many drowsy nods and absences of mind. It need not cause us to confuse failure to observe the usual causal attendant with observing its non-attendance, to confuse our absence with that usual attendant's absence. Should we blink at the crucial moment in our experiment, we will repeat the experiment, not discard the hypothesis.

Hume explains our belief that nature continues uniformly the same in our absence as much as in our presence by the principle of mental inertia, a principle that he had postulated earlier to explain how, from a series of progressively more equal pairs of observed things, we make up the idea of perfect equality (T. 48). Now he appeals to this habit of the mind to explain how we get the idea of a regularity in nature that is more "compleat" than what we have actually experienced. "Objects have a certain coherence even as they appear to our senses; but this coherence is much greater and more uniform, if we suppose the objects to have a continu'd existence; and as the mind is once in the train of observing an uniformity among objects, it naturally continues, till it renders the uniformity as compleat as possible. The simple supposition of their continu'd existence suffices for this purpose, and gives us a notion of a much greater regularity among objects, than what they have when we look no farther than our senses" (T. 198).

However, to explain "so vast an edifice, as is that of the continu'd existence of all external bodies" (T. 198-199), Hume finds mere coherence, or regularity of change, too weak. Some other constancy than constancy of conjunction, some lack of change, must buttress the edifice. But since we cannot keep the sun, the ocean and other relatively unchanging things under our vigilant gaze unremittingly, but can only give spot checks to confirm that they retain "like parts and in a like order" (T. 199), our interpretation of our data, as being data about the identical sun and ocean we have observed before, has to be checked for justification, and "very profound reasoning" finds "the greatest difficulties" precisely with what we (that is, we determined solipsists) make of constancy, rather than with what we make of coherence. "'Tis a gross illusion to suppose, that our resembling perceptions are numerically the same; and 'tis this illusion, which leads us into the opinion, that these perceptions are uninterrupted, and are still existent, even when they are not present to the senses" (T. 217). This "gross illusion" uses the idea of identity, which Hume takes to be a time-mediated "medium" between unity and difference (T. 200), the idea of a thing being the same individual at numerically different times. Hume here takes over Locke's use of the word "identity," a use that reserves the term for continuants. The sort of sameness with itself that a thing can have at any one point in time is taken to involve an assumed "simplicity," an absence of coexistent parts, or else a "feigned union" of its coexistent parts. So Hume can speak of minds as "suppos'd, tho' falsely, to be endow'd with a perfect simplicity and identity" (T. 207). Identity over time is his main concern in Sections II and VI of Part IV, but simplicity as well becomes important in Section VI, since "some philosophers" claim that we are conscious of "our SELF" as something that has "perfect identity and simplicity" (T. 251). Problems about identity bedevil our conceptions of ordinary physical continuants and of ourselves, but at least we are not tempted to attribute simplicity to the mountains and trees we see from our windows, or to our desk, our study door, or the logs in our fireplace. Natural philosophers of the "modern" atomist persuasion may purport to find physical continuants that they suppose to have perfect simplicity as well as perfect identity, but it is not the minute bodies they postulate that are Hume's concern in "Of scepticism with regard to the senses," since it is not primarily the senses that are taken to detect atoms or atomic particles. Boylean atoms become a target of Hume's scepticism in "Of the modern philosophy," and in a sense it is their simplicity that is the problem: denuded of all except primary properties, their primary properties reducing to solidity, which reduces to impenetrability, which is "nothing, but an impossibility of annihilation" (T. 229), they become shadowy entities, of which we have no "just and consistent idea." "Our modern philosophy, therefore, leaves us no just nor satisfactory idea of solidity; nor consequently of matter" (ibid.). But such problems are for these philosophers, not for the vulgar, who have a richer conception of the physical. They do not exclude color from their ideas of real mind–external existents, and they make no claims at all about what, if anything, are the simple parts of the bodies they perceive. Their views are found by Hume to be less inconsistent and "monstrous" than those of the atomist modern philosophers, especially when those philosophers add the unverifiable theory of representative (or misrepresentative) perception to their other "arbitrary" speculations. But the vulgar do, Hume thinks, face grave problems arising from their attributions of identity to "bodies." Simplicity problems are avoided, if simplicity is not attributed, but identity problems are found to be pervasive.

"'Tis a gross illusion to suppose, that our resembling perceptions are numerically the same; and 'tis this illusion, which leads us into the opinion, that these perceptions are uninterrupted, and are still existent, even when they are not present to the senses. This is the case with our popular system" (T. 217). The popular system is not as "loaded with absurdity" as that of the modern philosophers, but it is found to rest on an illusion, a "confounding" of constancy, resemblance between the content of episodic perceptions, with "perfect identity" or continued unchanged existence. Hume takes himself to be speaking with the vulgar, when he speaks of "perceptions" not present to the senses. "Almost all mankind . . . take their perceptions to be their only objects, and suppose, that the very being, which is intimately present to the mind, is the real body or material existence" (T. 206). In this passage, and in that just quoted from T. 217, Hume is using the term "perceptions" in the way he gave us notice of at T. 202, where he says that the generality of mankind reject the philosophers' notion of a body that is only represented by what we perceive. When speaking or thinking with ordinary people, he will not distinguish between objects and objects as perceived, and so will "suppose; that there is only a single existence, which I shall call indifferently *object* or *perception,* according as it shall seem best to suit my purpose, understanding by both of them what any common man means by a hat, or shoe, or stone, or any other impression, convey'd to him by his senses." This is to be Hume's usage between T. 202 and T. 211, when, while expounding the philosophers' views, he will let himself speak with them, and distinguish between inner fleeting mind-dependent perceptions, "different at every return," and outer "uninterrupted" mind-independent objects. Both these terms, "perceptions" and "objects," present problems for the contemporary reader, despite Hume's efforts to be explicit about his usage, and about the shifts he makes in it.

"Objects," before and after this section, include any objects of our attention, any contents of impressions or ideas. They were not, earlier, restricted to "solid and durable" objects. Hume's use of the term had been, and will soon again be, that which had been the standard one in earlier philosophers, the use we find in Descartes' "objective reality" of an idea. (The O.E.D. tells us that objects basically are things thrown before the mind, sometimes obstacles to its progress. Hume's cousin, Lord Kames, is cited for an example of the metaphysical usage of the term, referring to anything before the mind: "Every thing we perceive or are conscious of, whether a being or a quality . . . is with respect to the percipient termed an object.") Hume at T. 5 writes of scarlet, orange, sweet and bitter as "objects" which we can present to a child to give him the ideas of these qualities. To present the objects is "in other words, to convey to him these impressions." Objects here simply are the content of perceptions, whether those perceptions be of pain, of bitter taste, of color, or of a solid stone. Objects are intentional objects of perceptions. And indeed it is not clear that even Hume's "philosophers," who distinguish external objects from internal perceptions, are taken to intend anything other than intentional objects when they use the word "objects." But they, unlike the majority of mankind, intend their thoughts to refer to things the likes of which were never the contents of impressions, things which have shape but no color or texture, things that are taken to be represented (or misrepresented), not presented, in our perceptions. Our modern use of "object," for something solid, something that one might stumble over or choke on, coexists with the older use, as found in "object of affection" or "object of attention."[7] It is doubtless a result of the long obsession in scientific thought with solid uninterrupted atoms, a tribute to the influence of Boyle and Locke. (Locke's own use of "object," however, is the older one—ideas are the immediate objects of the mind.) One can see the modern use coming to consolidate its hold even within Hume's writings. The influence of the modern philosophers is felt, even by critics who dismiss their views as a "confusion of groundless and extraordinary opinions" (T. 218). Objects, then, are whatever we take ourselves to be attending to. If we are "modern philosophers" we will take the most important of the things we refer to in our thought to be merely represented in our mind-dependent sense perceptions; if we are ordinary persons we will admit a greater variety of objects, and may have less definite views about the relation between our perceptions and what they are of, that is to say, their objects.

What are perceptions, according to philosophers and non-philosophers? What are they for Hume? The first sentence of the *Treatise* speaks of "the perceptions of the human mind" as resolving themselves into impressions and ideas (T. 1). They do this resolving in virtue of the intentional objects of our ideas of perceptions, in virtue of our meta-perceptions. A single person's meta-perceptions will be ideas, or idea-involving impressions of reflection, not sense impressions (it would take a group of us to see, or seem to see, each other seeing, or at least seeming to see). The invaluable O.E.D. tells us that perceptions originally were collections of rents, then by a somewhat mysterious transition became receivings of the eucharist, and only then, by (now long-dead) metaphor, became the receiving cognizance of, or the becoming aware of, things in general. Perceptions are our receivings of the "sacrament" of the world we are part of, and they automatically have objects. "Perceptions" and "objects" are correlative terms. They are not quite interchangeable terms, as Hume makes them when he explores unphilosophical thought, but they are mutually implying terms. Does their standard use, as given by the O.E.D., encourage the "philosophical hypothesis of double existence," that our episodic perceptions are partly caused by, and partly represent, their somewhat mysterious but supposedly mostly non-episodic objects? It does not rule it out, but it certainly does not entail it. Representer and represented, like perception and object, are correlative concepts, but not all representeds need be absent, veiled, or mysterious. There are other ways of taking the doubleness of consciousness. We can talk of thought and content, perception and object, and yet avoid both the absurdities of the Lockeans and the confusions of the vulgar, who "take their perceptions as their only objects," and whose naive assumptions can supposedly be brought down by "a few . . . experiments" (T. 210).

Hume attributes to the vulgar the view that what they sense is and remains more or less the way they sense it, that their own presence or absence makes no particular difference to what they perceive. The experiments that are supposed to show that this cannot be right are ones inducing sensory illusions, such as pressing the eyeball and then seeing double. If even the question of whether there be one or two doors before us cannot be answered by simple attention to our perceptions, other questions about its (or their) other qualities, primary or secondary, will also require more than looking and seeing (feeling and knowing, listening and hearing, sniffing and smelling, and so on). But such experiments, while they do show that we cannot take all our perceptions to give us nothing but the truth about their objects, do nothing to upset the belief that bodies have the *sorts* of qualities we perceive them to have, and have them independently of our watchful presence. It is the pressed eye (a body, always affecting what we see, whether or not we attend to it), not our presence or absence, that makes the door appear to be twin doors. The vulgar easily learn to discount the perceptions that they have in circumstances that they can learn to recognize as abnormal, while continuing to treat their perceptions in normal conditions as "their only objects," if this is taken to mean that their perceptions show them the sort of world they are in, and usually show them the current state of the bit of it around them. This seems to be what Hume thinks when he criticizes the modern philosophers' distinction between secondary and primary qualities, two sections later. There may indeed be significant differences between, say, color perception and shape perception,[8] but not differences to warrant the downgrading of the reality of color. Hume, when he wants an analogy from sense perception for the correction of sympathy and sentiment that are needed for moral judgment, appeals both to correction of appearances of size, when distance is taken into account (T. 603), and to corrections of the appearances of a beautiful face when seen in non-optimal conditions for viewing. (I presume that beauty of face involves eye color, complexion, lip color and so on, as well as shape, size and having the approved number of each feature.) As by reflection we correct momentary appearances of shape, virtue and beauty, so we also in fact do correct those of color and number, when we take ourselves to be "viewing" from an odd point of view.

We trust the "testimony" of our senses, more or less as we do the testimony of our fellows. We learn from experience, and from reflection on that experience, that most testifiers can, in some conditions and on some matters, speak falsely, and maybe that some few rarely speak truly. But to judge that all speak falsely, when (as they all sometimes do) they attribute color to things, would be like resolving to disbelieve anybody who reported seeing the Loch Ness monster, because one's theory told one there could not be such a thing, even if one seemed to see it oneself. As we sort out how reliable human testimony is, in particular matters, and in particular conditions, by checking it against other testimony that we have already checked, as well as against our own sense perceptions, so we check our senses' veracity against other already accepted sensory data, both our own and that of others whose testimony we trust. The only objects we can have are the objects of our pooled perceptions. We reflect together on what points of view we should take as standard, as ones from which we correct what appears from other points of view. We have no doubt at all that, if we wish to count the spots on the wall, we should look with eyes that have not just been pressed hard, that if we want to know what color the cat's fur is, we should look at it in light, not in semi-darkness.

We *do* together arrive at fairly stable beliefs about what conditions for sense perception are optimal, what are normal, what are subnormal. But in "Of scepticism with regard to the senses" Hume deprives himself of our collective wisdom on this matter, and I suggest that the deprivation is deliberate. The sceptical systems are basically solipsistic systems, despite the continued use of "we," the references to "the greatest part of mankind," and the division of mankind into children and adults, moderns and ancients, peasants (or other vulgar) and philosophers. "Our popular system," whose illusions are being exposed, is a system that a single "vulgar" thinker could build up, unaided by her fellows, just as "our philosophical system" has Cartesian solipsistic foundations. The sceptical conclusion, or temporary pausing point, is that *I* "am more inclin'd to repose no faith at all in my senses" (T. 217), but the original assumption was that "*we* ought to have an implicit faith in our senses" (ibid., my emphasis). The scepticism is unstable, as it should be, if any system—popular, philosophical or sceptical—will in fact be "our system," and yet the sceptic ignores the rest of us, and pretends to limit his data to his own private observations, unaided by either other observers or by the guidance in interpreting it that comes from the language others have taught him. Hume's switches from "we" to "I" and back again, especially in the last two pages of this section, are significant, and gently force the reader to ask if it *is* "our senses," "our reflections" and "our system," or "my senses," "my reflections" and "my own system" whose reliability is here in question. For *our* faith in *our* senses may be justified, where mine alone would not be, were I not one of us, and so able to rely on others to correct the errors and illusions a single perceiver would be prey to.

The identity problem explored in Section II of Part IV arises primarily because of the perceiver's "absences" from the perceived thing to which continuity of existence is attributed. Unless a Berkeleyan god is included in the "us," who share our perceptions, this problem will still theoretically remain, even if it is a team of observers, rather than a single observer, whose perceptions pro-

vide "our" evidence for "our" beliefs about which existents have
continued existence, since even collectively we will not keep the
universe constantly under our unblinking gaze. There will be interruptions, even in our collective viewings. If they really are a
serious problem, if our overlooking of that problem is due to an
"illusion" that imagines continuity where all we know is episodic,
then that problem will not be solved, or that fictional continuity
made into fact, simply by our pooling our data. But if we *can* pool
it, if we can treat my viewing and your viewing as both viewings
of one mountain, at one time, at overlapping times, or at contiguous
times, then we have faith in an interchangeability of perceivers, a
way of getting a sort of continuous "us" out of a plurality of different "me"s, (or different "you"s). This merging of perceivers
into a relay team of perceivers, and into a standard perceiver, is
the "fiction" which is in fact correlative to the "fiction" of an "external" world's containing some continuants. Without the pair of
them, we would perish and go to ruin, and perish mutely, unable
to comment on or theorize about our sorry end. As Hume has his
sceptic allow, "The same continu'd and uninterrupted Being may
. . . be sometimes present to the mind, and sometimes absent
from it, without any real or essential change in the Being itself.
An interrupted appearance to the senses implies not necessarily an
interruption in the existence. The supposition of the continu'd existence of sensible objects or perceptions involves no contradiction" (T. 207–208). What we "feign," in our "fiction" of external
continuants is, *pace* Berkeley, perfectly coherent. We have no conceptual *or other* reason to disbelieve it. It cannot be fully confirmed, but neither is it in any way disconfirmed. If we, each of
us, take it that the human community of believers, as well as the
non-human world, will be in no essential way changed by our
personal absence from it, although in the nature of the case first-
person singular verification of this belief is ruled out (and surely
in our cool hours we do each believe this), no greater epistemic
rashness seems involved in our faith in a continuing non-human
"world" as environment for the continuing human community.
The two stand or fall together. So if the use of "we" throughout
these sections is anything other than royal, if the earlier claims
about the language dependence of our general ideas are taken se-

riously, if we can tell which philosophy is "antient" and which "modern," who is a philosopher, who a peasant, and who a down-to-earth honest gentleman, then faith in a human community is still uneasily present in Part IV of Book One, until an attempt at *consistent* fantastic scepticism is made, and made in vain, in its conclusion. Then, and then only fleetingly, is the completely general question "What beings surround me?" raised by the sceptic.

In "Of personal identity," too, we get plenty of references to the persons who surround the one who is thinking the thoughts expressed there. At T. 252 there are fellow reasoners (or those metaphysicians with whom one can no longer reason); there is the infant who becomes a man, sometimes fat, sometimes lean, at T. 257; there is the "other" into whose breast one tries to see (T. 260); and perhaps most significantly there are the persons who are the changing members of the republic or commonwealth to which the soul is most properly likened, for understanding the sort of "identity in an improper sense" (T. 255) that it truly exhibits. There are also, by implication, those whom the thinker relies on to get any answer to his question of what he was doing on the first of January 1715 (T. 262), to "extend" his version of his life back into his largely forgotten infancy, and those persons upon whose different identity he "pronounces," at T. 259. It is indeed "what we call our SELF" that is the topic, and even when that is restricted, it is restricted to "personal identity, as it regards *our* thought or imagination" (T. 253, my emphasis). Even when "I enter most intimately into what I call *myself*" (T. 252) I come out again fairly fast to seek confirmation from fellow persons about the sort of thing to be found by such intimate searches. One person can substitute for another in the *sort* of search the thinker is conducting. Each finds only the perceptions of which he or she alone is "intimately conscious," but the investigation is still taken as a (minimally) cooperative one. The person whose mind's identity is at issue is one who is a citizen, who had a childhood, who may have been an inhabitant of the parish that confers a borrowed identity on the rebuilt church, who might attend or act in a theater, or help to repair a ship, who has a non-private calendar, and a shared language that can give rise to verbal disputes. The thinker in this section is a person among persons, but nevertheless supposes that each person considers the identity of persons purely from a first-person singular perspective. Even when he pronounces on the identity of a second or third person, he does it by sympathetically becoming "intimately conscious" of that one's succession of perceptions, not by more commonsense ways, such as recognizing his face. What this thinker does is to suppose that he can "see clearly into the breast of another, and observe the succession of perceptions" (T. 260), to confirm his findings in his own case. (One breast, one person?) But the fact that he identifies and re-identifies the other by his confident recognition of face and breast, that he knows that others do the same of him, is not regarded as a significant datum. Our recognition of one another as the same persons we have previously met does not and could not depend entirely upon any attempt at sympathetic perception-by-intimate-perception reenactment of each's "successive existence." Our sympathy for each other's philosophical puzzlements about identity might involve that, but not our identifications. Why does this thinker's data exclude all perceptions of others' recognition of him, and his of them? Perhaps because this is recognition of expressive, living, embodied persons, with styles of talking and walking, and bodies have already been subjected to sceptical dissolution into successions of perceptions or of objects of perceptions. The cross-temporal "heap" that is a person's body, as ccountered by that person or by his fellows, may seem of not much help for ordering and uniting the "heap" that is the thinking person. At any rate, there is an eerily episodic coming and going of flesh-and-blood fellow persons in this discussion. They are absent when the data are first gathered: the data are exclusively from first-person singular introspection.[9] But they are present in the analogies, and by implication present as those whose first-person singular inward gaze might confirm the thinker's, and they are present in the end as those whose memories or records might fill in the gaps that exist in this thinker's memory of what he did on certain days. They flicker in and out of this thinker's recognition. Their stable presence there, I will argue in the following chapter, would transform the answer that can be given to the questions "What am I? And why do I take myself to have persisted as the same person through a fair stretch of time?"

Thinking persons, conceived of as the succession of their perceptions (or their more purely cognitive perceptions) are found to display "perpetual flux," "an infinite variety of postures," "constant revolution." This succession displays change and variety, little constancy except constant variation. "Our eyes cannot turn in their sockets without varying our perceptions. Our thought is still more variable than our sight" (T. 252–253). The variation to be disguised seems almost as great as it conceivably could be. So what explains our wish to "disguise" it, and what have we got from which to fashion the disguise? The answer given is the same one given to explain why we feign the continued mind-distinct existence of bodies, and so "remove the interruption" in our attention to them, namely mental inertia, our disinclination to change mental gears, our preference for "smooth slides," continuity of thought. Here we face a paradox.[10] Our thought is kaleidoscopically variable, yet also predisposed to "easy passage," "smooth slides," "apt to continue, even when its object fails it, and like a galley put in motion by the oars, carries on its course without any new impulse" (T. 198). This last passage gives us the clue that removes the paradox. The "objects" of our thought may fail it, or vary, while its movement or "action" continues smoothly on. Hume needs both the claim that our perceptions are constantly changing, and so display succession, diversity and some discontinuity, and also that the "action" of our imagination is resistant to discontinuity, predisposed to find constancies, reluctant to make the "effort of thought" needed to attend to a succession of diverse objects, taken as such. "The thought" associates the separable many, relates them, then "confounds" close relation with sameness, and so allows itself as smooth a passage as possible from moment to moment, perception to subsequent distinguishable, but not always distinguished, perception.

This spreading of our sluggish minds onto external objects is found to involve "confusion" and "mistake," when judged by "a more accurate method of thinking" (T. 254), but whatever its dangers, such inertial mental motion does give us a fine source for an idea of a relatively unchanging thinker, continuously persisting in mental contemplation, with the passage of time clocked by background awareness of the changing visual or other sensory field, or by the gadfly interruptions of our philosophical conscience as we "incessantly correct ourselves by reflexion" (ibid.). What Hume here calls "this biass of the imagination" in favor of continuity and minimal change, if it is a real feature of our minds, could give us a source for a perfectly "accurate" version of ourselves as persistent thinkers. The "mistake" is to spread the inertia of our thought onto the "objects" of our thought, but if our thought really has this inertia, then, when the "object" is ourselves, it will be no mistake to recognize the inertia. We will not need to *disguise* ourselves as unchanging, if our thought really is so conservative, obsessive and persistent. It would be equally much a "disguise" of our inertial thought to parade it as the sequence of its "objects," or available objects—to present it as adventurous and revolutionary, altering its "action" with every blink and turn of the eye. (There is more than one way in which I and my world can become one.) We are accused in Section II of projecting the qualities of our continuous and inertial thought onto the thought-about world. What seems to happen in Section VI is that all the variety and change of that world is projected back into the thinker's thought, so that it becomes "a perpetual flux." But only intermittently. The inertial slides still have to be acknowledged, as the stuff out of which the supposed "self disguise" is made.

The metaphors used for the mind are a "heap," a "bundle," and in the end a republic. Along the way, there is a brief discussion of the identity of rivers, but their flux is not directly related to the perpetual flux of our perceptions. Perhaps it should have been. "Thus as the nature of a river consists in the motion and change of parts; tho' in less than four and twenty hours these be totally alter'd; this hinders not the river from continuing the same during several ages" (T. 258). The flux of our perceptions, like the flowing waters, can display a fairly constant "motion." Both change of contents and relative invariance in "action" are found in rivers and in our streams of thought, so that the analogy is natural, familiar and apt. The thinker of this section does not avail himself of it, but prefers images in which the "parts" are less contiguous and more easily separated out than the waters of a river. But he needs the smooth passages of the thought as much as the sometimes abrupt changes of its objects, for the account he tries to give.

In the "Appendix" this same account is, with some justice, found labyrinthine, and internally inconsistent.[11]

The official story we are given in this section is that we discern causal relations between our earlier and later perceptions, as we remember them to have been, and we assume a causal relation between our memories of past perceptions and those perceptions as they originally occurred. So we discern a complex causal system in which vivacity is transmitted, beliefs are dependent on past experience, and many of the mental effects are "copies" of their likely causes. This makes the republic analogy seem apt, since there, too, the later generations of citizens depend upon earlier ones, show some resemblance to their ancestors and have the sort of complex interrelations to their contemporaries that our various coexistent perceptions have to one another. This "republican self," a system of discrete successive but organized and interdependent perceptions, is discerned by some self-contemplating self, the one who has projective proclivities and who is liable to "feign" more continuity and less variation in the contemplated than is in fact there, because of the "biass of the imagination," its tendency to use relations between its objects as an opportunity for smooth slides, easy passages and conservation of mental effort. But once this self-contemplating self turns its attention on its own contemplative activities and their usual features, their continuities, their constancies, their self-projections, a whole new set of data is available for the would-be accurate self-describer. It is as if the republic found itself to have not just a government and a constitution that changes less "incessantly" than its citizenry, but a constitution allowing there to be an intelligence service, a sort of FBI that is very resistant to change in its methods, and also a ministry of propaganda that often provides "fictional" versions of the state of the nation and of national unity, projecting their own conservatism and inflexibility onto the whole nation. That does not make the republic analogy any less "proper" than it is claimed to be, but it does complicate the question of which invariances are feigned, and which really there. "Did our perceptions either inhere in something simple and individual, or did the mind perceive some real connexion among them, there wou'd be no difficulty in the case" (T. 636). Perceptions, taken as episodic attention to "objects," do sort of inhere in the "action of the thought," and the slide-prone mind can, even in its sceptical moments, perceive the continuities of its own slides, and their connection with its beliefs about other continuities and other invariances.

Back in Part I of Book One, Hume, following Locke's division of complex ideas, characterized our ideas of substances as ones in which "the principle of union is regarded as the chief part of the complex idea" (T. 16). The principle of union between the united modes might be thought of as inherence in an unknown something, "or granting this fiction should not take place, are at least supposed to be closely and inseparately connected by the relations of contiguity and causation" (ibid.). Such a cleaned-up version of substantial union is indeed what the thinker about personal identity, in Part IV, has found for the "successive existence" of one mind. The contiguity is, in the nature of the case, temporal only. This loose flexible concept of what a "substance" is allows nations also to be substances. The substantial person, like the nation, unites many perceptions at one time (the data of different senses, thoughts, pleasures, anxieties) as well as over a stretch of time. The latter union of non-coexistent "modes" must be there, if causation is to unite the various modes of the substance, since causation is taken by Hume to imply temporal passage. This means that his fleeting suggestion, in "Of the immateriality of the soul," that a single perception might be a substance, can be squared with the earlier definition of "substance" only if the perception has some complexity, lasts and sustains itself. The perception-substance idea is only a fleeting one, and is intended to reduce *ad absurdum* the suggestion that anything is a substance if it may exist by itself. According to the earlier definition of substances as complex causal systems, they need not be closed causal systems, and there is nothing to prevent some mutual dependence between substances. We do not get very definite boundaries between substances, if the "principle of union" is specified as vaguely as Hume specified it in Part I. The union of simultaneous and successive perceptions in a person in "Of personal identity" is equally indefinite. Still, that section does give us the materials for an answer to the previous section's challenge: "I desire those philosophers, who pretend that we have an idea of the substance of our minds, to point out the

impression that produces it, and tell distinctly after what manner
that impression operates, and from what object it is deriv'd. Is it
an impression of sensation or of reflection? Is it pleasant, or painful, or indifferent? Does it attend us at all times, or does it only
return at intervals? If at intervals, at what times principally does it
return, and by what causes is it produc'd?" (T. 233). Armed with
the idea of a substance as a complex continuant whose essence is
its principle of union, namely some close causal interconnection,
we can answer: it is derived from the manner of appearing of *all* a
person's impressions, along with her ideas, and it arises only occasionally, when a somewhat painful effort of reflection is made,
such as that in "Of personal identity." It is greatly facilitated, however, if we already have some grasp of the principle of union holding together other equally variable lasting things, such as rivers,
and equally variable and intangible things, such as republics. It is
therefore to be expected that this idea of ourselves as lasting
things, as substances in the cleaned-up sense, will return less painfully once fellow persons, and social associations or unions of persons, move from the background more into the foreground of attention. For phenomenal wraiths to become stably substantial,
they must put on flesh and blood, and see themselves as fellow
persons.

6

Persons and the Wheel
of Their Passions

We are at all times intimately conscious of ourselves,
our sentiments and passions.   (T. 339)

Ourself, independent of the perception of every other
object, is in reality nothing.   (T. 340)

Every pleasure languishes when enjoy'd a-part from
company, and every pain becomes more cruel and intolerable. Whatever other passions we may be actuated
by; pride, ambition, avarice, curiosity, revenge or lust;
the soul or animating principle of them all is sympathy;
nor would they have any force, were we to abstract
entirely from the thoughts and sentiments of others.
(T. 363)

Book One's famous section "Of personal identity" was carefully
restricted, for the most part, to "personal identity, as it regards
our thought or imagination," leaving aside identity "as it regards
our passions or the concern we take in ourselves" (T. 253).[1] The
"true idea" of the human mind arrived at by the end of that section, namely of the mind as a causally interrelated system of perceptions, was one that was tersely said to be confirmed by "identity with regard to the passions," by what we find when we attend
to our "present concern for our past or future pains or pleasures"
(T. 261). In Book Two that concern is explored, and it does turn
out to be "*our* concern for *our* past or future pains or pleasures."[2]
It is not that the distinction between persons does not matter—it
matters enough to provide the difference between the subject matter of Parts I and II of Book Two. "As the immediate *object* of
pride and humility is self or that identical person, of whose

thoughts, actions, and sensations we are intimately conscious; so the *object* of love and hatred is some other person, of whose thoughts, actions, and sensations we are not conscious" (T. 329). But it does take "us" to make it possible for me to have any sustained pleasure or pride to be conscious of, and "ourself independent of the perception of every other object is in reality nothing" (T. 340). I can still be seen as the bundle of my perceptions, but those of them that are impressions of reflection become very important members, both for displaying the causal influence of past members and the influence of anticipation of future members, and for displaying my dependence on my fellow persons for a steady idea of myself.

Pride is the passion Hume begins Book Two with, and "nature has given to the organs of the human mind, a certain disposition fitted to produce a peculiar impression or emotion, which we call *pride:* To this emotion she has assign'd a certain idea, *viz.* that of *self,* which it never fails to produce" (T. 287). The idea of self, the identical person whose pleasures, pains, glories, shames, hopes, fears, ambitions, regrets, reputation, loves and resentments are all mine, and of which I have been at one time "intimately conscious," is produced by one "peculiar" sort of member of the bundle of perceptions comprising its object, that peculiarly reflexive impression of reflection, pride (and also, of course, by what Hume treats as its rival but obviously weaker twin, humility). There is, I think, no contradiction between what Book One said about the self and what Book Two says;[3] rather, there is supplementation and completion. If reason is and ought to be the slave of the passions, it is not going to be able to get an adequate idea of the self, one of whose "organs" it is, if it tries to abstract from the passions, those more vital and more dominant organs of mind and person. Hume never retracts his Book One denial of a "simple" persisting self, the sort of thing of which we might have a simple impression. The self is complex, changing, dependent on others for its coming to be, for its emotional life, for its self-consciousness, for its self-evaluations. Book Two explores these complexities, so that the reader will be ready for Book Three's account of our moral evaluations and self-evaluations. One's body, which Book One's discussion of personal identity ignored, but which Book Two treats as either "part of ourselves" or "near enough connected with us" (T. 298), supplies plenty of perceptions of itself, and presents itself to us as anything but simple and unchanging. Its identity, indeed, presents a parallel to personal identity, as Hume had analyzed it, that is as good as his Book One "most proper" analogy, a republic or commonwealth (which also always has a more or less clearly bounded physical territory). In Book Two he seems to realize that the best picture of the human soul is the human body, so he can speak of "qualities of our mind and body, that is *self*" (T. 303). Once the person becomes a person among persons, "languishing" when not in company, then there is no longer any temptation to treat oneself as something invisible and inaudible, a purely spiritual entity. To become recognizable, persons must become incarnate, and in Book Two they are treated as ordinary persons of flesh and blood, whose self-concern includes concern about their offspring, their address in dancing, their strength and vigor, their communicable diseases, as well as about their reputation, their wit and their virtues.

The investigation of pride and humility with which Hume begins Book Two takes up the theme of "contrariety" of passions, a theme that had been dramatically introduced into the conclusion of Book One, where, in the space of a few pages, despair and merriment, spleen and good humor, ambition and diffidence, compete for possession of the would-be self-understander's soul. And, as in Book One, one resolution of the conflict turns out to be alternation or turn-taking. Outright contrariety between two totally opposed passions (or ideas), if they are of equal force or vivacity, would lead to their mutual destruction, leaving the soul "perfectly calm and indifferent" (T. 278), passionless and "in reality nothing," insofar as passions and their objects are needed to make it something. Hume in his discussion here of the mutually destructive potential of pride and humility mentions only alternation as a non-destructive way out. He does not mention here the mingling without close destructive encounter that he later makes a possibility for mixed feelings when they are "direct passions" such as hope and fear, which may "like oil and vinegar" (T. 443) coexist in the soul. The point of introducing the rather contrived life-and-death conflict between being proud and being ashamed of oneself is to persuade us of the double intentionality of pride and humility, their need for a "subject" or "cause," as well as an "object," oneself.[4] Variety of subjects, and differing evaluations of their worth, can allow pride and humility somehow to mingle in the soul. I can be proud of the felicitous wording of what I am writing yet ashamed of the illegibility of my handwriting, displayed in the very same sentence. Hume can be proud of the "matter" of the *Treatise,* less proud of its "manner."

He divides the "cause" or occasion for pride (or humility) into a "subject" with its "quality" (T. 279), but in cases like Hume's attitude to the *Treatise* it is not clear whether the *Treatise* would be "subject," its pleasing matter its "quality," or whether the "subject" would be the matter of the *Treatise,* its pleasingness the "quality." Nor is it clear whether, when we do have mixed feelings, Hume thinks they must take turns, so that we fix our full attention alternately on what is good, and then on what is faulty, in something that is ours. He writes, "'Tis impossible a man can at the same time be proud and humble" (T. 278), but once we introduce the respects in which he is proud and humble, their "hundred different causes" (T. 288), there seems to be no impossibility, any more than it is impossible to have at one time the "oil and vinegar" mixture of hopeful and fearful anticipation of one event. Hume has a penchant for equating variety, mixture and opposition at one time, with the alternation over time of contrasting uniform "unbroken" mental objects, a penchant which showed in his treatment of probability.[5] It is as if we give each "chance" one moment's full attention, the resultant "imperfect belief" being a matter of interruption, or "breaking," of would-be perfect beliefs in perfect uniformities. Mixed feelings at one moment become transformed into a see-saw or attention-juggling of opposed feelings. We retain memory of the previous stretch of the juggling act, and have some anticipation of its continuation, since "after each stroke the vibrations still retain some sound" (T. 440). Thus, alternation leads to mingling. Hume seems to be using some version of Plato's principle, formulated in the *Republic* (IV 435), that we must recognize as much complexity in the soul (and its objects) as we need to, to save the principle that the same thing cannot act at the same time in the same respect in two opposed ways. The main point, for Hume here at the beginning of Book Two, is to arrive at an understanding of the complexity of the intentional objects of pride.

The distinction between direct passions, such as joy, that have one "object" (T. 292), even if its "qualities" may be a mixture of many rejoiced-over good ones and a few deplored bad ones, and an indirect passion, such as pride or love, which directs our attention to a person by the mediation of attention to the qualities of some "part" or "possession" of hers, so that such passions have "in a manner two objects," (T. 292), is one which provides the structure of Book Two, but which Hume mutes in the "Dissertation on the Passions," which begins with the direct, not the indirect, passions. There the whole complex machinery of "subjects," "qualities" and "objects," and the theory of the "double relations of impressions and ideas" that connect them, can be summed up in these simpler terms: "Besides those passions . . . which arise from a direct pursuit of good and aversion to evil, there are others which are of a more complicated nature, and imply more than one view or consideration. Thus *Pride* is a certain satisfaction in ourselves, on account of some accomplishment or possession which we enjoy."[6] To understand Book Two of the *Treatise,* and its place in the *Treatise* as a whole, we need to see why he there begins with pride, and why its "indirectness' is important.

Contrariety and quick emotional changes were a feature of the end of Book One, so there are literary as well as philosophical reasons for the early concentration in Book Two on conflict and on emotional see-saws. They are also important topics for Hume's later account of how morality depends on a calm steady sentiment, and of how its role is to prevent or end unwanted conflict, both within a person and between persons. But why begin with conflict in the indirect passions, and why begin with pride rather than love? The need to supplement Book One's incomplete account of self-awareness may be one reason. But Book One was also virtually silent about our awareness of fellow persons, and so that topic needs even more supplementation. As we have seen, it was only as porters, as anonymous agents of a postal service, as faithful printers, as testifiers (in which capacity they become less reliable purveyors of information than when they are operating printing presses or delivering letters) or as members of a hostile public who expel philosophical dissidents, that other persons figured in Book One. As one of the first reviewers of the *Treatise* noted,[7] it is full of "egotisms," at least in its first half.

The chosen opening of Book Two shows us something about its relation to the books that precede and follow it, and about its author's philosophical priorities. Reflexivity, indirectness, conflict—these are the opening themes, and they are all themes that are of importance for understanding Hume's version of morality, as well as being themes that are carried over from Book One. The pride of place given to pride is not so much a case of egotism as it is of preoccupation with reflection and reflexivity. Book Two's look at first-person singular self-evaluation, at the "seconding" that others may give us of our self-evaluations, at our capacity for sympathy with one another's evaluations—all prepare us for the first-person plural reflexivity that morality involves, for its judgment of different human character traits from the point of view of "the party of human kind" (E. 275). For it is "characters" (that is, human character traits)[8] and combinations of them, not individual human persons, that Hume makes the proper object of moral evaluation.[9]

The moral sentiment is at least as complicated as any indirect passion, but has characters of persons, not persons, as its objects. It indeed seems to involve a reversal of the scheme Hume uses to define indirect passions:[10] from a non-moral point of view, we love a certain person because of the achievement, wit or beauty that are his. His wit is the "subject" and he is the "object" of our love. But if we morally approve of his wit or his gentleness, that will be because we approve of such qualities wherever we find them, and approve of them because of the agreeable sort of "company" they usually make their possessors to be. Wit seems to be the "object," and pleasingly witty people more the mediating "subject," of any moral passion we have for wit. Person-evaluations seem to mediate our moral evaluations of character traits, as moral evaluation of character traits may mediate the person-evaluations that Hume thinks pride and love involve.

Our moral evaluations are general, and made from a general point of view, whereas the evaluations on which personal loves are founded are more particular and more directly hedonic. Moral approval is for passions; it is a passion directed on passions. It is an impersonal passion, felt from a general point of view, directed on passions because of their general effects on persons. Non-moral passions, including the indirect ones, may but certainly need not involve any passion-evaluation. If we want to be proud of our virtue, we will have to evaluate our passions, but if we are proud of our cloak, our house, our strength, our address at dancing, we will not need to direct our passion on any passions. The reflexivity of the moral sentiments is special, and not the same as the reflexivity of pride. But it is a close relative to it. Hume begins Book Two with pride, because his main concern is with what can, and what cannot, bear its own survey.

The indirectness of the indirect passions, which later becomes simply the complication of their objects, is a matter of the relationship between a person and what is hers, in all the "hundred" senses of the possessive personal pronoun. So this indirectness and complication should shed light on Hume's reflective views about persons, their perceptions and whatever objects of their perceptions they see as their own, as either part of themselves or some sort of possession of theirs. Me and my character traits, me and my abilities, disabilities, virtues and vices, me and my brain, heart, nerves, skin, pores, muscles, me and my life, me and my heap of perceptions, me and my reputation, me and my family, me and my loves, me and my ambitions, me and my country, me and my preferred vacation place and its climate, me and my evaluation of the importance or unimportance of whether the beautiful fish in the ocean is or isn't in any sense mine rather than yours, ours or no one's.[11] What is the 'I' who claims this manifold as her own? Hume's answer in Book Two, Part I, seems to be "just that, the concerned claimant, and out of the relation to these other things, it is in reality nothing." I and my world are "cor-relatives". But once we get to Part II of Book Two, with its thesis that the object of love is of exactly the same type as the object of pride, and that, if our passions are not to be absurd (T. 332), we must see other persons in relation to what is theirs, and ourselves in relation to what is ours, in precisely the same way, then we can make out the general lines of another answer to the question inherited from Book One (and the "Appendix" to it), the question of what unites the "monstrous heap" of things that are simultaneously or successively mine.

The answer is that I must be to what is mine whatever I take you to be to what is yours, and what you take me to be to what is mine. I must not so much "see clearly into the breast of another" (T. 260) as see myself clearly reflected in her eyes, let her and her views of me as expressed in words, gestures, behavior, help me shape my own self-conception. It is not just the minds of men that are "mirrors to one another" (T. 365); it is the expression of those minds, and the eyes, hands, breasts, and voices through which they are expressed, that gives us our mirrors. Since our conception of a fellow is of a flesh-and-blood person, then whatever conception we have of the identity over time of a living expressive body will be the core of our notion of a person's identity, and so of our own identities. Since we can see the separateness of human bodies (once the umbilical cord is cut), we know what makes one person different from another, and the experience of disagreement and conflict will reinforce that knowledge. Equally we know about the inter-dependence of flesh-and-blood persons for normal growth, for belief formation, for self-knowledge and for the sustaining of pride. Although Book One had referred to the breasts and eyes of persons ("Our eyes cannot turn in their sockets without varying our perceptions"—T. 252), the treatment of personal identity there abstracted from the fact that thinking persons have eyes and breasts. Hume had there alluded to the identity over time of the human body, despite its "total change" when "an infant becomes a man, and is sometimes fat, sometimes lean, without any change in his identity" (T. 257). But he there took the identity of mind to be only analogous to, not intimately linked to, the identity of a human body. Although his topic supposedly was the identity of persons, not just of minds, he had abstracted not only from personal identity "as it regards our passions or the concern we take in ourselves," but also from the identity of flesh-and-blood persons, and from the contribution made to "identity as it regards thought or imagination" by identical eyes, hands, nerves and brain. The approach there, in that part of his work devoted to "sceptical systems," was not merely intellectual; it was "spiritual" and solipsistic. A person's body, and his fellow persons and mirror images, were all left, along with his passions and self-concern, for Book Two.

In the "Appendix," commenting on the "labyrinth" he finds in his own attempt to elucidate personal identity in Book One, Hume concludes the comment by saying that "the difficulty is too hard for my understanding. I pretend not, however, to pronounce it absolutely insuperable. Others perhaps, or myself, upon more mature reflection, may discover some hypothesis, that will reconcile those contradictions" (T. 636). The "Appendix" was written later than Book Two; so if Hume thought, when he wrote it, that Book Two does give us more mature reflections about persons, and ones freer of internal incoherence than Book One's reflections on the identity of pure bodiless, friendless, passionless thinkers, if he believed that it was only his understanding, as that was understood in Book One, that was powerless to avoid the labyrinth, he certainly does not say so in so many words. But "the understanding" was what explored itself within Book One, and we can perhaps take it as implied that what was too hard a difficulty was to give a coherent account of personal identity within the constraints thus imposed—that is, while excluding attention to self-concern, except as a very brief afterthought. Hume may here be insinuating, by indirection and irony, that successful maturer reflections about persons, made when body-acknowledging self-concern becomes self-conscious, have proved easy enough for him. Neither Book Two nor Book Three advances any "hypothesis" intended explicitly to "reconcile the contradictions" that worry the author of the "Appendix," nor to clarify exactly what they were, but in neither of those books is there any shadow of worry about our ordinary assumptions concerning the identity and difference of persons. "The idea of ourselves is always intimately present to us" (T. 354) and seems to be an unproblematic if complex idea, as it presents itself from Book Two onwards. The

surface contradictions that the interpreter of Hume must reconcile
are those between the worries expressed in the "Appendix" and
the calm assurance of Books Two and Three.

The labyrinth and the difficulties of getting out of it exist only
for solipsistic intellectualist views of unique inner selves, the sort
of view contrived by Hume in Book One, Part IV, when he deliberately made himself a "strange uncouth monster," unable to
"mingle and unite in society" (T. 264). He showed us the mon-
strousness of what such "forelorn solitude" (ibid.) produces. It
produces monsters trapped in the intricacies of their own intellectual labyrinths. Once the Ariadne thread of mutual recognition is
firmly held and followed, it is fairly easy to get out of the maze.
Once we remember how vital the recognition of faces, voices,
styles of talking and walking is to our recognition of others, we
can bring our bodies back into our self-conceptions, and see ourselves through the eyes of our fellows. For in ordinary life we do
not find ourselves caught up in contradictions in our recognitions
of who is who and whose is whose. We often need legal decisions
to decide the latter, and may very occasionally need to make
"grammatical" (T. 262) decisions to settle the former, if there are
two sincere claimants to one name or social role. But so far, these
grammatical puzzles about identity are mostly intellectual, not
real, dilemmas. Amnesia and abrupt personality change may be
grounds for divorce, but not for issuing new identity cards. We
have no cases of brain transplants or of teletransportation, and so
do not know what our beliefs about persons would be in a world
that did have them. If in our armchairs we conjure up "scenes, and
beings, and objects, which are altogether new"(T. 271), we should
not be surprised if real-world concepts lose their grip. In this
world, where persons are flesh-and-blood persons, with non-
exchangeable brains, the beginning of a person-history is between
conception and birth; its end is death or brain death. There are no
other person-beginnings, no other person-endings. Abrupt unusual discontinuities along the way, long periods of unconscious-
ness, amnesia, surprisingly sudden knowledge, will, like Hume's
abrupt change as a young man from very lean to very fat, be
treated as part of one person's uneven life history, not as evidence

of switch of spiritual person-selves in and out of various bodily dresses.

In the "Appendix," as well as in Book One's discussions, at T. 252, Hume alludes to "the annihilation, which some people suppose to follow upon death, and which entirely destroys this self" (T. 634). He is himself one of those persons, and an account of identity satisfactory to him must keep person-beginnings and person-endings geared to biological birth and death.[12] Book Two emphasizes our generation, our "ties of blood" to parents, our initial non-separateness, and our continuing inter-dependence. Persons here are ones who bear their father's name (and wonder, as at T. 309, why they do not bear that of their mother, to whom the close tie is more obvious). Their name, like their character and reputation, is "of vast weight and importance" (T. 316). Persons in Book Two are inhabitants and sometimes inheritors of social roles, they are members of a moderately sociable species of mammals, and their self-conceptions do not, like the solitary bloodless "I" of Book One, Part IV, Section VI, fail to reflect those plain facts. The metaphysics of persons in Book Two are the socio-bio-physics of human reality.

The treatment of love of persons shows very plainly how well anchored in a biological and social world Humean persons have become within Book Two. The causes of love, which with a few interesting exceptions are said to reflect (or to be reflected in) the causes of pride, range from esteem for social power to captivation by "the little faults and caprice of his mistress" (T. 420), from admiration for wit to appreciation for a well-turned leg, or other "signs of force and vigour" (T. 615). Hume's short section on "the amorous passion" exhibits very clearly the central place of the human body in Book Two's conception of the person. The very title of this section shows us that Hume has been using the term "love" as a generic term that includes many passions rather different from "the amorous passion, or love betwixt the sexes." "Love" ranges over all forms of a person's pleasure in "some other person, of whose thoughts, actions and sensations we are not (intimately) conscious" (T. 329, parenthesis my importation from the earlier part of the sentence, describing pride's object). "Love may shew itself in the shape of *tenderness, friendship, intimacy, esteem, good will,* and in many other appearances" (T. 448). One of these variants of love is the "tender" passion of "lovers" for one another. Concerning this, Hume writes that it combines esteem for the "wit and merit" of the beloved with fancying that she is "more beautiful than ordinary" (T. 395) and with "the bodily appetite for generation" (T. 394). Nor is this just a mixture, like oil and vinegar, in which the different elements, "however mingled, never perfectly unite and incorporate" (T. 443). In the amorous passion they "transfuse" into one another, and they can do this, Hume writes, because of the mediating role of love of bodily beauty. Esteem for merit and the appetite for generation "are too remote to unite easily together. The one is, perhaps, the most refin'd passion of the soul; the other the most gross and vulgar. The love of beauty is plac'd in a medium betwixt them, and partakes of both their natures: from whence it proceeds, that 'tis so singularly fitted to produce both" (T. 395). It partakes of the refined passion, because of the link between bodily grace and "a grace, an ease, a genteelness, an I-know-not-what . . . which is very different from external beauty and comeliness, and which however catches our affection almost as suddenly and powerfully" (E. 267). Different though this "comeliness" is from physical beauty, we have the same group of words for both. (In the *Treatise,* Hume uses "lovely" and "handsome" [T. 611–612] rather than "grace" and "comeliness" for this important aspect of personal merit.) Physical beauty is not independent of expressive grace and loveliness. As Hume emphasizes, it involves the "promise" of the purely physical traits of capacities for various sorts of "commerce" with others (T. 614–616). What enables the amorous passion for persons to "incorporate" its varied elements is the "just medium" of love of human beauty of body, a beauty that Hume is willing to call "the beauty of our *person*" (T. 300, my emphasis).

It is the fact that human persons are essentially incarnate, that they are flesh and blood, generated, born of women, coming into the world complete with blood ties, and acquiring other social ties as they mature, grow and with others' help acquire self-consciousness, that banishes the ghost of that Book One worry, "Who am

I or what?" I am a living, more or less loved and more or less loving person among persons. The "real connexion" that Book One and the "Appendix" despaired of finding is not to be found by fragmenting a person-history into separate perceptions, out of physical or social space, but by seeing persons as other persons see them, as living (really connected) bodies, with real biological connections to other persons, in a common social space, depending on them for much of our knowledge, depending on them for the sustaining of our pleasures and for the comfort in our pain, depending on them also for what independence and autonomy we come to acquire. (No one severs his own umbilical cord.) Even if we achieve the greatest independence, even if we turn our backs on the ties of blood, or on any other ties, Hume believes that "we can form no wish, which has not a reference to society . . . Let all the powers and elements of nature conspire to serve and obey one man: Let the sun rise and set at his command: The sea and rivers roll as he pleases, and the earth furnish spontaneously whatever may be useful or agreeable to him: He will still be miserable, till you give him some one person at least, with whom he may share his happiness, and whose esteem and friendship he may enjoy" (T. 363).

One could scarcely have come further from the solitary would-be know-it-all-for-oneself of Book One's sceptical systems. "Where am I or what? From what causes do I derive my existence, and to what condition shall I return? Whose favour shall I court, and whose anger must I dread? What beings surround me? and on whom have I any influence, or who have any influence on me?" (T. 269) These were Book One's questions, when the "affrighted and confounded" solipsistic philosopher realized how forlorn his unnecessary solitude was, once he admitted that he did occupy some place, did depend upon some causes, was influenced by the beings around him, by their anger and their favor. Book Two answers these questions in a sensible realistic manner. I move around in a physical and social world. I derived my existence from parents and other nurturers of body and soul. My body will return to earth, my soul to the nothingness from which it came. I must court the favor of those whose judgment I respect, and dread their disapproval. The most important beings who surround me are fellow persons, since we (to varying degrees) influence each other, influence each other's welfare, and each other's self-conceptions. Book Two's turn (or continuation of the turn) from solitary reason to sociable passions answers Book One's despairing questions, and makes light of the intellectual puzzles found in the "Appendix."

Book Two does not take back Book One's conclusion that a person is a system of causally linked "different existences," which "mutually produce, destroy, influence, and modify each other" (T. 261), but the system of perceptions is now seen to be inseparable from the system which is the living human body. The "republic or commonwealth" of the person acquires a native soil, and a place in the family of fellow commonwealths, once it does become a public thing with a place in a social and a physical world. Hume "dropped" contiguity, in his Book One treatment of personal identity, claiming that it was "evident" that it has "little or no influence" on the case when we consider "the successive existence of a mind or thinking person" (T. 260). Temporal contiguity seems to have been too blithely assumed to be trivially present, in selves who present no "interruption" to be removed, and spatial contiguity is deemed inapplicable to thoughts and other perceptions which can *"exist, and yet be no where"* (T. 235). Only when we attend to those "parts" of our concept of persons that concern what does appear to be somewhere, thus reintroducing spatial contiguity, can we get a problem-free version of ourselves. We must know, if not where we are, at least that we are somewhere, if we are to grasp what we are.

In Book Two the self is the "correlative" of all the things that belong to it, mental, physical, cultural, as the self of Book One was the correlative of its heap of perceptions. Enlarging the heap to include the percipient body as well as its perceptions, to include riches and promotions, poverty and failure, as well as memories and transitions of the mind, reputation and name as well as self-image and introspective musings, might seem to make the heap even more monstrous. The indirectness of our self-concern, its detour through the self's correlatives, through all the hundred sorts of things that belong to it, may seem at first to increase, not solve, the difficulties. Am I correlative to my favorite old socks, as well as to my character? Structure, and with it a way of sorting the trivial from the less trivial correlatives of the self, is, however, introduced into the heap both by the inclusion of the expressive body, and by the inclusion of character and the reputation the person has with others. The body provides a continuity lacking in the sleep-interrupted "stream" of perceptions; the views of others are needed to complete one's own partial view of one's continuing body, and to supplement, correct and render "firm and stable" (T. 324) one's less purely bodily self-conceptions, as the "secondary" (T. 316) causes of pride and humility either "second" one's self-viewings, or "shock" one with opposing views (T. 324).

One's own view of others and their identities imposes another constraint on one's own self-conception, if to avoid "absurdity" one must let one's conception of other persons have a "line of communication" to one's self-conception. Hume gives us dynamic instances of how this communication works, in his "experiments" (thought experiments) to confirm his "exact system" of the person-directed passions. It is in this section (Section II, Part II, Book Two) that Hume uses the metaphor of our person-concerned passions "wheeling about" (see T. 336) from self-concerned to other-concerned, and back, as contrived variations are made in the relations of impressions and ideas on which these passions depend. Hume has "compleated the round" (T. 337) by having the affections come to rest in pride, that agreeable passion in which he thinks our minds tend to rest and invigorate themselves whenever possible. But the communication through sympathy with others' passions is vital to pride, and so also is its communication with esteem for others when they have the sort of attribute or possession we would ourselves be proud to have. In his examples of how pride and love or esteem communicate, Hume emphasizes both the mind's preference for self-preoccupation, and its interest in other persons and their passions. Our idea of ourselves must have greater "vivacity," he claims, than that of our idea of any other person, because of our constant consciousness of "ourself." This superior vivacity, invigorated by pride, overflows in sympathy to vivify our ideas of the feelings of others, indeed to raise them into impressions, into shared feelings (T. 320). But it also "engages the attention, and keeps it from wandering to other objects" (T. 339). So our wheeling passions, even loving and sympathetic ones, do tend to come to rest in self-concern.

We gladly let our thoughts dwell on those who second our pride. Here pride is "transfus'd into love" (T. 346), since "nothing more readily produces kindness and affection to a person, than his approbation of our conduct and character" (ibid.). The flatterer, however, is not the only case of another person as cause of pride, correlative of self. Hume also allows that one can be proud of the qualities and achievements of those we already love, of our friends, brothers, children (T. 337–338). It may be that he believes that these close ties will not persist unless there is some mutual seconding of pride going on, but at least the reason for the love need not be just the fact that this person flatters the lover's vanity, the case that he gives us at T. 346. The very strong claim that nothing produces affection so readily as praise seems to be taken back later, in sections such as "Of the love of relations," where parental love is said to be "the strongest tie the mind is capable of" (T. 352). (Whatever the reason parents love their infant children, it can scarcely be that these children offer them flattery.) In the intervening section, "Difficulties solved,"[13] Hume had pronounced that "whoever can find the means either by his services, his beauty, or his flattery, to render himself useful or agreeable to us, is sure of our affections" (T. 348). This at least makes the flatterer compete with the handsome and the subservient to obtain our love.

Even if offspring are sometimes seen to "favour" their parents by inheriting their mutually perceived beauty, and so in a sense to "flatter" them, this is not what Hume stresses when he discusses family love. It is not flattery but candor and ease of communication that seem to be the goods that close blood ties can bring. What wakes the melancholy man from his lethargic dream, and gets his blood to flow "with a new tide," is the arrival not of a deputation of flatterers but rather of an intimate, who "communicates to us all the actions of his mind; makes us privy to his inmost sentiments and affections; and lets us see, in the very instant of their production, all the emotions, which are caus'd by any object" (T. 353). Thus, it seems that the full "vigour" of a person requires not just that other persons second her pride, but that she have candid intimates with whom she shares love, and it requires also that the ones who second her pride be ones that she independently respects. We are "better pleas'd with the approbation of a wise man than with that of a fool" (T. 321), and we will not esteem "plagiaries" who "are delighted with praises, which they are conscious they do not deserve" (T. 324), or feel any self-esteem on account of our taste for such dubious delights, or feel very proud if we become aware that our love of fame has degenerated into love of flattery. Pride conscious of itself is conscious both of its dependence on others and of its line of communication with esteem. Pride made reflexive, pride of which we can be proud, depends on others whom we do not judge to be fools, and its line of communication is with other loves than love of flatterers. However "readily" the latter love is produced, it can scarcely be calm and steady, since it does not survive reflection.

I HAVE HERE BEEN TRYING to reconcile a few apparent contradictions in what Hume writes about the relationship between self-concern and concern for others, and in doing so I have anticipated what Hume kept for Book Three, an account not just of pride but of due pride, of pride the virtue (T. 596), not just of love but of steady love, of friendship the virtue (T. 603). Within Book Two he restricts himself to portraying the conflicting tendencies we have, and to giving us an explanatory "system" that accommodates them all. He portrays opposed passions as mainly alternating, wheeling us about from love of undeserved praise to contempt for our flatterers, from disinterested benevolent love to a "great partiality in our own favour" (T. 321). Hume had written in Book One that "if you wheel about a burning coal with rapidity, it will present to the senses an image of a circle of fire" (T. 35). The fiery circling of our successive passions allows many that threaten to extinguish each other to wheel together, without this threat being realized. The sorts of "contrariety," opposition and hostile coexistence that human passions exhibit is one of Book Two's recurrent themes. I leave until Chapter 7 the discussion of opposition in motivating "direct" passions, and the "violence"

Hume finds that it causes, restricting myself in this chapter to the conflicts among our indirect person-directed passions, and among the "principles" governing their working.

The most difficult opposition both to explain and to overcome is that between the human tendency to feel sympathy for others' feelings and thus to share them, and the equally real tendency to think of other people's pleasures and pains merely as a (preferably contrasting) backdrop to enhance our own pleasures. Hume calls this latter "the principle of comparison," and invokes it in his account of respect and contempt, as well as in his account of the "appetites for evil"—malice, envy and mixtures involving them. We had a hint of this principle much earlier, when, in the "Limitations of this system" (that is, the limitations of the systematic account of pride that he had given), he noted how we do not feel proud of real goods we possess, such as health, if they are seen as commonly possessed, as the human norm, and not in any way "peculiar" to ourselves. We "judge of objects more from comparison than from their real and intrinsic merit" (T. 291). If, on "comparing ourselves with others, as we are every moment apt to do, we find we are not in the least distinguish'd" (T. 292), then we will not feel pride. Pride's "delicacy" in spurning the common implies that "the persons, who are proudest, and who in the eye of the world have most reason for their pride, are not always the happiest" (T. 294). Unless we are the most distinguished, comparison makes us miserable, and can poison our enjoyment of normal health and "the common beauties of nature." What it poisons are those "natural pleasures" that we normally do not compete with others to enjoy (see E. 283–284).

Hume does not say that love is as "delicate" as pride in its demand for distinction—people can be loved for qualities, such as good nature, that are fortunately common. What happens with love is not that there is a judgment made of the comparative superiority of a person's qualities, which then grounds the love, but rather that, once love is present, caused by "good" but not necessarily "better" qualities in the loved one, what follows is that the lover "fancies her more beautiful than ordinary" (T. 395). As Hume describes the two passions of pride and love, the latter is much less comparison-dependent than the former. This is one reason "good nature, good humour, facility, generosity, beauty, and many other qualities . . . have a peculiar aptitude to produce love in others; but not so great a tendency to excite pride in ourselves" (T. 392). These qualities may be too common to be grounds for jealous pride. Their presence in others will evoke love, rather than humility-tinged respect. Hume invokes this closer link between "pure love" and pride to account for what seems to him a fact—that we can love a person for his common good nature, while not taking any pride in our own good nature, or feeling any great respect (as distinct from liking) when we encounter people more good-natured than ourselves. He stops just short of saying, indeed, that we may despise them for too much good nature, that we may judge them to be *"too good"* (E. 258).

Is it just a brute fact that sometimes we judge by comparison, grade on the curve, and sometimes not—that sometimes we sympathetically share another's joy, sometimes envy it? Hume goes to considerable lengths to try to find some explanation of when "our fancy considers directly the sentiments of others, and enters deep into them," in sympathetic sharing (T. 381), and when sympathy is limited or blocked by "the principle of comparison," so that "the misery of another gives us a more lively idea of our happiness, and his happiness of our misery. The former, therefore, produces delight; and the latter uneasiness" (T. 375). When do we feel delighted at another's happiness, and when uneasy? Hume the empiricist, the curious collector of human foibles, lists some factors that tend to block sympathy, in the sections devoted to malice and envy, and mixtures involving malice. He then takes up the question again in Book Three, when he faces the question of what form of pride we can recognize as a virtue, and how much sympathy we can have with the pride of others. The question of when sympathy is blocked by envious or malicious "comparison" is one of obvious importance for the moralist, especially for the moralist who hopes not just to morally evaluate envy and malice, but to discourage them. Hume's findings in Book Two are that the "reverst sensations" of displeasure is another's pleasure, pleasure in another's displeasure, tend to arise when the other is already "close" to one in the respect in which the comparison is made. Great displeasure can be felt when men "perceive their inferiors approaching or overtaking them in the pursuit of glory or happiness" (T. 377). But they must be in the same "race," so to say, and fairly close to the jealous person. "A common soldier bears no such envy to his general as to his sergeant or corporal; nor does an eminent writer meet with so great jealousy in common hackney scriblers, as in authors, that more nearly approach him" (T. 377). So it is rivals for some honor, prize or promotion who have difficulty sharing the pleasures of one another's successes. Whenever two or more persons are in situations such that "the success of one is perfectly incompatible with that of the other" (T. 383), then sympathy and benevolence will be blocked, and hatred likely.

The flip side of this is that when persons "enter into co-partnership together, the advantage or loss of one becomes immediately the advantage or loss of his partner" (T. 383). Hume imagines business partners "living in different parts of the world," whose gains and losses are thus shared, and whose common interests lead to "love" for one another. This love is unlike that of brothers or fellow countrymen, which is not based on such an intentional gearing together of gains and losses. At this point Hume does a little hedonic calculation, which shows him that a rival may bring one, through his failures, as much pleasure as a successful partner brings through his successes; and a partner may bring as much pain from his failures as a rival from his successes. Why then do we not love our rivals as much as our partners? This is one of the places in the *Treatise* where we see how Bentham could have been inspired to invent utilitarianism by reading Hume. Hume, however, is not content just to conclude that partnership and rivalry turn out to be equal in hedonic "fertility"; he pushes on to complicate his moral psychology, to try to explain why we do not love our rivals, despite the hedonic returns we may get from them. The explanations seem to do as much to compound as to clarify the problem. Our concern for our own "interest" (here significantly not reduced to any concern to maximize our pleasures) is said to give a "parallel direction" to our pleasure in our partners' pleasures, and our pleasure in our rivals' pain. In both cases the pleasure is taken in our "advantage," in the satisfaction of the "interested affection." Hume also says that pleasure in a partner's pleasure occurs "after the same manner as by sympathy we feel a sensation correspondent to those, which appear in any person, who is present with us" (T. 384), where the latter sympathetic pleasures seem disinterested, seem to have no obvious link with "advantage" and "our own interest," in the limited sense in which Hume is using those concepts. The sameness of manner lies merely in the unblocked sympathetic communication of pleasures. In pleasure in a rival's failure, by contrast, comparison blocks sympathy. So there can be "a parallel direction of the affections, proceeding from interest" both to what is "deriv'd from sympathy and from comparison" (ibid.).

To this only partially successful "explication," Hume adds the general observation that we tend to come to love those whom, from whatever motives, we benefit (our successful business partners?), and to hate those we in fact injure (our less successful rivals?). But this observation would seem to make it likely that we will come to hate our partners when we drag them down with us, and come to love our rivals when our downfall entails their rise; so one is left more dazzled than illuminated by the epicycles of Hume's explanatory principles. What is impressive, however, is the seriousness with which he takes the variations in our sympathy for others. Since the sympathy-dependent moral viewpoint has to correct for these baroque variations (T. 581), Hume has good reason to take them seriously, however limited his success in showing that "not only the variations resolve themselves into the general principle, but even the variations of these variations" (T. 347).

Sympathy takes "a great effort of imagination" (T. 386), to enable us to "enter deep" into others' sentiments, so deep that we become "sensible of all the passions" we survey (T. 381). More than mere beliefs about others' passions are involved—we actually feel with others. To treat others' pleasures as a mere standard of comparison with our own, less effort is involved, and we need not enter so deeply. Mere ideas of their passions will suffice. So one might have expected Hume to suppose that our more natural and immediate reaction to others' feelings would be the easier and more selfish reaction, when "the principle of comparison" merely uses them as a measure for our own pleasures. Hume does not take this line. Sympathy, despite the "effort" it involves, is treated as the "direct" and natural response to others' feelings, and, even when the principle of comparison is at work, it blocks rather than preempts sympathy. "The direct survey of another's pleasure naturally gives us pleasure, and therefore produces pain when compar'd with our own" (T. 376). This suggests that at first, briefly, we do sympathize with the other's pleasure, and the contrast is at first between our "own" pleasures and our sympathetically shared pleasure, not just between the former and the pleasures we merely *believe* another to have.[14] Indeed, the very complication of Hume's explanation of the principle of comparison and its involuted workings, the fact that he makes it an application, to the passions, of a more general principle of the understanding or imagination (that "objects appear greater or less in comparison with others"), all show how "secondary," "indirect" and derivative he finds this principle to be. It is also significant that he recognizes no principle of antipathy, no full negative analogue to sympathy. As some of his Christian opponents in moral theory strove to show that the force of evil was not coordinate with that of good, but was a perversion of a drive to good, so Hume treats the appetites for others' evil that the principle of comparison excites as something not as lively and "original" in us as sympathy. What is more, "comparison" is seen to presuppose our capacity for sympathy. When, in Book Three, he comes back to this secular "problem of evil," and to reconsider "what general rules can be form'd, beside the particular temper of the person, for the prevalence of the one or the other" (T. 594), he repeats his earlier claim that sympathy takes greater "force" of perception of another's state of mind than does comparison, and he takes physical proximity to another (a clear sight of the distress of the shipwreck victims) to be enough to guarantee sympathy. The workings of "comparison" are here made to depend on the blurriness of our vision of another's state, on a defect in our cognitive capacities. Once we see the others' state vividly, sympathy will operate. "No man has so savage a heart as to reap any pleasure from such a spectacle" as a shipwreck witnessed at close quarters (T. 594). Many or most persons will still in some sense be "glad" that they themselves are not among the victims; few will leap into the waters simply to show solidarity with the victims, but most will do what they can to save them, and will feel sympathetic distress.

In this Book Three scenario, no already guaranteed conflict of "interest" is involved, no gearing of the seafarers' material "advantage" to the landlubbers' disadvantage, or vice versa. Hume clearly does think that plenty of men have savage enough hearts to reap pleasure from their rivals' misery and failure, from their enemies' defeat and destruction. The special scenario of the disinterested spectator's capacity for sympathy is selected in Book Three because it is the best analogue for the moral judge's position—a fellow person who feels with the judged, but whose own "interest" is either not involved or is "overlooked." Neither the rivals nor the partners are disinterested spectators of each others' fates, so their reactions may differ, without necessarily thereby showing "a savage heart." The partners' reactions to each other's fate do not, however, differ *very* much from that of the disinterested sympathetic bystander. Partnership and common "interest" reinforce the sort of more spontaneous sympathy and passion-sharing that Hume takes to be natural to us. What can interfere with it are both rivalry and blurred vision. Defects of the imagination and defects of social organization (if Hume does think that zero-sum games are defective social games) are the root of secular evil. Rivalry and opposition of interests are the "sin"; copartnership and vivid mutual awareness are the general lines of any salvation. (Can this be Hume, the supposed defender of cut-throat capitalist competition?)

The concern with contrariety and conflict between different passions, between different persons' interests, between principles that communicate passions, between persons and principles that block or reverse that communication, continues throughout Books Two and Three. But although Hume finds conflict a virtually ever-present problem, he also criticizes some of his philosophical opponents for inventing conflicts where none really exist. Before he looks at conflict of motivation—that is, at contrariety among the "direct" passions—he first confronts the traditional contenders for sovereignty over the human will, in the supposed combat of eternal, invariable, divine "reason" and blind, inconstant, deceitful "passion." That pseudo-combat, and the battleground where it is supposed to occur, are the topics of the next chapter.

7

The Direction of Our Conduct

Of all the immediate effects of pain and pleasure, there is none more remarkable than the WILL. (T. 399)

In short, as nothing more nearly interests us than our own actions and those of others, the greatest part of our reasonings is employ'd in judgments concerning them. (T. 405)

Our actions are more voluntary than our judgments; but we have not more liberty in the one than in the other. (T. 609)

Hume is often criticized for taking a spectator's, not an engaged agent's, attitude to human action. It is true that he seems more impressed with the human will as effect than with its role as cause. From the introduction of the will as a topic in Book Two, "tho', properly speaking, it be not comprehended among the passions" (T. 399), he treats it as an effect of our past experience and our anticipation of pleasure and pain, an effect as predictable as any other. "Is it more certain, that two flat pieces of marble will unite together, than that two young savages of different sexes will copulate?" (T. 402). It is not only savages whose intentional action is predictable, and not only lust that in certain conditions predictably dominates among influences on the will: "A general, who conducts an army, makes account of a certain degree of courage. A merchant looks for fidelity and skill in his factor or super-cargo. A man, who gives orders for his dinner, doubts not of the obedience of his servants" (T. 405). We count on others' voluntary actions, and count on them not primarily because we have (as the factor's laird may well have) been given solemn undertakings, but because, "as the *union* betwixt motives and actions has the same constancy, as that in any natural operations, so its influence on the understanding is also the same, in *determining* us to infer the existence of one from that of another" (T. 404). Where we think we know the motives and their relative influence, we confidently predict what people will do.

Does Hume think that our judgments about our own future actions take this same purely predictive character? Has he no place for practical reason,[1] for deliberation about what to do? He certainly allows that it occurs: the merchant who calculates his debts does this not out of idle curiosity but to decide whether now is the time for repayment (T. 414), and if I hesitate before picking and eating an attractive-looking fruit, and you, my tried and true advisor, tell me that although it looks good it is juiceless and tastes unpleasantly bitter, then I will quickly decide against it. "Whenever you convince me of my mistake, my longing ceases" (T. 417). (Practical deliberation is here interestingly interpersonal.) Hume readily grants this correction of the presuppositions of our intentions, as well as of our means-end practical reasoning, and our occasional need to keep our accounts straight by a bit of calculation. But he sees deliberation about our own conduct to involve exactly the same sort of reasoning as that which we would use before counting on our troops' limited courage, our factor's fidelity, our servant's obedience, our lover's lust. The only place where a difference might arise in our own case (and in that of our friends), is where we try to correct mistakes, rather than simply taking the agent's beliefs as a fixed given. If, from a distance, I see you admiring that deceptively attractive persimmon, I will predict you will pick it and bite into it, whereas were I beside you I might attempt to disillusion you. We do try to "clean up" our friends' as well as our own will-influencing desires, to minimize regret and disappointment. We may not do the same for many other people's will-influencing desires, partly because of powerlessness, partly because of ill will or limited good will, partly because of the fear of being thought to be busybodies.

Another difference between our attitude to our own actions and to those of others is that we are more prone to blindness to passion-causes in our own case than in that of others. Although on reflection we may agree with Hume that "while we act, we are, at the same time, acted upon" (E. 99), nevertheless, while deciding how to act, "we feel that our actions are subject to our will on most occasions, and imagine we feel that the will itself is subject to nothing" (T. 408). We have "a false sensation" of liberty, false because we confuse ignorance of cause with absence of cause. "We may imagine we feel a liberty within ourselves; but a spectator can commonly infer our actions from our motives and character" (T. 408).

Hume does try to superimpose the detached observant spectator's viewpoint on what he sees as the self-deceiving agent's viewpoint, to correct it, but he does not ignore the interest that the less detached outsider can have in the question of whether the agent should be held responsible for his action, whether, when his action harms us, he merits our anger, our revenge or our magisterial punishment. The spectator may be the moral judge, as well as the recording curious scientist of human nature.[2] What does this judgmental one, who presumably must sympathize with the agent's "false sensation of liberty" as much as with the other human affects involved in the action and its consequences, say about the predictability and "necessity" of the agent's decision and of its implementation in action?

Hume claims that our actual practices of response to intentional actions reveal our sometimes unavowed reliance on the same will-determining causal forces that the scientist of human nature will recognize. There is no real incompatibility between the presuppositions of our punitive practices, or the better-considered of them, and acceptance of the view that our intentions have psychological causes, that our wills are subject not just to influences but to "compleat" or determining causes. Hume does not, like some contemporary compatibilists, try to show that we must reassure ourselves that a person, at the time he did some resented thing, could have acted differently, before we can admininister what we see as appropriate punishment. He does think it relevant to ask if the offender will in the future act differently as a result of the punishment. Presumably, therefore, he might concede some relevance to the question of how an offender might have acted had he earlier committed the same offense and been punished for it in the way we now contemplate punishing him, but he himself shows little interest in counter-factual conditionals, this one or any other. As a consistent determinist (that is, as a confident searcher for uniformities), he takes it that the facts that determined our past actions were themselves determined, so that it would only be in some fairyland that exhibited our causal constancies along with different initial or "original" facts that any fact could have been other than it was. It may be harmless, when we are considering the truth of causal generalities, to do thought experiments in which facts are imagined away and replaced by counter-facts, but Hume typically does not indulge in this. His historical writings are full of causal attributions, but are singularly free of speculations concerning what would have happened had conditions been different, or had different decisions been taken. He prefers confirming his generalizations by looking at what did happen in varying actual conditions; he prefers real "experiments" to thought experiments. So on his version of when a person deserves punishment, the question "Could he have acted differently?" is not asked.[3]

The questions that are asked are whether the action was intentional (T. 348–349), whether the intention flowed from enduring motives in the person (T. 411–412), whether these motives can be changed by reward and punishment (T. 609). These are the questions properly asked by anyone in a "magisterial capacity" (T. 410) who intends his punishments and threats of punishment "to produce obedience." There are other, more primitive reactions to actions perceived as harmful to the agent's fellows that Hume also notes—revenge for "odious" or hurtful actions, regardless of the agent's intentions, and a certain vengeful or malicious attitude to any behavior perceived as showing "deformity" (T. 411). But he claims that even these unreflective responses to what others do, and show themselves to be, tend to get rationalized into responses to ill will, to intentional injury. Any offense or harm we suffer from another person can "excite our hatred, and . . . afterwards we seek for reasons upon which we may justify and establish the passion. Here the idea of injury produces not the passion, but arises from it" (T. 351). Hume includes revenge (along with the desire of happiness for our friends) among the primitive appetites we have, ones that, "properly speaking, produce good and evil, and proceed not from them, like the other affections" (T. 439). But the magisterial punisher will not be a mere avenger, rationalizing revenge by imputing intention and ill will wherever there is humanly caused harm. The conscientious magistrate will check for intention, and will look carefully both at motives and at the probability of punishment's effecting their reform.

Hume, then, does give intention an important role to play in the causal sequence that will be of greatest interest to a judge of actions, or to an agent responding to another person's actions. The reason intention is important, however, is not that it is "freely" formed, and could have been formed otherwise, not that it is more a person's "own" than the motives which animate her. Hume finds intention important because it "shews certain qualities, which remaining after the action is perform'd, connect it with the person" (T. 349). These qualities may be individual lasting motives, but they may also be qualities such as "strength of mind," the prevalence of calm over violent passions (T. 418), prudence, "facility," impulsiveness or thoughtlessness. We will be as interested in our factor's "skill" as in his "fidelity." Hume sees actions to be "temporary and perishing" (T. 411), of relevance to our person–evaluations only as "signs or indications of certain principles in the mind and temper" (T. 477). Intentions are links between these perishing actions and their more "durable" agents; they are better indications of their mind and temper than "external performance" (ibid.). It is because Hume sees our main evaluative concern to be with lasting persons that he is willing to grant that "by the intention we judge of actions; and according as that is good or bad, they become causes of love or hatred" (T. 348). It is not because intentions display our freedom of uncaused will, but rather because they anchor our sometimes capricious-seeming actions (T. 403) in the lasting "system" of our passions and the various cognitive and non-cognitive strengths and weaknesses that they and their satisfaction display. Hume grants that good intentions are an appropriate cause of love, and perhaps an essential cause of any deliberate moral "rewards" (as bad intentions are of proper punishment). He instantly adds, however, that our loves and hates may be caused not by any actions of the loved and hated ones, but merely by their beauty or deformity, and that actions can be causes of love and hatred only when they do indicate something "durable" in the agent (or at least as durable as beauty or ugliness). So his treatment of merit and desert is nicely calculated both to make some concessions to those who see the human will as the appropriate focus of human judgment of human persons, and also to infuriate them by demoting will to mere transmitter and indicator of the motivational forces that constitute a person. He takes these forces to be as really one's own as any standing intention, any momentary choice, any "temporary and perishing" voluntary action. To get the whole Humean story on this topic, and to appreciate both its internal coherence and the extent of its calculated challenge to received voluntarist modes of moral thought, we need to look not just at the first three sections of Book Two, Part III, but also at the earlier discussion of intention in Book Two, Part II, Section III, and at Book Three's discussion of "this distinction betwixt voluntary and involuntary," in Section IV of Part III. Voluntary or intentional actions are allowed to be the proper focus of minds intent on rewarding and punishing, but only because of what intentions reliably indicate about the less voluntary motives, and the strengths and weaknesses that are the focus of the less restricted person-evaluations involved in love and hatred, pride and shame, moral approbation and disapprobation.

Hume's targets in "the greatest part of moral philosophy, antient and modern" (T. 413) are what he regards as false claims about the human will's freedom, undue emphasis on reward and punishment (mainly in the moderns, not in the ancients) and, linked with both of these, a false version of the role of reason in human intention formation. In Section III of Book Two, Part III, he moves to this third target. It is one of the *Treatise*'s most often cited and most often attacked sections. As with every other section, however, its meaning will be properly understood only if the connections to earlier and later sections are appreciated. It was written not as an essay, but as an integral part of a treatise. As early as Book One, Part III, Section X, "Of the influence of belief," we get anticipations of its themes, in a discussion of the influential role that thinking does play in intention formation. This earlier discussion, usually neglected by the commentators on "Of the influencing motives of the will,"[4] was prefaced by Hume's diffident estimate of how few "proselytes to his opinion" the *Treatise* would win, but he did not adequately foresee how many would reject his opinions on the basis of very selective reading. It took experience to persuade him that "so vast an undertaking" as the *Treatise* demanded more "stretch of the thought" than most readers would sustain.[5] At the beginning of Book Three, after experiencing the distortions and incomplete quotations to which the first reviewers of Books One and Two subjected him, he notes this intolerance for any "long chain of reasoning, where we must preserve to the end the evidence of the first propositions" (T. 455), but hopes against hope that his long reasonings about morality will be read, and that they will be found to "corroborate whatever has been said concerning the understanding and the passions" (ibid.), even in an age when "the greatest part of men seem agreed to convert reading into an amusement, and to reject every thing that requires any considerable degree of attention to be comprehended" (T. 456).

Philosophical reading habits still seem to be resistant to Hume's attempt to link the theses of Book One with those of Books Two and Three, indeed resistant to treating the *Treatise* as a treatise, as distinct from a series of self-contained section-long philosophical essays.[6] Such habits condemn the reader to miss out on what Hume found (initially at least) most satisfactory about his "system of philosophy": that it acquires "new force as it advances" (T. 455) from book to book, that the later reflections depend upon, corroborate and extend the earlier, more tentative conclusions. It certainly condemns such readers to getting only part of Hume's views on reason's role in the causation of action, if they read only the most famous bits, "Of the influencing motives of the will" and the first section of Book Three. The theses advanced there are bound to appear very puzzling, if excerpted from the "system" they are embedded in.

Book One's discussion of the influence of belief directs our attention not to the impotence of reason's products (the conclusions of our reasonings, causal or demonstrative) but rather to the dangerous potency of thought. Our ideas about the sources of pleasure and pain, good and evil, "are always wandering in the mind; and were it mov'd by every idle conception of this kind, it would

never enjoy a moment's peace and tranquillity" (T. 119). Wise nature has "chosen a medium, and has neither bestow'd on every
idea of good and evil the power of actuating the will, nor yet has
entirely excluded them from this influence" (ibid.). Firm beliefs
about what is good can actuate the will and influence the passions
almost as strongly as do present pleasures. Hume here extends to
beliefs about pleasure and pain his earlier claim that beliefs about
matters of fact have a vivacity derived from and approaching that
of sense impressions. Beliefs about what is good do actuate the
will. Having noted this empirical fact, Hume claims that it cor-
roborates his general thesis about the relation of our beliefs to our
current and past impressions, and says that it "may give us a notion after what manner our reasonings from causation are able to
operate on the will and passions" (T. 120). It is mediately, through
effect on our passions, that beliefs either about pleasure ("good"),
or about the causes and effects of our pleasures, influence our will.
Our vigilant prevailing or ruling passions are on the watch for
information that feeds or strengthens them (the coward "readily
assents to every account of danger that he meets with"); our desires are on the watch for recipes for their own satisfaction. Belief
and obsessive or even passing thoughts influence our passions and
motives, and so influence our will. Hume takes this point to be
already established long before he gets to his most famous and
infamous Book Two claims about the impotence of "reason alone"
to produce or prevent any action.

He begins the resumed discussion by claiming that popular and
traditional philosophical talk of "the combat of passion and reason" is strictly nonsense (T. 413–415). Since passions incorporate
the influence of reason, since they presuppose beliefs, they would
be in combat with themselves if they resisted the influence of belief. (This of course may happen, in self-deception and in weakness of the will, but these pathological cases point up rather than
disprove the normal influence of belief.) So Hume, relying in part
on his earlier exploration of the influence of thought on our passions and our wills, can claim that "we speak not strictly and philosophically when we talk of the combat of passion and of reason"
(T. 415), and he can dismiss as fallacious not just "popular decla-
mations" but also "the greatest part of moral philosophy, antient

and modern," when they urge us to let our blind, inconstant and deceitful passions be subdued by divine unchanging reason. What is fallacious is to think that any sense can be given to the idea of a combat between "reason alone" and passion. A careful look at what reason is, added to the careful look at our passions that Hume is in the middle of giving us, will show us that it is non-sense to see reason and passion as potentially opposed combatants.

Hume is partly to blame for the misunderstanding to which this one brief section has given rise. First, because he does not remind us that he is picking up a discussion begun in Book One in "Of the influence of belief"; second, because he writes as if he is "prov-ing" the fallaciousness of talk of reason battling passions simply by establishing points about one of the mythical combatants, pure reason, when in fact he needs to remind us also of some already established facts about passions; third, because his own famous metaphor of master and slave suggests, at least to post-Hegelian readers, the possibility of the very combat he finds impossible; and fourth, and most deplorably, because he wrote one very silly para-graph that has perversely dominated the interpretation of his moral psychology—the paragraph asserting that passions are "original existences" that "contain not any representative quality" (T. 415). This is, at the very least, unrepresentative of Hume's claims about passions in the preceding and following parts of Book Two.

Hume had begun Book Two by reminding us of Book One's classification of impressions into those (including pleasure and pain) of sensation and those "of reflexion." "Original impressions or impressions of sensation are such as without any antecedent perception arise in the soul, . . . Secondary or reflective impres-sions are such as proceed from some of these original ones, either immediately or from the interposition of its idea" (T. 275). All the passions that Hume analyzes do involve the "interposition" either of an idea or of a sense impression, and some of them (respect, envy) involve complex relations both of ideas and of impressions of pleasure and pain. So the claim that they are "original exis-tences" has to somehow square with the earlier claim that they are secondary and often idea-mediated impressions. They are reflex reactions to what we take to be the case. This does not give the impression of reflection itself any "representative character," but it would not be an impression "of reflexion" except for the fact that it has an idea to introduce it. Impressions of reflection do not "without any introduction make their appearance in the soul," but are introduced by our thoughts about what is or is likely to become the case. The purely hedonic components in, say, pride, are, on Hume's analysis, two pleasures—one, the "separate pleasure," an enjoyment of some fine thing, the other the pleasant glow of pride itself, of proud ownership. But for it to be pride, rather than some other passion, one must believe the fine thing to be one's own. The belief is crucial in identifying the passion as pride, and some idea must be present for it to be a passion rather than just a pleasure.

Hume had spent over a hundred pages explaining the intricacies of his theory of "the double relation of impressions and ideas" involved in the "indirect" or person-directed passions, and in the course of it he had given us an account of anger. Now suddenly he writes: "When I am angry, I am actually possest with the passion, and in that emotion have no more a reference to any other object, than when I am thirsty, or sick, or more than five foot high" (T. 415). How can he write this after his earlier account of anger? How much or little reference to other objects, in any case, is involved in being thirsty, sick, or more than five feet tall?

Anger, as discussed by Hume earlier in Book Two, is always directed at someone for some perceived insult, injury or harm. In the terminology he has been using, it has an "object" of its own, namely the person one is angry with, and has also a "subject" or cause, the perceived injury that person is thought to have done one. So, like all passions, it does seem to refer us to at least one intentional "object" of the passion, and it involves the ideas of its object or objects. Anger is a passion that "compleats" hatred in the way benevolence completes love, Hume has told us. It "attends" hatred. It may be aroused simultaneously with hatred, and share its cause. In the already discussed Section III of Part II, Book Two, before his official discussion of anger in Sections VI and IX, Hume had raised the question of whether an injury need be thought intentional to cause anger at and hatred of the injurer. "A violent anger for injuries," he there notes, may be sustained a short

while even when the injuries are known to be "entirely involuntary and accidental" (T. 350), but they will not then be enough to
sustain "a lasting enmity."

In Part II, Section VI, he further spells out the relation between
lasting hatred for relatively enduring features of the hated person,
and the less lasting anger which expresses hatred. It is in this section that we get one of the clearest recognitions by Hume of the
multiple "references" a passion may have. He considers the hypothesis "that love and hatred have not only a *cause,* which excites
them, *viz.* pleasure and pain; and an *object,* to which they are directed, *viz.* a person or thinking being; but likewise an *end,* which
they endeavour to attain, *viz.* the happiness or misery of the person belov'd or hated" (T. 367). He rejects this hypothesis, which
would fuse hatred and anger into one passion, as "contrary to experience" (ibid.), since experience shows that the lover need not
think much about the happiness of the beloved, or the hater much
about the misery of the hated. Should they think of them, they
will desire them, but "the passions may express themselves in a
hundred ways, and may subsist a considerable time, without our
reflecting on the happiness or misery of their objects" (T. 368). So
it is best to regard anger as an "attendant" on hatred, not as a
necessary part of it. It does, like every desire, have an "end," in
this case to hurt the one we are angry with. It shares the "object"
of the hatred that it "attends," and its distinctive causes, some
"painful" injury or disservice, are among the many possible causes
of hatred. So although Hume rejects the hypothesis that gives
hatred an object, a cause and an end, he is accepting that triple
intentionality for benevolence and anger. To adapt his phrase
about pride (T. 292), they "have in a manner three objects, to
which they direct our view." They do not copy these things, but
they certainly refer to them.[7]

In his exposition of the "parallel direction" of anger to "comparison"-dependent malice (T. 384), in the section discussed in the
previous chapter, Hume continues his exploration of the causes of
hatred and anger. We become angry at our victims, and come to
hate them, as we come to feel good will to those we have (perhaps
unintentionally) benefited, and come to love them. This is supposed to happen by association of impressions, accompanied by

some rationalization. Uneasy sympathy with our victims leads to uneasy anger at them, and the latter to finding painful and hateful lasting attributes in them. This remarkable and already remarked-upon passage shows, among other things, that when Hume directs his view directly on the passion of anger, rather than on his rationalist opponents' views, he certainly does find that anger refers beyond itself to its causes, object and end, as well as to its attendant passions. And this clear recognition of the complex intentionality of anger continues right up to the section immediately preceding his surprise announcement that anger is an "original existence." While discussing punishment, he had written that "the constant and universal object of hatred or anger is a person or creature endow'd with thought and consciousness" (T. 411). (Hume failed to foresee how later generations would find their recalcitrant cars, computers and other machines apparently appropriate objects of anger.) Anger refers us at the very least to the person, god, angel, animal or machine we are angry with, and it also "directs our view" to what offense this one is guilty of, and to the harm we at least fleetingly want to inflict on it.

When we attend to thirst, or nausea, or even to being more than five feet tall, we will also find reference to (but not copies of) the drink that is desired, the vomiting that is expected, the standard foot that is our measure. "Hunger, lust, and a few other bodily appetites" are included by Hume among those non-hedonic appetites that "produce good and evil, and proceed not from them, like the other affections" (T. 439). This means that they need not include reference to the idea of the pleasure of drinking or the painfulness of retching; they may simply refer to the ideas of drinking and retching. Hume's more considered view is that they, like any other desire or appetite, have their "objects." So what happened here at T. 415? Did Hume forget his own account of the "objects" that passions must have, in order to be passions at all, and to be the particular passions that they are? Is this passage a temporary aberration, an atypical and counter-productive blind swipe at his rationalist opponents? Was he so "possest with the passion" of antirationalist zeal, so "carry'd away by the Heat of Youth & Invention"[8] that he misrepresented his own views, the views he had been spelling out with such appreciative detail in the preceding parts of Book Two? Whatever the explanation, Hume's overselective readers have given him and his ghost occasion to repent his "Haste" in this "defective" passage "a hundred & a hundred times." We find no repetition of the claims in this paragraph in the *Enquiries* or the *Dissertation on the Passions,* so we have every reason to think that Hume himself came to see their defects. The first appendix to the *Enquiry Concerning the Principles of Morals,* "Concerning Moral Sentiment," makes no such claims for the non-intentionality of passions and sentiments. Sentiments are preferences for things, and the moral sentiment is a preference or feeling "for the happiness of mankind, and a resentment of their misery" (E. 286). It refers us to its object, both general and particular. Our disapprobation of murder is of intentional killing, our special disapprobation of the murder of a parent is of the knowing murder of a parent, so our feeling about Nero is a different feeling from that about Oedipus. The disapprobation refers us to its proper "objects" and to its "causes" or appropriate reasons.

One other partial explanation of how Hume could have written that unfortunate paragraph at T. 415 is that the claims made there are perfectly plausible for "emotions,"[9] though not for passions. Since a passion, especially a typically violent one like anger, usually brings "some emotion or movement of spirits" (T. 373), Hume may have extended the claims true of "emotion" to the passions they help constitute. As Hume and his contemporaries use the term "emotion," it is a bodily disturbance, much more appropriately classified, like some pleasures and pains, as an "impression of sensation," than as an "impression of reflexion." (Hume could have reflectively accepted the James-Lange theory of emotions for "emotions," but not for passions.) Still, this gives us only a partial explanation of this anomalous paragraph. It remains an anomaly.

The main claim of this section, that reason alone is insufficient as a cause of action, is perfectly in accord with Hume's considered views, and does not require the expulsion of the influence of reason from what does cause action, namely passion. Desire is the usual passion to play this role, but after reason has more fully influenced desire, we usually call it "preference," as Hume often does. Since belief does naturally influence preference, and reason produces beliefs, then passions and preferences can be "unreasonable" if they are uninfluenced by relevant beliefs that we possess, or if they are influenced by false beliefs we possess. If we prefer the destruction of the world to the scratching of our little finger, that usually will be unreasonable, since it will depend on the obviously false belief that our little finger is not part of the world. But if the particular destruction we opt for does mysteriously leave us and our fingers unharmed—perhaps firing the rocket that shoots us to some other planet—then the criticisms to be made of our choice will have to be in terms like "vicious," "callously indifferent to the fate of the majority of humankind," or, if the chooser is indulging a mere passing enthusiasm, "imprudent, showing weakness of the mind, a regrettable prevalance of violent over calm passions." "Contrary to reason" is not the strongest criticism that a critic of rationalism will make.[10] "Immoral" or even "imprudent" will be much stronger. For such criticisms will be directed at all our responses to what we know or believe, not just to our purely cognitive limitations (and not just to our lack of enterprise in collecting and verifying relevant beliefs). As Norman Kemp Smith[11] put it, "Though it is not contrary to reason to prefer the destruction of the world to the scratching of my little finger, it is less 'humane' to do so, i.e. less in keeping with the *sentiments* which, as members of the human species, we *naturally* entertain."

The traditional rationalist moralist, who criticizes a person for acting contrary to reason, for having a will that is not a rational will, intends to criticize mainly the person's will, not the reason that should have guided it. Reason for such a person is by definition unchanging and beyond criticism. But for Hume, human reason is a mix of animal intelligence and language-dependent calculative ability, which varies from person to person, from animal to animal. Particular instances of it can indeed be criticized—stupidity and thoughtlessness are vices. But to criticize the will of a person, we will need to consider not just the "influence of belief," and the beliefs that did the influencing, but also the motives that led to the acquisition and retention of these beliefs, and the motives that these beliefs influenced. It is the world-destroyer's desires and preferences that make his will faulty. The person whose desire for her present lesser good is more ardent than for her greater long-term good, which she sees and acknowledges as such, is guilty of "weakness of mind," but not of irrationality or acting contrary to "reason alone." For reason alone merely tells her that she is sacrificing later and greater goods. If she does not care about that, then the fault lies in her caring, and through that, in her will. She acts contrary to her long-term good, not contrary to reason. How could one's intention be contrary to reason if one acknowledges what reason tells one, that one is sacrificing one's greater good, and that very likely one will regret it? Reason has had its say—its voice has not been silenced. The intention to invite later regrets, to sacrifice one's greater good to one's present plea- sure (by continuing to smoke, for example) incorporates what rea- son informs one of; it is the sort of intention that only a rational being with foresight could form. We deplore it when people form such intentions, but not because we are more influenced than they are by our reasoning. We are simply differently influenced.

Why do we deplore weakness of the mind, and call it a weak- ness? For one thing because, as sympathetic persons, we will have to sympathize with and so have a share in the weak-minded per- son's later misery, as well as in her lesser present pleasure, and as citizens and as moral persons we may have to try to alleviate it. We have very good reasons, given our own concerns, to deplore what Hume calls "weakness of mind," and to encourage our fel- lows not to prefer their present lesser good to their overall greater good. Our intentions, like theirs, will be formed by passions and by such beliefs as inform those passions and "concur" with them in their expression and satisfaction. Our intentions, like theirs, will be "unreasonable" only if "founded on a false supposition," or if we "chuse means insufficient for the design'd end, and de- ceive ourselves in our judgment of causes and effects" (T. 416). But though the weak-minded person's intentions are not contrary to reason, they may be contrary to moral sense, to humanity or to prudence.

Hume explains the error of thinking that "reason alone" could be in a combat with our belief-influenced passions by the hypoth- esis that the popular declaimers and the moral philosophers who talk of this combat (both groups seem to lack "a strict philosophic eye") confuse two different sorts of mental occurrence, because both occur "without producing any sensible emotion" (T. 417). Calm passions motivate us without any discernible turbulence in the soul or in the body, just as reasoning can go on in "calmness and tranquillity." This explaining away of rationalist error depends crucially on the distinction between "emotion" and "passion." Hume has no special quarrel with moralists who preach the subduing of "emotion" to superior principles, but he takes the superior principles to be calm passions, ones that "cause no disorder in the soul." Violent passions, such as anger, are ones that do cause emotion and disorder.

Violence in passion is the topic of the section following "Of the influencing motives of the will." Hume finds its causes to be the contiguity of the desired good, contrived delay or obstacles to getting a temptingly close good, conflicting feelings about it, uncertainty about getting it. (It is not clear to me how to apply Hume's fifth rule for judging causes [T. 174] to get a unification of these various causes of violence in passions.) Calm passions are typically for remote but fairly secure and often familiar goods. Hume gives us a list of desires that he (fairly optimistically) takes to be typically calm, and so presumably typically secure, unconflicting, regularly satisfied and demanding no sacrifice of contiguous to remoter goods. These are "either certain instincts originally implanted in our natures, such as benevolence and resentment, the love of life, and kindness to children; or the general appetite to good, and aversion to evil, consider'd merely as such" (T. 417). The last seem merely formal goods, harmonious by definition. The others may be calm in good conditions, but as Hume goes on to note, they certainly have their violent moments—resentment can turn to disorderly anger, when, as it often is, it is in conflict with other desires. But when our passions are calm, then there will be no internal "combat," so no violence. Hume claims that such emotion-free passions get confused with emotionless reason, and so become what is "vulgarly call'd . . . *reason*" (T. 419). But any one of them can become violent when the violence-inducing factors are present.

Among these violence-inducing factors is conflict of motivation. If such conflict is enough to make the conflicting desires violent, then Hume really has no explanation of how the rationalists can falsely believe in a combat of reason and passion. He can explain how they can mistake passions for reason, but only so long as the passions in question remain clam. The moment there is any conflict of motivation, then there will be the danger that all parties in the soul will become violent. How then can any of these passions appear emotionless and calm? Hume's account of the causes of violence in passions, especially his thesis that "an opposition of passions commonly causes a new emotion in the spirits, and produces more disorder, than the concurrence of any two affections of equal force" (T. 421) seems to threaten to make nonsense of his own previous talk of calm passions counteracting violent ones (T. 418). The most that could be expected to occur would be that a typically calm passion counteracts a typically violent one, by becoming briefly violent during the time of opposition. It is, however, only "commonly" that opposition of passions causes disorder, so in theory there might be occasional calm negotiated victories of more considered preferences over momentary gusts of more violent opposed passions. But the victory will not often be won without resort to counter-violence, if "when we wou'd govern a man, and push him to any action, 'twill commonly be better policy to work upon the violent than the calm passions" (T. 419). Presumably this is as good a policy with oneself as with anyone else.

Hume makes this claim about the efficacy of appeal to violent passions as a qualification to the immediately preceding statement that "we must, therefore, distinguish betwixt a calm and a weak passion; betwixt a violent and a strong one" (T. 419). But how is relative strength to be measured if not by frequency of victory in cases of opposition? If opposition usually leads to violent combat, then the victors will be as guilty of violence as the vanquished. The best way to save Hume's theses here is to suppose that "calm passion" usually means "typically calm," not "necessarily calm, even when it meets opposition." The typically violent passions may derive their typical violence as much from the other causes of violence (tempting closeness of the goods they are bent on, insecurity, and so on) as from their frequent disharmony with other passions. So then we could save Hume's claim that the rationalists and popular moralists have mistaken the desirable prevalence of the calm over the violent passions for a supposedly welcome victory for reason in a combat between reason and passion. There really is frequent "combat," and the winner can be a force that typically avoids rather than causes "emotion" or disorder in the soul. But equally typically it may create a little violent disorder in order to win.

Hume's discussion of motivation and variety of kinds of motive in these sections is obviously intended to prepare the ground for Book Three, and for his own account of morality and of what natural motives in us it flows from and endorses. It is therefore interesting that one of the causes of violence in a passion that he singles out for mention is the passion's being opposed by a prohibition. "Hence we naturally desire what is forbid, and take a pleasure in performing actions, merely because they are unlawful. The notion of duty, when opposite to the passions, is seldom able to overcome them; and when it fails of that effect, is apt rather to encrease them, by producing opposition in our motives and principles" (T. 421). This forewarns us that the version of duty that Hume will endorse is geared to be in accordance with at least some of our strong passions, so as not to have counter-productive effects. The version of morality that he will endorse will minimize flat prohibitions, and the version that he will criticize most strongly will be that which sees it as a set of "thou shalt not...s" stemming from some source external to the passionate human person. A morality that can expect to do more good than harm will have to avoid exciting to fever pitch the very passions that it wants to regulate, and avoid adding to the very disorder that it aims to replace with order.

There are also some hints in Sections V and VI of Part III, Book Two, about how, other than by issuing prohibitions to their opponents, some passions can come to predominate, and to remain strong without resort to violence. Custom and habit strengthen desires for pleasures coming from our own activity, since custom brings "facility." "The pleasure of facility does not so much consist in any ferment of the spirits, as in their orderly motion" (T. 423), and thus such pleasures will be calm joys. But surprise and novelty also please, particularly where our more "passive" tastes are concerned. Hume cites pleasure obtained from "the fair sex, or music, or good cheer" (T. 424) as among those that pall or turn to aversion on too frequent repetition. (He was himself no musician, but were his pleasures in company so passive?) Some passive contemplative pleasures, such as those got from "the clouds, and heavens, and trees, and stones" (T. 423) may rarely cause much "ferment in the spirits," but they do not pall, "however frequently repeated." Hume sees a trade-off between intensity and durability in our passive but not in our active pleasures. The former feed much more than the latter on novelty, change and surprise.

Hume culls his wisdom in these matters as much from his wide reading as from his own steady pleasure in writing, his mild enjoyment of nature, his boredom at concerts, and his inconstancy in love affairs with members of the fair sex. When it comes to the question of how some morally endorsed desire can be gotten to prevail over some less approved desire, he turns to "a noted passage in the history of *Greece*" (T. 425). The Athenians could vote to sacrifice advantage to justice, when Aristides told them that Themistocles' secret plan, if carried out, would bring them very great advantage, but would also be very unjust, only because they did not know the details of the plan, and were not told just what advantage they were sacrificing. To let one's thoughts dwell on the details of what one is giving up is to risk change of mind. The clever governor of self or of others, then, presumably will draw a veil of ignorance or attempted forgetting over what, for example, the sensible knave gains and the just person sacrifices, but will encourage her imagination to dwell on the less feverish satisfactions of "inward peace of mind, consciousness of integrity, a satisfactory review of our own conduct" (E. 283), and any other mild but lasting pleasures that virtue may bring. The wise moral reformer will try to engage our "active habits" in activities that do not offend against justice or other moral values; she will provide for a few circuses and an occasional change of moral heroines, as well as for non-tedious moral anthems. She will try to arrange things so that attention is not drawn too often to those "feverish, empty amusements of luxury and expense" (E. 284) that the successful knaves may be ostentatiously enjoying. The psychology of the passions that Hume gives us here, the implicit recipes for arranging for the prevalence of "calm" orderly passions over disorderly troublesome ones, not merely prepare the ground for his moral theory, but forewarn us of what to expect in his own moral, rhetoric: "Nothing is more capable of infusing any passion into the mind, than eloquence, by which objects are presented in their strongest and most lively colours" (T. 426). In the *Enquiry Concerning the Principles of Morals,* though not in the *Treatise,* Hume tries to perform this service for our calm but sometimes flagging desire for justice and for other moral virtues.

Section VI, "Of the influence of the imagination on the passions," directly continues the themes of Book One's discussion, "Of the influence of belief."[12] Our passions and their relative strengths are the products not just of "original instincts" and our sensitivity to pleasure and pain, but of what we know and what we are kept in ignorance of, what we vividly portray and what we keep hidden, what others who matter to us believe and how eloquently they express it. Hume here discusses the factors determining patterns of attention, and the relative salience of different evaluative judgments which we have accepted, only some of which, however, on any given occasion become "lively" or vivacious enough to affect our will. "We may of ourselves acknowledge, that such an object is valuable, and such another odious; but 'till an orator excites the imagination, and gives force to these ideas, they may have but a feeble influence either on the will or the affections" (T. 426–427). Recent "tastings" of the value in question keep evaluative judgments young and vigorous; orators can revive old, tired, nearly forgotten evaluations; our friends' "bare opinion," expressed sincerely but not necessarily eloquently, can make us attend to acknowledged values we would otherwise have neglected. Practical deliberation, and especially its correction, are once again interestingly interpersonal in this account. We depend on others to remind us of overlooked values, to "represent in their strongest and most lively colours" important pleasures, the memories of which may in our own case have grown dim and faded.

In the *Abstract,* as a puff for his associationist account of how the human mind operates, Hume wrote: "For as it is by means of thought only that any thing operates upon our passions, and as these are the only ties of our thoughts, they are really *to us* the cement of the universe, and all the operations of the mind must, in a great measure, depend on them" (T. 662). It is because thoughts influence passions (including the passions that direct conduct), that thought matters so much, and that we need each other's help in correcting the vagaries of the thoughts of good and evil that "wander in our minds."

At the end of this survey of our motivating passions, their conflict, and the factors determining their relative strength, Hume turns to that peculiarly human desire, the desire to accumulate a fund of truths. Its strength, he writes, comes in part from the belief that these truths will one day prove useful. But "the principal source of that satisfaction we receive from the sciences" (T. 449) comes from "the exercise of genius," "the game alone." The most pleasant and agreeable exercise of our minds is to "stretch" our powers of thought, to "exert our genius." Thus, finally, Hume does concede the real motivating force of "reason alone"—we enjoy reasoning. His earlier claims about sustainable active pleasures, about the stimulus of surmountable difficulties, about custom bringing a facility that enhances these pleasures, about the calm strength of desires for such active lasting pleasures, are all corroborated by that "peculiar" affection (T. 448), the love of truth. Pleasure in the expected utility of the truths we collect combines harmoniously with pleasure in "the action of the mind." This desire for truth rarely conflicts with other desires; it serves all of them, it helps us harmonize them, and it brings its own harmless joys.

Is it one of the calm desires that we can confuse with pure reason, or is it reason itself? Is it always calm? Hume, perhaps looking ahead optimistically, supposes that "when we are reading the history of a nation, we may have an ardent desire of clearing up any doubt or difficulty" (T. 454). There may be sudden and violent changes, "transports" from idea to idea, doubts and painful "uneasiness." The reasoning that he portrays in this final section of Book Two is prone to temporary violence, is not free from internal conflict and from doubt. Not merely has he animated the inert reason of Section III; he has disturbed its "calmness and tranquillity," and introduced considerable emotion into it. His "somewhat extraordinary" opinion at T. 415 that "reason is, and ought only to be the slave of the passions, and can never pretend to any other office than to serve and obey them" becomes even more extraordinary when one of the dominant passions turns out to be the enjoyment taken in sometimes turbulent reasoning. "Our attention being once engag'd, the difficulty, variety, and sudden reverses of fortune, still farther interest us" (T. 452).

There are enough difficulties and reverses of fortune in Book Two to keep the reader from boring fixity of belief about Hume's beliefs. Passions suffer sudden transport from being secondary impressions to being original existences, then back again. Reasoning's fortune is reversed from emotionless calm calculation to ardent doubt-interrupted dialectic. Book Two certainly exemplifies the latter, not the former. Is its own unfortunately famous section, "Of the influencing motives of the will," then, intended only as a passing moment in the sustained display of the workings of curiosity about human passions? Has Hume turned the adventurous love of truth onto the passions, and eventually onto itself? Book Two's concluding section is less dramatic and self-dramatizing than the conclusion of Book One, but like the latter, it is a piece of subtle "reflexion." It may not be a perfectly coherent reflexive turn. Difficulties remain unsurmounted. If, as Hume claims, the *Treatise* acquires "new force as it advances," then the fully coherent turn on themselves of the love of truth and the other intelligent human passions that it can harmonize with must wait until Book Three. There the direction of our thought, as well as of the rest of our passion-displaying conduct, is shown to be subject to the very special sort of reflection that moral evaluation involves.

8

The Contemplation of Character

> An action, or sentiment, or character is virtuous or vicious; why? because its view causes a pleasure or uneasiness of a particular kind. In giving a reason, therefore, for the pleasure or uneasiness, we sufficiently explain the vice or virtue. To have the sense of virtue, is nothing but to *feel* a satisfaction of a particular kind from the contemplation of a character. (T. 471)

> When we form our judgments of persons, merely from the tendency of their characters to our own benefit, or to that of our friends, we find so many contradictions to our sentiments in society and conversation, and such an uncertainty from the incessant changes of our situation, that we seek some other standard of merit and demerit, which may not admit of so great variation. (T. 583)

What standard of merit and demerit does Hume think that our moral contemplation of character employs? What reason can we give for the satisfaction or dissatisfaction we feel with one another's characters, when we take those feelings to be moral approbation and disapprobation? Hume's characterization of moral evaluation is given to us within Book Three in gradual stages. He warns us at the start that there is to be a "long chain of reasoning" which will, like the *Treatise* as a whole, "acquire new force as it advances" (T. 455), and he expresses his hopes that, because "morality is a subject that interests us above all others" (ibid.), we will tolerate the lengthiness of his "abstruse reasoning." If we are to understand it, then, we must follow it to the end, not rest in the antirationalist ground-clearing that goes on in Part I, nor think that Part II is self-contained and Part III an optional extra. In Part I we get first a negative characterization of morality as "not conclusions of our reason" (T. 457), then a sketch of Hume's positive theory and some preparations for its full development. It is, however, only in Parts II and III that we find out what sort of "reasons" can be given for moral uneasiness, what particular kind of pleasure we get from contemplation of a morally good character. Part I is insistent that this is a *"peculiar* kind" of satisfaction (T. 472), but does not analyze the peculiarity—that is left for Parts II and III. Since I believe that Hume's antirationalist arguments in Part I, as much as his own alternative to rationalism, acquire new force as his whole argument advances, and are more easily understood once we see the details and not just the outlines of the "system" he is offering to replace it, I shall draw on the later parts of Book Three as well as on Part I to present Hume's position in its full force. In this chapter, I will consider his own positive views about moral approbation in general. I leave the details of his list of virtues and the special complexities of the "artificial virtues," as well as fuller discussion of his apparent antirationalism, for later chapters.

The *Treatise* has accustomed us to its author's penchant for reversing "that method, which at first sight seems most natural" (T. 8). Ideas were discussed before impressions, or at least before those "which principally deserve our attention" (ibid.); indirect passions were discussed before direct passions; and now artifice is discussed before nature. But only at first sight is it more natural to discuss nature before artifice, and Hume has his good reasons for the order he follows in Book Three. As with all these contrasting pairs, he begins with a short discussion of the contrast, before settling in to a sustained discussion of one member of the contrasting pair, in this case artifice. In this short discussion, at the end of Part I, he prepares us for his later willingness to speak of the artifice of justice as "natural" (T. 484) by explaining the usual opposition of the terms "nature" and "artifice" as due to the fact that "we readily forget, that the designs, and projects, and views of men are principles as necessary in their operation as heat and cold, moist and dry: But taking them to be free and entirely our own, 'tis usual for us to set them in opposition to the other principles of nature" (T. 474). The artificial is simply the contrived or designed.

Hume's attention to the more contrived parts of human morality, the rights and obligation of "justice," before he attends to the more spontaneous and so more unvarying elements in it (the "natural" virtues) serves several purposes for him. First he balances the statement that moral distinctions are "not the conclusions of our reason" with the acknowledgment that reason nevertheless plays a vital role in establishing our obligations, since these obligations arise from "artifice." Justice, as Hume understands it, is a remedy for the "inconvenience" of insecurity and scarcity of transferable goods, and "the remedy, then, is not deriv'd from nature, but from *artifice;* or more properly speaking, nature provides a remedy in the judgment and understanding, for what is irregular and incommodious in the affections" (T. 489). For the love of gain to regulate itself, collective reason must work out an acceptable cooperative scheme. Justice depends on reason's "concurring" with the desire for "commodious" and "convenient" conditions, the desire to improve the climate of life. Hume's analysis of justice describes the vital role that reason plays in this part of morality, and corrects the over-emphasis in Part I on what it cannot do. It cannot provide the basic motivation, but it must provide the foresight and the calculation that go into acceptance of a cooperative scheme.

Another good reason for Hume to move directly to the virtues that depend most on human understanding, on the design of cooperative schemes, and on "convention," is that the account of them that he gives demonstrates beautifully how a philosopher can "observe and explain" the transition from *is* to *ought,* that transition "of the last consequence" (T. 469). Hume complained, at the end of Section I of Part I, that rationalist moralists slur over it too quickly. They should be able to "deduce" the *ought* relation, if they purport to derive morality from their version of reason, but such a deduction of, say, the conclusion that we ought to have no other gods before Jehovah, from the premise that this is what Jehovah commands, "seems altogether inconceivable" (ibid.). Hume has been saddled by some commentators[1] with "Hume's law," which says not just that no Humean "demonstration" can be given getting us from premises about matters of fact to conclusions about obligations or *oughts,* but that no sound inference or reasonable transition from *is* to *ought* can be made. This is not what Hume writes, and I take this famous little "observation" of his, tacked on to the end of his attack on rationalist moral theories, to be directed at their deficiencies, not to be any sort of general impossibility claim.[2] The unrestricted claim that Hume makes here is that any transition from *is* to *ought* is "of the last consequence," and that the move to *ought* "shou'd be observ'd and explain'd." Then he adds the particular observation that a deduction of an *ought* from any set of *is*-claims "seems altogether inconceivable." Here he uses the rationalists' own rules against them, as he did in his discussion of their use of the principle of induction. But he does not share their view that the only good inferences are demonstrations, so it is still open to him to move from *is* to "should," and to give a carefully explained account of a transition from facts about human agreements or conventions to conclusions about our "natural obligations." This is precisely what he does in his account of the obligations not to rob, steal, break promises and so on. This discussion, in Part II, is appropriately placed to be a discernible follow-up to the brief discussion of *is-ought* transitions in Part I. Hume first "wou'd subvert all the vulgar systems of morality" (T. 470) which take a leap of faith from supposed facts about divine commands to conclusions about what ought to be done, then constructs his own sophisticated system that explains the sort of facts from which the transition can be made.[3] He observes and explains the transition from facts about importance to claims about norms, from facts about conventions to conclusions about rights, and makes them reasonable.[4]

There is a third good reason for Hume's leaving the natural virtues and the full story about the points of view from which they are recognized until after his account of the artifices that morality involves—namely that some artifice, in the sense of thoughtful design and contrivance, seems involved in that point of view itself. Hume repeatedly postpones fully describing it. In Part I we get mere hints: it is not that of the wine connoisseur or the appreciator of good music, nor is it that of the general who is anxiously assessing the qualities of the enemy forces. It is a viewpoint from which a *"peculiar"* kind of pleasure in human character is felt. In Part II he gives us only "a few words" (T. 498) about the viewpoint from which we recognize obedience to the rules of certain established human institutions as virtues, and the obligations they give rise to as moral obligations. He writes there that "for farther satisfaction the reader must wait till we come to the third part of this book" (ibid.). Just why the reader is kept waiting is not said—perhaps partly to whet interest, in accordance with the psychological principles Hume had endorsed in Book Two. What is said here is that not just self-interest but sympathy is exercised, and that there is "a general survey" of the kind of conduct whose virtuousness or viciousness is being decided. Hume writes that he can be brief at this point, "after the principles that we have already established." The relevant established principles presumably include Part I's claims that virtue is recognized by getting a special sort of pleasure from contemplating a human character, and also Book Two's claims about our capacity for sympathy, when envy, "comparison" and cut-throat competition do not interfere with it. But he may also regard his just completed discussion of how we can come to agree on a cooperative scheme for mutual advantage as a step on the way to showing how we can agree in moral evaluation. If we are reasonable enough to agree to have our "interested affection" regulate itself, and to agree on a convention that initiates a particular cooperative scheme—then we must be capable of considerable coordination of intention, judgment, action. Adoption of the viewpoint needed for moral evaluation exercises those same capacities for understanding our fellows' outlooks, and for coordinating with their ways of judging. The motive for the coordination is different, but some of the capacities it exercises are the same.[5] So Hume's discussion in Part II of how we can reach an "interested" agreement does make it easier for him to explain the sort of special agreement in judgment that moral evaluation must, on his view, expect to attain.

J. L. Mackie finds the sort of correction and regulation involved in the recognition of what Hume calls the natural virtues to be so similar to what goes into the social construction and recognition of the artificial virtues that he is willing to conclude that Hume's natural virtues "are, after all, a further set of artificial virtues," and to criticize Hume for overemphasizing the distinction. Whereas Hume sees the artificial virtues as a special subset of natural ones, special in their reliance on social contrivance and convention, Mackie thinks "that this distinction should be broken down in the opposite way: our interpersonal, impartial, objectifying approval of the natural virtues, no less than of the artificial ones, should be understood as a system of evaluation which has much the same social function as the artificial virtues themselves."[6] I postpone discussing just what special function Hume thinks the virtues he calls artificial do serve, and just what is especially artificial about them, but for present purposes I can agree with Mackie that some "artifice" is needed for the recognition of all the Humean virtues, since some artifice is essential in adopting the viewpoint needed for "seeing" them. Hume's delay in spelling out the details until after he has, in Part II, explained social artifice and agreement in convention, and, at the beginning of Part III, discussed the relation of natural to artificial virtues, can be taken as implicitly conceding at least part of Mackie's point.

Hume's good reasons for proceeding in the order he did are not necessarily decisive reasons for a commentator to follow that order, especially after two and a half centuries of critics who too often ignored Part III, and concentrated, like Reid, on making fun of an oversimplified version of the sketches Hume gives in Part I. Speaking of Hume's version of the moral judge, Reid scoffs, "Mankind have very absurdly called him a *judge;* he ought to be called a feeler."[7] After the account in Part III of how sympathy's natural partiality has to be corrected, how self-interest has to be overlooked and coordination with other person's reactions achieved, before any sentiment counts as the moral sentiment, and of how our actually felt sentiments may be stubborn and lag behind what we know we would feel if we could properly "overlook our present situation" (T. 582), so that the words in which we frame our moral verdicts may not express our actual occurrent "sentiment," but rather express what we predict we would feel if we made the appropriate corrections of sentiment—after all of this, the Reid parody looks pretty silly. Hume gives thought and judgment indispensable roles to play in the process by which we get ourselves into the right point of view for our evaluation to count as moral. He does this unmistakably in the *Enquiry Concerning the Principles of Morals,* but in the *Treatise* he delays spelling out the sort of thought-requiring "corrections of our sentiments" that moral evaluation involves, and so lays his views open to mistaken interpretation, especially from impatient and selective readers. The proper corrective for these emotivist oversimplifications is due attention to the accounts in Part III of the special points of view needed to discern virtues.

T. H. Green, in his introduction to Book Three, when commenting on the first passage quoted at the opening of this chapter, writes that if we "revert to the account of the passions, we can have no difficulty in fixing on that of which this peculiar pleasure, excited by the 'mere survey' of an action without reference to the spectator's 'particular interest,' must be a mode."[8] What he takes to be obvious is that it must be a form of sympathy. The reader who reverts to Hume's account of the passions will also have no difficulty in grasping that passions and sentiments are not "raw feels," but are necessarily thought-caused. Hume's word for the sort of thought-free feeling that Reid is contrasting with judgment is "emotion," and he never says that morality arises from our "emotions." Strictly speaking, Hume is no emotivist. His theory of morality bases it on reflective passions and corrected sentiments, and thought is as essential to them as it is to pure reasoning.[9]

Peter Jones, discussing the ambiguity of the term "sentiment" as used in the French by Dubos, and in the English by Hume, writes of "Hume's term 'sentiment,' by which he sometimes means 'emotion, passion,' and sometimes 'judgment, opinion'."[10] This remark assimilates Hume's term "passion" to "emotion." Jones a few lines earlier had noted that "Hume found it quite natural to talk of looking for reasons to justify a passion."[11] It is not just a matter of the possibility of looking for reasons, it is a matter of the necessity of having some (even if bad or unreasonable) reasons, or "causes," for one's passion, some idea that is seen to make one's particular passion the relevant one to have on a given occasion. If we remember that passions and sentiments are, for Hume, impressions of reflection, then we will not be able to forget their indispensable idea "subjects" (or "causes") and "objects." If we also remember Hume's Book One reduction of judgments to ideas (T. 96, note), then we see that "sentiments" and "passions," as Hume uses those terms, are far from excluding thought and judgment. They positively require them. So Jones seems to be wrong when he writes that, when Hume uses "sentiment," "the term treacherously covers both feeling and thought, which are otherwise often kept apart by the notions of impression and idea."[12] Hume's terms "passion" and "impression of reflection" explicitly unite feeling and thought. (If anything in this region is treacherous, it is to forget Book Two's definitions and long elaborations, in interpreting Book Three.)

Hume is partly to blame for the distortions of his views, because he does in Book Three, Part I exaggerate the difference between his view and "the system, which establishes the eternal rational measures of right and wrong" (T. 471), as earlier at the beginning of Book One he had overstated the difference between thought and feeling. None of these exaggerations is repeated in his later writings, and we get a more interesting version even of his early "heated" enthusiastic work if we attend as much to its later qualifications and conciliations as to the initial stark oppositions. I shall therefore take it that the later, perhaps calmer, formulations do correct the earlier ones—that Hume's theory not merely acquires more force as it proceeds, but corrects itself so as to acquire this force.

What Part II adds to Part I's characterization of that peculiar pleasure, moral approbation of human characters, is that sympathy must be exercised before this pleasure (or displeasure) can be felt. Just as the pleasure that a good wine affords requires us first to smell and taste it, so the pleasure that a morally good character affords requires that we first share, by sympathy, the impact of that character on the person whose it is, and on all those who have any sort of "commerce" with her. What Part III adds is that we must "correct" our initial sympathy-based evaluation by allowing and correcting for the biases to which we know felt sympathy to be subject. If we are distant from the one we judge, we must try to sympathize with the way those close to the judged person feel (especially to see the virtues that make her "good"). If we are close, we must sympathize with those who have more distance (especially to judge if she is "great"). We will in this way correct our tendency to overvalue those who serve or matter most to us, to undervalue the virtues of those whose virtues make no perceptible difference to our own lives. Our faithful living servant, bringing us meals when we request them, may not really be morally superior to a worthy long-dead Roman senator, but it is easier for us to appreciate her value, to feel warmly about her virtues. Biases due to our particular historical and social position, and to where our own advantage or affections lie, all must be corrected in our moral discourse and moral evaluations. But it is not a "view from nowhere";[13] it is a view from a common *human* viewpoint, expressing the sentiments of "the *party* of humankind against vice or disorder" (E. 275). It aims not at detachment from human concerns but at impartialty, and interpersonal agreement. "Every particular man has a peculiar position with regard to others; and 'tis impossible we cou'd ever converse together on any reasonable terms, were each of us to consider characters and persons, only as they appear from his peculiar point of view" (T. 581). Hume likens these corrections of our less impartial assessments of people to getting into the right position to view an object so as best to discern its beauty (T. 582), and to the corrections of appearance that we make more or less automatically in judging the size and shape of bodies. "All objects seem to diminish by their distance: But tho' the appearance of objects to our senses be the original standard, by which we judge of them, yet we do not say, that they actually diminish by the distance; but correcting the appearance by reflexion, arrive at a more constant and establish'd judgment concerning them. In like manner, tho' sympathy be much fainter than our concern for ourslves, and a sympathy with persons remote from us much fainter than that with persons near and contiguous; yet we neglect all these differences in our calm judgments concerning the characters of men" (T. 603).

Hume's version of the point of view from which moral evaluation is made has some striking similarities to the version of the general will given by his temporary friend and ungrateful beneficiary, Jean-Jacques Rousseau. Both require that the individual expect her verdict to be the same as her fellows' verdicts; both restrict the subject matter on which these shared preferences are to be formed to matters of general concern for a common good. Rousseau restricts them to general policies of general concern, and I will later in this chapter argue that Hume's version of the objects of moral evaluation, as human "characters," makes a similar restriction. It picks out repeatable, frequently repeated, fairly long-lasting human traits, and it restricts our evaluation to them. It tolerates attention to the temporary and fleeting only when these are signs of something that is a lasting characteristic of the person, and a characteristic that we expect to reencounter, a characteristic that we have a word for in our moral language. The differences are of course enormous, if instead of a "will," issuing laws for persons to obey, we have a sentiment, expressing its pleasures and displeasures in human characters, and if, instead of independent votes, we have verdicts reached after full discussion and attempted persuasion. But with due allowance for these big disagreements, the formal constraints that Hume and Rousseau impose on their respective versions of the court of ultimate moral appeal show striking agreement. (They should have been able to sustain their friendship longer. But one of them was really of two minds about whether individuals should submit their preferences to the scrutiny of other persons, and was uncomfortable under the apparently disconcerting gaze of the friendly Scottish stranger.)

The sentiment that Hume takes to be expressed in our sincere moral evaluations is a peculiar one. Like Rousseau's general will, it requires a viewpoint from which we expect no "contradiction" from other judges, no fluctuation in our own judgment. It is calm, because it has resolved any conflicts between close and distant views. Does it, like the General Will, make a significant difference to the direction of our conduct? It certainly motivates us to express moral judgments, but Hume is cautious about assuring us that it will motivate us to much else, should our "heart" be not much involved. "Tho' the *heart* does not always take part with those general notions, or regulate its love and hatred by them, yet are they sufficient for discourse, and serve all our purposes in company, in the pulpit, on the theatre, and in the schools" (T. 603). This and other similar passages in Part III impose interesting constraints on the way we should interpret Hume's more famous claim in Part I, the claim that "morals excite passions, and produce or prevent actions" (T. 457). On calmer reflection, it may turn out that the actions they most dependably produce are the expressive ones occurring in evaluative discourse, in the pulpit, at the lectern, and on the stages of theatres specializing in morally instructive plays (like John Home's *Douglas,* which presents intense mother love, leading to a heroic suicide, and in whose first performance Hume took part).

Hume's own version of morals finds them to be derived from a sentiment so calm, so different from "the heart's" more fiery passions, and so limited in its dependably action-producing power, that those who confuse it with "indolent" reason seem to have ample excuse for their confusion, and more excuse than Hume seems to allow in Part I. If Humean morals should excite only those passions needed for our purposes in discourse, and the pulpit, then they will excite the same sort of speech acts that reasoning itself does—verbally expressed judgments. So was Hume insincere in his famous claim in Part I, that morality has to be founded on "an active principle" (T. 457)? The better conclusion, I believe, is that Hume in this early section is appealing to the rationalist moralists' own presuppositions, and trying to reduce their positions *ad absurdum,* just as he did in Part IV of Book One. Their morality typically takes the form of commandments or laws, which are supposed to produce obedience. Hume's own version of morality is a list of approved "characters" with reasons why we approve of them, not a set of would-be authoritative prohibitions. The only Humean virtues that resolve into such directly action-regulating prohibitions are the ones he calls "artificial," and they are carefully limited in their scope. Hume devotes much attention to the question of how they motivate us to obedience to them, and this is a most important question for him, given his Book Two psychological maxim that "we naturally desire what is forbid" (T. 421). It is the rationalists, not Hume and his enlightened fellows, who see morality as a "multitude of rules and precepts" (T. 457). Moralists who take morality to be a multitude of rules and precepts expected to "influence action" are Hume's targets in Part I, Section I. I suggest that his argument against them is an *ad hominem* one, and that his disagreement with them is not just over whether some set of agreed action-influencing moral commandments, which we feel guilt at disobeying, rests on reason or on passion. Hume's disagreements with traditional moralists go deeper. He disagrees about the role morality plays, the content it has, and about the form it takes, as well as about its source.[14]

So does morality, on his version of it, and of the passion or sentiment from which it is derived, not reliably produce or prevent any actions except speech acts? That would be a doubly improper conclusion. First because speech acts, especially those directing the design of places of moral education, and passing legislation, can be very powerful and influential actions,[15] and second because the "influence" of our pleasure in good character does often go beyond influence on our discourse. The heart does not always regulate its love and hatred by its calm and moral evaluations, but it sometimes does, and when it does, then there will be "a hundred ways" in which this love can be expressed, some of them active and virtue-encouraging ways. There will be no dependable link between moral approbation and commensurate "love" or esteem, but some esteem will be there, if "*virtue* is the power of producing love or pride" (T. 575). There will be no assurance of benevolence towards the virtuous, even when they get our esteem, but there will at least not be malice (T. 367–368). Virtue may remain in rags, in Hume's moral scenario, but will at least not be reduced to rags by those who recognize it as virtue. Virtue will have the reward of esteem from moral judges, but otherwise it will often have to be its own reward.

Páll Árdal[16] puts a lot of weight on Hume's claim near the beginning of Part III that "since every quality in ourselves or others, which gives pleasure, always causes pride or love; as every one, that produces uneasiness, excites humility or hatred: It follows, that these two particulars are to be consider'd as equivalent, with regard to our mental qualities, *virtue* and the power of producing love or pride, *vice* and the power of producing humility or hatred" (T. 575). As he emphasizes, "love," for Hume, takes a great many forms, and the love normally excited by virtue will be "esteem" rather than, say, the amorous passion. The qualification that later passages in Part III introduce is that the esteem we feel for virtue may find expression mainly in our discourse, and may not "regulate our love and hatred" in ways it theoretically could. We will

1ot always love the more virtuous more than the less virtuous;
'r will our esteem for virtue always trump our esteem for wealth
power. So the influence of the Humean moral sentiment on
ou₁ motives and actions is real, but weaker, more circumscribed
and less dependable, than Part I might have led us to expect.
Hume is "sceptical," in the vulgar sense of the word, about the
impact of even sincere moral evaluations on human conduct. We
may "embrace" virtue (E. 172) once we recognize it in others, but
the embrace can be a fairly formal one.

To embrace virtue, in the sense of welcoming it into ourselves,
it must already be there to welcome. "Men may well be sensible
of the value of virtue, and may desire to attain it; but it is not
always certain, that they will be successful in their wishes." So
speaks Hume's sceptic (*Essays,* p. 169), and in his own voice the
claim is even stronger: "it being almost impossible for the mind
to change its character in any considerable article, or cure itself of
a passionate or splenetic temper, when they are natural to it" (T.
608). If morality is to be, as Hume says it is, "a practical study"
(E. 172), its practical impact on conduct and character will have
to be indirect. Human persons "cannot change their natures. All
they can do is to change their situation" (T. 537). "To teach us our
duty," in the sense of getting us to do it, precepts will not be
enough, and may be fruitless or even counter-productive. "I may
have recourse to study and reflexion within myself; to the advice
of friends; to frequent meditation, and repeated resolution: And
having experienc'd how ineffectual all these are, I may embrace
with pleasure any other expedient" (T. 536). The best expedient is
changing our situation.

Even indirect impact of our recognition of what characters are
good ones may not be easy to achieve. Hume sees us as naturally
concerned about the lives and characters of our children, and ex-
empts young children from his gloomy estimates of the inflexibility of character. (Parents are said to smooth off "rough corners"
in their children's minds—T. 486.) Thus, wise design of children's
"situation," of child-rearing practices, could effect moral reform
at a generation's remove. But only if adults have both the wisdom
and the motivation to make any sacrifices needed to set in operation the wise practices, and have good enough characters them-

selves to play their part within these practices not too splenetically. It is not impossible that these conditions of indirect impact of adult recognition of virtue be met, but it may be "almost impossible" for the products of bad practices to design, implement and successfully operate the better practices that would produce better characters in the next generation, or in later ones.

There is, however, one point that my gloomy estimates of the limited practicability of Humean morality has neglected, and that is Hume's often criticized insistence that the qualities picked out as virtues be ones that human nature regularly does turn up. Parental solicitude is a virtue, not just because of its obvious desirability, but because it is not too much to expect—it is "natural" in the sense of not at all rare or unusual (T. 474). One constraint that Hume imposes on the moral point of view is that it be non-Utopian, that it find value in the available human material. It looks for what is better in us, and so any practicability its findings have will depend on appeal to those better actual tendencies. In his essay "Of the dignity or meanness of human nature," Hume deplores those moralists who set impossibly high standards of virtue and then find us all contemptible because we do not measure up. His version of moral approbation restricts our approbation to motives that are regularly found, and found to be effectively strong, in human nature. There is a realism constraint built into his theory, which amounts to the requirement that vice be the exception, virtue the rule. So the prospects for moral progress by indirect means become brighter. Morality, Humean style, does not excite passions that produce actions by mere moral precept, but may direct the natural motivation that it finds and evaluates into wiser "artifices" for forming character while it is still malleable, and it may also effect a reform or two in retributive reformative practices, putting a stop to those that do nothing to improve character or conduct. The "tendency to regulate our lives and actions" (E. 172) that we can expect from the moral contemplation of character will be indirect, and will work through approved natural motivation, through concern for the happiness of still malleable loved ones, and ability to control their "situation," through sympathy, through desire for esteem, through pride in virtue. Character may be indirectly changed for the better by these means, especially when they work over several generations, and direct the design of wise artifices.

WHAT EXACTLY IS "character" for Hume? It is what is evaluated from moral points of view. Is it the same as personality? We use the term today primarily to refer to the whole cluster of "character traits" that a person has, but Hume's usage shifts from this fairly inclusive sense, in which one person has only one character (or only one character at a time), to a use closer to Theophrastus' "character,"[17] and so closer to our "character trait." Hume often speaks of persons having "a character for . . .," where the phase is completed by a word like "honesty," naming a specific trait. Character in this sense is also said to be "given one" by those who attribute it to one, and can be "character with" specific others. I might have (be given) a character for honesty with my family, a character for dishonesty with my business rivals. Hume's term "character" refers to some aspect of a person that is recognizable by her fellows, and so is "given" to her by their recognition of the "inner principles" expressed in her behavior with them. In Book Two he refers to the vast importance to us of "our reputation, our character, our name" (T. 316). "Character," for Hume, can have the same grammar as "reputation" and "name"[18]—it can be *for* a characteristic, *with* some group who discern that characteristic in a person. It is not, or not always, identical with reputation, since reputation can be false, but it is related to reputation much as facts are to propositions—character is what reputation is about, but it requires reputation, recognition by others, for its ontological security. Only as expressed, recognized and "named" does inner principle count as character.

"Character" for Hume can be "character for" a single attribute, such as honesty, but it can also be the referent of a characterization that attempts to sum up all of a person's morally interesting traits or qualities. In his *History of England,* and in the second *Enquiry,* one richly differentiated "character" per person is attributed, so "character" then refers to the mix of character traits that a person has exhibited—pretty much what we today mean by character. Hume regularly sums up his verdicts on monarchs and officials, in his *History of England,* under the heading "Death and character."

And in the conclusion of the second *Enquiry* he delineates an imaginary person, a really incredible bundle of virtues: the perfect son-in-law, Cleanthes. After listing his remarkable virtues, Hume writes that "a philosopher might select this character as a model of perfect virtue" (E. 270). "This character" is what the long list of virtues specifies, the total mix of described character traits. (Cleanthes combines, in an unlikely fashion, honour and humanity with justice and kindness, all of these with legal acuity and business sense; he has gaiety with genteelness, gallantry without affectation, wit without bad manners, a tranquil soul despite trials and hardships.)

All these virtues are attributed to Cleanthes by those who know him in the various spheres where these characteristics are shown—his "character with others" (E. 265) is a character for a whole rich mix of virtues. It is significant that the mix includes "a perpetual serenity on his countenance" (E. 269), as the outer face of the "tranquillity in his soul." Even when the virtue is one that is valued mainly for its agreeability to the person who has it, it will show and be recognizable to others. Virtues that "keep us in humour with ourselves" (E. 282) will, by their expressive outward face, also help keep us in humour with such others as are around. Virtues are approved passions, and passions get expression whether or not they lead to intentional actions towards other people. The contemplator of character will be on the watch not just for benevolence but for serene countenances.

Hume can speak of "virtue in rags" as still approved virtue—a virtue like serenity which normally makes its possessor agreeable or useful in human affairs may, in a particular case, fail to deliver its usual contribution, but we still approve of it and esteem its possessor for it, "into a dungeon or desart, where the virtue can no longer be exerted in action, and is lost to all the world" (T. 584). Where we cannot love the man for his contagious serenity, or for his current witty contributions to human company, since he is (let us say) in solitary confinement, and his serenity and wit are lost to the world, we still from an impartial point of view approve of serenity and wit, and so of *his* serenity and wit, and esteem him for them.

Since moral evaluation is applied to character, and since a person can have character for a single virtue or vice,[19] then we may recognize and approve of some virtue in a person while still reserving judgment about the whole mix of traits that the person exemplifies. King Henry the Eighth of England can be given moral credit for being "sincere, open, gallant, liberal, capable of at least temporary friendship," yet at the same time censured for "violence, cruelty, profusion, rapacity, injustice, obstinacy, arrogance, bigotry, presumption, caprice."[20] He was "great" rather than "good," Hume judges, using the distinction between two sets of natural virtues that he had first drawn in the *Treatise,* Book Three, Part III. It may not in many conditions be possible to be a "great" king, and at the same time to be a "good" person. One has to have moral luck to combine, like the mythical Cleanthes, the "greatness" of public success with "good" qualities like kindness and good humour. "Perfect virtue"—that is, possession of all the virtues—will be rare, though each individual virtue need be in no way rare.

The design of practices aimed at producing good characters will of course aim at "perfect virtue," at making the human and social world safe for the coexistence of all the desirable character traits within each person. But often trade-offs will be made. Girls may be formed to be "good" while boys are trained to be "great." Some schools will sacrifice the companionable virtues to the useful ones, teach all mathematics and no music, train young people to be diligent and prudent, but neglect to help them become charming or witty. It will take an exceedingly clever designer or redesigner of social conditions to turn out a population of characters like Cleanthes', and a wise designer will want to recheck Hume's judgment that we really would welcome him and his clones.

Character, the object of the moral sentiment, and the target of such indirect moral reform as will be possible, is a cultural artifact and a somewhat abstract thing, abstracted out with the aid of a special vocabulary, from the array of persons and personalities that we encounter. To discern character, a special and especially "steady and general" point of view is necessary. From such a point of view, we will discern traits and mixtures of traits that repeat themselves in human populations, and that affect human happiness. From this general standpoint, we will not look at each person as a unique, never-to-be-repeated individual, but will look for common features, ones for which we have coined names in our moral language. Here the moral viewpoint is very different from that of the lover, whose "object" is a concrete unique person. "Desire this passionate lover to give you a character of his mistress: He will tell you, that he is at a loss for words to describe her charms" ("The Sceptic," *Essays,* p. 162). The moral evaluator cannot be at a loss for words to describe what she approves—she must be able to "give you a character for" what she approves in you. From the moral viewpoint, particular repeated and repeatable "characters" have been singled out for notice, and a special language evolved for referring to them. We "invent a peculiar set of terms, in order to express those universal sentiments of censure or approbation, which arise from humanity, or from views of general usefulness and its contrary. Virtue and Vice become then known; morals are recognized" (E. 274). It is essential to Hume's version of moral evaluation that it be shared and articulated, and it is equally essential that what is discriminates be generally recurring human characters or character traits, ones we have names for, and ones whose value we can discuss and make explicit. Far from being the sort of Hurrah-Boo theory that some twentieth-century emotivists held, Hume's theory of moral evaluation restricts it to what we can spell out and articulate in our special moral discourse. Only because we are talkers, testimonial-givers, capable of learning the meaning of terms such as honesty, honour, integrity, fidelity, patience, discretion, lenity, generosity, moderation, tenderness, can we be moral evaluators of one another.

"It may be establish'd as an undoubted maxim, *that no action can be virtuous or morally good, unless there be in human nature some motive to produce it, distinct from the sense of its morality*" (T. 479). What we morally approve is what is there, not too rarely occurring in human nature, and, like parental solicitude, there independently of our approval of it. It is more often present than absent; it has a name; it is generally welcomed; and general reasons can be given as to why it is welcome. The claim that morally approved motives must be there independently of whether or not they are evaluated does not contradict the claim that we have a special moral language for naming and praising good characters. They could be there, unnamed, until our moral discourse got going and took an interest in them. But in fact Hume thinks that they are not unnamed in other human discourses. The scientist of human nature, the author of Book Two of the *Treatise,* had no trouble finding names for human passions, some of them the very same names that the author of Book Three uses for virtues and vices. So we do have a certain amount of language-sharing between the psychological and the moral points of view. When we speak as psychologists, we will be as interested in human characters as when we are moral evaluators. But we will then refrain from explicit evaluation and concentrate on explanation. When we are moral evaluators, we will need the explanations that our psychologists provide, in order to do the evaluating in an appropriately knowledgeable way. Hume believes that attempts at moral evaluation of character are as constant a feature of human nature as any we could find—"if ever there was any thing, which cou'd be call'd natural in this sense [opposed to rare and unusual], the sentiments of morality certainly may; since there never was any nation of the world, nor any single person in any nation, who was utterly depriv'd of them, and who never, in any instance, shew'd the least approbation or dislike of manners. These sentiments are so rooted in our constitution and temper, that without entirely confounding the human mind by disease or madness, 'tis impossible to extirpate and destroy them" (T. 474). These are very strong claims for the universality of the phenomenon of a moral viewpoint with its moral language.

No parallel claims are made by Hume for the scientific viewpoint—he sees the science of human nature, in the "Introduction" to the *Treatise,* as a new enterprise, lagging behind both other "moral" enterprises and other scientific ones. It was new to aim to have a science of the moral animal, to want to have an explanation of the explainers and the moralizers. The ultimate in scientific reflection is to turn our science on ourselves, as the ultimate in moral reflection is the sort of impartial contemplation of the moral judge that Hume is attempting in Book Three. But we all naturally become judges much more automatically than we become scientists of any sort, let alone scientists of human nature. So the vocabulary of psychology could be the vocabulary of a

somewhat special and esoteric viewpoint. For Hume it wasn't—
he simply borrowed from the commonsense vocabulary, indeed
from the moral vocabulary, that was ready to hand. His psychology really is his moral psychology, in that its descriptive categories are taken over from moral discourse. We know what envy
and malice are from our evaluative discourse, and Hume's attempts to graft an explanatory discourse onto this pre-existent one
produced somewhat ptolemaic psychological principles.

It may, in any case, be a mistake to try to separate our explanatory goals very sharply from our evaluative goals. Commonsense explanations of human behavior abound, and are as inevitable a human phenomenon as moral sentiments. We are as
naturally curious about one another as we are natural mutual evaluators. "Some people have an insatiable desire of knowing the
actions and circumstances of their neighbours" (T. 453). Our explanations of each other's reactions may lack the systematic generality that Hume hoped a "science of man" would introduce, but
then what we take as our moral sentiments equally often lack that
detachment and generality of concern that Hume makes the particular hallmark of proper moral evaluation. For both our explanatory and our evaluative activities, Hume sketches what we can
now call a "character," or ideal type. As we can draw the character
of the priest or the soldier, as Theophrastus drew the character of
the boor and the back-biter, so we can also draw the character of
the moral evaluator and of the scientist of man. "Character" is
contemplated or reflected on by both these characters, with different but coordinated goals.

Virtues are "characters" or character traits that are welcomed
from the special point of view that we take when we make moral
judgments. The names of most of these traits are not reserved for
what we see only from that viewpoint, but are part of the vocabulary of anyone curious about people, anyone who studies human
abilities, passions and motivation. Such traits are "really there" in
the strongest sense that Hume can allow.[21] They, or some of them,
such as perseverance, are needed if one is to be a serious student
of human nature, and they are also included in the subject matter
of that study. When Hume, in the second *Enquiry,* speaks of "another language," that of morality (E. 272), it is not the names of

particular virtues that he gives as examples of that special language, but rather very general terms such as "vicious" and "virtuous." It is the status of actually occurring character traits such as serenity and cheerfulness *as virtues* that require the special viewpoint. But such qualities must be there in some persons, in order for the moral judge to welcome and approve of them, and so deem them virtues. Hume's "undoubted maxim" guarantees some "realism" in his "moral epistemology." These latter terms are anachronistic when used of Hume, and it is very doubtful that, could he have followed contemporary debates, he would have welcomed characterization of his views under any such labels. My only reason for mentioning them is their current fashionability, and the insistence of many other Hume commentators[22] on trying to pin him down as a "realist," a "non-realist," a "quasi-realist" or a "projectionist." I myself do not find this language very helpful for reflection on moral evaluation, or for reflection on Hume's views about it, but I will make some brief concessions to current philosophical tastes.

Hume famously writes that our moral evaluations "gild" the human world that they evaluate "with the colours, borrowed from internal sentiment," and raise "in a manner a new creation" (E. 294).[23] Moral status as virtuous or vicious, and concern with that status, are the new creation that moral judgment raises, but *what* it gilds or stains with evaluation are psychologically real traits, as real as any other qualities. Hume in this passage likens virtues and vices, insofar as they are *judged* traits, as distinct from traits *simpliciter,* to colors gilded onto some thing, furniture or natural object, that presumably had some color already, before the staining or gilding. There is no good reason to see him as likening the status of virtues to that of "secondary qualities" if these are seen as somehow less real than others, labelled "primary" ones. Hume himself had criticized that latter Lockean doctrine in "Of the modern philosophy," and he is as happy to liken moral judgments to judgments of size and shape as to those of color and beauty (T. 603, 581–582). The human mind does have a great propensity to spread itself on external objects, but in moral evaluation the "internal sentiment" with which it gilds is spread on *internal* not external objects, since it is some human minds and characters that are "gilded" with the impartial human mind's approbation of them. If we like, we can call this "projectionism," but it is no "error" theory of moral virtue.[24] There need be no illusion of something "out there" when in fact it is really "in here." The character traits *are* "out there," in the people in whom they are found. The "gilt," or approval, is in the approvers, but their actual approbation makes a real difference to the approved persons—it gives them a particular status in a moral community, and it may give them pride, or encouragement in conserving or strengthening the approved character traits. (Perhaps we could call this "internal realism"?)

It is moralists whose preferred moral entities are "laws" and "obligations," rather than virtues and vices, who may be prone to illusion, to thinking that there is something *outside all members of the human moral community* which gives "reality" to these things, and "truth" to their moral codes. It is hard to get an illusion going with Hume's preferred vocabulary of virtues and vices, seen as "certain principles in the mind and temper" (T. 477). Since "we must look within to find the moral quality" (ibid.), that is, since we must look within the person we are judging, the fact that we must also "turn our reflection into our own breasts" to see why we call that quality a *moral* one, call it a virtue, rather than just a cluster of "certain passions, motives, volitions and thoughts" (T. 468), need not surprise or upset us, or convict us of being auto-illusionists. *Of course* it takes something in a human (or at least in a sensitive animal) breast to recognize and evaluate what is in human breasts, and *of course* it takes a community of mutual moral evaluators to "create" a particular moral status, such as "depraved," or "of perfect character." Hume's moral "ontology" (if we must use such notions) of virtues and vices, necessarily in human breasts if they are anywhere, along with his "undoubted maxim," which limits the "creative" ability of the moral sentiment to mere gilding or repainting, protects him effectively from any basis for worry about the "reality" of what his moral language refers to. It is the deontologists, not the virtue recognizers, who are the easiest targets for the "error theorists."

What is peculiar about the moral sentiment, then, is the generality of its concern, the abstractness of its objects from the human reality in which they are found, the social construction of the means of finding them, the generality or extensiveness of the sympathetic understanding of human reactions required, the expected agreement from others who have met these earlier requirements, and so the calm or steadiness of verdict from time to time as well as from person to person. The moral sentiment is a sentiment or pleasure taken in other human pleasures or passions, and it is a sentiment aiming at agreement with other persons' similarly reflective sentiments. It is the sentiment of humankind for kinds of human sentiment. Hume's and Cicero's[25] undoubted maxim, that human nature must first supply the motives and passions before the moral sentiment can react to them, is a maxim that ensures not only the reality of our moral subject matter, but also the special reflexivity of moral pleasure. It is an "impression of reflection" that takes as its objects other "impressions of reflection." It needs less reflective materials as the original objects of its contemplation, the causes of its pleasure. But it can also reflect on itself, and in the "Conclusion" of Book Three Hume sketches but does not develop this turn of the moral sentiment on itself.[26] If all goes well, it will find itself to have improved, not worsened, the lot of "the party of humankind." It will bear its own survey. "It requires but very little knowledge of human affairs to perceive, that a sense of morals is a principle inherent in the soul, and one of the most powerful that enters into the composition. But this sense must certainly acquire new force, when reflecting on itself, it approves of those principles, from whence it is deriv'd, and finds nothing but what is great and good in its rise and origin" (T. 619).

But is it the case that when we look at our moral sense, its approbations, and their power and force, we find that "nothing is presented on any side but what is laudable and good"? Hume suggests that a morality like his, which is founded on "extensive sympathy with mankind," will be "the most perfect morality with which we are acquainted" (E. 276), that it can approve of itself. But of course the success of morality's reflection on itself will depend on the form, content and method of the morality in question. The true "most perfect" morality will survive its own survey, but false moralities will be shown up as false by the same test.

To see why Hume thought he had outlined a morality better able to pass the test of reflection than those he attacked, we need to look in more detail at the details of his list of virtues, and at how they compare with the "multitude of rules and precepts" (T. 457) issued by the moralists he is attacking.

9

A Catalogue of Virtues

And 'tis a most certain rule, that if there be no relation
of life, in which I cou'd not wish to stand to a particular
person, his character must so far be allow'd to be perfect. If he be as little wanting to himself as to others, his
character is entirely perfect.   (T. 606)

Each of the virtues, even benevolence, justice, gratitude, integrity, excites a different sentiment or feeling in
the spectator. The characters of *Caesar* and *Cato,* as
drawn by *Sallust,* are both of them virtuous, in the
strictest sense of the word; but in a different way . . .
The one produces love; the other esteem: The one is
amiable; the other awful: We cou'd wish to meet with
the one character in a friend; the other character we
wou'd be ambitious of in ourselves. In like manner, the
approbation, which attends natural abilities, may be
somewhat different to the feeling from that, which
arises from the other virtues, without making them entirely of a different species.   (T. 607–608)

Hume's catalogue[1] of moral virtues includes agreeable ones as well
as useful ones, self-regarding as well as other-regarding ones, "awful" as well as amiable ones, qualities of the "head" as well as those
of the "heart" and will, voluntary as well as involuntary abilities
and habits. "There are few, who are not as jealous of their character, with regard to sense and knowledge, as to honour and courage; and much more than with regard to temperance and sobriety"
(T. 607), Jealousy of character is the acid test. As Hume puts it in
the second *Enquiry,* to compile a catalogue of virtues all a person
has to do is "enter into his own breast for a moment, and consider
whether or not he should desire to have this or that quality as-

cribed to him" (E. 174). The test is not "What qualities would I wish to have?" but "What qualities would I wish my fellows to find in me?" One has to enter into one's own breast but also to listen for others' verdict.

This test lets in a great range of mental qualities, whose only common feature is that they are all generally welcomed.[2] From a moral point of view, we "reap a pleasure" (T. 591) from finding any of them in a person. I now list the qualities that Hume, in Part III, Book Three of the *Treatise,* says that, from the moral point of view, we will recognize as ones we are pleased to find in persons. I leave aside the implications of his more ambiguous citings, in Part I, of parricide, murder and incest as generally acknowledged "crimes," and leave for the following chapter his list of and commentary on the "artificial" virtues. The "natural" virtues that he lists in Part III and that he appears, sometimes with qualifications, to endorse, are: meekness, beneficence, charity, generosity, clemency, moderation, equity (T. 578), prudence, temperance, frugality, industry, assiduity, enterprise, dexterity, humanity (T. 587), "a certain easy and disengag'd behaviour" (T. 590), "a genuine and hearty pride, or self-esteem, if well conceal'd and well founded" (T. 598), courage, intrepidity, ambition, love of glory, magnanimity ("and all the other shining virtues of that kind," T. 599–600), compassion, gratitude, friendship, fidelity, zeal, disinterestedness, liberality ("and all those other qualities, which form the character of good and benevolent," T. 603), due self-assertiveness (T. 605), good sense and genius, wit and humor (T. 608), perseverance, patience, activity, vigilance, application, constancy, economy, resolution, eloquence, good humor, cleanliness (T. 610–611) "a certain *je-ne-sçais-quoi* of agreeable and handsome," and decorum (T. 612). In addition there is parental solicitude, which is clearly endorsed in Part II, Section I. Hume refuses to reduce all the "virtues" on this list to one category, such as the useful. He refuses equally firmly to exclude any, such as wit and humor, because the satisfaction they afford is not "serious" or "weighty" enough, or because, like sense and good judgment, they, while granted to be important, are found "almost invariable by any art or industry" (T. 609), and not much changed "by the motives of reward and punishment" (ibid.). He includes the "natural abilities" in his catalogue, since they pass his test. We do wish to be found to have good sense and wisdom. We do want our friendship and our enmity to be "of moment" (T. 613), not made negligible by our stupidity. "Who did ever say, except by a way of irony, that such a one was a man of great virtue, but an egregious blockhead?" (E. 314).

Hume includes cleanliness in his list of virtues (perhaps to compensate for the absence of godliness), and barely restrains himself from including "the ability to give enjoyment" that is possessed by "those we call good *women's men*" (T. 614). He does separate purely "bodily advantages" from mental ones, restricting virtues to mental qualities, but he cannot forbear noting the "great resemblance" between all the different pleasures we get from contemplating different sorts of good things, from convenient houses and "broad shoulders, a lank belly, firm joints, taper legs" (T. 615) to a scrubbed-clean appearance, wit, good humour and generosity. "The flexibility of our sentiments" (T. 617) enables us to be pleased by all these promises of pleasure, even if, like the virtuous women who welcome the company of men "whose make of body promises any extraordinary vigour," we ourselves "have no prospect of receiving that enjoyment" (T. 614–615). Whenever we are pleased by a person, whether by his character or his advantage of body, "we consider him as a person capable of contributing to the happiness or enjoyment of his fellow-creatures, whose sentiments, with regard to him, we naturally embrace" (T. 616). The moral sentiment becomes a special case of a broader, impartial, sympathy-dependent evaluation of persons. To James Beattie's horror, handsome faces are approved of, as well as handsome deeds.[3] Moral judges and judges in Miss America or Mr. Muscle contests are implicitly assimilated to one another. Hume is at his puritan-baiting cheekiest in this section, which is innocently entitled "Some farther reflexions concerning the natural virtues." As the human body is "near enough connected with us" (T. 298), whose characters the moral sentiment is pleased or displeased with, so the sentiments we have about human bodies will be near enough connected to our moral sentiments to be worthy of comment. Hume does not blunt the difference between attention to a person's heart and mind and attention to the "advantages of the body," but he does dwell on the similarities. Both give pleasure or displeasure from the "mere survey." Hume is willing to use the term "approbation" widely enough to cover our satisfaction in convenient houses and "the beauty of men" (T. 615) as well as in virtuous character, as long as this satisfaction does arise from a calm survey of them "without any particular interest[4] in them" (T. 617). Human beings have a great range of capacities to give pleasure, and signs of these capacities can yield a disinterested reflective pleasure.

We could schematize Hume's comparisons and distinctions as shown in the figure below. I choose the term "psychological," rather than "non-bodily," to label the qualities that count as moral virtues, since many of them are expressive excellencies, necessarily involving the body, and others, like cleanliness, involve our attitudes to our own bodies. The cut is between what is only bodily,

Varieties of approbation

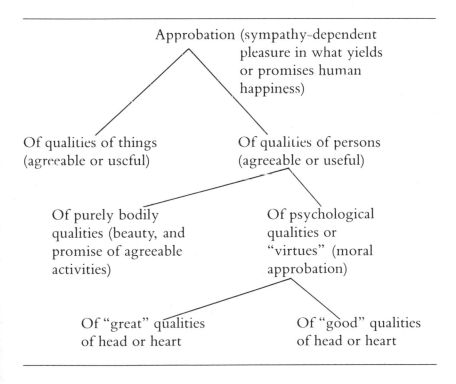

and what is expressive of personality. Much that goes into beauty of face, movement and voice is not purely bodily (as are bone structure, height, eye color) but expresses some of the virtues that Hume wants on his list. There are "all those qualities, which render a person lovely or valuable, there is also a certain *je-ne-sçais-quoi* of agreeable and handsome, that concurs to the same effect" (T. 611–612). About the last, Hume in the second *Enquiry* writes that "this class of accomplishments, therefore, must be trusted entirely to the blind but sure testimony of taste and sentiment; and must be considered as a part of ethics, left by nature to baffle all the pride of philosophy, and make her sensible of her narrow boundaries and slender acquisitions" (E. 267). But his own philosophical pride is not so baffled—he can accommodate what puritan moralists cannot, the fact that there is such a thing as moral charm, and can grant its very close link to other sorts of charm. "There is a manner, a grace, an ease, a genteelness, an I-know-not-what, which some men possess above others, which is very different from external beauty and comeliness, and which, however, catches our affection almost as suddenly and powerfully. And though this *manner* be chiefly talked of in the passion between the sexes, where the concealed magic is easily explained, yet surely much of it prevails in all our estimation of characters, and forms no inconsiderable part of personal merit" (ibid.). Hume can afford to admit moral charm, even magic moral "pheromones," where other moralists would find them an embarrassment; for his moral system is a happiness-bent one, and gives a central place to the agreeable. The Humean moralist will want to know what does please us, both spontaneously and more reflectively, and charm by definition pleases. We may sometimes be suspicious of its magic, we may look for some compensatory *gravitas* to give it moral weight, but Hume is surely right that it does catch our affection, and that we are pleased to have it attributed to ourselves. Other things equal, it counts as personal merit, so it is on Hume's list of moral virtues.

The catalogue is pretty clearly calculated not just to present the truth about our sincere mutual evaluations, but also to create a murmur among the zealots. Although Hume leaves his explicit demotion of the puritan "virtues" into vices until the second *En-*

quiry, the *Treatise* can have left his readers in no doubt that here, as Alasdair MacIntyre has recently insisted,[5] was an apostate from Calvinism. The hedonism of Hume's theory is one of its most striking features, and one calculated to outrage those who had invested in the manufacture of a supply of dismal dresses for morality. Hume strips them off, "and nothing appears but gentleness, humanity, beneficence, affability; nay, even at proper intervals, play, frolic, and gaiety. She talks not of useless austerities and rigours, suffering and self-denial" (E. 279). John Laird characterizes Hume's description of the natural virtues as "rather jejune," summing it up inadequately thus: "His theory was, in brief, that our motives were moral or virtuous when they were humane or kindly."[6] There need be nothing very kindly about proper pride, and insinuation and charm are more human than humane. Hume's presentation of his catalogue of virtues is part of a young rebel's daring attempt to topple a puritan establishment. Those Scottish elders who blocked his appointment to a university chair may not have read this far in the *Treatise*; but if they had, these later sections would have added plenty of fuel to fire their determination not to have ethics taught to their sons by the author of the *Treatise*. Moral charm, and other sexy moral virtues, were quite an innovation to the Calvinists. Perhaps it is more correct to say that the open valuing of them was a departure from the dominant tradition, since, as Hume himself emphasizes, veils, disguises, even perhaps dismal dresses, along with other obstacles, prohibitions and delays, can enhance rather than really deny pleasure, and the puritans were not unaware of this.

Hobbes and Spinoza, before Hume, had in their ethics been quite free of puritan scruples about the pleasurable. But their emphasis was on power, on the means to obtain a future apparent good, and so they were with the Christians in advocating a concentration on "glory," the pleasure of knowing one has power, riches in heaven. Hume balances the useful, along with pleasure in utility, against the immediately agreeable, against pleasure taken in goods other than utility—in wit, charm, beauty. His ethics encourages enjoyment, including enjoyment now, not endlessly delayed gratification. In the special areas of life where the artificial virtues impose constraints, the agreeable may have to take second place to the useful, but even there Hume strains to show that new pleasures as well as new powers are made possible by justice, and by other virtues valued primarily for their usefulness. He thinks he must show that utility naturally *pleases* us now, not just that it promises us future pleasures. The virtues that are undoubtedly socially useful, and valued for their usefulness, virtues such as benevolence and kindness, are also "sweet, smooth, tender, and agreeable" (E. 282), both to the benevolent person and to companions who are in no direct way the beneficiaries of his benevolence. "These feelings, being delightful in themselves, are necessarily communicated to the spectators, and melt them into the same fondness and delicacy" (E. 257).

In his later economic essays we can discern a parallel reverse attempt on Hume's part to show the usefulness of enjoyment and consumption, but he does not in his ethics feel any need to justify agreeability by linking it to utility. The bottom line is hedonism, and a hedonism suspicious of the wisdom of the inherited maxims that require delay of gratification. In his ethics, as much as in his cosmology, Hume reacts sharply against all those who take our present condition to be "merely a passage to something farther; a porch, which leads to a greater, and vastly different building; a prologue, which serves only to introduce the piece" (E. 141). He is not just this-worldly; he has prudence in this world, and other aspects of the *utile,* balanced by wit, gaiety, charm, grace and other aspects of the *dulce.* He is suspicious of demands for self-denial, even when they do not come from pulpits, since self-denial tends to "sour the temper" (E. 270) and temper is what counts. Prudence has its place, since avoidance of future harm is only sensible, but temperance is not of self-evident value. "If the unlimited use of strong liquors, for instance, no more impaired health or the faculties of mind and body than the use of air or water, it would not be a whit more vicious or blameable" (E. 280).

This emphasis on pleasure as the good for the sake of which we sensibly act, and as what we sensibly have in view when we endorse enlightened versions of morality, is what Bentham found so enlightening in Hume's writings on ethics. But Bentham blunts Hume's distinction between the useful and the agreeable, distorting the agreeable into cash utility. The kind of calculative thinking appropriate for judging what has greater utility is carried over into evaluation of the agreeable, in a way that Hume avoids. Bentham not merely extends the label "utility" to cover the value of the agreeable, but he extends to the whole of ethics the accountant's style of thinking which Hume invokes only for justice, that relatively dismal virtue whose value does lie much more squarely in utility, as Hume uses the word, than in any agreeability. It is *disagreeable* to take from the poor to get rich creditors paid, disagreeable, to humane people, to insist on penal statutes being inflexibly carried out. The cost of this useful virtue is very great sacrifice of the agreeable, and that is one reason Hume finds it to be such an exceptional case, among the virtues.

One very good reason for attending to the details of Hume's treatment of the natural virtues, then, is to appreciate the hedonism, rather than the utilitarianism, of his thinking about ethics, to see the dominant place the agreeable has there, a place it does not have in his account of cautious justice. The agreeable virtues are not cautious virtues, and some of the useful virtues, such as generosity, enterprise and courage, can be as far from caution as are wit and high-spiritedness. Hume writes in the second *Enquiry* that, just as when we call a person "*too good*" we are implicitly acknowledging that benevolence *is* one virtue (but only one), so when we call a person too high-spirited, or too full of amorous enterprise ("Harry the IVth of France"), we "imply more esteem than many panegyrics" (E. 258). Harry's amours may have "hurt his interest and his cause," but interest is not everything, and even those who see such amorous enterprise as a weakness in a monarch will "allow that this very weakness . . . chiefly endears that hero, and interests them in his fortunes" (ibid.). Hume repeats Polybius' account of how Dicaearchus, the Macedonian general, "erected one altar to impiety, another to injustice, in order to bid defiance to mankind" (E. 240). Hume's own altar to impiety stands beside a modest altar to sensuality, and, like those of Dicaearchus, they are erected out of defiance. In Hume's case, it was defiance of the moralists whose "perpetual cant"[7] of puritan virtue seems to have provoked some disgust at the very notion of self-denial. There is some spleen, as well as irony, in his discussions of their favorite virtues.

Such moralists took humility as well as self-denial to be a virtue. Their reason for preaching self-control was not just the future cost to the self of any self-indulgence now, but the sinfulness of the to-be-controlled self, the lowness of its current tastes in pleasure. Humility was therefore in order. Hume inverts these values, making humility a vice, one of those dismal counterfeit virtues that "stupify the understanding and harden the heart, obscure the fancy and sour the temper" (E. 270). This is the open censure of the *Enquiry,* but the *Treatise*'s more "indirect manner of insinuating blame" is no less forceful. Vanity is found to be "a social passion, and a bond of union among men" (T. 491), and the first natural virtue to be given an extended discussion, after the preliminaries of Part III, Section I, is proper pride. "Nothing is more useful to us in the conduct of life, than a due degree of pride, which makes us sensible of our own merit, and gives us a confidence and assurance in all our projects and enterprizes" (T. 596–597). Not only is such pride useful; it is "always agreeable to ourselves." If well-founded and decently veiled, it need not be disagreeable to our fellows. It is one of the virtues that make a person "great" rather than "good" (in the narrow sense of benevolence, in which a person can be "too good"). Indeed, for Hume, who distrusts the traditional heroic virtues, it is the main component of "greatness of mind."

Hume includes modesty as a virtue, as well as pride. As pride is a due sense of our own force, modesty is "a just sense of our weakness" (T. 592). Modesty in others is always welcome, but in oneself it "produces often uneasiness" (T. 597). Whether or not it does this will depend on the sort of weakness we have, and its importance. To know one's own strength or force justly is necessarily to know its limits, and so, in all but the omnipotent, due pride will be accompanied by due modesty. In a society where division of labor is encouraged, where cooperation works best when different persons' particular strengths are complementary and not reduplicative, a modest sense of what one cannot do but that others can, of where one is weak while others are strong, need not cause uneasiness, when it is accompanied by a due sense of what strengths one does have. Modesty is not humility, that necessarily disagreeable, debilitating passion, that dejection of the spirits which Hume had, with significant brevity, discussed in

Book Two. Humility is a painful dwelling on shameful features of oneself, features one would like to hide. But modesty is simply a recognition of the limits of one's grounds for pride. Only the "conceited," who need to believe that everything that is theirs is the best of its kind, will shun modesty. Such a fool will want to find "some person, that is more foolish, in order to keep himself in good humour with his own parts and understanding" (T. 596). The person with due virtuous pride will not have to find inferiors, in order to keep her good humour, since her pride will be accompanied by correlative modesty, by calm acknowledgment of such weakness where others have strengths.

In his discussion of virtuous pride, Hume lifts one of the "limitations" imposed in Book Two on pride's conformity to "the general system, *that all agreeable objects, related to ourselves, by an association of ideas and of impressions, produce pride, and disagreeable ones, humility*" (T. 290)—namely the second limitation, which restricts the causes of pride to things that are "peculiar to ourselves, or at least common to us with a few persons" (T. 291). This restriction not only introduced comparison with others into our self-evaluations, but ruled out pride whenever, "upon comparing ourselves with others, as we are every moment apt to do, we find we are not in the least distinguish'd" (T. 292). Now, in Book Three, pride in its moralized form is freed from this restriction. Only those with "an ill grounded conceit of themselves, are forever making those comparisons, nor have they any other method of supporting their vanity. A man of sense and merit is pleas'd with himself, independent of all foreign considerations" (T. 596). What Book Two termed normal pride now becomes "conceit," and the term "pride" is promoted to the name of virtue. This is to some extent just part of Hume's Christian-baiting. He can't resist the opportunity, not just to transfer the monkish vices to the column of the virtues, but to give the first of the natural virtues he treats in detail the name of the first cardinal sin. But this is not merely impudent verbal legerdemain. Pride, as Book Two had analyzed it, requires a judgment that something about one is relatively fine, and the most natural relativization is to what, in that line, other people have. It is natural but not inescapable. Pride in virtue still requires the verdict that something about one is good of its kind, but that verdict is now less directly based on a simple comparison with what other persons have. The original restriction was, as Hume wrote, "deriv'd from the very nature of the subject" (T. 290). What feature of its nature? Presumably from its vulnerability, its need to have other persons second the evaluations on which it is based. It is linked to the third limitation, that the cause of pride be something fine that is "very discernible and obvious, and that not only to ourselves, but to others also" (T. 292). But already in Book Two, comparison was extended to cases where one compares one's present state, achievement or position with one's own earlier state, and is therefore able to let one's own earlier self stand in for another person, as object of comparison. "The comparison being the same, as when we reflect on the sentiments of others, must be attended with the same effects" (T. 376). Hume in this passage explains how, by this alienation of our earlier selves, we can "rejoice for our pains, and grieve for our pleasures. Thus the prospect of past pain is agreeable, when we are satisfy'd with our present condition" (ibid.). Our less accomplished earlier selves can also play the role of "inferiors" on whom our present self has satisfactorily advanced, giving ground for pride. When we take pride in such increase (or good maintenance) of a socially valuable quality, others will usually second it, and we will not need to find ourselves at the top of the heap to sustain pride.

Hume, in his essay "Of the dignity or meanness of human nature," written very soon after Book Three of the *Treatise,* reports that he has heard thoughtless people observe "that there are few women possessed of beauty, in comparison of those who want it; not considering, that we bestow the epithet of *beautiful* only on such as possess a degree of beauty, that is common to them with a few. The same degree of beauty in a woman is called deformity, which is treated as real beauty in one of our sex" (*Essays,* p. 84). If we are determined to honor only the top few, then whom we honor will depend on what comparison-class we take; we can almost always alter a person's comparative standing by widening or narrowing the comparison class. A morality intent on selecting the few who are to pass through the narrow door into heaven may be forced into invidious comparisons, but there are other ways open to us to fix and to adjust our standards of personal merit.

The standards of excellence that govern our pride, when it is virtuous pride, will be those appropriate to our special circumstances, and the merit we look for will be "real and intrinsic merit" (T. 291). Of course our understanding of it, our recognition of it as *merit,* will depend on our participation in social life and on our understanding of a shared language. But that does not restrict it to evaluations in which other persons' achievements set the relevant standards. Just as, even when we do compare persons with one another, we praise some children for accomplishments that adults would not take pride in, and admire adults for accomplishments that would shock us if we found them in children, so our reflective sense of what is of value in persons, and of what is reasonably aimed at and expected of different sorts of persons, can lead us to have standards for ourselves that, while they depend on interaction and social learning for their very possibility, are still in the relevant sense "independent of all foreign considerations."

Hume had made a point in Book Two of insisting that virtue is an appropriate reason for pride. "The most rigid morality allows us to receive a pleasure from reflecting on a generous action" (T. 298), and Hume's less rigid morality encourages us to feel pride also in "pleasing by our wit, good humour, or any other accomplishment" (T. 297). He extends the list of prideworthy virtues to include some agreeable ones that "the vulgar systems of ethics" (ibid.) had excluded, and with this extension comes that special case of reflection: due virtuous pride as a proper cause of due virtuous pride. Just as we can be proud of generosity the virtue, so we can be proud of pride the virtue, and our pride in both cases will have to be "due" and duly modest, in order to be virtuous. Even when it is virtuous pride, and virtuous meta-pride, it will still need the "seconding" of fair-minded sympathetic others, and so will retain the close link that Book Two established with "the love of fame." Hume writes in "Of the dignity or meanness of human nature" that "to love the fame of laudable actions approaches so near the love of laudable actions for their own sake, that these passions are more capable of mixture, than any other kinds of affection; and it is almost impossible to have the latter without some degree of the former" (*Essays,* p. 86). The close linking of "our reputation, our character, our name" (T. 316), and of proper concern for them, persists into the *Enquiry,* where Hume writes, "Another spring of our constitution, that brings a great addition of force to moral sentiment, is the love of fame . . . By our continual and earnest pursuit of a character, a name, a reputation in the world, we bring our own deportment and conduct frequently in review, and consider how they appear in the eyes of those who approach and regard us. This constant habit of surveying ourselves, as it were, in reflection, keeps alive all the sentiments of right and wrong, and begets in noble natures, a certain reverence for themselves as well as others, which is the surest guardian of every virtue" (E. 276). This self-"reverence" is a solemn version of self-esteem, or proper pride. It needs the nourishment of the esteem of those one esteems. It also needs their verdict to confirm or correct one's own self-evaluations, especially evaluations concerning how proper and properly veiled one's pride is, whether or not it is verging on conceit. "No one can well distinguish *in himself* betwixt the vice and virtue, or be certain, that his esteem of his own merit is well-founded" (T. 597–598).

Any catalogue of virtues, Hume's included, includes courage. Among the great or "shining" virtues are "courage, integrity, ambition, love of glory, magnanimity" (T. 599–600), all with their strong admixure of self-esteem. "An excessive courage and magnanimity, especially when it displays itself under the frowns of fortune, contributes, in a great measure, to the character of a hero" (T. 600). But Hume has almost as many doubts about the character of the hero as about the character of the humble saint. Or rather, he has reservations about specifically *military* glory and heroism. "Men of cool reflexion are not so sanguine in their praises of it. The infinite confusions and disorder, which it has caus'd in the world, diminish much of its merit in their eyes. When they wou'd oppose the popular notions on this head, they always paint out the evils, which this suppos'd virtue has produc'd in human society" (T. 600–601). Heroism on the battlefield and intrepid leadership in war may "dazzle" us into admiration, but Hume reminds us that it is dazzling war heroes who are the authors of all the "mischief" of the devastation of provinces, and the sack of cities (ibid.).

Book Two had prepared us for this verdict on military heroes. There Hume had commented that our unreflective admiration of valour tends to be reserved for our own troops and generals, especially when victorious. The equally courageous leaders of the enemy are often detested "under the character of cruel, perfidious, unjust and violent," as "bloody minded," taking pleasure in death and destruction (T. 348). It is not easy to form steady impartial judgments of military virtue. In the second *Enquiry,* Hume quotes Demosthenes' generous praise of Philip of Macedon's courage and ambition, which show that an enemy's courage can be recognized, but his treatment there of the military virtues is as cool as in the *Treatise.* He cites Tacitus' description of the warlike Suevi, aiming even in their hairstyles at striking terror in their enemies; he cites Herodotus' account of the Scythian esteem for those of their fellows who had collected the largest number of enemy scalps (tanned and used as towels); he cites Thucydides on Homeric robber heroes, and Spenser's description of the customs prevailing in "many barbarous parts of Ireland." The moral is that military courage is valued by "barbaric" peoples, and in times when civilized life reverts to barbarism. Martial bravery, and the conditions under which it flourishes, destroy "sentiments of humanity; a virtue surely much more useful and engaging" (E. 255).[8]

In the *Enquiry*'s cool reflections, Hume moves immediately from courage as a virtue to another "of the same class," namely "that undisturbed philosophical tranquillity, superior to pain, sorrow, anxiety, and each assault of adverse fortune" (E. 256). There is a form of peaceable courage which is rightly admired, even if it is less "shining" and "dazzling" than courage on the killing fields. After Demosthenes' representation, under "shining colours," of Philip "exposing himself to every wound; his eye gored, his neck wrested, his arm, his thigh pierced, whatever part of his body fortune should seize on, that cheerfully relinquishing" (E. 254), we get Hume's parallel, less gory representation of the philosophic "grandeur" of Socrates' "perpetual serenity and contentment, amidst the greatest poverty and domestic vexations" (E. 256). Hume does not even mention Socrates' death here, contenting himself with the forms of "magnanimity" shown by "the heroes in philosophy" in the ancient world, even before their noble deaths. He tries to shift the mantle of "greatness" and "grandeur" from the military hero to those whose courage could not, even by their enemies, be termed courage in a cruel enterprise. "The most detested of all vices" (T. 605) is angry cruelty. Just as a person may find it difficult to distinguish in herself conceit from due pride, so she may find it difficult to distinguish cruelty, love of death and destruction, from military heroism. While Hume encourages us to rescue the virtue of due pride from its confusion with vicious conceit, he is not so keen to preserve the good reputation of military courage, or to distinguish it from ruthless violence. We are warned that in encouraging it we may be encouraging war, cruelty and destruction. Courage has to be transferred from the battlefield to more peaceful fields (or to merely domestic battlefields), before it gets approved as a virtue. Once there, it becomes scarcely distinguishable from patience, serenity and the virtues that Hume usually puts under the heading of the "amiable" rather then the "awful," the good rather than the great.

The virtues that make a person morally "good" rather than morally "great" are those we naturally value in our companions, even if we have some trouble being proud of them in ourselves. (Hume takes it for granted that we would all naturally prefer awed respect to mere affection. It takes the special moral point of view to get us to welcome good nature in ourselves as much as in our companions.) The good but not necessarily great qualities of a person are those that render him "a safe companion, an easy friend, a gentle master, an agreeable husband, or an indulgent father" (T. 606). This is not the character of that "great" man, Cato, whose "character we wou'd be ambitious of in ourselves" (T. 608). Here is what Sallust writes of Cato, in comparison with the more amiable Caesar: "Caesar was held great because of his benefactions and lavish generosity, Cato for the uprightness of his life. The former became famous for his gentleness and compassion, the austerity of the latter had brought him prestige. Caesar gained glory by giving, helping, and forgiving; Cato by never stooping to bribery. One was a refuge for the unfortunate, the other a scourge for the wicked. The good nature of the one was applauded, the steadfastness of the other."[9] Cato, like Caesar, was "virtuous in the strictest sense of the word" (T. 607), but he does not come across as "an easy friend, a gentle master, an agreeable husband, or an indulgent father." Hume really does give us a *catalogue* of virtues, and, like any catalogue, it contains diverse items, not necessarily easily combined. The "good" affections or passions are different from the "awful" ones, and what makes a person an indulgent father may unfit him from being a successfully ruthless general, or even an austerely upright man like Cato, who could argue against "womanish entreaties" and against Caesar's plea for mercy for the conspirator Publius Lentulus, and successfully convince the senate that Lentulus should receive the legally prescribed punishment for the murder and arson that he had planned but not carried out. As a result of Cato's austere uprightness, Lentulus was duly taken to a dark stinking dungeon and there executed by strangling. Cato *was* "a scourge for the wicked." To see his austere virtue, it will be better not to ask if "there be no relation of life, in which I cou'd not wish to stand" (T. 606) to him, better not to "confine our view to that narrow circle, in which any person moves" (T. 602). A larger circle, a view to public good, forefathers' laws, and deterrence to other world-be traitors have to be considered, to appreciate Cato's unamiable virtues.

Hume, in the section "Of goodness and benevolence," is not giving us a general description of moral virtue as such, as Laird and others[10] seem to have thought. He is supplementing his earlier section "Of greatness of mind" with one on goodness of mind. Benevolence does not swallow up all the other virtues: as this section itself emphasizes, there are equally important, not so benevolent virtues, such as the capacity for appropriate anger, the want of which "may even be a proof of weakness and imbecility" (T. 605). In the second *Enquiry* we get both warnings about some thoughtless and counter-productive forms of benevolence, and a reminder that as wise a moralist as Epictetus "scarcely ever mentioned the sentiment of humanity and compassion, but in order to put his disciples on their guard against it" (E. 319). Hume does not put us on our guard against it, but he does put us on our guard against some forms of it, and he balances it with more self-assertive virtues. From the virtuously benevolent person "the hungry receive food, the naked clothing, *the ignorant and slothful skill and industry*" (E. 178, my emphasis). Lest we miss the point, Hume adds a couple of pages later: "Giving alms to common beggars is naturally praised; because it seems to carry relief to the distressed and indigent: but when we observe the encouragement thence arising to idleness and debauchery, we regard that species of charity rather as a weakness than a virtue" (E. 180). The person with benevolence the virtue will feed and clothe the indigent by giving them, where possible, skill and industry. On cool reflection, Hume has doubts about the traditional virtue of charity, as well as about its companions, humility and the willingness to fight the good fight. All the Christian virtues, and many of the ancient ones (Roman martial valor), get overhauled and qualified before being endorsed. And even the endorsed ones can be in some tension with each other, as the "great" and "awful" ones seem to be with the "good" and "amiable."

The good and the great may compete, and so on occasion may the useful and the agreeable. One contrast that Hume tries to play down is that between the virtues of the heart and the excellencies of the head. He does his best to reject this bit of recent intellectual inheritance, whereas he seems happy enough to work within a scheme that recognizes the difference between the *dulce* and the *utile,* as well as that between the amiable and the awful. He sees the rejected distinction to be a theological invention of the modern era, one without which his more admired ancient moralists managed very well. So although he devotes a section to "natural abilities," he spends most of it arguing that there is no good reason to try to distinguish abilities from the other internal principles of the mind, to persuade us that abilities are virtues, and virtues abilities. Motivational forces and intellectual capacities are not sharply separable, and neither are under any very significant control either of the will or of those who try to act on others by "motives of reward and punishment, praise and blame" (T. 609). Neither a "slow apprehension" nor "a splenetic temper" will be changed much by any reformer's or self-reformer's schemes, so there is no reason to pick out bad temper as a moral vice, while treating faulty apprehension as a god-given limitation. Stupidity, Hume rather cruelly notes, is insupportable in a companion—it takes parental love to tolerate it. Only philosophers who are "divines under that disguise" (E. 322) will insist on treating moral evaluation as primarily a preamble to reward or punishment, and so make "this circumstance, of *voluntary* or *involuntary,* the foundation of their whole theory" (ibid.). And even they, if they are realistic, will soon see that not just stupidity but "cowardice, meanness, levity, anxiety, impatience, folly, and many other qualities of the mind, might appear ridiculous and deformed, contemptible and odious, though independent of the will" (E. 321). Moral beauty and loveliness, like beauty of body and face, is more the gift of fortune than an accomplishment of strength of will.

It was some divines, of course, who had included in their lists of virtues that set of gloomy habits of life that are significantly absent from Hume's *Treatise* list, and that are explicitly demoted to vices in the second *Enquiry.* These "monkish" pseudo-virtuous habits are there listed as "celibacy, fasting, penance, mortification, self-denial, humility, silence, solitude" (E. 270). The reasons given there for their demotion, as we have seen, are that they "cross all . . . desirable ends; stupify the understanding and harden the heart, obscure the fancy and sour the temper" (ibid.). A mind cultivated and expressed in a more cheerful and friendly mode of life is, he writes, "a more animating and rejoicing spectacle, than if dejected with melancholy, tormented with anxiety, irritated with rage, or sunk into the most abject baseness and degeneracy" (E. 277). "Degeneracy" is his verdict on the alternation of debilitating depressive states and manic furies that the religiously devout often display.[11] In the twelfth part of his *Dialogues on Natural Religion,* and in the *Natural History of Religion,* as well as throughout the *History of England,* he offers similar characterizations of the peculiar states of mind for which "religion as it has commonly been found in the world," and in particular the Christian religion that he knew at close quarters, had been responsible, or for which it had at least provided expression and deadly license.

This raises an awkward question, namely whether to such anxious, rage-filled, self-hating persons, with their hardened hearts, stupefied understandings, obscured fancies and soured tempers, such character traits do not bear their own survey as successfully as do those on Hume's preferred list, to his preferred non-Puritans. The sour may well approve of sourness, the hard-hearted of ruthlessness. In a sense I think this is undeniable. But the self-hating cannot coherently love themselves for their self-hatred. If self-hatred *is* properly put on the list of monkish supposed virtues, if the sort of "humility" that is required of the devout is a sense of their baseness, then whatever approval they can give to it had better not elevate their self-assessment enough to bring sinful pride. Humility as a virtue faces a paradox, namely that the very approval of it seems to threaten to destroy the thing approved. Pride in due pride presents no paradox, and neither does shame for shame, but pride in shame and shame for pride are at best unstable, degenerate cases of reflexivity. Whatever point of view the religious adopt from which to do their approving of humility and their disapproving of all pride, it cannot be the Humean moral point of view, from which approbation is indistinguishable from pride in virtue and love of the virtuous (T. 575). The religious, in any case, do not take the moral point of view to be the point of view *of humanity;* they take it to be the point of view of an outside judge, external to the judged. It is bearing God's survey, not bearing their own survey, that they aim at. The failure of the monkish and self-denying virtues to meet the Humean test of successful reflexivity is not likely to worry the monks and self-deniers too much, since they must deny or disown any trust in their own unaided powers of surveying. The disagreement between the self-deniers and the self-affirmers, the party against humanity and the party for humanity, can scarcely be settled by simply prejudging matters by using the latter's standard of judgment.

Hume can and does (for example, in his discussion in the *History* of Becket's character) point out the falseness of any pretense the religious may make of denying ultimate authority to any human judge—it will always be the survey of one of us, priest, pope, prophet or accusing self, that is taken as the crucial survey. Some human *persona* for the divine judge must always be found, if moral judgment is to be made here and now. The religious seem to have had no difficulty finding human moral judges and recognizing their authority. The cost of the self-denial of the judged is the self-aggrandizement of those they recognize as judges. The alternative to reflexivity, as the moral test, is a division of labor into active and passive, into judges and judged. The alternative to requiring *us* to bear *our* own survey is requiring *most* of us to face the survey of a *few* of us, or, as in Kant's solution, requiring most of each person's passions to face the survey of one privileged one. Self-denial cannot be denial of *all* of oneself, or collective abasement the debasement of everyone. The longer story about what is wrong, what is false, what is self-deceived, what is unstable, and what is self-contradictory in the religious moralists' alternative to Hume's version of morality is given in Hume's later works, not in the *Treatise* or in the second *Enquiry*. Where the latter inveighs against the evaluations of the furious and gloomy purveyors of dismal dresses for morality, I have read into its rhetoric hints of that longer story about the "degeneracy" of most religious moralities. The case for "the charms of a facetious wit or flowing affability" (E. 277) over the anxious torment of a sense of sin is made in the *Treatise* more with facetious wit than with any anxiety to rebut a foreseen charge of circularity. To be facetious, the circularity of appealing to the survey and judgment of cheerful friendly wit-loving people to get approval of cheerfulness, friendliness and wit seems to be taken to be a wholly virtuous circularity.

Hume does not himself raise the question of whether, in order to take up the moral point of view as he characterizes it, to do any moral surveying, one will not need a modicum of the very qualities that one will approve from that viewpoint. Clearly one needs the capacity for sympathy, and surely also equity, delicacy of discrimination, delicacy of taste in pleasures, and lack of stupidity. The hard-hearted, stupefied, unimaginative, and sour-tempered will be effectively disqualified as moral judges, as "judicious spectators." They will be incapable of sympathizing with all those affected by the particular character trait that is up for judgment, of putting themselves imaginatively into the shoes of representative persons who have "commerce" with a person with such a character trait. Even before equity comes in to correct the natural bias of sympathy, there has to be the capacity for sympathy, for understanding, for a wide-ranging imagination. Certain sorts and degrees of vice, and indeed precisely those of which Hume accuses the monks—namely hardened hearts, stupefied understandings, obscured fancies and sour tempers—are the ones that would positively disable a person from taking up the moral point of view. This at least saves the monks from self-condemnation from the Humeanly moral viewpoint, and gives them what they profess to respect: judgment from an *external* judge. But I am not sure that it can count as generosity to them.

Hume's catalogue of virtues has challenging inclusions and exclusions. The absence of the "monkish virtues," the prominent position of due pride, the presence of non-solemn virtues such as wit and good humor, the qualifications on the heroic virtues, the presence of intellectual, expressive and body-involving excellences, all give Hume's list the character more of a proclamation than of a summary of received moral wisdom. They are so many theses nailed to the Chirnside kirk door, or at least pinned up in its austere porch. Hume wrote to Frances Hutcheson that he wanted to "take my Catalogue of Virtues from Cicero's *Offices,* not from the *Whole Duty of Man,*"[12] but it is not so much Cicero's rather pompous *Offices* as Theophrastus' *Characters* that Hume seems at times to be emulating in his list of vices. Theophrastus gives us the character of the "nasty" person, with his exposed scabs, bad nails, unshaven body hair, dirty clothing, black rotten teeth; the person who blows his nose at table, showers one with spittle as he talks, hiccups in one's face while drinking, goes to bed with one with his hands unwashed, his shoes still on his feet. Hume's mention of stinking breath and unwashed bodies is more in the spirit of the late peripatetic philosophy than in the spirit of Cicero's pompous advice to public servants, or equally smug advice to the aging, who are enjoined to welcome the failing of their sexual powers,[13] to brace up and avoid drowsiness, sloth, forgetfulness and moroseness (all taken by Cicero as avoidable by strength of will). Theophrastus, with a lot more facetious wit than Cicero, fills out Aristotle's account of what makes a person an unwelcome companion or fellow citizen with his vivid portrayals of the stupid who salt their lentil soup twice over, making it inedible; of the surly who curse the stone they stumble over; of the officious who add, to a woman's name on her tombstone, the names of her husband and parents, adding "All those were worthy people"; of the tactless who inveigh against womankind at weddings and drag those sunk in unconvivial moods into their drunken dances; of the garrulous person who sits down by a stranger and launches into a eulogy of his wife, followed by an account of his last night's dreams, and the dishes he ate at dinner; of the buffoon who lifts his shirt in the presence of freeborn women, who beats time as the lute-player plays, "and when he would spit something out, spits it across the table at the servant."[14] Hume's catalogue of virtues could well be an intended reconstruction of Theophrastus' missing version of good characters, so well do they agree in the vices they choose to highlight, and in their delight both in sly satire and in occasional open abuse.[15]

At least part of Hume's campaign as a moralist is directed against moral nastiness, against the moral equivalents of bad breath, dirty nails, going to bed with one's shoes on. Other equally important parts of it are directed against cruelty, vindictiveness, masochism and self-hatred, especially in their pseudo-moral disguises. The test for virtue, for what makes a quality an approved quality, is "tendency to the good of mankind" (T. 578), recognized by impartial sympathy with all of those affected by the presence of that quality of mind. Vices are anything that renders "any intercourse with the person dangerous or disagreeable" (ibid.). Human happiness is the touchstone, and Hume takes it to be obvious that happiness requires fellowship, commerce, intercourse. Consistently with this test, he includes in his catalogue of virtues all and only the qualities of head, heart and expressive body that he believes we will agree do make a person a welcome fellow, whether in "that narrow circle, in which any person moves" (T. 602) or in "the greater society or confederacy of mankind" (E. 281).

10

The Laws of Nature

The first and original principle of human society . . . is
no other than that natural appetite betwixt the sexes,
which unites them together, and preserves their union,
till a new tye takes place in their concern for their common offspring.   (T. 486)

By the conjunction of forces, our powers is augmented:
By the partition of employments, our ability encreases:
And by mutual succour we are less expos'd to fortune
and accidents: 'Tis by this additional *force, ability,* and
security, that society becomes advantageous.   (T. 485)

. . . to prove that those laws, however necessary, are
entirely artificial, and of human invention; and consequently that justice is an artificial, and not a natural virtue.   (T. 526)

Hume is one of many (Plato, Cicero, Grotius, Hobbes, Rousseau)
who tell us a story about "the origin of justice." Hume's moral tale
is told to make clear the sense in which justice is an "artificial"
virtue, the sense also in which its rules are not improperly called
"Laws of Nature" (T. 484). His tale is of natural human inventiveness, and of the self-gratifying self-regulation of our vigilant and
inventive passions, in particular one of them that the story highlights, since it poses the problem to which justice is the solution.
He calls this passion "the interested affection." Although only one
among many human passions, this one is especially troublesome,
especially vigilant and especially inventive. It shows an alarming
tendency to become a ruling passion, indeed to cannibalize the
other human passions. The history of the word "interest"[1] reflects
this tendency. Indeed, Hume's own account of the self-regulation

of "the interested affection" tends to be read today as an account of the self-regulation of one all-encompassing desire, which comes to be labelled "self-interest"; and so justice, the sensible and virtuous self-regulation of the interested passion, swells to become the core of all of morality.

Hume's "justice" is no such imperialist virtue. It does have several guises, but it does not comprehend every moral excellence. Equity, considerateness, non-cruelty, obedience to the law of one's land are all different virtues from Humean justice. It is concerned only with the restraint of the "love of gain." It does not even seem, except incidentally, to include restraint of aggressive impulses, respect for any right to life. (Unlike Locke, Hume does not include one's own body within one's property.) Humean justice redirects the desire to accumulate transferable goods, and is not, or not directly, concerned with any passion to inflict non-transferable evils, such as insult, wounds or death. Hume's "justice" can be criticized for not being imperialistic enough. It could have included wrongs against persons as well as against property without swelling into either Aristotle's "complete virtue in relation to others"[2] or that catch-all dubious virtue of twentieth-century moralists, the disposition to maximize one's personal "utility" by constraining one's natural willing of its "direct" less cooperative apparent maximization.[3] On some versions of this modern "complete virtue," it becomes almost a puritan Kantian virtue, a strange merger of self-restraint or continence with the duty to join the collective dance towards capitalist accumulation.[4] A forced willing of oneself to an against-the-grain cooperativeness, a disciplining of what are taken as one's natural predatory instincts, a denying of oneself the tempting thrills of secret free-riding, then come to replace Hume's very different and much more naturally sociable virtue of justice. Cautious and jealous that virtue may be, but its caution is not that of the converted predator, nor its jealousy that of the one who has no concern for anyone else's concerns.

Hume's justice-initiators are parents who care about their children's concerns, and friends who care about each other's cares. They are limitedly sociable persons with limited generosity, as well as a dangerous but productive love of gain. They are prone to sympathy, even with total strangers. And they seem to be amazingly gentle persons, since the problem that they see facing them, and solve by their inventiveness and ability, is not that of danger to life and limb from bloodthirsty aggressive strangers intent on removing competitors for scarce material resources, or on bloody vengeance for fancied insults, or on putting the fear of death into those they want to master and enslave. Hume's justice-initiators face and solve a much milder problem, that of insecurity of possession of transferable goods.

Implausible and optimistic though this scenario may seem to us, to whom Hobbes's description of "the naturall condition of mankind" seems to carry the ring of twentieth-century verisimilitude, Hume's version of our prehistory should come as no great surprise to us, after Book Two's version of our natural passions. If every pleasure languishes when enjoyed apart from company, then of course our life will not be solitary, even when it is poor. If we have not merely needs for nourishment, raiment and shelter, but also a natural pride in our gardens, cloaks and houses, then of course we will be jealous of their secure possession, and we may also be prone to envious designs on the better-looking transferable goods of passing strangers. Security and increase of fine possessions will be natural goods to Humean persons. In conditions of scarcity of external goods, this socially harmless or even socially beneficial wish to have something fine that is securely one's own will take the dangerous form of "avidity," on one's own or one's loved ones' behalf. It is this that Hume sees to be the problem that the artifices of "justice" are to solve. Humean justice is an essentially distributive virtue, distributing rights to the secure possession of transferable goods, and to their transfer by consent and by contract. Vanity or pride in itself is not a problem, since it is or can be "a social passion, and a bond of union among men" (T. 491). The problem is avidity, the love of material gain. In conditions of scarcity, natural needs or appetites, fear of want and pride of possession all may feed into this avidity.

Avidity *can* lead to ruthless and violent seizure, and so to insecurity of life, but Hume seems to see no "natural" general problem of aggression or bloodthirstiness, parallel to the problem of dispossession and thirst for gain. Like Rousseau's more solitary savages, Hume's pre-civilized persons are perfectly tolerant of each other's presence, unless and until squabbles over possessions break the peace. Not only is their condition not "the Warre of every man against every man"; it is not a condition of war at all, even against unfamiliar strangers. It is more a condition of intermittent scuffles over possessions. Hobbes writes, "For Warre consisteth not in Battell onely, or the act of fighting; but in a tract of time, wherein the Will to contend by Battell is sufficiently known" (*Leviathan,* Chapter 13). By this definition, Hume's state of nature becomes a state of war, but Hobbes's definition is an unhelpful one. If the will to contend by battle is known to be conditional—say, to fight if attacked, and not to fight unless attacked, or to attack only for gain—then whether there is a state of real battle-involving war or not will depend upon which conditions hold. The will to fight only if attacked is as much a conditional assurance of peace as it is of battle. Hobbes's definition of "Warre," as absence of assurance that there will be no fighting, makes war trivially ever-present, since we have and can have no absolute assurance that no one will ever for any reason strike us. Hume's natural persons have reasonable assurance that their mates and children will not attack them, and that no one else will either, if they avoid acquiring enviable possessions. If, like Epictetus (E. 256), they content themselves with obviously non-enviable possessions, then they need not fear dispossession, and so need not fear attack. Since they are rarely like Epictetus, they are occasionally dispossessed, and so do feel undesirable insecurity of possessions. But seizure with violence will come only in occasional "showers," not continuous or severe enough to count as Hobbes's "foule Weather." What Hume's convenors of justice aim to eliminate is not a climate of violence against persons, but a climate of incommodious insecurity of possession of material goods.

Only when property rights have been invented, profitable contractual exchanges made possible, and a cooperative surplus accumulated, does Hume see that anything like Hobbes's misnamed "natural condition" will come about. Once "encrease of riches" (T. 541) and property in *"absent* or *general"* goods (T. 520) tempt people to fraud and other acts of contagious injustice, then and only then by frequent "violations of equity" is "the commerce of men, by that means . . . render'd very dangerous and uncertain"

(T. 535). Then and only then, when the three invented laws of justice, *"that of the stability of possession, of its transference by consent,* and *of the performance of promises"* (T. 526), have changed conditions by both their observance and their non-observance, so that the stage is set for the invention of magistrates to detect and penalize injustice, does Hume start to mention the dangers to human life and limb that "the commerce of men" may bring. Earlier, when the first convention is adopted, there is no mention of insecurity of life due to human aggression. Society first becomes advantageous not as a control on aggressive impulses, but for what it brings in increased power, ability and mutual aid to make us less vulnerable to "fortune and accidents." Only later does the likelihood of intentional human attack join fortune and accident as a source of insecurity of person. Although Hume in Part I had called willful murder vicious (T. 468), and called parricide as well as incest a "horrid crime" (T. 466–467), he forgets to give us his own superior-to-the-rationalists' account of what exactly is criminal or vicious about them, precisely why the moral sentiment comes down against them, more than against murderous impulses that are restrained. This is a shortcoming in his account, but it is one that has its compensatory theoretical advantage—it makes it very clear that "the interested affection" is restricted in its scope, not simply a meta-passion for the satisfaction of all our passions. Our instinctive "love of life" (T. 417), and the threats to its satisfaction posed by our equally instinctive anger at and resentment of insult and injury (ibid.), are either to be reconciled by the moral sentiment's recognition of the natural virtues of clemency, kindness and moderation, and of the natural vices of cruelty and murderous desires, or they have to await the regulation that magistrates will give them. For all that Hume says in his account of justice, there is nothing unjust about willful murder, any more than there need be about incest.

Hume's account of this limited "justice" is justly famous. Particularly in our time, when game-theoretical models of cooperation are the fashion, Part II of Book Three has been hailed[5] as a remarkable accomplishment. In lucid prose, without any formal tools, Hume presents to us the essentials of several society-wide coordination problems and their different solutions. As later in his essays on economics, where he combines depth of analysis with simplicity and non-technicality, so here, in his first assay on "the interested affection," he lays bare the special problems it gives rise to, and a sketch of their multi-staged solutions, with depth of insight and with great subtlety. He was helped by Thomas Hobbes's earlier discussion of how, despite or even because of the strength of our selfish passions, we might cooperate to ensure more "commodious" living, and helped also by Bernard de Mandeville's witty demonstration of how "private vices" such as greed might feed into the "public virtues" of business enterprise and general prosperity. Locke's disagreements with Hobbes about what we would have been like before we invented governors (if indeed that is what Hobbes took his "naturall condition of mankind" to describe), about whether or not our conduct could then be at all effectively constrained by any recognition of agreed rights and obligations, must also have raised the questions to which Hume's account of "convention" gives an answer, one that agrees neither with Hobbes nor with Locke. Hume's immersion as a law student in the Scottish Natural Law jurisprudential tradition, his acquaintance with the writings of Stair,[6] Grotius, and Pufendorf (as well as with Voet and Vinnius),[7] would make it natural for him to ask if all binding agreements must be promises or covenants. His acquaintance with English common law, at least during his time in Bristol, if not earlier as a law student, would make it natural that he ponder the function of undeclared and of declared laws. Locke's writings would also raise the question of when we need official penalizers, and when we can do better without them. Hume brought to the complex issues he addressed the mind of a well-read drop-out law and business student, combined with the mind of a future economist and historian. This was a very fruitful mixture. The mix was in some ways typical of the Scottish enlightenment, encouraged by the Scots' penchant for natural histories of society, even by the form of the standard syllabus in moral philosophy. Hutcheson's lectures, Adam Smith's lectures and later writings, Adam Ferguson's lectures and writings, Dugald Stewart's lectures and writings—all mixed questions of morality, law and economics in the same way as do Hume's writings. The "genius of the age" was for natural history and political economy.

An interesting comparison case is Jean-Jacques Rousseau, who had a quite different background. Works like his *Discourse on Inequality* and *Essay on the Origin of Language* shows the same taste for instructive mythical history, the same interest in social and economic change and its consequences for moral psychology, but no one could accuse Rousseau of having a legal mind. He lived "amidst scolding and mutual reproaches" without having or developing any expertise about how quarrels could be handled. Hume's sure grasp not just of the essentials of economics but also of the law of property, contract and other instances of a "kind of superstitious practise in civil laws" (T. 515) shows throughout his *Treatise* discussion of justice. He thinks as a comparative lawyer as well as a moralist, as a historian as well as an economist. This makes the attempt to get anything like the measure[8] of Part II a hazardous but rewarding adventure. Despite the many helpful guides[9] to this part of Hume's text, it remains a part which should humble, even when it no longer baffles, the pride of other philosophers (see E. 267).

THE STORY ABOUT the supposed "origin" of justice is told to make clear, first, what problem it is that justice is invented to solve. Once limited generosity over transferable good is seen to be the problem, the general lines of the solution follow immediately. And one thing that is striking about that solution is not just its cleverness and profundity but Hume's plain cheek. He is correcting not only Grotius, Pufendorf, Hobbes and Locke, but also the book of *Genesis*. His ongoing campaign to counter the influence of the Bible is conducted here with particular verve and brilliance. (Mossner relates that Hume estimated the population of Scotland in his time at one and a half million, the number of Bibles it contained as three million, so that it deserved the title "land of Bibles".) Hume's version of our moral history is nicely calculated to contrast with the version he had been given in his Christian upbringing. We find Hume's Adam not in any garden of Eden, where fruit drops into his lap, and no garments are needed, but in harsher (more Scottish?) conditions where "not only the food, which is requir'd for his sustenance, flies his search and approach, or at least requires his labour to be produc'd, but he must be posses'd of cloaths and lodging, to defend him against the injuries of the weather; tho' to consider him only in himself, he is provided neither with arms, nor force, nor other natural abilities, which are in any degree answerable to so many necessities" (T. 485). Far from being the creator's favourite, our species appears to have been singled out for "more cruelty" from mother nature than any other species. To us and us alone nature has given "this unnatural conjunction of infirmity, and of necessity" (ibid.). Only by team-work can man "raise himself up to an equality with his fellow-creatures, and even acquire a superiority over them" (ibid.). Whereas in the biblical genesis we began superior and non-needy, then fell from grace into living by our own collective wits and the sweat of our brows, in Hume's story we begin in exceptional need, incompetence and inferiority, then rise by our wits and the bootstraps of our natural passions to being able to hold our own, if necessary, against other voracious species, or at least becoming their equals.

What exactly saves us from the want and insecurity which was our natural portion? The theoretical solution is that cooperation would save us. "By the conjunction of forces, our power is aug-mented: By the partition of employments, our ability encreases: And by mutual succour we are less expos'd to fortune and acci-dents. 'Tis by this additional *force, ability,* and *security,* that society becomes advantageous" (ibid.). That is the recipe for our salva-tion, but how can we adopt it, if we are naturally so disadvan-taged? Hume rules out any social instinct—we have only limited benevolence, and so do not naturally fly to one another's succour, or team up by instinct to divide employment, or automatically join forces against marauding lions. Had nature given us social instincts, she would not even have appeared cruel in her endow-ment to her human offspring. Hume's answer to the question of how we can get ourselves into a position to see and use the general recipe for our salvation is one that we might have predicted from the story so far, with its point-for-point inversion of the biblical story. What saves Adam is the presence of Eve. What saves both of them is lust: "Most fortunately, therefore, there is conjoin'd to those necessities, whose remedies are remote and obscure, another necessity, which having a present and more obvious remedy, may

justly be regarded as the first and original principle of human society. This necessity is no other than that natural appetite betwixt
the sexes, which unites them together, and preserves their union,
till a new tye takes place in their concern for their common offspring. This new concern becomes also a principle of union betwixt the parents and the offspring, and forms a more numerous
society" (T. 486). What enables us to see that cooperation is the
key to increased force, ability and security is our experience that
it already has proved the key to that, in our spontaneous cooperation with lovers and children. We are not natural cooperators
with our fellow persons, but we are naturally cooperative with
lovers and children, and, crucially, we are smart enough to see
both the advantages that this brings, and the disadvantages that
accrue from the restricted scope of family cooperation.

Some fellow persons are neither known kin nor lovers (although we can always remember that "a man, that lies at a little
distance from us, may, in a little time, become a familiar acquaintance"—T. 581) and the existence of different family groups leads
to conflict. It is not the Hobbesian war of all against all; it is the
very different conflict of "ourselves and our friends" against those
others and their friends. The conflict will be in some ways worse
than the Hobbesian conflict, since some "conjunction of forces"
will already have increased individual striking power. But it is in
other ways better, since its participants not only know the theoretical recipe for ending it, but require no psychological conversion to put that recipe into effect. They do not face the problem
that Hobbes's natural men improbably faced, of knowing the
theorems of peace, but not knowing how they could put them
into practice. Hume's justice-inventors know from prior experience that cooperation and mutual trust are both possible and advantageous. Behind the conventions of justice lie the ur-conven-
tions of sexual love, family life and friendship.

The "convention" or conditional agreement that initiates cooperation between non-friends, non-lovers (and those who are not
intended lovers) and non-kin (or those not recognized as kin) is
one that stabilizes possession, turns possession into property. It is
"a general sense of common interest; which sense all the members
of the society express to one another, and which induces them to

regulate their conduct by certain rules. I observe, that it will be for my interest to leave another in possession of his goods, *provided* he will act in the same manner with regard to me. He is sensible of a like interest in the regulation of his conduct. When this common sense of interest is mutually express'd, and is known to both, it produces a suitable resolution and behaviour. And this may properly enough be call'd a convention or agreement betwixt us, tho' without the interposition of a promise; since the actions of each of us have a reference to those of the other, and are perform'd upon the supposition, that something is to be perform'd on the other part" (T. 490). This pithy account describes a transition from a shared, expressed, recognized sense of common interest to mutually referential, mutually expressed, conditional intentions to act to further this interest, to behaviour conforming to these intentions. Many features call for comment.

First is the emphasis on expression. A common interest that each sees but does not know that the others see will be furthered only by a miracle, or by the "interposition" of some omniscient coordinating party. It is essential to Hume's story that the parties to the convention recognize each other's state of mind, that those states get expression, and expression in some already shared "language." Does Hume suppose that all of them already know how to speak English, or French? Surely not, since "in like manner are languages gradually establish'd" (T. 490). The mutually comprehensible expression that plays an essential role in the fundamental (since first) convention must be non-verbal expression. And Hume's moral psychology has prepared the reader for this apparent assumption that "the *party* of humankind" do not need Esperanto or any other spoken or written language to "see into each other's breasts." We can see and understand breasts heaving, tears starting in the eye, clenched fists, outstretched hands, warning frowns and encouraging smiles, and the Humean story of human cooperation would collapse with a dull thud if this assumption were removed. We need not be supposed incapable of veiling our sentiments or of faking them (indeed, we must be able to learn "some disguise" [T. 598] of our sentiments, and on occasion to "wear a fair outside" when it is not so attractive inside). What is important is that, when we want to make our intentions on some

basic matter clear to a stranger whose cooperation we want, we
need not depend on a learned language to do so. If cooperation
were limited to those with the same "mother tongue," then it
could extend no further than that mother's rule extends. A common language would go no further than the extended family, if its
spread were not assisted by other forms of cooperation, enough
to motivate and facilitate language-learning outside the family circle. Hume includes facility of expression in the second *Enquiry*'s
extended catalogue of virtues, and with good reason. Expression
in general, not just verbal expression, is a key plank in the raft of
morality as Hume understands it. It is essential for sympathy, and
for the mutual understanding that underpins the artificial virtues.

One of the marks of artifice, and of the artificial virtues, is cultural variation, and it might be thought that localized communication, rather than humanity-wide communication, would be
enough to start the cooperation whose rules are the laws of justice.
After all, the series of conventions that Hume describes leads up
to that of the authority of magistrates, which is of course local and
restricted. Hume emphasizes not just the plurality of authoritative
governors, each with limited territory, but also the variation from
community to community in details of the pre-government conventions. In Scotland, the ceremonies of consent by which property is transferred are different from those in Turkey, and recognized property rights vary from group to group. Would it then
matter if the mutual communication presupposed by the first convention were restricted and local? If what is built upon it is to be
restricted and local in its force, why should its foundations not be
equally restricted? The answer is that the role of the first convention is to extend trust beyond the confines of friendship and family, so it is essential that it rest upon some fairly dependable feature
of strangers. The language they have evolved or picked up is not
dependably our own language, so it had better not depend on that.
Rousseau later wrestled with the problem of how the cooperation
people need in order to speak intelligibly to each other relates to
other forms of cooperation. Had he read the *Treatise,* he could
have come to the problem from T. 490.[10] Hume's story here involves no claims about temporal priority—the conventions of a
shared native language could grow up at the same time as property

conventions. Speech becomes unmistakably present in Hume's story only when he gets to the account of promise and contract. Once promises and contracts are being made, we will also expect a monetary currency to become accepted,[11] as "common measures of exchange" (T. 490).

We can, then, take it that a shared language evolves in a group along with a commonly recognized set of property rights, and common customs for signifying consent to transfer of property. Words, as well as gestures such as the handshake, would naturally come to serve this latter purpose. Before "the interposition of a promise" there would be the interposition of other, less complicated symbols, including verbal consent. Cooperation in the verbal exchange of sentiments will accompany other mutually advantageous exchanges. The whole process is made possible by the fact that there is both some instinctive cooperation, and some automatic communication.

Convention, in Hume's sense, involves not just mutually comprehensible expression of sentiments, but expression of mutually referential and parallel sentiments. I express my sense that we would all do better (that we have "a common interest") if you all would join me in a cooperative scheme to stabilize possession, and each of you expresses a parallel sentiment. We all think, "If only we could cooperate, we would all gain." We all express that sentiment, and so we know we agree in sentiment. Because of that, we can move to conditional intentions, each again referring to the others' intentions, and each again mirroring the rest: "I will not dispossess you, so long as you similarly intend not to dispossess me." The mutual expression and mutual recognition of these mutually referring conditional intentions is enough to satisfy their conditions, and so there is not merely "resolution," but behavior in accordance with resolution. There seems to be no "compliance problem," and no Hobbesian "fooles" saying in their hearts that they will gain even more if they merely pretend to cooperate. Hume's non-fools resolve to cooperate, and carry out their resolve. As Hume (a little later) puts it, "No more is requisite to induce any one of them to perform an act of justice, who has the first opportunity. This becomes an example to the others. And thus justice establishes itself" (T. 498).

An "act of justice," in this context, is simply a refraining from taking from another person some possession of hers that one could take. It becomes an act of justice, a refraining from injustice, only because of the expressed and known conditional intentions, whose conditions are met and known to be met by the very fact that everyone has such intentions. The will to cooperation, by its very expression and replication, becomes the fact of cooperation. Justice is initiated by confident example-setting, and is established or made settled by the fact that the first or early performers' example is followed, their confidence confirmed, general expectation of further conformity strengthened and so a general custom launched. What, before the recognized coordination of conditional resolutions, would have been simply an act of dispossession, becomes, after the first actions to carry out those intentions, an act of injustice. Hume is insistent that it would be "a very gross fallacy" (T. 491) to suppose that there is any obligation not to dispossess, or any right to keep what one has in one's possession, before there is any "convention," any mutual according-to-fact conditional resolve, as "the origin of justice." It is in this sense that justice is artificial. Justice is indeed a matter of the will to render every person his or her due, as Aristotle, Justinian and others maintained. But Hume insists that nothing is "due" anyone until a cooperative scheme is successfully launched. All our dues are dues to and from "co-ops" of one kind or another. Some dues are duties arising from the basic cooperation of family members, and of friends. Hume tends to call these "duties," not obligations. The sorts of dues that justice involves rely upon very general convention-dependent cooperative schemes, not instinctive or natural ones like that of parent and child or friend and friend. It is only after the successful launching of the reciprocal agreement to abstain from seizure that anything counts as robbery, that any possession counts as property.

Hume mentions no penalty for not conforming to his first convention; indeed, he seems to rule penalty out. "No more is requisite" for conformity than a "common sense of interest . . . mutually express'd, and . . . known to both." This sense of interest, motivating conformity, does depend on "repeated experience of the inconveniences of transgressing[12] it" (T. 490), as well as on the experience of the convenience of having it generally conformed to, but "inconvenience" would be an odd way to describe contrived penalty. What the convenors know is that, just as it is unpleasant to tangle oars, so it is unpleasant to scuffle over possessions. The reason for conformity is the improved climate of life that coordination brings, not the threat of punitive measures against non-conformers. Tit for tat still lies in the future. Just as responding to an uncoordinated rower by a deliberate off-stroke of one's own would be counter-productive, so attempting to rob the robbers would increase, not decrease, discord. Hume makes no mention of any penalty, and certainly not of tit for tat.

This suggests that the problem solved by the first convention has not the structure of the "prisoner's dilemma," but more that of the "assurance game."[13] Conforming is preferred over nonconforming, so long as the sweets of coordination are achieved by conformity. There is the prospect of an indefinitely long (life-long) iteration of situations presenting a choice between acts of justice (not seizing) and injustice (seizing), so no endgame problems threaten.[14] In any case, the love of gain would be an odd passion to release from self-restraint once one did know that the end approached. "Enough of restraint. Let me give my last days over to the heedless and impetuous movement of the love of gain," would be an odd resolve, unless one did it for one's heirs. The love of gain is intrinsically future-oriented, and when the perceived future is limited, this future-oriented passion will naturally and commensurably lose its grip, even more than our other passions. There will be no very strong self-interested motive to seize others' goods in one's known last weeks of life, any more than there is in normal conditions of others' respect for property rights, and one's own ignorance about the timing of one's end. Hume seems to take it that the desire for order and stability will at this stage be stronger than the impulse for quick easy gain, so his convenors will conform in order to get and maintain order, to avoid breakdown of order. It is only much later, when conditions have changed and order has broken down, that there is any temptation to respond to injustice with tit for tat: "Your example . . . pushes me forward in this way by imitation . . . by shewing me, that I should be the cully of my integrity, if I alone shou'd impose on myself a severe restraint amidst the licentiousness of others" (T. 535). This comes after the invention of all three laws of nature, not after the first of them, and it comes about through the accumulation of property, through change of conditions and change of the sorts of injustice that are tempting—cheating and breach of contract, not seizure and highway robbery. In the simple uncultivated conditions when the first convention is initiated, fear of reversion to the insecurity of the state of nature will be sufficient reason for sensible self-interested conformity. There is at this stage neither need for nor point in Hammurabi-style tit for tat response to non-conformity. One conforms because one does better by conforming, by not tangling oars. The reason one does better is not that one fears retaliatory responses in kind for any out-of-rhythm strokes.

But for this first convention to be taken as the solution to a coordination problem,[15] we must be able to see it as really in everyone's best interest to go along with the cooperative scheme that institutes property rights. Some problems seem to present themselves when we probe the exact gains or "interest" that these apparently eager cooperators expect from this cooperation. The cooperative scheme is to fix possession, to transform it into own-ership. Whether stable possession will really be such a gain in con-venience will depend upon just what property the scheme allots one. Hume separates out the in-principle agreement to have some scheme from the agreement to have a particular scheme, that which freezes present possession into rightful property. But if in the relevant "present" I have no possessions, or almost none, while others have more, I will not gain from the scheme. Our ancestors would surely have to have been more fools than Hume thinks they were to agree to adopt a totally unspecified system of rights. Unless they had some assurance that each would get some tolerable minimum share of rights, they would have to have been desperate or crazy to agree to accept an unknown scheme. The most generous construction to put on what Hume writes about the general terms and the specific details of the agreement invent-ing property is that there is not really a two-stage process—first a reciprocal willingness to recognize rights, whatever their details turn out to be, and then a settling of a "method . . . by which we may distinguish which particular goods are to be assign'd to each particular person" (T. 502). After all, these fairly smart ancestors will be able to see that an agreement to stabilize possession "can never serve to any purpose, while it remains in such general terms" (T. 501–502), so they will not agree on it until its terms are made less general, or at least until it is made clear that each of them will be assigned goods. Only if the state of nature were much more Hobbesian than Hume seriously wants to portray it would it be sensible to risk beggary, let alone risk slavery, for the sake of stability. To have the stable possession of almost no property would be no improvement over unstable possession of ever varying amounts of goods, which is what one could expect when cooperation was restricted to families and friends.

To persuade us that society-wide cooperation is indeed sensible, Hume sometimes portrays its alternative as a "solitary and forlorn condition" (T. 492, 497), as if our ancestors had suddenly switched from being family members with some friends to being all of them rogue males, on their own against the world. If we look closely, we find that these Hobbesian descriptions depict what would happen should society "dissolve" (T. 497)—what would "follow" from "universal licence" (T. 492). They are not descriptions of the state from which the hypothetical convenors moved, when they improved their lives by adopting a general cooperative scheme setting up property rights. There is no reason to think that what we would revert to, after the breakdown of social cooperation, would be the same as what preceded it. One striking feature of Hume's story, like that of Rousseau's later story, is that there is not just a one-shot change, from nature to civilized cooperation and culture, but a series of changes, and that each convention alters the conditions, both by its success and by its limitations. When cooperative schemes go wrong, or break down, then the problems will be different from, perhaps worse than, those that such schemes were evolved to solve. Hume shows a good awareness of this, but he does not altogether avoid ambiguity in what he takes the state of nature to be. Some of his accounts of it, those in which its human inhabitants are portrayed as "solitary and forlorn," are more plausible as descriptions of breakdown than of initial conditions, and if we look closely we can take it that they are intended as such. Hume's original portrayal of the first convenors depicts them as family members, hoping to cooperate outside the family. They are not solitary, and not so forlorn. But should the new scheme of cooperation break down, then they may well end up worse than they began. The proper comparison to make, in order to see the reasons they have to start the scheme, is a comparison with the way they were, not with the way they will become if the scheme breaks down. The latter may yield a reason for keeping it going once started, but not for starting it in the first place. The inherently stabilizing tragicomedy of long-term cooperation is that whether or not it was rational to initiate it, it so alters its participants that it unfits them for any other style of life, so that it becomes rational to continue it.

When Hume is trying to persuade us of the advantage of recognized property rights, however unequal they are, and of the "pernicious consequences" of disregarding them, he asks such rhetorical questions as, *"What must become of the world, if such practices prevail? How could society subsist under such disorders?"* (E. 203). He claims that if we ceased to recognize established property rights, we would "fall into that savage and solitary condition, which is infinitely worse than the worst situation that can possibly be suppos'd in society" (T. 497). This is analogous to the argument of a husband who is trying to keep his wife from leaving him by pointing out how lost each would be without the other, how unfitted for independence each is, how infinitely worse a life alone would be, and who takes that argument at the same time to show that the marriage has been of infinite advantage to each. Hume has good arguments to show what we risk by upsetting an existing order of property rights, less good arguments to show that it was so advantageous to institute them, especially if this is to be done more or less blindly when it comes to what their details are to be.

The point of the scheme is to settle what was inconveniently unsettled. Nothing will be settled if endless arguments take place about what would be a fair distribution of property. In the second *Enquiry* Hume stresses the social chaos that results when meritarians insist on distribution according to their version of merit. In the *Treatise* he simply says that some general principle that is easy to apply without too many disputes is obviously needed, and that the salient one is present possession. This is to fix initial endowments, and it will be supplemented later by other principles such as occupation, prescription (long possession), accession and succession. These, Hume writes, are the four "most considerable" circumstances that he finds to "give rise to property after society is once establish'd" (T. 505). Significant by its absence, or its absorption into other principles, is what Locke took to be the obvious ground of entitlement: having mixed one's labor with some external thing. Hume dignifies this famous suggestion with a footnote, in which he points out that unless one already owns the thing one improves by one's labor, one's property in it is not indisputable. If one does already own it (by "occupation," if not by long possession) then the principle of "accession" will account for one's right to any extra value the thing acquires by the alteration one's labor has effected in it. But whether the extra value comes from the sweat of one's brow, from one's lying on the beach and letting the bananas and the coconuts grow undisturbed, ready to drop into one's hands, or from waiting for one's cows to calve in nature's good time, or for the river to beach a few shoals of edible fish on the bank that one occupies, is all one. Labor has no pride of place as the basis of a claim to property. Appeal to it is either question-begging or "a needless circuit" (T. 505, note). (It may be less question-begging if, like Locke, one treats one's own body as one's ur-property. Hume limits property to goods that are external and transferable.)

These rules that determine property are "principally fix'd by the imagination, or the more frivolous properties or our thought and conception," as well as by some concern for public utility (T. 504, note). They do not pretend to be equitable. Their merit is salience and relative ease of application. This is as true of the rule of distribution used to launch the scheme, present possession, as of the others. "It must immediately occur, as the most natural expedient, that every one continue to enjoy what he is at present master of, and that property or constant possession be conjoin'd to the immediate possession" (T. 503). Hume thinks we would "easily acquiesce in this expedient," since we all miss what is taken from us more than what we never had. But if the cooperative scheme is

broached just after a raid in which I lost most of my former (temporary) possessions, so that I now have almost nothing, I will not
so easily acquiesce to fixing present possession as rightful possession. If some males have formed a spontaneous confederacy to
reduce females to slavery, to treat them as possessions not possessors, then a rule which fixed present possession would render the
females "incapable of all property" (E. 191). Sensible women,
then, will not acquiesce in just any scheme that fixes rights. Neither they nor other sensible people will, without some conditions,
accept a scheme that fixes present possession as initial endowment.
Only if they know that possession is at present not intolerably
unequal will they sensibly agree on the rule that Hume supposes
they did agree on, one stabilizing present possession.

Hume's story makes sense only if his earlier description of how
things stood before general cooperation is taken quite seriously.
At that time, "the *parents* govern by the advantage of their superior strength and wisdom" (T. 486, my emphasis). Should there
be any male or female confederacies, then cooperation will have
already gone beyond the natural family. If there are patriarchs or
matriarchs dispossessing those in their power, then the convention
will not get the sensible acquiescence of the dispossessed. If they
are excluded, if their acquiescence is not even sought, then they
can be expected to make their resentment felt, and the convenors
will not then be able to expect their cooperative scheme to be stable. It cannot promise infinite advantages if it faces the prospect
of recurrent slave rebellions. Nor can it expect general acceptance
if it freezes into property rights possessions which are at the time
of fixing grossly unequal, due to one's bad luck, or to one's fellows
predatory triumphs. The only way to save Hume's account here
is to suppose that the convenors do include both sexes, and that
there is no great and greatly resented discrepancy of possession
between one possessor and her fellows. Otherwise it will just be
false that the scheme offers infinite advantages to all parties.

By the time Hume wrote the second *Enquiry,* he realized that
there were problems here. The actually adopted property rights
have, as a matter of historical fact, reduced women in many nations to slavery, "incapable of all property" (E. 191). And in many
systems of property, inequality is such that "we rob the poor of

more satisfaction than we add to the rich, and . . . the slight gratification of a frivolous vanity, in one individual, frequently costs
more than bread to many families, and even provinces" (E. 194).
Would rational convenors, if they foresaw such developments for
their descendants, be so sure of the infinite advantages of what
they were initiating?

Hume is not attributing to the original convenors either any
prophetic insight into the long-term future or any indefinitely extended concern for their descendants. They clearly do not foresee
the horrors to come. They adopt a system which seems to them
an improvement for each person and for her children and grandchildren, despite the "frivolous" nature of the principles determining property distribution, principles whose only virtues are sal-
iency and the relative definiteness of the decisions they yield.
Compared with principles like "The saints shall inherit the earth,"
or "To each according to his labor," they yield relatively clear decisions about who is to get what when. But unless there were not
only "motives of public interest for most of the rules, which determine property" (T. 504, note) but also some rough equity, it is
hard to see how the scheme could be rationally agreed to. We
make best sense of Hume's claims about property if we suppose
that there was a golden age when things did more or less work
out better for all, so that the more settled conditions enabled a
surplus to be produced and enjoyed. There was "accession" to the
lot of each, skills increased and began to be specialized, and mutual
aid was strengthened within small groups, perhaps extended more
widely when it came to defense of property rights. (One might
help one's neighbor fend off an invading robber, without thereby
becoming part of a citizen militia intent on policing and punishing
crimes against property.)

THE ADVANTAGES OF fixing possession, of converting present
possession into property, are by Hume's own account accompanied by grave (and surely foreseeable) inconvenience, until the
rules determining property are supplemented by a second set of
rules, a second "law of nature" enabling the "adjustment" of the
rights that the first complex law had just fixed. "As these depend
very much on chance, they must frequently prove contradictory

both to men's wants and desires; and persons and possessions must often be very ill adjusted. This is a grand inconvenience, which calls for a remedy" (T. 514). The remedy is transfer by proprietor's consent. Hume describes this convention, inventing gift and barter, as a "medium betwixt a rigid stability, and this changeable and uncertain adjustment"—that which would be effected by reversion to violent seizure (ibid.). First possessions get fixed. Then they get unfixed, enough to adjust them better to people's wants and desires. The grand inconvenience of property holdings inappropriate to one's wants and desires is remedied by enabling barter and gift, "mutual exchange and commerce." Once we have this grand remedy, specialization of labor can advance. "Different parts of the earth produce different commodities; and not only so, but different men both are by nature fitted for different employments, and attain to greater perfection in any one, when they confine themselves to it alone" (ibid.). So the initial promise that cooperation-enabling conventions would increase ability as well as force and security (T. 485) is slowly being kept.

Hume emphasizes that the mobility of possession that this second law introduces should not bring "wars and dissensions," since it is not violent seizure, nor is it the sort of transfer that threatens to occasion disputes. "The proprietor's consent, who alone is concern'd, is taken along in the alienation" (ibid.). Consent is presumably a response to a request to take. One party requests and the other consents or refuses consent. The full panoply of offer and acceptance does not come in until promise is invented, until we move from the second to the third law of nature. All that the first party offers here is to give or to take something, and what is consented to is a taking. When this is done reciprocally, we have barter; when it is done unilaterally we have loan or gift.

There is no "interposition of a promise," but there can come to be interposition of some other simpler symbols. These are symbols for particular individual goods, not representations of the value of those goods—that is, money.[16] What is literally transferred at the time that consent to transfer is given may be a mere stand-in for the goods that are alienated, the property that is "translated." "*Symbolical* delivery," of a key to the house transferred, or of a stone for the land transferred, satisfies the fancy,

Hume writes, and may deceive us into thinking that we have given sensible and so comprehensible form to "the mysterious transition of the property," the alienation and acquisition of rights. It is a superstitious practice "resembling the *Roman catholic* superstitions in religion. As the *Roman catholics* represent the inconceivable mysteries of the *Christian* religion, and render them more present to the mind, by a taper, or habit, or grimace, which is suppos'd to resemble them; so lawyers and moralists have run into like inventions for the same reason, and have endeavor'd by those means to satisfy themselves concerning the transference of property by consent" (T. 515–516). Here speaks not just the lapsed Christian, but the lapsed Protestant, and puritan. Rights, property and their transfer are insensible, are normative fictions, useful inventions of the collective human mind. They are not the same as claims, possession and delivery. They cannot be adequately represented by sensible symbols, and such symbols as we use "deceive the mind, and make it fancy, that it conceives the mysterious transition of the property" (T. 515). Better to be undeceived, to admit mystery, or to be quite clear that "the property of an object, when taken for something real, without any reference to morality, or the sentiments of the mind, is a quality perfectly insensible, and even inconceivable; nor can we form any distinct notion, either of its stability or translation" (ibid.).

The mention of morality reminds us that "the laws of nature" are not simply the rules of human cooperative schemes that in fact have been adopted, as property rights, gift and barter obviously have, but of schemes that get moral endorsement. Hume distinguishes between the "natural obligation" that any accepted cooperative scheme generates and the "moral obligation" which morally endorsed schemes generate (T. 498). He drew this distinction before discussing the determinate form of the first law of nature, as if to warn us that not every actually adopted social practice, perhaps not every actually adopted set of property rights, need give rise to any moral obligation to respect such conventional rights. But what he is most interested in are the schemes that can be approved from a moral standpoint, when we overlook our own special interests and attempt to sympathize with all right-holders in the scheme, and with "the public interest." Interest here is still

concern for increase, for accession, for good investments. The
public interest is the increase of the public goods of order, and of
safe and commodious commerce or interpersonal relations. *"Thus
self-interest is the original motive to the* establishment *of justice: but a*
sympathy *with public interest is the source of the* moral approbation,
which attends that virtue" (T. 499–500). The public interest had earlier been rejected as the reason people pay their debts, and Hume
is not retracting that earlier claim that "men, in the ordinary conduct of life, look not so far as the public interest, when they pay
their creditors, perform their promises, and abstain from theft,
and robbery, and injustice of every kind" (T. 481). What is inadequate as a motive may be perfectly adequate as a reason for approbation of other, less "sublime" motives. Hume had also, in that
earlier discussion of the motive for just acts, claimed that observation of the rules of justice comes to serve the public interest only
"after an artificial convention for the establishment of these rules"
(T. 480), not "naturally." It takes contrivance or artifice to create
a public interest, a means of increase of public goods, and so an
interest in which we all share. Each person's motive, in observing
the rules of justice, can be enlightened self-interest, awareness of
her own share in the public interest, but when it comes to approving such motivated acts, her own and others', it is the public interest as such that becomes the relevant concern, not just any one
person's share in it. The moral judge must sympathize with the
public interest, as well as with each individual's sense of private
interest. In the *Second Enquiry* Hume writes, "After the laws of
justice are fixed by views of general utility, the injury, the hard-
ship, the harm, which result to any individual from a violation of
them, enter very much into consideration, and are a great source
of that universal blame which attends every wrong or iniquity"
(E. 310). Sympathy with other passions that right-holders have
may also be involved—sympathy with parental concern, with
worry about how the scheme will work out for one's children's
children. Not every scheme that passes the test for an acceptable
convention, that can be reasonably felt by each person to be in her
interest, so that it generates "a general sense of common interest,"
need pass the moral test (nor, perhaps, vice versa). If morally appropriate sympathy with concerns other than the love of gain out-

weighs sympathy for that particular passion, then the moral judge will withhold endorsement, even though the public "interest," and every private interest, might be served.

The public interest is not the common good, but only one component of it. Hume seems to require that, for something to be a moral obligation, it must first satisfy the test of self-interest which convention imposes; in addition, he seems to require that the public interest be served, and that these interests be ones whose precedence over other components of private and public good can be impartially approved. This is a tough test, and yet Hume seems confident that some version of property rights, and of their transfer by consent, can satisfy it. Only if the moral test is satisfied will there be any moral reality to the rights that are exchanged in barter. They may have only social or conventional reality derived from "the sentiments of the mind" that are not yet moral sentiments. Serving self-interest and the public interest are necessary but not sufficient conditions for a cooperative scheme giving rise to moral obligations.

THE COOPERATION THAT IS instituted by the second law is both the general cooperation needed for respect for that law, and the cooperation needed for those private cooperative transfers of particular goods which the second law facilitates. The convention or general agreement to accept this second law is an agreement to respect private agreements to transfer of particular rights, and so transfer of what the rights are rights to. The third convention, instituting promises and contracts, is also a general agreement concerning particular agreements, this time more fully reciprocal and future-involving ones.[17] The reflexivity increases as the general agreements succeed one another, correcting for their predecessors' limitations. The first convention is a stable collective resolution to make individual possessions in the future more stable. The second is an adjusted general resolve to require the proprietor's consent before adjusting distribution to suit particular need or wish. The third is a general resolve to fix or secure private mutual agreements involving agreement to future delivery, or delivery of "general" rather than "individual" goods,[18] by the interposition of a "promise," a form of words that is taken to bind the speaker to the specified delivery, on pain of never being trusted as a promisor again, should she fail to deliver. This third invention makes explicit, at the private level, what all along was implicit at the general level—that those who encourage others to depend upon their expressed resolves regarding behavior affecting others, and do not carry out these expressed resolves, incur appropriate distrust, which will make future exchange, "commerce" or "intercourse" more difficult for them, unless they can move beyond their reputation for unreliability. Trust, and distrust as the inevitable consequence of disappointed trust, now assume center stage, whereas in the discussion of the earlier conventions they had been implicit only. Promise licenses the promisee to disable the defaulting promisor from future promises or contracts with her and her acquaintances, by initiating distrust of her word.

Promise depends doubly on the spoken word—it is a verbal agreement to a verbally specified future action, and it incorporates consent that one's reputation as a normally trustworthy person be taken from one, should one fail to perform what one promised. This reputation, and its destruction, will normally take a verbal form, just as promises do. This is not to say that one first has to be "given a character for trustworthiness" before that character can be taken away by the victims of one's broken promises. But character is close to "name," and to have any sort of name is to be a member of a group with a language, language used for record-keeping concerning its members, as well as for expression of intention, threat, request, consent, acceptance, offer, contract, prediction and several sorts of evaluation. A special sort of evaluation, person-evaluation, has to be present, and, included centrally in that, an evaluation of a person's trustworthiness that is preserved, updated and shared. This mutual policing was not mentioned by Hume in his discussion of the earlier artifices. It introduces coercion into the story, and sets the stage for the specialization of the policing task, which comes with the next artifice, government.

Coercion was not present from the start, or, if it was, was not important enough to deserve mention. The first important coercive measures, threats to deter promise-breaking, are scarcely contrived, since some distrust is the inevitable psychological consequence of disappointed trust. What is contrived or "artificial" is both its spread from the immediate victims to possible future victims, and also its specific focus—this person is distrusted, not all promisors. Only once we have names and records, to facilitate recognition of who and what we are, can distrust be restricted to those particular persons who are known to have proved themselves untrustworthy.

Detection of promise-breakers is easy, compared with detection of robbers and thieves. But detection would serve no protective purpose if we could not reidentify the offender. If we live in a small society we may remember his face, but we cannot warn our friends against him unless he has a name, and so a character he can forfeit. The informal penalty of distrust as the more or less spontaneous response to untrustworthiness is possible with this special sort of untrustworthiness, infidelity to promises, in a way it is not with many others. When a promise made to us is broken, we can be in no doubt who made it, and so who has let us down. If we are the victims of theft, or of rape by masked men, we may become generally suspicious of others who, for all we know, will steal or rape, but our distrust will be diffuse. We may harbor suspicions against specific persons, but usually suspicions are the most we can have, so it would be manifestly unfair to brand these people as thieves or rapists.

Promise-breakers are necessarily "caught red-handed," that is, known for who they are. But that may be the only sense in which they are caught. If they move beyond the field within which we can spread the word, then they escape this spontaneous penalty. It is just this limitation of the informal enforcement of promise and contact that is remedied by the next artifice, the invention of magistrates as official penalizers and record-keepers. Their net is cast wider than any victim's punitive net could be cast. We increase our collective ability to identify rule-breakers as such, and limit their power to break the rules again, by specializing the jobs of detection, labelling, record-keeping and penalizing. But all of that lies beyond the scope of what Hume includes in the *"Laws of Nature."* When those laws are no longer seen as the laws of a Divine Lawgiver, then they seem to include none that deal specifically with retributive justice. Retribution lurks threateningly in the offing once we have the third law of nature, the one requiring the performance of promises, but all that it actually incorporates is acceptance of the threat of the natural response of distrust, and the deliberate communication of that by the victims.

Hume goes out of his way to liken both the ceremonies signifying consent and the verbal act of promising to religious superstitions. They both are acts that dramatically alter rights, that suddenly attach, to individually selected individuals, rights that they did not possess before the "magic" acts of consent or of promise. Only if the second and third laws of nature are kept does their magic extend from the moral world to the real world, where they make their participants not just "tolerable" but also "advantageous" to one another. Hume is unequivocal in his claim that these are "useful" artifices, and that respect for them is of enormous social importance. Nevertheless, there is something less than wholehearted in his endorsement of them.[19] He certainly does not want them taken as paradigm sources of obligation, and even in their own rightful sphere, private transfers, he seems to delight in making them look ridiculous, albeit useful. They are a kind of secular "baptism, or communion, or holy orders" (T. 525). They tempt us into "feigning" that impossibilities have occurred; they "deceive the mind" about their own real nature. Neither property rights nor magistrates come in for the sly satire to which Hume subjects promise and the symbolical versions of consent. The artifices that empower single individuals, through their own wills, to change the moral–cum–legal situation, seem to incur his suspicion. Promises are "mere artificial contrivances for the convenience and advantage of society" (ibid.). They are useful contrivances, but in endorsing their force, and so recognizing it as moral force, the thoughtful moral judge will realize that this artifice is known to invite its own elevation to predominance, to pride of place among the sources of obligation. It flatters the individual will, and it civilizes and blesses a relatively ruthless form of self-interest, that which lacks "any kindness" to others. Hume contrasts the cooperation it facilitates with that which occurs between friends in a much more stark way than when he described the transition from family and friendly cooperation to the general cooperation needed to get property instituted. Indeed, he implies that it is not until promise is invented that "the self-interested commerce of men begins to take place and to predominate in society" (T. 521). In theory, it should not "entirely abolish the more generous and noble intercourse of friendship and good offices" (ibid.), but it is known in practice to threaten them. Why should those consumed by the interested affection bear anyone a real kindness, or expect anyone to have any kindness for them, if they can get the services they want by unsentimental contract, with its implied threat of penalty for breach of contract? Kindness and friendship seem to be seen by Hume as threatened by contract in a way they were not threatened by property rights and consent. The threat lies primarily in the very resort to threat.

The situations that call for the use of contract are typically ones where there is a known temptation for the second or later performer in a cooperative scheme to free-ride on the contributions of earlier performers. I gladly accept your help in getting my corn in, but am tempted then to break my promise to give return help. Only the knowledge that I will be just as glad of your help next year, and that neither you nor your neighbor will help me if I am known to welsh on such deals, keeps me to my word. Hume shows a very clear awareness of the essential structure of iterated prisoner's-dilemma-type games, when he summarizes the nature and point of contract: "Hence I learn to do a service to another, without bearing him any real kindness; because I forsee, that he will return my service, in expectation of another of the same kind, and in order to maintain the same correspondence of good offices with me or with others" (T. 521). Tit for tat comes into its own, and becomes not just an individual but a social strategy. The "correspondence" of good offices is not just one on one, but between each and another who communicates with others, and so between each and all.

We should compare this description of why each party observes the terms of an individual contract with the description Hume gave of the reasons the first general convention was adopted. There the first performer was confident that the others would imitate her example. A sense of common interest was enough to "induce any one of them to perform an act of justice, who has the first opportunity" (T. 498). Common interest, the interest of the whole as well as of every part, motivated conformity. But what motivates people to keep contracts is plain self-interest, and it takes the power of initiating penalty to give a first performer assurance that the second performer will also perform. The preference structure has changed. Bringing in the corn is another and somewhat nastier game than not grabbing one's neighbors apples, or burying the garbage, or dowsing one's campfire (to use the sort of examples that game theorists such as Howard Sobel[20] have used to illuminate the structure of different and differently motivated sorts of cooperative games).

I have emphasized the dynamics and dialectical character of Hume's account. There is not one problem of cooperation; there are many, and the solution to one creates the conditions for the emergence of different and sometimes tougher ones.[21] The invention of contract is a solution to the need to induce persons without any kindness for one another to work together to mutual advantage. Property rights, on Hume's construal of them, initially solved a different sort of problem—the problem of extending cooperation from those who do feel kindness toward one another to a larger group towards whom they may or may not feel any kindness. That slight difference can make all the difference between contract and convention, and so between contractarian and non-contractarian moral theories.

It is individual contracts that presuppose a preference-ordering in which, but for penalty, each party would prefer that only the others perform. The convention which invents contract, which gives the words "I promise . . ." or "I solemnly undertake . . ." their force, does not itself presuppose this plain opposition of interests. There is a common interest in these words' having binding force, and whoever has opportunity to take them to have this force when others use them will have unproblematic reason to interpret them in an "exemplary" fashion. If I hear you promising him to help with his harvest and then hear him complain that you reneged, I will have every reason to cooperate in branding you a promise-breaker. I lose nothing by this cooperative act, and we all are supposed to gain. We unite to maintain the vault of the institution of contract, by continuing to take that special form of words as binding, and as subjecting the speaker to conditional penalty, whenever the words are spoken with understanding of their meaning and without obvious intent to jest or to make believe. As Hume puts it, the words must "be a perfect expression of the will, without any contrary signs" (T. 524). Since their point is to make the one addressed by them believe in the speaker's solemnly expressed resolution, then we need very evident contextual or other signs if they are to be taken as mere make-believe.

Other things equal, "I promise" binds. For it to bind, all speakers have to "by concert, enter into a scheme of actions, calculated for common benefit, and agree to be true to their word" (T. 522). Hume at this point should have added "and to help spread the word," for we have to agree to help force others to be true to their word, if the scheme is to work. Hume goes on here, echoing his earlier formulation of what a convention is, and what motive there is for accepting it: "Nor is there any thing requisite to form this concert or convention, but that every one have a sense of interest in the faithful fulfilling of engagements, and express that sense to other members of the society. This immediately [without interposition of threat of penalty?] causes that interest to operate upon them; and interest is the *first* obligation to the performance of promises" (T. 522–523, bracketed question my interposition). The interested obligation to the performance is two-fold. First, there is the interest each has in the general dependability of promises, and so in the credibility of the threat each promise incorporates. This interest obliges each to help spread distrust of promise-breakers, as well as to trust other promisors, and be a trustworthy promisor. Second, there is the particular interest one has, in virtue of this scheme to penalize, in avoiding the conditional threat accepted when one makes a particular promise—there is an interested obligation to keep each promise one makes.

It is in this complex way, through concerted and sustained social action to motivate participants in isolated undertakings to be true to their word, that we "give each other security of our conduct in any particular incident. After these signs are instituted, whoever uses them is immediately bound by his interest to execute his engagements, and must never expect to be trusted any more, if he refuse to perform what he promis'd" (T. 522). Through our concerted scheme of actions, particular business deals between partic-

ular parties become secured. Promise can become "a bond of security" among profit-oriented non-friends only through the less
secured, more trusting cooperation of the whole community—of
friends, partners, rivals and neutral sympathetic bystanders. It is
only because people are able to cooperate without threat of penalty
for non-conformity that they are able to set up a scheme to penalize non-conformers to the rules of promising. The third law of
nature depends upon the very possibility, as well as upon the details, of the first and second laws. Threat-secured cooperation, cooperation despite the temptation to free-ride, cooperation between
those who have no kindness for one another, itself free-rides on
the unsecured but tolerably safe cooperation of fellow persons,
each of whom has at least some kindness for at least some of the
others.

IN VIEW OF THE recurrent attempts[22] of others to pin some contemporary label on Hume's account, I shall permit myself a few
"farther reflexions" on Humean justice. His account of the three
"laws of nature," it should now go without saying, is neither utilitarian nor contractarian, and not merely because it would be anachronistic to foist either label upon it. Having said this,[23] I shall
now say it once more, with feeling.

It is not utilitarian because, although social utility plays a major
role in the story, the requirement for the adoption of a social artifice is that it be deemed "infinitely advantageous to the whole,
and to every part" of society (T. 498, my emphasis). "A regard to
public interest, or a strong extensive benevolence, is not our first
and original motive for the observation of the rules of justice" (T.
495–496). A concern for or sympathy with the public interest *is*
the source of the reflective approbation we give to justice, but the
driving motivation which is then approved is that of enlightened
self-interest, or family interest, enlightened enough to appreciate
a common interest with other persons and other families. Hume's
term "utility," like his term "interest," in any case does not cover
every aspect of a person's or a society's happiness; it covers only
those things that he classifies as "useful" rather than "agreeable."

The account is not contractarian because neither the first convention, setting up private property, nor the next two conven-

tions, instituting transfer by consent and by contract, are general agreements made by persons whose preference structure is that for which contract is designed. Unlike the typical contractarian's parties to a hypothetical social contract, Hume's convenors do have sympathy with each other's concerns and a limited amount of generosity. They have friends, lovers and children, and care about their interests, and they are capable of feeling sympathy for total strangers. They are also mindful that "our situation, with regard both to persons and things, is in continual fluctuation; and a man, that lies at a distance from us, may, in a little time, become a familiar acquaintance" (T. 581).

Hume's account of justice does make it rest on agreements between the persons who are to come to have recognized rights, and these agreements or conventions could be seen as hypothetical *express* agreements. But they are neither contracts nor hypothetical contracts. This is true not just because "even promises themselves . . . arise from human conventions" (T. 490), but because they lack the typical features of contracts. As Hume expresses their content, they do not specify exactly what each party must "deliver," or when it is to be delivered, and so they do not specify what would count as breach of contract, or when one party's failure would cause the other parties' contractual obligations to lapse. They do not incorporate penalty clauses. If I were a party to the Humean convention setting up the right to transfer property, to make gifts, and to engage in barter, exactly what counter conventional behavior of mine would justify my fellows in concluding that their conventional obligations, to me at least, had lapsed because I had not delivered what I had agreed to deliver? Would it be only seizure without the owner's consent that would make me a non-cooperator? Seizure, presumably, is what it would take to break the *first* law, creating stability of possessions. The transgression of the second law can scarcely be the very same as the transgression of the first. What then must I do to transgress specifically the second law, to go against the second agreement? Well, I might repossess what I had consented to have "translated" into the property of another, without her consent to the repossession. Or I might *receive* from another, with that person's consent, goods that I know to have been earlier transferred without the consent

of the person then the owner. Or I might recognize the false right
of other such receivers of stolen goods. Or I might refuse to recognize the right of those who did acquire property by barter or
by free gift. Any of these actions would go against the agreement
to allow the transfer of property, so long as it is transferred with
the owner's consent. But not all of these actions, if indeed any of
them, would give my fellows cause to think that the general
agreement had broken down, so that their obligations lapsed—
that *they* were now free to repossess, to seize without consent, to
exchange stolen goods, to refuse to recognize any rightful transfers, or even to do any or all of these in their dealings with me.

Hobbesian covenants become invalid "where there is a feare of
not performance on either part,"[24] and Lockean social contracts
incorporate penalty for non-performance. Humean conventions
are agreements that are not deemed invalid simply because an occasional person transgresses them, and they do not incorporate
penalty clauses. The convention setting up promise and contract
as a form of private agreement *does* incorporate a penalty for
promise-breakers, but not a penalty for those who transgress the
general convention on which promises rest, the agreement to invent, recognize and respect promises. "All of them, by concert,
enter into a scheme of actions, calculated for common benefit, and
agree to be true to their word; nor is there anything requisite to
form this concert or convention, but that every one have a sense
of interest in the faithful fulfilling of engagements, and express
that sense to other members of the society" (T. 522–523). No penalty is requisite, and no penalty is likely to be levied against those
who, having expressed this sense of interest in fidelity to promises, fail to do their bit to enforce it—who accept promises from
known promise-breakers, or who in any other way, short of actual
promise-breaking, fail to be true to their expression of agreement
to establish promise and contract.

The fact that few if any contemporary social philosophers calling themselves contractarians see their version of the social contract as incorporating penalty clauses, let alone as becoming invalid once any party to the hypothetical contract fails to deliver,
once she fails to discharge any of her hypothetico–contractual obligations, means that they mislabel themselves, not that Hume

should be labelled "contractarian." He is neither a contractarian in his social theory, as Hobbes, Locke and Rousseau might well be seen to be, nor a fake contractarian, like many of our contemporaries. Jean Hampton, although very clear about the mislabelling, is willing to be a party to it, and to absorb Hume into the supposedly *true* contractarian tradition.[25] If Hume's "conventionalism" is seen as the correction and the truth of earlier contract theories, then it will be very difficult to see twentieth-century representatives of that tradition as anything but false to this truth, so long as they insist that the parties to the agreement would really prefer non-compliance to compliance. Once Humean convention, rather than Hobbesian covenant, becomes what Hobbes calls "the fountain and original of justice," then the old Hobbesian covenanters must become Humean convenors in their psychology, in their prior understanding of the rewards of cooperation, in their understanding of the sort of goods they gain by it, in their willingness to set examples, and to take some risks. For Hume's convenors, in virtue both of their psychology and of their grasp of what sort of common interest we share, can in consistency risk more in return for more than can either Hobbes's covenanters or the hypothetical parties to most contemporary contractarians' versions of the social contract.

It is for the sake of increased force, increased ability and increased security that the parties to Hume's general agreements enter, in concert, into their cooperative schemes of action. But their security against free-riders is not very great. The presence of flourishing sensible knaves is a risk that has to be accepted by the equally sensible full cooperators.[26] So long as they too are also flourishing, as judged by their own values, Hume's convenors need not be unduly perturbed by the fact that the unjust are not reliably "brought to justice." Given these Humean persons' enlightened psychology, they can easily tolerate a few parasites. So long as the cooperative scheme is not wrecked by the knaves' defections, knaves and non-knaves can afford to despise each other's values, each lot dismissing what the other gets as "worthless toys and gewgaws." The Humean agreement can accommodate a small incidence of fundamental value-disagreement better than any Hobbesian covenant could. Unlike Hobbes's "Foole," transgressors of Humean conventions cannot in reason expect that, if discovered, they will perish, through being "left, or cast out of Society."[27] If their misdeeds are bad enough, sufficient to excite very great resentment, and to be made crimes, they may if caught be executed, imprisoned or shipped to Australia, but some of them will get off with no more than a reputation for lack of integrity, which, given their values and the wealth they may have accumulated before being found out, they may not much mind. Hume's just persons do not have to be obsessed with the problem of how the less just can be made to suffer. But they do have their pride, and are not proud of becoming "cullies." Like their benevolence, their long-suffering has its limits. Eventually, official penalizers for violations of the laws of justice do get invented, by a fourth convention, a law which is not itself a "law of nature," but one to enforce "the three laws of nature." That convention is the topic of the following chapter.

11

The Shelter of Governors

Here then is the origin of civil government and allegiance. Men are not able radically to cure, either in
themselves or others, that narrowness of soul, which
makes them prefer the present to the remote. They cannot change their natures. All they can do is to change
their situation, and render the observance of justice the
immediate interest of some particular persons, and its
violation their more remote. These persons, then, are
not only induc'd to observe those rules in their own
conduct, but to constrain others to a like regularity, and
inforce the dictates of equity thro' the whole society.
(T. 537)

The state of society without government is one of the
most natural states of men, and may subsist with the
conjunction of many families, and long after the first
generation. Nothing but an encrease of riches and possessions cou'd oblige men to quit it. (T. 541)

By means of these two advantages, in the *execution* and
decision of justice, men acquire a security against each
others weakness and passion, as well as against their
own, and under the shelter of their governors, begin to
taste at ease the sweets of society and mutual assistance.
But government extends farther its beneficial influence;
and not contented to protect men in those conventions
they make for their mutual interest, it often obliges
them to make such conventions, and forces them to seek
their own advantage, by a concurrence in some common end or purpose. (T. 538)

Governments, Hume believes, are invented to make what is in our
long-term interest also in our short-term interest, so that our "violent propension to prefer the contiguous to the remote" (T. 537)

will not lead us to sacrifice our greater to our lesser good. They are also invented to help us "concert" complicated cooperative enterprises such as building bridges, opening harbours, digging canals. They are to give us "shelter," so that we can taste at ease the sweets of society and mutual assistance. Shelter from what? The panegyric of government, as "one of the finest and most subtle inventions" of our ancestors, now has to take on a slightly grimmer note. Magistrates are to shelter us from potential criminals in our midst, as well as from external attack. Their first task is the "execution and decision of justice," and, among the cooperative enterprises of complicated design that they are to coordinate are the raising of ramparts and the disciplining of armies. It is because there are public enemies that we need the shelter of governors. Once we have them, we use them also to add to "the sweets of society and mutual assistance," by having them coordinate the building of bridges and opera houses, in addition to air raid shelters and prisons.

Hume's account of the artifice of government and the artificial duty of "allegiance," or non-passive obedience, to non-tyrannical governors is itself fine and subtle, avoiding the infirmities of most of its competitor accounts. Some of its finest features are ones that must be highlighted through comparison. Only if one comes to the reading of Hume from reading not just Hobbes and Locke, but also Hooker, Filmer, Stair and Pufendorf, is one, for example, likely to appreciate what his contemporaries clearly did appreciate, that the duty of obedience, in Hume's hands, gets drastically pruned of the luxuriant growth that centuries of slave-owning, patriarchal and feudal forms of life had encouraged to flourish. Hume explains and endorses one and only one form of the traditional duty to obey the powers that be, namely "allegiance to magistrates." Authority is a human artifice, and the one form of it that Hume endorses is the authority of governments over their subjects. All those subdivisions of the duty to obey that Stair's *Institutions,* or even Hutcheson's *Institutio,* had listed and dwelt on—servants obeying their masters, wives their husbands, children their parents,[1] lay persons their pastors—get quietly swept away. All that remains is the duty to obey non-oppressive magistrates and the officers whom they appoint to assist them. This could, of course, include all the old bosses, should the sovereign choose to depute power to all husbands, fathers, employers, popes and bishops. But that is unlikely, and none of these would-be commanders have any moral right to command obedience unless and until some artifice empowers them, and until this artifice secures moral endorsement. If Hume thought that all these authoritarian structures were useful artifices whose right-holders' sense of their rights could be sympathized with, from a moral point of view, he kept that belief from the readers of the *Treatise*. I take his silence on the duty to obey anyone other than magistrates to be an eloquent silence, given the multitude of noisesome rules of obedience that it followed. Even Locke has the natural law containing some duties of obedience, in particular those of children to parents and wives to husbands.[2]

Hume does see wives as having some special obligations, but not of obedience. He diagnoses the evils of the institution of marriage as it existed in his own day as due primarily to male pretensions to and abuse of authority. "Tyrants, as we know, produce rebels; and all history informs us, that rebels, when they prevail, are apt to become tyrants in their turn. For this reason, I could wish there were no pretensions to authority on either side; but that every thing was carried on with perfect equality, as between two equal members of the same body" (*Essays*, p. 560). Hume's wish was counterfactual. He never married, and he withdrew this essay. (Because it provoked so many offers of marriage? Because it so offended his more patriarchally inclined male friends? We know only that he came to judge it "too frivolous for the rest, and not very agreeable neither even in that trifling manner.")[3]

Governors, and with them the very idea of authority, are invented to gear everyone's long-term interest in an orderly society, and in a good reputation as a trustworthy member of that society, to their inclination in favor of short-term gain. Our violent propensity to prefer the contiguous to the remote is to be contained or redirected by the threat of violence from official law enforcers. This "infirmity" of our nature, this failure of our imagination to make vivid enough to us, at moments of decision, the real costs of allowing our love of gain "heedless and impetuous movement," becomes a "violent" and socially troublesome propensity only

when the existence and success of the artifice of contract has produced the conditions where false pretenses and fraud[4] can flourish.
It is the temptation to cheat, whenever one judges one can get
away with it or whenever one does not mind the penalty of acquiring a reputation as a cheat with the limited group with whom
one's victims can communicate, that makes this general infirmity
a grave problem. One may pretend that one is willing to do one's
share of draining the meadow (see T. 538), along with one's nine
hundred and ninety-nine fellow villagers, but one may be insincere, and count on one's fellows' inability to check up on just who
has and who has not done his share, or not mind becoming known
as untrustworthy in such communal undertakings. Before long,
no one will be willing to be the cullies of such cheats, so no mead-
ows will get drained, and all will lose.[5] As David Miller has
noted,[6] on Hume's account it is not selfishness which creates the
main problem that government is to cure or at least contain; on
the contrary, it is the unenlightened limits of our self-interested
passion that pose the problem—it is our imagination's failure to
properly serve our interested passions. Governments are to be
their subjects' collective "prospective glasses,"[7] to remedy the defects of their self-interested sight, defects that lead them to "act in
contradiction to their known interest" (T. 535). The remedy that
governments provide against contagious fraud and the consequent
threat of a breakdown of trust in consent, promise and contract
consists in changing the human situation so that contiguous and
remoter goods "shock in a direct line," and do not oppose one
another. Book Two has prepared the reader for this general type
of remedy. "'Tis certain, that when we wou'd govern a man, and
push him to any action, 'twill commonly be better policy to work
upon the violent than the calm passions, and rather take him by
his inclination, than what is vulgarly call'd his *reason*" (T. 419).
The violent propensity to prefer the contiguous is to be controlled
by itself, by removing the opposition between contiguous and remote goods. The magistrate is to take us by our inclination to
avoid the risk of arrest and punishment, and by our wish to have
the chance of winning a medal, a taxbreak, a legal profit or a government contract.

Who are to be governors, and what ensures that they can and will perform the task of aligning everyone's close and remoter interests? Those suitable to fill this role, at least to get the invention of government off to a successful start, will be those who "have no interest, or but a remote one, in any act of injustice" (T. 537). One must find, and agree on, exemplary rule-observers, and then agree to make it in their power and their interest to "constrain others to a like regularity, and inforce the dictates of equity thro' the whole society" (ibid.). What has freed them from a troublesome form of the preference for close over distant goods? Hume describes the candidate magistrates as those "who being indifferent persons to the greatest part of the state, have no interest, or but a remote one, in any act of injustice; and being satisfied with their present condition, and with their part in society, have an immediate interest in every execution of justice, which is so necessary to the upholding of society" (ibid.). These exemplary rule-observers are exemplary not in "strength of mind," but in their moral luck. They have no immediate interest in anything except law-abiding acts. Are they ones, like Epictetus, who are content with earthenware lamps that no one wishes to take from them? Or are they so rich that they have no temptation to add to their riches by quick unlawful gains, not rich or not generous enough, however, to say, "What are my parasites to me? . . . May they live and prosper: I am strong enough for that!"[8] Hume gives us too few indications of exactly how circumstances have managed to turn up a few persons whose nearest interest already lies in the observance of the laws of justice, persons who have escaped the general contagion of sensible knavery, which "pushes me forward in this way by imitation, and also affords me a new reason for any breach of equity, by shewing me, that I should be the cully of my integrity, if I alone shou'd impose on myself a severe restraint amidst the licentiousness of others" (T. 535). By some lucky turn of events, a few persons retain their integrity without either needing to impose severe constraints on themselves, or risking becoming cullies. These fortunate persons, with their cost-free integrity, are to push the rest of us forward to imitate their integrity, but they do it by imposing costs for rule-breaking. Integrity will now pay, or at least it will if all goes well, if the magistrates retain their own integrity and continue to find it in their interest to "inforce the dictates of equity thro' the whole society." The interested passion is correcting its own heedlessness by a fine and subtle turn onto itself.

In this section, "Of the origin of government," there are frequent references to equity and inequity as well as to justice and injustice. Magistrates are to end a rash of breaches of equity, and prevent their recurrence. They are to "inforce the dictates of equity." How did equity get so closely allied with Humean justice? Is it as artificial as the justice it now seems to accompany? Hume sometimes lists it among the natural virtues (T. 578), and he never says that it is artificial. What does he take it to be? Is it a constraint upon the content of property rights and contracts? Or is it a constraint merely on their interpretation, on "the decision and execution of justice"? Is it the formal virtue of equality before the law, of non-preferential treatment, treating all parties to some transaction evenhandedly? If so, then even a set of property rights that made no bows to any demands for equality might be observed and administered with utmost equity. Contracts that took exploitative amounts of service in return for miserable wages might be equitably kept by the employer to each exploited employee. What are the "breaches of equity" that are so tempting and so contagious when conditions are right for the invention of governors? Presumably various exemptions of oneself from obligations that one hopes others still fulfill, such as doing one's share of the swamp-draining. Breaking an agreement will be, *qua* breach of agreement, unjust. *Qua* exemption of oneself from a rule that applies to one, *qua* a laying of the whole burden on others, it will count as inequitable. In Hume's story, it is inequity as well as injustice that drives people to respond to fraud with official force. Equity and inequity in this sense could be displayed by parents towards their children, perhaps even among friends. As Hume uses it, it is closer to fairness than "justice" is. Hume may take an "equity as fairness" view pretty much for granted, and it is a pity that he did not say more about the link between artificial justice and natural equity. But there is no doubt that it is "violations of equity," as well as of injustice, that it is government's job to avoid and prevent.

Governors are to be models of contagious equity and justice. But the main job they do, the execution and decision of justice, is their monopoly. Their use of force must not become contagious, otherwise the invention fails. Governors are invented to give us shelter against a climate of inequity and violence. They are invented on occasions when "violations of equity . . . become very frequent in society and the commerce of men, by that means . . . render'd very dangerous and uncertain" (T. 535). If state terrorism comes to make life equally dangerous, or if state inequity and violence lead to counter-violence, then the invention will have failed. The subtlety of any successful invention of government will lie in the balance it achieves between giving magistrates enough power to perform their appointed task, and giving them a strong enough interest in setting an example of equitable conduct and of enterprising mutual assistance. "Thus bridges are built; harbours open'd; ramparts raised; canals form'd; fleets equip'd; and armies disciplin'd; every where, by the care of government, which, tho' compos'd of men subject to all human infirmities, becomes, by one of the finest and most subtle inventions imaginable, a composition, that is, in some measure, exempted from all these infirmities" (T. 539).

In some measure exempt. Among magistrates' accomplishments is the disciplining of armies, and sometimes the armies are used to put down rebellions. After his panegyric for government in Section VII, Hume in the subsequent sections qualifies this high praise of what government might be. What we actually invent is often not so subtle, and gives plenty of scope for the human infirmities of magistrates to weaken the sheltering structure that the artifice is supposed to provide. What is more, "though government be an invention very advantageous, and even in some circumstances absolutely necessary to mankind; it is not necessary in all circumstances, nor is it impossible for men to preserve society for some time, without having recourse to such an invention . . . And so far am I from thinking with some philosophers, that men are utterly incapable of society without government, that I assert the first rudiments of government to arise from quarrels, not among men of the same society, but among those of different societies. A less degree of riches will suffice to this latter effect, than

is requisite for the former" (T. 539–540). The disciplining of armies turns out to be the magistrates' first task, even before they turn
to "the execution and decision of justice." "Civil government . . .
succeeds the military" (T. 541), and camps are the true mothers of
the cities that come with settled government.

As Hume recognizes in the *History of England,* when he looks at
the Germanic tribes and the evolution among them of the artifices
of property and of the authority of leaders, quarrels between
neighboring groups (which need not always be quarrels over
property) can provide an opportunity for the rudiments of government to develop before stable property rights, at least in land,
have been recognized. There are many reasons people can have to
invent that subtle but dangerous thing, a superior. In the *Treatise,*
the claim that property is the first and most fundamental social
invention commits Hume to treating government as a later invention, which arises when new problems about property develop—
problems that arise from the successes and the limits of the earlier
inventions. So in the *Treatise* we should suppose that the warfare
between groups that gives rise to the rudiments of government in
the form of military leaders is warfare which ends in the victors'
having the spoils of war. "Now foreign war to a society without
government necessarily produces civil war. Throw any considerable goods among men, they instantly fall a quarrelling, while
each strives to get what pleases him, without regard to the consequences" (T. 540). (This is a fine description also of what happens to allies after a victory.) Hume here mentions "life and limbs"
as "the most considerable of all goods" at stake in foreign war, but
this should not be taken to imply that life is now assimilated to
property, that Hume has suddenly become Lockean. By the time
government is invented, according to Hume's story, there will be
many forms of property, some of them fairly abstract, but all
property will still be "external" to the proprietor, and transferable
to others. The only way one's life and limbs could become one's
property, within Hume's conceptual system, would be by the advance of the medical profession to the point at which we are now,
where organs and limbs are transferable. We may be able to accept
both Hume's definition of property and Locke's version of its ex-
tensio   ⌐ cover life and limb, but Hume could not. He sees gov-

ernment as needed to prevent or end "commotion" and disorder arising primarily, although not exclusively, out of quarrels over transferable property. The "opposite passions of men" now come to include some that are not "the love of gain." The problem seems to have become more general. It now includes all forms of violent propensity to prefer the contiguous to the remote. Violence in a passion typically comes from conflict in motivation, and leads to social conflict. The job of governments is to bring or restore "calm."

Inventing these artificial pacifiers is one thing; keeping them going with calm transitions from one to the next, another. Hume thinks it quite plausible to suppose that the first magistrates, or the first military-into-civil leader, were appointed by some promise-involving convention. After all, promise and contract are devices lying ready to hand, and it is their very "progress" that sets the stage for government. The general recipe is to turn a troublesome force on itself, in order to find a remedy for the disorder it is causing; and so using a special form of promise to get us out of the mess that promise has landed us in would be a true Humean remedy. Promise would work very well for the task, since "the same convention, which establishes government, will also determine the persons who are to govern, and will remove all doubt and ambiguity in this particular" (T. 554), and "a *promise* fixes and determines the persons, without any uncertainty" (T. 555). Hence it is likely that "the authority of the magistrate does *at first* stand upon the foundation of a promise of the subjects, by which they bind themselves to obedience; as in every other contract or engagement. The same promise, then, which binds them to obedience, ties them down to a particular person, and makes him the object of their allegiance" (T. 554). Promise includes acceptance of threat of penalty, and there certainly are penalties for non-compliance with this magistrate-creating promise! Contract would thus become reflexive, as the victims of freedom and of breach of contract freely contract to recognize the authority of a given magistrate who, by his penalizing power, makes the commercial world safe again for trusting and trustworthy contractors, and even may "force them to seek their own advantage, by a concurrence in some common end or purpose" (T. 538). A few unfree agreements may be the price of the protection of freely made agreements: "Not contented to protect men in those conventions they make for their mutual interest, it often obliges them to make such conventions" (ibid.). The reflexivity of contract and promise is negative, not positive, feedback. The contract to create a government is a contract to limit as well as to protect freedom of contract, a contract to remedy the ills of a contractual society, by introducing new obligations that only *at first* arise from contract or promise. Hume's concessions to contractarian theories of political obligation are as fatal as his more famous attacks. Government begins in contract, as a homeopathic cure for the evils that reliance on contract has wrought. Contract alone, like reason alone, cannot save us. Contract must be accompanied and guided by other sources of obligation to be really beneficial.

Once government is started, and the first governors, those to whom allegiance has been promised, die or become incompetent, or outlive those who promised them allegiance, then the strength of the invention gets tested. For it to do any useful work beyond the first generation, some mechanism for transfer of power must be in place, some rule by which subjects can discern who is the new "object" of their allegiance. Promise may once have fixed it; but what fixes it as generation succeeds generation? Hume's most famous answer is the negative one, "not re-negotiated contracts." Were we like silkworms and butterflies, one generation going "off the stage" at once, another succeeding it, then a sequence of social contracts would be a possibility. As it is, with the population of subjects constantly changing, "one man every hour going out of the world, another coming in to it" ("Of the original contract," *Essays,* p. 476), we must find some other way of legitimating and replacing governments. Contractarianism is for the butterflies.

We need the shelter of governments, and we begin to learn conformity to law, long before we reach the age of consent. Once we do reach it, we still cannot reasonably expect to have veto powers over "the established constitution." If there is to be stability and order (the very ends that justify having any governments), then "the new brood should conform themselves to the established constitution" (ibid.) and make their criticisms or grievances grounds for appeal, orderly change or peaceful protest, rather than rebellion. "Some innovations must necessarily have place in every human institution, and it is happy where the enlightened genius of the age gives these a direction to the side of reason, liberty, and justice: but violent innovations no individual is entitled to make: they are even dangerous to be attempted by the legislature: more ill than good is ever to be expected from them" (*Essays*, p. 477). These are Hume's words in 1748, after the "unhappy troubles" of the Jacobite rebellion in 1745. His pronouncements about justified rebellion changed a little in tone, emphasis and refinement as he rethought this politically charged topic throughout his life, lived through the Jacobite rebellion, observed the workings of freedom of the press and studied and wrote history. The changes we find in his last thoughts about this question, in "Of the origin of government" (written 1774, published in 1777), differ from his first thoughts, whose title they echo, more in their differentiations between the various arms of state power than in the substance of their conclusions. "The factitious duty of obedience" (*Essays*, p. 38) is clearly presented for what it is—factitious or artificial. The question is what artifice is best, how power can be distributed or balanced within it so that it is best freed from the infirmities of those who occupy its several offices, people to whom obedience, deference or allegiance is due in virtue of the offices they hold. In the *Treatise*, the chief task of magistrates is the execution and decision of justice. In his last round on this topic, Hume refines this point: "We are, therefore, to look upon all the vast apparatus of our government as having ultimately no other purpose but the distribution of justice, or, in other words, the support of the twelve judges" (*Essays*, p. 37). This disambiguates "magistrates" and demotes monarchs, ministers, lords and elected representatives to the role of "a number of officers, civil and military, to assist them in their government" (T. 537). "Magistrates" turn out, in the end, to be magistrates.

Rebellions are rarely directed against judges; and rebellions against monarchs, their militia and other officers are sometimes motivated by the wish to restore a constitutional balance of power between executive, legislative and judicial power. The right to rebel against constitutional powers in their constitutional balance is not one which any constitution is likely to recognize. Hume, after noting how the British monarch, as supreme magistrate, was in his time in some ways above the law, in that only his ministers could stand trial for any injury or wrong, writes, "But though the constitution pays this salutary compliment to the prince, it can never reasonably be understood, by that maxim, to have determined its own destruction" (*Essays,* p. 491). The laws cannot expressly provide any remedy against abuse of power by the highest authority, and so cannot give any *entitlement* to resistance. But neither must or can they establish "a tame submission." The extraordinary remedy is resistance, but it is a remedy that goes with a liberty or moral right, not with an express entitlement. When there are disputes about divisions of power for which the constitution provides no adequate means of settlement, or disputes about the constitutionality of proposed ways for making innovations to the constitution, the limits of the artifice of government will show themselves. However subtle an invention we make it, "it is well known, that every government must come to a period, and that death is unavoidable to the political as well as to the animal body. But . . . one kind of death may be preferable to another" (*Essays,* p. 51).

The right to attempt to overthrow the constitution by violence is one that no constitution can formally acknowledge and protect without building in not just its own obsolescence but its own violent destruction. But does this mean that it cannot formally recognize any right of subjects to fall back on violence when perceived abuse of powers, or controversies over division of powers and over constitutional amendment, cannot be settled by peaceful means? Hume is not in favor of constitutional recognition of the right to appeal to force as a last resort of the aggrieved, even when their grievance takes the form of a charge of unconstitutional uses of power by others. The American Constitution, guided here more by Locke's recipes than by Hume's,[9] does protect the right of citizens to bear arms, and that dangerous-seeming protection has a pretty good record, so far as violent rebellion goes. (Its effect on violence against private citizens is another matter.) One civil war in two hundred years is a fairly enviable record, about as good as that of Britain, where that dangerous right is not recognized.[10] When Hume writes that "on some occasions it may be justifiable, both in sound politics and morality, to resist supreme power" (T. 553), he is not contradicting his claim that there can be no express *entitlement* or constitutionally protected right to rebel against the present constitution. On occasions best left only vaguely specified, it may be sound morals and sound politics to jettison an unsatisfactory or evil artifice, even at the cost of temporary disorder.

The twelve judges for whose sake the whole apparatus of government exists will be the official experts on the constitution, and so on their own authority in relation to monarch, army, legislature, voters and other subjects. When Hume designs a "perfect commonwealth," he does not completely separate judicial, legislative and executive powers. In "Of some remarkable customs," he had argued that two separate "wheels" of government, each balancing the other in power, could in some conditions work well enough, without any explicit rules giving one the right to correct the workings of the other. In "Idea of a perfect commonwealth" he has the Lord Chancellor, and other officers of the law, appointed by a complexly elected senate, who act in an executive capacity and also form part of the legislature. Laws can be proposed by the county representatives who elect the senators, and also by the county magistrates elected by the representatives, so that there is legislative initiative from many levels. Hume's non-utopian utopian scheme (non-utopian in its assumptions about human nature, utopian in its non-provision for any transition to it from any actual constitution) has the interesting innovation of a "court of competitors," consisting of unsuccessful candidates for senator who received more than one third of the vote. This body, a sort of second-rung loyal opposition, can propose legislation, and its members also act as a sort of court of appeals. Should their proposed legislation be rejected by the senate, they may "appeal to the people, that is to the magistrates or representatives" (*Essays*, p. 520). In this multi-tiered "perfect" system of government, authority is widely distributed, and checks and balances abound. It is designed with an eye to providing orderly processes of extensive debate, appeal, and non-violent innovation initiated at any of several levels among elected officers, and those appointed by them. Hume criticizes Harrington's *Oceana* for not providing "a sufficient security for liberty, or the redress of grievances. The senate must propose, and the people consent; by which means, the senate have not only a negative upon the people, but, what is of much greater consequence, their negative goes before the votes of the people" (*Essays,* p. 515). Hume is well aware of the power that lies in the mouths of those who set the agenda, who do the proposing. The "distribution of justice," which is the chief business of government, will, in a perfect commonwealth, distribute the power of proposing, as well as other powers, and do so with justice and equity.

Hume's blueprint has not, to my knowledge, been tried,[11] nor was he sure that it could be tried in Britain (see *Essays,* p. 52). It fails his own test of experiment. I cite it here mainly to show how, throughout his life, he wrestled with the problem of how a constitution could, without arranging for its own destruction, arrange for processes of orderly innovation, initiated at any of several levels.[12] There can be no coherent entitlement to violent rebellion, but there can be entitlement to challenge, protest, appeal and propose innovations. Hume stops short of including in his draft of a perfect constitution any entitlement to resort to arms as a last resort, but one of his chief criticisms of monarchies is that "the sword is in the hands of a single person, who will always neglect to discipline the militia, in order to have a pretence for keeping up a standing army" (*Essays,* p. 527).

"'Tis certainly impossible for the laws, or even for philosophy, to establish any *particular* rules, by which we may know when resistance is lawful; and decide all controversies, which may arise on that subject" (T. 563). The laws cannot coherently give us the permission to break them,[13] so we will always lack entitlement if we resist "the present constitution." If moral philosophers issued maxims attempting to tell us in detail how to identify "egregious tyranny" (T. 549) and "flagrant instances of tyranny and oppression" (T. 522)—so that, say, Hume's own general moral rule that there is nothing wrong or unjust, nothing to be morally condemned, in resisting tyrants, were to be made specific enough to be applied to particular present cases—they would then be setting themselves up as a supreme moral court, and would merit Hobbes's criticism of those who "think themselves wiser than all others, clamor and demand right Reason for judge, yet seek no more, but that things should be determined, by no other mens reason but their own . . . bewraying their want of right Reason by the claym they lay to it" (*Leviathan*, Chapter 5). If there were any particular rules to apply to tell when resistance is morally justified, when a virtuous person can resort to it, they would have to be agreed on by all who take up the moral point of view, agreed on as not merely right in theory but right given the anticipated application of them by those tempted to resistance. Clearly there are no such specific rules that command general acceptance. Hume is right: philosophy cannot do much to guide the perplexed when it comes to the identification of intolerable tyranny. Discretionary powers of moral judgment to moral agents are unavoidable. We will find out what is intolerable by seeing what is not tolerated.

We can reach moral agreement more easily in retrospective judgments about which past rebellions did some good, and brought beneficial innovations, than we ever can about rebellions and proposed rebellions whose success and whose results are still uncertain. Hume can and in his *History of England* does welcome the innovations brought into British life by many past rebellions, including the "Glorious Revolution" of 1688. But to welcome its results, from a moral point of view, and to accept its present authority, is not to claim either that there was a moral entitlement to rebel against the Stuarts or that the rebels were, although without entitlement, morally justified. To have had moral justification, they would need to have been right in finding James II an intolerable tyrant (and Hume's view, in "Of the Protestant succession," is that he was tyrannical at most in matters of religion). They would also have to have had reasonable confidence both in the success and in the good consequences of the Hanoverian venture. In the *Treatise,* Hume refrains from concurring with their judgment that rebellion was justified, but he judges that things did in fact work out well. Duncan Forbes, an invaluable guide to the political context and background influences on Hume's thoughts and second thoughts about the objects and measures of allegiance, accuses him of "twisting and turning" in the *Treatise* on the question of the Whigs' right to depose James II. "The plain fact seems to be that although Hume can defend, quite unambiguously and consistently with his general principles, the present establishment, he cannot unambigously and consistently defend those who brought it about."[14] But the very distinction between defensible grounds for institution and defensible grounds for preservation is part of Hume's consistently maintained general position, and there is nothing ambiguous about the claim that those who had no moral entitlement (that is, no morally endorsed legal or customary right or privilege) may still have a moral liberty, may have acted "without injustice." Hume warns us that his own position ("Government is a mere human invention for the interest of society. When the tyranny of the governor removes this interest, it also removes the natural obligation to obedience. The moral obligation is founded on the natural, and therefore must cease where *that* ceases"; T. 552–553) is "too subtile for the vulgar." The combination of that position with a denial of any *entitlement* to disobedience even against tyrants has sometimes proved "too subtile" for the philosophers, too.[15]

Moral obligations and entitlements are founded on natural obligations—that is, on the obligations and entitlements that beneficial artifices recognize. Not only do they cease when the artifice fails; they do not come into being until a beneficial artifice is in place. Persons who judge, rightly or wrongly, that the Stuart dynasty has become tyrannical, so that the obligations of obedience and the entitlements to political power that those supreme magistrates recognize all lapse, cannot claim any *entitlement* for their political actions to depose and replace the Stuarts, until they have successfully initiated a new acceptable form of government, whose recognition of obligations to obey and entitlements to political power can become morally endorsed. At the moment of revolution, the only rights and obligations that exist will be those of "natural justice," and they are, on Hume's view, silent on the question of who is to obey whom. At most, they give us a moral liberty to resist. There is a moral liberty to resist oppressive powers; there could be a contract-based moral entitlement to insist on a magistrate's fulfilling some actual contract that he or she had made; but there cannot be even a conditional general moral *entitlement* to disobey, if there is no longer any established legitimate "authority" to grant the entitlement. Authorities and titles stand or fall together. Since authority is an artifice, and is the same artifice as that of entitlement to govern and to confer titles, if we rebel against all established authorities it cannot be done on higher authority. Hobbes's distinction between a right as a liberty and a right that is protected by the voice of the law (not just tolerated by its silence) will serve us well enough to see how Hume can in perfect consistency say both that no one can have entitlement to resist the present constitution, and that resisting tyrannical institutions need be neither wrong nor unjust. "Those who took up arms against *Dionysius,* or *Nero,* or *Philip the second,* have the favour of every reader in the perusal of their history; and nothing but the most violent perversion of common sense can ever lead us to condemn them" (T. 552). Only deontologists need express permissions and entitlements before they feel morally justified in any action. Hume's ethics make all strict obligations artificial, and make "the factitious duty of obedience" a particularly derivative one. Its "strictness" is purely formal, correlative to its factitiousness. Hume, in "Some farther reflexions concerning justice and injustice," makes this strictness and absoluteness a hallmark of artifice. But it is not a hallmark of moral approval and disapproval, and the ultimate moral court of appeal is the moral point of view.

In his account of the origin, source, measures and objects of "allegiance," Hume shows at least implicit awareness that at the root of that very concept is the concept of a free or "ledig" person. (According to the O.E.D. the word is a derivative of "liege," which is itself most probably a borrowing from the Old High German "ledig," meaning "free.") Authority is an invention of free persons, who bind themselves to a superior not in order to renounce their liberty, but to keep their liberty from degenerating into disorderly unjust license. Liberty is prominent in the *Treatise* account of government,[16] less prominent but still clearly there in the later accounts. "A great sacrifice of liberty must necessarily be made in every government; yet even the authority, which confines liberty, can never, and perhaps ought never, in any constitution, to become quite entire and uncontroulable" (*Essays,* p. 40). We do not need to be contractarians to see that we are not morally bound to submit to tyrants, and we do not need to be conservatives to agree with Hume that for moral philosophers to spell out in detail the criteria for tyranny is both a hopeless and presumptuous task, and one the very attempt at which may, if their views catch on, rebound upon them, turning subjects into either hamstrung servants[17] or too-ready rebels, and turning governors into self-protective tyrants. Both in the silence of the laws and in the silence of deontological moral maxims, " 'Tis certain, that the people still retain the right of resistance; since 'tis impossible, even in the most despotic governments, to deprive them of it. The same necessity of self-preservation, and the same motive of public good, give them the same liberty in the one case as in the other" (T. 563–564).

Hume's account of the artificial virtues "acquires more force as it advances" (T. 455). The points made at the beginning about the advantage of restraining one's pursuit of advantage get generalized from private interest to the public interest, when Hume argues that government, perhaps begun by an interested promise or contract which would "fix" the "object" of allegiance, is continued by allowing other principles to select subsequent rulers. "The same interest, therefore, which causes us submit to magistracy, makes us renounce itself in the choice of our magistrates, and binds us down to a particular form of government, and to particular persons, without allowing ourselves to aspire to the utmost perfection in either" (T. 555). As avidity restrained itself when an agreement was reached to stabilize possession, so the broader interest in having orderly "distribution of justice" restrains itself when, after government is instituted, we agree to let succession be determined by principles other than direct appeal to public interest. It is in the public interest to restrain the appeal to public interest, as it was in each person's private interest to restrain *its* direct pursuit. What is more, the rules by which governors are selected, after the hypothetical first governor, are the same "frivolous" but salient ones that Hume invoked to explain the details of property distribution. Long possession or "prescription," present possession, conquest as the analogue of "occupation," succession in the form of the passing of authority from father (or at least from parent) to eldest son (or at least to child)—all these "principles of the imagination" can serve to fix the objects of our allegiance. There is also a fifth principle, positive laws, which Hume treats as derivative of the others. The constitutional law on succession of authority may be changed suddenly by the legislative power, but "few subjects will think themselves bound to comply with this alteration, unless it have an evident tendency to the public good: But will think themselves still at liberty to return to the antient government" (T. 561). Jacobites are a natural human phenomenon, and wise legislatures will give their innovations the appearance of a return to old and fundamental laws. As Hume put the matter in "Of the origin of government," it is "from necessity, from inclination *and from habit*" (*Essays,* p. 37, my emphasis) that society, and political society, is maintained.

Habit reinforces what interest first justified, and it is in the interest of our governors and ourselves to let habit have some authority. However, only royalists lacking all sympathy with those who rebelled against Charles I will maintain that "the true rule of government is the present established practice of the age" (*Essays,* p. 498), without adding the qualifying clause, "provided the practice is not tyrannical." Hume's views on the royal prerogative, the powers of parliament, the right to resist, are subtle, and subtly presented. As David Miller has said, "A more carefully balanced standpoint it would be hard to imagine!"[18] Authority is factitious or artificial, and its confinement of natural liberty must be carefully monitored. Allegiance is "imperfect obedience," not servitude. The job of government is the prevention of inequity and injustice, and assistance in enabling us to enjoy at ease the sweets of society. The perfection of government is the protection of liberty. We invest liberty, in the hopes of a return in more secure rights and liberties. Locke put it memorably: "The end of law is not to abolish and restrain but to preserve and enlarge liberty" (*Second Treatise,* section 57).

HUME ADDS TWO last sections to Part II of Book Three, one concerned with the obligations of governors to one another, and one concerned with the obligations of modesty and chastity imposed by society on women who intend to be wives and mothers. The "laws of nations" impose weaker obligations on the governors of nations, in their relations with the governors of other nations, than the civil or natural laws impose on ordinary persons. Sexual mores impose weaker obligations of chastity on possible fathers than on possible mothers. "As to the obligations which the male sex lie under, with regard to chastity, we may observe, that according to the general notions of the world, they bear nearly the same proportion to the obligations of women, as the obligations of the law of nations do to those of the law of nature" (T. 573).

The point of the obligation of female chastity is to keep track of paternity, to enable each child to know its father, each father his "own" children. This interest requires that women, by "the voluntary conventions of men" (*sic,* T. 570), be subjected to what is a "conspicuous example" of artifice, the demand that they be chaste. "What restraint, therefore, shall we impose on women, in order to counter-balance so strong a temptation as they have to infidelity? There seems to be no restraint possible, but in the punishment of bad fame or reputation; a punishment, which has a mighty influence on the human mind" (T. 571). The temptation, Hume goes on, is "the strongest imaginable," and women would "over-look remote motives in favour of any present temptation" were they not, from childhood, trained to an against-the-grain modesty, what Hume cleverly calls "a preceding backwardness." This training is intended to give them "a repugnance to all expressions, and postures, and liberties, that have an immediate relation to that enjoyment" (T. 572). Here speaks the young man whose sister and female companions were reared on *The Ladies Calling,* which did its best to persuade young women that it was natural of them to resist sexual advances, so that courage would be required of them on their wedding night. Hume clearly thinks this gets matters backwards, and, helped by Pufendorf and Mandeville, works out why the "conventions of men" have invented the unnatural artifice of female modesty. In later years he had relations with women whose "fame" was somewhat dubious, and who seemed neither daunted by that fact nor too prone to that "peculiar degree of shame" which the world tried to inflict on sexually unrestrained women.[19]

What Hume says about the relaxed duties of governors in international relations, and the relaxed sexual morality of males, raises "curious questions" once we ask what social interests are at stake that justify the obligations that are customarily imposed on princes and on males. Although the obligations of nations and their leaders are said to be weaker versions of the ordinary obligations of justice, the consequences of violating some of these obligations, those of respect for other nations' property or territory, are grave enough: "Where possession has no stability, there must be perpetual war" (T. 567). The Hobbesian state of perpetual war comes, according to Hume, not before property is invented, nor even in the more disorderly conditions that occasion the invention of government, when there is frequent fighting between and within groups; it comes only after governments have been invented, have disciplined their armies and have conceived designs on each other's territories, unconstrained by the "law of nations." This worst threat, of perpetual war between territory-hungry nations and subsequent discord within the camp of the victors over the spoils of war, is avoided if nations respect one another's territories, and also respect those rules which are peculiarly theirs, "the sacredness of the persons of ambassadors, the declaration of war, the abstaining from poison'd arms, with other duties of that kind" (ibid.). "Where possession has no stability, there must be perpetual war. Where property is not transferr'd by consent, there can be no commerce. Where promises are not observed, there can be no leagues nor alliances. The advantages, therefore, of peace, commerce, and mutual succour, make us extend to different kingdoms the same notions of justice, which take place among individuals" (T. 567–568).

Is there a parallel threat of "perpetual war" if males do not take their relaxed duties of chastity so seriously? And must they, too, abstain from poisoned arms? Just how far does the analogy between the special though not so demanding obligations of males and the special though not so demanding obligations of nations go? And why, if the danger of breach of these obligations is perpetual war, does Hume think that "the *natural* obligation to justice, among different states, is not so strong as among individuals" (T. 569)? Mackie remarks how questionable in Hume's lifetime, let alone in ours, is the judgment that the interest we have in observance of the laws of nations is less urgent than the one we have in justice within nations. When we excuse nations for pursuit of apparent self-interest, even when that involves breach of treaty or disregard of other nations' rights, as Hume notes that we often do excuse them, Mackie proposes that "the reason is not that international justice matters less, but that as yet there is much less of an established system of justice between states."[20] To taste at ease the sweets of society and mutual assistance, we need observed international conventions, and also "domestic" peace, in both senses of that term.

For Hume, the point of government is the peaceful distribution of justice, and the justification for resisting governments is tyranny. Wherever we have forms of cooperation that give some authority over others, we need safeguards, such as the freedom of the press, to which Hume devotes one of the first essays he wrote after the *Treatise*. We need them to prevent the tyranny that would justify rebellion and endanger cooperation. We need them also to watch for the new injustices that the presence of official guardians of justice can bring. "History, experience, reason sufficiently instruct us in this natural progress of human sentiments, and in the gradual enlargement of our regards to justice" (E. 192). Our safeguards against inequity and tyranny require commensurate enlargement. Hume's own emphasis on the evil of discord, the evil of inequity, the evil of tyranny, shifts as the "perpetual intestine struggle" in his own society appeared to give ascendancy now to authority, now to the forces demanding equity and liberty. "There is no more effectual method of betraying a cause, than to lay the stress of the argument on a wrong place" (*Essays,* p. 501). Different places are wrong at different times, and Hume's emphasis shifts from time to time. But the goal, a form of government that shelters us from inequity and injustice without involving us in war or in tyranny, remains constant. At the end, in the essay "Of the origin of government," he "owns" that liberty is the perfection of civil society, even though he acknowledges a "but . . .",[21] It was his own thesis in the beginning. "Rara temporum felicitas ubi sentire quae velis, et quae sentias, dicere licet" ("Rare the happy times when we can think what we like, and are allowed to say what we think").

12

Reason and Reflection

With what confidence can we afterwards usurp that glorious title, when we thus knowingly embrace a manifest
contradiction? (T. 266)

But the heart of man is made to reconcile contradictions. (*Essays*, p. 71)

But this sense must certainly acquire more force, when
reflecting on itself, it approves of those principles from
whence it is derived, and finds nothing but what is great
and good in its rise and origin. (T. 619)

The glorious title of inventive philosopher should go to one who
not merely shows us how to avoid, or at least to reconcile, the
contradictions into which we continually stray, but also demonstrates how we may achieve reflexive self-acceptance, agreement
with ourselves. Absence of contradiction is reason's minimal demand. Reflexive self-understanding is the perfection of theoretical
reason; reflexive self-approval, that of practical reason. This, in
effect, is what Hume at the end of Book Three claims for his version of moral judgment.

But can it be practical reason that, in its moral guise, achieves
this higher-level self-award, if reason is and ought only to be the
slave of our passions? It is the moral sentiment that is said by
Hume to approve of itself, but at points during his exposition of
its workings his antirationalist mask slips revealingly, and we are
reminded that the love of truth is as inventive and lively a passion
as any other, and one that freely cooperates with our moral passions. It is no slave. When Hume is intent on persuading us to
agree with him that the moral authority of government is not de-

rived from any promise of obedience made by their subjects, he confides that he has "all along endeavour'd to establish my system on pure reason" (T. 546), and then he assimilates popular opinion on this matter to the conclusions of his "pure" moral reasoning, since "the opinions of men, in this particular, carry with them a peculiar authority" (ibid.).

Hume's project all along has been not so much to dethrone reason as to enlarge our conception of it, to make it social and passionate. Within Book One, Part III, "reason" is enlarged from deductive reason to inductive, experience-informed, "animal" reason. The antirationalist arguments of Book Three, Part I, are directed against the sufficiency, for morals, of a reason that includes causal reasoning and probability estimation, as Hume has analyzed them. The "pure reason" which shows us that the authority of governments does not rest on any promise is not just the ability to follow the arguments that Hume has given about the separate functions of the artifices of promise and of government, the limited temporal scope of the former, their common foundation in interest; it is also the ability to respond to his appeal to our capacity for enlarged sympathy in seeing which forms of these artifices are morally acceptable forms, and our ability to adjust our views to those of our fellows in order to be capable of any convention and any moral agreement. This capacity for mutually adjusted intention and agreement is the capacity to be reasonable,[1] and the "peculiar authority" that Hume here accords to the "universal consent of mankind" is but a moderate extension of the sort of "reason" that his argument has already appealed to. "Pure reason" is already socialized and sympathetic reason.

The "authority" accorded to popular opinions about moral vice and moral obligations in this passage is not authority on the intricacies of any argument or stretch of reasoning, but an authority on matters of fact and of feeling. (Once we have invented authorities, we can transfer the concept of authority to spheres beyond the political.) Each person knows whether or not the characters of dishonesty, infidelity and treachery displease her, and whether or not she expects other moral judges to share her displeasure. (She also may know whether she regards these as three different vices, or as only variants of two or of one.) She knows as well or better than others whether or not she made a promise to obey some government, and she knows whether or not she feels obligated, and expects her fellows to regard her as obligated, to pay her deceased parents' debts. She knows what she thinks about the moral force of any promise of obedience that they may have made on her behalf. "No man can either give a promise, or be restrain'd by its sanction and obligation unknown to himself" (T. 549). The artifice of property that Hume thinks reasonable people do agree on is one which allows heirs to inherit debts, but the artifice of promise that he defends as useful, if kept in its limited place, is one by which a particular person, for a particular purpose, binds himself to some limited particular payment, to be made within a particular limited time. He does not defend serfdom (or marriage vows of lifelong obedience). "A man, who acknowledges himself bound to another, for a certain sum, must certainly know whether it be by his own bond, or that of his father; whether it be of his mere good will or for money lent him, and under what conditions, and for what purposes, he has bound himself" (T. 547). We have some authority about what promises we have made, to whom, for what and by when, and about what similarly limited promises have been made to us. We also have authority on the question of whether we would disapprove of someone who, after being sold into slavery or sworn into serfdom by another, disobeys her "master." The "reason" that leads us to agree with Hume about which artifices are and which are not morally tolerable is not "pure" in Kant's sense. It is guided by wide sympathies, and by pleasure in mutually beneficial cooperative schemes and in the human traits that enable such schemes to work.

Hume's *Treatise* campaign to show the limits of "reason," to point up what it cannot do alone, was a campaign directed first against deductive reason or "demonstration," then against a wider-ranging inferential reason that was limited to fact-finding, fact-relating and fact-predicting. This latter needs to "concur" with some motivating passion before it goes to work for any practical or evaluative purpose. But the love of truth is among our passions, and it can motivate us to reason, to write treatises, to become moral anatomists who tell ourselves that our systems might also serve practical morality, might concur with other passions besides the love of truth. "Reason," by the end of the *Treatise,* has effectively teamed up with the calm passions it has served within the *Treatise.* It is no longer "reason alone" (T. 414), and the splenetic humour against it has spent itself, replaced by a "serious good humour'd disposition" (T. 270). "Where reason is lively, and mixes itself with some propensity, it ought to be assented to" (ibid.). Nor is it merely tolerated, as a human capacity that demands its regular exercise, and enjoys an agreeable "stretch of thought or judgment." Its final status in the *Treatise* is as a very important natural virtue or ability. (Only grammarians will care which term we use.) "'Tis impossible to execute any design with success, where it is not conducted with prudence and discretion; nor will the goodness of our intentions alone suffice to procure us a happy issue to our enterprizes. Men are superior to beasts principally by the superiority of their reason . . . All the advantages of art are owing to human reason" (T. 610). The slave has earned manumission. Reason joins the virtues, and may even be put high on the list.

It is, however, a transformed reason. It is accompanied by other abilities and virtues; it is answerable to the shared moral sentiment; it is itself a social capacity, both in its activities and in the standards of excellence by which they are judged.[2] If we ask what is more important, "whether a clear head, or a copious invention, whether a profound genius, or a sure judgment? In short, what character, or peculiar understanding, is more excellent than another? 'Tis evident we can answer none of these questions, without considering which of these qualities capacitates a man best for the world" (T. 610). The world for which virtuous reason capacitates a person is a peopled world in which the value of a good memory or good computational ability will depend on whether or not some art or invention has supplied a substitute for them. Writing, orderly record-keeping, libraries, information retrieval systems, computers, as well as the social tasks we set people, will make a difference to the value put on different mental abilities (E. 241). There may even be modish pretenses to inability to do in one's head what some invented thought-aid will do for one. "'Tis so far from being a virtue to have a good memory, that men generally affect to complain of a bad one" (T. 612).

Hume is confident that there is one ability that will never be handed over to our artificial intelligence-aids. This is judgment. "The defects of judgement can be supplied by no art or invention" (E. 241). Judgment we reserve for ourselves, in part because we would not trust any invention of ours enough to entrust judgment to it, in part because "that faculty is never exerted in any eminent degree without an extraordinary delight and satisfaction" (T. 613). There are some things we do not trust, or want, our robots to do for us. It is significant that this special human mental prerogative has the name, "judgment," that Hume uses for the deliverances of the moral sentiment as well as for those of the intellect.[3] Both our moral judgments, and those other more purely intellectual affirmations that we also reserve for ourselves, resist full intellectual analysis. We cannot fully spell out any rules or standards that determine our judgments, and so we could not, even if we wanted to, construct anything else to do our judging for us. We have a mighty addiction to general rules and they do influence our judgments, but we attribute our formulated rules to our judgments (T. 149), not vice versa. Our capacity for judgment outruns our capacity to reduce our judgments to rule. We trust our powers of judgment more than we trust our ability to generalize about what determines our judgment. We judge judgment to be somewhat mysterious, a wonderful unintelligible instinct in our soul, still somewhat unintelligible even after our best efforts to understand it and to turn it on itself. Hume had formulated rules for judging causes and effects, but his own judgment of those rules was that they do not instruct us in their own application, and so they leave the most difficult questions to a judgment for which we have and can have no useful rules. There will always be some "stretch of judgment" where no rules guide us, and where we need "the utmost sagacity to choose the right way" (T. 175).

Judgment, theoretical and practical, has been turned on itself in the *Treatise,* and the judgment passed on the usefulness of general rules to guide it is guarded. We are addicted to trying to formulate rules, but their usefulness is limited. In the practical sphere, we need them in the form of rules and laws to regulate our more impersonal dealings with one another, but in Hume's full version of morality, rules play a very minor role. It is judgment, not higher laws, that we must use to endorse, or refuse to endorse, habits, customary rules, the conventions of justice and the laws of our land. The character traits that we judge to be virtuous include the willingness to conform to the beneficial conventions of justice and of non-tyrannical government, but most of them do not consist in conformity to rules, nor are there any useful rules to tell us what count as virtues. Moral judgment has to be exercised to know how, say, the virtue of gratitude is best expressed in given circumstances, and it takes moral judgment of a more general sort to recognize that any sort of gratitude is a virtue. The moral sentiment is a faculty of moral judgment that, in judging what habits, motives, actions and reactions are virtuous, has to judge when ordinary moral discretionary judgment has been well or badly exercised. That is not the only thing that it judges, but it must judge powers of judgment, since most virtues call for them when expressed in action. Even with the artificial virtues of justice and allegiance, judgment will be needed to decide when, for example, an emergency is pressing enough for the strict laws of justice to be suspended (E. 186), or when a magistrate is tyrannical enough for disobedience to her[4] to be no moral wrong. To judge who is and who is not a morally vicious traitor, and whether Robin Hood was a common robber or a public benefactor, knowledge of accepted customs and popular moral maxims will not be enough to guide us.

Reason in its new guise is the power of judgment, along with the aids we judge helpful for judgment. These include some general rules, especially rules of inference, and include also the habits and customs that support and nurture our best powers of judgment and inference—those, that is, that we judge to be best. In the first *Enquiry,* Hume makes explicit what had been implicit in many of his *Treatise* discussions: that linguistic customs are among the most important of these social roots of reason, roots from which it draws its nourishment and its powers. When he lists the factors that explain why human reason (by its own judgment) outstrips other animal reason, he includes, as the final factor, our ability, through conversation and books, to learn from one another, to share, pool, accumulate and pass on information and the other fruits of experience. We "enlarge the sphere" of our experience by talking, writing, reading (E. 107, note).

This great enlarger of our reason works only if we "acquire a confidence in human testimony," or at least a confidence in our powers of collective dialogue and dialectic. The *Treatise* is a single thinker's work, but it is one that submits its own findings to confirmation or criticism from its readers. It invites response. It puts trust in its eventual readers and in their powers of "the most critical examination" (T. 272). In the conclusion of Book One, as I noted in Chapter 1, Hume submits his "system" not just to his readers but also to "honest gentlemen" who do not read philosophy treatises. Their worldly experience is the proper testing ground for philosophical systems of the sort that Hume aims to establish, ones in which the "fiery particles" from the imagination will be tempered with "a share of this gross earthy mixture" that is found in non-philosophical honest citizens. In the first *Enquiry,* this combination of deference and high ambition is repeated and elaborated, when Hume expresses his hope that "though a philosopher may live remote from business, the genius of philosophy, if carefully cultivated by several, must gradually diffuse itself throughout the whole society, and bestow a similar correctness on every art and calling. The politician will acquire greater foresight and subtility, in the subdividing and balancing of power; the lawyer more method and finer principles in his reasonings; and the general more regularity in his discipline, and more caution in his plans and operations" (E. 10). Hume himself gained some earthy mixture for his fiery philosophical principles (and perhaps gave philosophical cautionary advice) when he served as aid to General Conway. He did a little subdividing and balancing of political power for a year as undersecretary of state for Northern Britain, and certainly he argued enough with his lawyer cousin Lord Kames, trying to impart finer principles to his reasoning. So there was a two-way exchange, in Hume's lifetime, between philosophical and non-philosophical callings. It might even be said that many of his own philosophical principles have gradually diffused themselves through the whole culture, not just in Britain and France, whose culture he knew and hoped to influence, but also

in America, about whose culture he was uncharacteristically optimistic. He expressed himself thus: "I am an American in my
Principles, and wish we woud let them alone to govern or misgovern themselves as they think proper."[5] He hoped not just for
American self-government, rather than British colonial misgovernment, but also for philosophically influenced public opinion in
America. In 1772 he wrote to Benjamin Franklin complaining of
British prejudice against his views, and adding, "I fancy that I
must have recourse to America for justice."[6]

   What one must have confidence in, for a literate and non-tyrannical culture to flourish, is not just testimony but ability and willingness to engage in civilized debate, including philosophical debate once philosophy is "carefully cultivated by several". Hume
ended the conclusion of Book One predicting that his own philosophical enthusiasm would lead him to overconfident claims for
his system, and acknowledging his trust in his public's ability to
administer "the test of the most critical examination". In his "Advertisement" to the *Treatise,* he had written: *"The approbation of the
public I consider as the greatest reward of my labours; but am determin'd
to regard its judgment, whatever it be, as my best instruction"* (T. xii).
This is not undue deference, or sycophancy. What determines
Hume to be instructed by responses to what he wrote is his own
social view of reason. Reason in solitude becomes not just abstruse
but monstrous. Reason's appropriate nourishment is civilized debate within "the republic of letters," along with thoughtful response even outside that republic, wherever reason hopes for influence. Hume's "deference" to his readers is required of him by
his own reconstruction of reason as social, concerned and responsive.

   The selection between different versions of reason, solitary or
social, passion-hostile or passion-friendly, formal or less formal,
primarily practical or primarily theoretical, is made by "reflection." The final arbiter is reflection both in the wide sense, in
which it is simply sustained attention, and in the strict narrow
sense, in which it is the turn of a faculty or movement of mind
back onto itself. Reflection in the wide sense showed that "demonstration" is limited in its achievements, and that sound causal
inference is inductive. Reflection in the strict sense showed that

inductive causal reasoning could validate itself, but that, when the combination of inductive and demonstrative reason was turned on demonstrative reason, its evidence is "reduc'd to nothing" (T. 182). The scepticism about reason expressed in the conclusion of Book One is the outcome of the tests of both sorts of reflection. It is a scepticism about a solitary intellectualist reason in which induction plays second fiddle to "demonstration," and it is also a scepticism about solitary intellectualist modes of both kinds of reflection. "Very refin'd reflections have little or no influence upon us; and yet we do not, and cannot establish it for a rule, that they ought not to have any influence; which implies a manifest contradiction" (T. 268). This was the contradiction, or manifest internal conflict, that destroyed the *Treatise* protagonist's confidence in this version of reason, and temporarily plunged him into "the deepest darkness". The contradiction is between a norm enjoining reflection and a practice of ignoring its awkwardly negative outcomes. "Most manifest absurdities" and "express contradictions" resulted when intellectualist reason was turned on itself, and when our expressive reflective practice was compared with the content of the conclusions of this solitary and argumentative reflection.

The reason which is a lively love of truth along with an ability to search for it was turned on itself at the end of Book Two, with less dramatically negative results. It looked a little ridiculous, but not manifestly absurd. There was amused acceptance of it, not philosophical melancholy, let alone despair. By the time reason in Book Three is fully reconstructed, moralized and made sociable, there is no longer any hint of melancholy or of derision when it is turned on itself. The moral anatomist is proud of his work, and particularly proud of his reinstitution of the intellectual virtues. They are not, like Aristotle's version of them, dominant over other abilities and other virtues, but they are given very high praise. When the reason of moral philosophers is turned on practical and socialized reason, we find that "all the advantages of art are owing to human reason" (T. 610).

"Lively reason," reason as not merely "mixed with some propensity" (T. 270) but seen as itself that particular propensity that we call "curiosity or the love of truth," returns us to the postponed question of what Hume takes truth to be. Reason, when it works properly, produces truth as its effect (T. 180). Truth consists in "an agreement . . . either to *real* relations of ideas or to *real* existence and matter of fact" (T. 458). And what is it for an idea to "agree" with real matter of fact? Agreement is what we have when two or more people say the same thing, when the second or third parties reaffirm what the first affirmed, do not contradict it. So an idea agrees with a matter of fact when it repeats it, when it says what some impression also "said," when it is true to its original. It is no accident that both "agreement" and "truth" are terms used by Hume in his ethics as well as in his succinct account of the epistemological value of truth. It is true that he writes "as nothing can be contrary to truth or reason, except what has a reference to it, and as the judgments of our understanding only have this reference" (T. 415–416), but this isolated claim is contrary to his own usage of "truth." The moral virtue of truth, which has complicated sources (E. 238), is surely some variant of fidelity, and comprises a bit more than simply veracity accompanied by fidelity to promises. The latter two virtues do include reference to the sort of truth that "the understanding" is concerned with, but go beyond that. And being a true friend is not just a matter of avoiding lies and broken promises. Truth the virtue is a wider-ranging and more sustained "agreement" than just that of one's words with one's beliefs or one's deeds with one's words. It is trustworthiness, a sustaining of all the forms of trust that are there between friends.

The English word "truth" shares its roots with those of "troth" and "trust," and Hume's use of it, in a moral context, exploits this ancestry. His use of the term in epistemological contexts can, on his behalf, be linked up with his use of it in moral contexts, to eke out the very meager amount he himself says about the real nature of the truth that the understanding is concerned with. Even in that context, he can speak of some versions of reason as "false" (T. 268), where this seems to mean false to their own pretensions. Whatever is true is trustworthy, whether it be a friend, a belief or a version of reason. In all cases truth involves some sort of agreement, some confirmation of expectations. The confirming in the moral case is done by the faithful conduct of the one who has the virtue of truth, who lives up to the self-representations she has previously given. In the case of ordinary beliefs, the confirming is done by the encountered facts. In the case of reason, it is done by its own ongoing record. If my claims about Hume's use, in his epistemology, of metaphors taken from the social and personal realm are correct, then it should come as no surprise that true reason and true beliefs are abstract variants of true friends. True reason keeps its own rules, and produces reliable ideas, ones that do not let one down, whereas false reason betrays its own pretensions. Like false friends, both false reason and false beliefs do not live up to their own pretensions, do not prove firm and solid.

It cannot be claimed that Hume actually says what I have just said about truth, agreement and representation for the whole mind of which the understanding is only one part or aspect. But it is, I hope, true to most of what he does say. It agrees with the manner of his epistemology as well as with the matter of his ethics. Truth is trustworthy representation,[7] whether of reason, of the world or of oneself (a part of that world itself capable of making representations). The love of truth is the appreciation of trustworthiness or reliability, and it shows in our wish to get a true version of reason, to get true beliefs and to find the virtue of truth in our fellow persons.

"A mind will never be able to bear its own survey, that has been wanting in its part to mankind and society" (T. 620). Reason passed the test of reflection only when it became not just the lively love of truth, but also a moral virtue, only when it came to incorporate shared sentiments and a shared cooperative love of truth. Its "part to mankind and society" had been extracted from it somewhat forcibly and dramatically in the *Treatise,* but at the end there is peace between the once-warring contenders for control of the throne.[8] After Hume had employed scepticism to subvert both rationalist reason and fantastic scepticism itself, and placed moral sentiment on the vacated throne, the power drama is repeated, as reason is given shelter under the throne occupied by calm moral sentiment. But this time, once reason gets its seal and patent from the moral sentiment, it proves not the imbecility of its sovereign but her competence, so that it strengthens rather than weakens the governing power. Once true cooperative reason works for a sympathy-based moral sentiment, it prescribes fewer draconian laws and maxims, and avoids both tyranny and imbecility. Then "nothing is presented on any side but what is laudable and good."

The *Treatise* used reflection first to destroy one version of reason, then to establish the sort of customs, habits, abilities and passions that can bear their own moral survey. It thereby reestablished[9] a transformed, active, socialized reason to a "likeness of rank, not to say equality" with sovereign moral sentiment. In the course of the *Treatise,* this subdividing and the balancing of power has been accomplished with the foresight and the subtlety of an accomplished dialectician. Hume's literary tastes were, however, ahead of his time. His anxious questions to his friends, when the *Treatise* first appeared, concerned its manner as much as its matter. "Have you found it sufficiently intelligible? Does it appear true to you? Do the Style & Language seem tolerable?" he presses Pierre Desmaizeaux.[10] Hume's contemporaries' negative judgment on the *Treatise*'s style and intelligibility, and his own "due deference" to them, have held critical sway for too long.[11] Philosophers who agree with Hume in seeing philosophy as part of "the republic of letters," and who read the *Treatise* in its entirety, must deferentially disagree with its author's famous final public judgment on it.[12] Hume should have been more diffident about his own second thoughts concerning the manner of the *Treatise*. But it does not become an admirer of Hume to have a "conceited idea of my own judgment" (T. 274). Safer to fall back on that reflexively authenticated Humean maxim that the true philosopher and the true sceptic will, although diffident of both her doubts and her convictions, "never refuse any innocent satisfaction which offers itself on account of either" (T. 273). Not even Hume can refuse us satisfaction with his *Treatise,* with its manner, its matter, and the aptness of the one to the other.[13]

Chronology
Notes
Index

Hume as a thin young man, from an unauthenticated portrait in the possession of the National Portrait Gallery of Scotland, reproduced with their permission.

Chronology

1711: On April 26, in Edinburgh, David Home (pronounced "Hume") is born to Katherine Falconer and Joseph Home of Ninewells, their third child.

1713: Joseph Home dies.

1713–1722: David spends his childhood at Ninewells, in a household of which his mother, widowed at age thirty and never to remarry, is head.

1722: The family moves to Edinburgh, to a house in the Lawnmarket, so that David and his brother John can study at Edinburgh University.

1723: David matriculates at Edinburgh University. "I passed the ordinary course of study with success." The ordinary course includes Greek (under William Scott), logic and metaphysics (under Colin Drummond), natural philosophy (under Robert Stewart, a convert from Descartes to Newton), possibly ethics (under William Law and John Pringle), and mathematics (under James Gregory). David develops "a passion for literature, which has been the ruling passion of my life."

1725–1726: David returns to Ninewells, with winters spent in Edinburgh. He is encouraged to study law, but finds "an unsurmountable aversion to everything but the pursuits of philosophy and general learning."

1729–1730: After abandoning the study of law, and attempting to express in philosophical writing his "new Scene of Thought," David suffers a breakdown of health, which he self-diagnoses as psychosomatic, "the disease of the learned."

1731:   A new, less sedentary regime of life turns the "tall lean rawboned" young man into "the most sturdy robust healthful-like fellow you have seen, with a ruddy complexion and a cheerful countenance . . . a better companion than I was before."

1734:   David leaves Ninewells for London, then Bristol, where he works as a clerk to Michael Miller, who imports sugar from the West Indies (and possibly is also engaged in the slave trade). He changes the spelling of his name to "Hume," to avoid mispronunciation by the English. In Chirnside, in Hume's absence, he is named by Agnes Galbraith as the father of her illegitimate child. In Bristol, he tries to improve Miller's epistolary style, and to rid his own of Scotticisms. Miller is unappreciative, and, after a quarrel, Hume leaves for France.

1734–1735:   Hume resides in Rheims, learning French, studying, and writing.

1735–1737:   Hume resides at Yvandeau, La Flèche, writing, using the library of the Jesuits' College, and "gravelling" the monks with his arguments about miracles. He completes the *Treatise*.

1737–1739:   Hume is in London, arranging to publish the *Treatise* anonymously. Books One and Two are published by John Noon, January 1739 (price: 10 shillings).

1740:   Book Three of the *Treatise* along with the "Appendix," is published by Longman (price: 4 shillings). *Abstract* of the *Treatise* is published, also anonymously.

1739–1745:   Hume lives at Ninewells, with visits to Edinburgh, awaiting and being disappointed by reviews, writing and publishing *Essays, Moral and Political,* and applying unsuccessfully for the chair of Ethics and Pneumatical Philosophy at Edinburgh University.

1745:   Death of Katherine Home, Hume's mother. "An immense void in our family."

1745–1746:   Hume is tutor to the (mad) Marquess of Annandale, living in London and at Weldehall near St. Albans. He works on *Philosophical Essays* (later *Enquiry*) *Concerning Human Understanding,* "containing everything of Consequence relating to the Understanding that you would meet with in the *Treatise.*" In Scotland the Jacobites rebel.

1746–1748: Hume is secretary to General St. Clair, during the War of Austrian Succession, on a military mission which is supposed to take him to Nova Scotia but in fact takes him to Brittany ("unsuccessful, tho without any Loss or Dishonour"), Ireland, Vienna, and Turin.

1748: First publication of works bearing Hume's name *(Philosophical Essays Concerning Human Understanding,* new edition of *Essays, Moral and Political).*

1749–1763: Hume lives in Edinburgh with his sister Katherine. He applies unsuccessfully for the chair of logic at Glasgow, works on the *Enquiry Concerning the Principles of Morals* (1752), *The Political Discourses* (1752), *The History of England* (1754–1762), the controversial *Four Dissertations* (1757) and the *Dialogues Concerning Natural Religion* (not published in his lifetime). He holds the position of keeper of the Advocates Library, 1752–1757, then resigns after being found guilty of ordering "indecent Books and unworthy of a place in a learned library."

1763–1766: Hume resides in Paris, as private secretary to Lord Hertford, the British ambassador. He is acclaimed, is a favourite of the ladies, (especially of the Comtesse de Boufflers) and develops friendships with Diderot, D'Alembert, d'Holbach, Helvetius, Buffon, and, briefly, Rousseau. Returns, with Rousseau, to England.

1767–1769: London. Hume becomes undersecretary of state, Northern Department, "a Philosopher, degenerated into a petty Statesman."

1769–1776: Hume, with his sister Katherine, lives in Edinburgh. He advises his nephew David on his education, builds a house in the New Town (in St. Andrew's Square) becomes very attached to Nancy Orde, corrects his *History* for new editions, continues to work on the *Dialogues.*

1776: Hume dies peacefully in Edinburgh on August 25, after two years' illness of the digestive organs.

1777: *My Own Life* (which acknowledges the *Treatise*) is published.

1779: *Dialogues Concerning Natural Religion* are published, as arranged on his deathbed by Hume with his nephew David, after Adam Smith declines to take responsibility for their publication.

Hume towards the end of his life, from an engraving used in some editions of his *History of England*.

Notes

1. Philosophy in This Careless Manner

1. Book Two is discussed by John Laird in *Hume's Philosophy of Human Nature* (London: Methuen, 1932); and by Norman Kemp Smith in *The Philosophy of David Hume* (London: Macmillan, 1941). Both find little in it except associationism. Kemp Smith regards it as both an inappropriate sequel to Book One and an inappropriate introduction to Book Three. He says that the extended discussions of pride and love "have no very direct bearing upon Hume's ethical problems and play indeed no really distinctive part in his system" (p. 160). The first to look closely at the links between Books Two and Three was Páll S. Árdal, in *Passion and Value in Hume's Treatise* (Edinburgh: Edinburgh University Press, 1966). Terence Penelhum, *Hume* (London: Macmillan, and New York: St. Martins, 1975), and Barry Stroud, *Hume* (London: Routledge and Kegan Paul, 1977), each devote a rather unenthusiastic chapter to Book Two; and Robert Fogelin, *Hume's Scepticism in the The Treatise of Human Nature* (London: Henley, 1985), attends only to one of its thirty-four sections, "Of the influencing motives of the will," dismissing the rest as mostly "tedious" (Fogelin, *Hume's Scepticism in the Treatise of Human Nature*, p. 109). Nicholas Capaldi gives a good survey of the neglect of Book Two in *David Hume, The Newtonian Philosopher* (Boston: Twayne, 1975).

2. Charles Taylor, too, likens Hume's neo-Lucretian philosophical journey towards self-acceptance to Wittgenstein's philosophical pilgrimage. The destination is "a home-coming to a garden, a grateful acceptance of a limited space, with its own irregularities and imperfections, but within which something can flower." *Sources of the Self* (Cambridge, Mass.: Harvard University Press, 1989), p. 346. For a recent example of the more usual view that pits Wittgenstein against Hume, see S. L. Hurley, *Natural Reasons: Personality and Polity* (New York: Oxford University Press, 1989), p. 101, and n. 38, p. 399.

3. The importance of this dialectic for waking Immanuel Kant from his dogmatic slumbers is persuasively argued by Manfred Kuehn in "Kant's Conception of 'Hume's Problem,'" *Journal of the History of Philosophy* 21 (1983), 175–193.

Kuehn points out that a German translation of this section of the *Treatise* was published in the *Königsberger Zeitung* in July 1771. See also Manfred Kuehn, "Hume's Antinomies," *Hume Studies* 9 (1983), 25–45.

4. See Jan Wilbanks, *Hume's Theory of Imagination* (The Hague: M. Nijhoff, 1968), especially chapter 2, for a study of Hume's claims about the human imagination.

5. In Chapters 5 and 6, I discuss the relations between Book One's discussion of personal identity and the developments in Books Two and Three. An earlier discussion of them can be found in "Hume on Heaps and Bundles," *American Philosophical Quarterly* 16 (1979), 285–295.

6. Hume indicates in several places that he does not consider the reconstruction of causes an activity symmetrical with the tracing of effects. To "mount up" (E. 137) to causes is a different intellectual activity from what we do when we "descend downwards," and he seems to have regarded it as a more speculative and dubious activity. For practical purposes we need to foresee effects, and only the historian (with the aid of records), not the theorizer, can trace causes. In the *Dialogues Concerning Natural Religion,* ed. Norman Kemp Smith (Indianapolis: Bobbs-Merrill, 1947), Philo agrees that "similar causes prove similar effects and similar effects similar causes" (p. 147), but his main emphasis is on *variety* of possible causes for one type of effect. Hume's apparent belief in the asymmetry of cause-tracing and effect-tracing does not fit well with his casual "definition" of a cause as *"an object followed by another, and where all the objects similar to the first are followed by objects similar to the second. Or in other words where, if the first had not been, the second never had existed"* (E. 76). If we could dismiss the whole of this last sentence, and not only its first phrase, as a slip of Hume's pen, then he, if not Philo, would be committed to an account of cause which makes it a sufficient but not necessary ancestor of an event, and then his greater confidence in effect-tracing than in cause-tracing success would be appropriate. "Nothing is more requisite for a true philosopher, than to restrain the intemperate desire of searching into causes . . . his enquiry wou'd be much better employ'd in examining the effects than the causes of his principle" (T. 13).

7. I will substantiate this finding in Chapters 3 and 4.

8. The reviewers and religious readers of the *Treatise* got the underlying message perhaps better than Hume had bargained for, and never ceased to regard him as a dangerously antireligious thinker. When this reputation was destroying Hume's chances as a candidate for the job of professor of philosophy at Edinburgh University, Hume wrote to Henry Home of the dilemma of Principal Wishart, his main attacker on the appointing council. "The Principal found himself reduc'd to this Dilemma; either to draw Heresies from my Principles by Inferences & Deductions, which he knew wou'd never do with the Ministers & Town Council. Or if he made use of my Words, he must pervert them and misrepresent them in the grossest way in the World." Hume's letter of June 13–15, 1745, to Henry Home, in *New Letters of David Hume,* ed. Raymond Klibansky and Ernest Campbell Mossner, (Oxford: Clarendon Press, 1954), p. 17, is

quoted in Ernest Campbell Mossner, *The Life of David Hume* (Oxford: Clarendon Press, 1980), p. 15. Wishart is accused by Hume of much prudence but very little honesty for embracing the latter horn of the dilemma, but the same charge might well be made of Hume's own indirect presentation of his views on religion.

9. Laird, in *Hume's Philosophy of Human Nature,* discusses and criticizes this argument. More recently Fogelin has emphasized its importance for Hume's general attack on intellect's pretensions, in his study of Hume's scepticism. See Fogelin, *Hume's Scepticism in the Treatise of Human Nature,* ch. 2.

10. See Ian Hacking, "Hume's Species of Probability," *Philosophical Studies* 33 (1978), 21–37.

11. See Chapters 3 and 4.

12. The Pyrrhonian sceptic professes to be able to live without turning his inevitable habits of assent into rules. Myles Burnyeat, in "Can the Sceptic Live His Scepticism?" (*Doubt and Dogmatism: Studies in Hellenistic Epistemology* [Oxford: Clarendon Press, 1980), accuses Hume of dogmatism in the first *Enquiry* in asserting without proof that the sceptic must not merely act but reason and believe like other men (E. 160). However dogmatic the *Enquiry*'s assertion, the *Treatise* is more guarded. Hume grants that some people *can* forget the "difficulty" of living by habits which they cannot endorse, and presents his *own* inability to rest in this position with careful restriction, "for my own part. . . ." The "intense" reaction, despair rather than *ataraxia,* is his own reaction to the sceptic's prescription. As Burnyeat later concedes, the sceptic's divorce of habits of assent from any normative endorsement may be a possible policy for a life, but scarcely for a fully human one. Hume's supposedly dogmatic claim in the *Enquiry* was a claim about the condition of *mankind,* not about intelligent life. If it were possible for the mind of man to "rest, like those of beasts" (T. 271) in unreflective instinctive assent, then the sceptic could live his scepticism. If the causal result of his balanced intellectual pros and cons *were* the cancelling out of his peculiarly human need to endorse his habits, then he would have rid himself of his humanity. But what he *cannot* then claim is that his absence of belief is grounded on, rather than merely caused by, his arguments. If the sceptic's methods work to destroy belief, they also destroy retrospective recognition of those arguments as *arguments* at all. This is Burnyeat's own point: "Certainly it appears to him that dogmatic claims are equally balanced, but this appearance, so called, being the effect of argument, is only to be made sense of in terms of reason, belief and truth—the very notions the sceptic wants to avoid" (p. 50). Hume, at T. 268, claims only that *he* can't avoid using norms, wanting to turn habits into rules, but he does later extend this into a thesis about what is "almost impossible for the mind of man" (T. 271).

13. By all accounts it certainly was not reading Hume that awoke Wittgenstein from his dogmatic *Tractatus* slumber.

14. This attempt to contradict his own mental ancestry is precisely what the Pyrrhonian sceptic attempts.

15. This seems to be the policy that Fogelin calls theoretical as distinct from

prescriptive scepticism. He attributes it to Hume (Fogelin, *Hume's Skepticism in the Treatise of Human Nature,* p. 46), despite the evidence here that Hume finds it a manifest contradiction.

16. I have done Descartes an injustice by using him as the fall guy in this exposition of Hume's moves, since the actual Cartesian position gives the passions of the soul a vital role to play in the search for truth. Hume recommended René Descartes' *Meditations on First Philosophy* to his friend Michael Ramsay as proper preparation for understanding his own *Treatise,* and Descartes does in that work show reason concurring with wonder and adoration, as well as with anxiety, but it is usually assumed that Descartes' *Meditations* were to serve as point of contrast, rather than as training exercises in Humean philosophy. (See Mossner, *The Life of David Hume,* pp. 626–627, for the text of Hume's letter to Ramsay.

17. Burnyeat, in "Can the Sceptic Live His Scepticism?" emphasizes the fact that the sceptic's suspension of belief was an avoidance of all existence claims, since to believe was to believe true of some real thing. Hume is showing the middle way of acceptance of norms which are free of both intellectualist baggage (since truth is no longer primarily truth for intellect) and of metaphysical baggage.

18. Gilles Deleuze, in *Empirisme et subjectivité: Essai sur la nature humaine selon Hume* (Paris: Presses Universitaires de France, 1953), writes, "Hume est un moraliste, un sociologue, avant d'être un psychologue" (p. 1).

19. Volume 4 of *The Correspondence of Charles Darwin,* ed. Frederick Burkhardt and Sydney Smith (New York: Cambridge University Press, 1985), lists the entries in Darwin's reading notebook, and there are frequent Hume entries, covering almost all of Hume's works. Among the first to note the way in which Hume paves the way for Darwin were T. H. Huxley, in his book *Hume, with Helps to the Study of Berkeley* (New York: D. Appleton, 1896); and Georg von Gizcki, *Die Ethik David Hume's in ihrer geschichtlichen Stellung* (Breslau: Louis Koehler's Hofbuchhandlung, 1878), pp. 232–242. Several recent Hume commentators discuss the foreshadowing of Darwinian theses in Hume's *Dialogues Concerning Natural Religion.* See João-Paulo Monteiro, "Hume, Induction, and Natural Selection," in *McGill Hume Studies,* ed. David Fate Norton, Nicholas Capaldi, and Wade L. Robison (San Diego: Austin Hill Press, 1979), pp. 291–308; and J. Howard Sobel, "Hume, Darwin and the Resolution of National Theology," unpublished.

20. For a contrary view, see James Noxon, *Hume's Philosophical Development: A Study of His Methods* (Oxford: Clarendon Press, 1973).

2. Other Relations: The Account of Association

1. John Passmore, in *Hume's Intentions* (Cambridge: Cambridge University Press, 1952), ch. 6, takes Hume's associationist project to be Newtonian (p. 106), so he would presumably disagree with my claim here. Passmore also quotes the

same passage from Locke (*Essay Concerning Human Understanding,* ed. P. H. Nidditch [Oxford: Clarendon Press, 1975]) that I quote, saying that his "contribution to associationist psychology is often underestimated" (p. 106). Doubtless my own estimation of it is largely due to Passmore's formative influence on my understanding of Hume.

2. Donald W. Livingston, *Hume's Philosophy of Common Life* (Chicago: University of Chicago Press, 1984).

3. Its pre–eighteenth-century connotations were astrological, or legal. Causation exculpated an agent from responsibility for an action. Hume seems to be asking his readers' permission to free the term from its association with fatalism. His contemporary, James Beattie, finds Hume's use of the term surprising. In a note to p. 214 of his *An Essay on the Nature and Immutability of Truth, in Opposition to Sophistry and Scepticism,* 10th ed. (London: Lackington, Allen & Co., 1810), Beattie says that the term rarely occurs in English authors, and never in Hume's sense, as the name of a relation. "It properly signifies *the act or power of causing.*" He himself uses it in this sense, of causal power or efficacy.

4. Locke, in his *Essay Concerning Human Understanding,* Book III, Chapter III, Section VII, says that children begin with the "well framed" ideas of their nurse, their mother, "confined to these individuals," then note in the larger world certain "agreements of Shape, and several other Qualities," and so acquire the ideas of 'nurse,' 'mother,' 'woman,' as general ideas. Generalization is an action of the mind, the sort of thing that supposedly converts Lockean simple ideas of sense into complex ideas, so these general ideas are more complex than the particular ones the children began with. The initial ideas are not themselves simple, but they are at least simpler than their generalizations.

5. Hume here repeats Locke, *Essay Concerning Human Understanding,* Book III, Chapter IV, Section XI, "He that thinks otherwise, let him try if any Words can give him the Taste of a Pine-Apple, and make him have the true *Idea* of the Relish of that celebrated delicious Fruit."

6. For a contrary view see Passmore, *Hume's Intentions,* p. 110.

7. Robert J. Fogelin, in *Hume's Skepticism in the Treatise of Human Nature* (London: Routledge and Kegan Paul, 1985), p. 176, uses the term "dependent relation" for this subset of Humean relations.

8. Passages like this give support to John P. Wright's plausible hypothesis that Hume is not merely (like Locke) influenced in his treatment of association by Book II of Malebranche's *De la Recherche de la vérité* (Paris: J. Vrin, 1945), but also agrees with Malebranche in supposing that all association is due to the motion of animal spirits in pathways that have been worn smooth in the brain. See John P. Wright, *The Sceptical Realism of David Hume* (Minneapolis: University of Minnesota Press, 1983), pp. 205ff.

9. There may indeed *be* conditioned emotional responses, particular contingent passion sequences reenacted because of their experienced temporal contiguity in our pasts (say, sadness and hunger in some people, sadness and lack of appetite in others), but it is Descartes and Freud, not Hume, who drew our attention to them.

10. Blind faith that there are any such things as perceptions, ideas, thoughts, beliefs, desires, hopes, suspicions, will also be involved, if we are to believe some recent philosophers of mind, such as Paul Churchland, in *Matter and Consciousness: A Contemporary Introduction to the Philosophy of Mind* (Cambridge, Mass.: MIT Press, 1984); Stephen Stich, *From Folk Psychology to Cognitive Science: The Case against Belief* (Cambridge, Mass.: MIT Press, 1983); and Stephen Schiffer, *Remnants of Meaning* (Cambridge, Mass.: MIT Press, 1987). Such philosophers are less sceptical about the intellectual descendants of Hume's "animal spirits rummaging the brain" than they are about contentful Humean thoughts, beliefs and passions (in their updated form of "propositional attitudes"). For a helpful and critical discussion of the new scepticism about our knowledge of our own mental states, see Paul A. Boghossian, "The Status of Content," *The Philosophical Review* 99 (1990), 157–184. Hume, I think, would find it an ironic twist that the new way of ideas should lead its latter-day wayfarers into such self-subversion. Against the privileged ontological position accorded to such things as must be somewhere in order to exist, Hume could adapt the arguments of Book One, Part IV, Section V, directed there against Spinozist claims to be able to understand the universe (a universe including the understander) entirely under the attribute of extension, with thought itself unacknowledged.

11. Malebranche may be his philosophical grandfather. At the end of Book II of his *Recherche,* he attributes the evils of undisciplined association to the lasting effect of our original intimate union with our mothers, in the womb. (Did Freud read Malebranche?)

12. I advanced this thesis earlier in "Helping Hume to 'Compleat the Union,'" *Philosophy and Phenomenological Research* 41 (1980), 167–186.

13. Hume thinks the minds of those in cultures where the artifice of marriage ensures that "the male sex has the advantage above the female" (T. 308–309) will trace a family line with greater "facility" through the male line. Tracing through the female line will go against the grain of patriarchs, and may be difficult to bring off in patrilineal societies.

14. Pride is taken in the things that others value and notice (T. 292), and curiosity is a love of such truths are as "esteem'd important and useful to the world" (T. 450), fit for the world's table (T. 451).

3. Customary Transitions from Causes to Effects

1. I have myself learned most from Barry Stroud, *Hume* (London: Routledge and Kegan Paul, 1977). Stroud treats what he terms "the negative phase" of Hume's account of cause in ch. 3, "the positive phase" in ch. 4. He does not subordinate the latter to the former, nor say that what he terms the "phases" are two sequential moves within Hume's own treatment of cause. (The term, however, has its dangers.) A recent interesting addition to the literature on Hume's treatment of causation is Galen Strawson, *The Secret Connexion: Causation, Re-*

alism, and David Hume (Oxford: Clarendon Press, 1989). It came to my attention after this chapter was written.

2. Yves Michaud, *Hume et la fin de la philosophie* (Paris: Presses Universitaires de France, 1983), p. 164, gives a nice diagrammatic summary of the structure of Part III.

3. Hume's "sceptical doubts" in Section IV of *An Enquiry Concerning Human Understanding*, ed. P. H. Nidditch and L. A. Selby-Bigge (Oxford: Clarendon Press, 1975), concern the ability of demonstrative "argument" or "ratiocination" to establish a conclusion such as "this bread will nourish me." It is the rationalist's "reason" whose limits are shown, or perhaps more generally, it is our ability to give any algorithm to spell out how we perform causal inferences that Hume has real doubts about—"we cannot give a satisfactory reason, why we believe, after a thousand experiments, that a stone will fall, or fire burn" (E. 162). We cannot even say *when* we generalize, and when not. "Nothing so like as eggs; yet no one, on account of this appearing similarity, expects the same taste and relish in all of them" (E. 36). Hume almost anticipates Nelson Goodman's "new problem of induction," and sees it as just as grave as that other problem of induction that he is credited with inventing. But his sceptical doubts have their "sceptical solution," and it is the true meta-sceptic who provides that solution. For just what have we shown once we have shown the limits of "ratiocination" and algorithmic thinking? The mind has other resources, other abilities. "If the mind be not engaged by argument to make this step, it must be induced by some other principle of equal weight and authority" (E. 41). What we call induction, and the causal inferences that depend on it, rest on our minds' being "induced" by custom, and by experience of nature's customs. In the final section of this *Enquiry,* where Hume contrasts "antecedent" with "consequent" scepticism, and "mitigated" academic scepticism with "extravagant" Pyrrhonian scepticism, he repeats that "it is only experience which . . . enables us to infer the existence of one object from that of another" (E. 164). The true meta-sceptic, whose diffidence about his doubts mitigates those doubts, sees how little is shown once the limits of our algorithm-addicted reason are shown. Hume's *Enquiry* treatment of varieties of scepticism is different from that of the *Treatise* (and perhaps truer to ancient scepticism and its varieties). Different also is the mood in which the *Enquiry* ends— a book-burning mood. But then that work, unlike the *Treatise,* does not deal with the calm passions that the understanding serves, and so the understanding's self-understanding can there only be partial.

4. Robert J. Fogelin, *Hume's Skepticism in the Treatise of Human Nature* (London: Routledge and Kegan Paul, 1985), p. 38.

5. Ibid. Tom Beauchamp and Alexander Rosenberg, in *Hume and the Problem of Causation* (New York: Oxford University Press, 1981), document and dispute this common interpretation. Despite their careful efforts to rebut it, Galen Strawson, eight years later, still refers to it as the "standard" view. Strawson, *The Secret Connexion: Causation, Realism and David Hume,* p. 8, and passim.

6. Wade Robison, in "David Hume: Naturalist and Meta-sceptic," in *Hume: A Reevaluation,* ed. Donald W. Livingston and James T. King (New York: Fordham University Press, 1976), pp. 23–49, takes "meta-scepticism" to be the view that we have no good reasons for a given belief, but cannot help holding it, i.e., scepticism about our ability to really doubt what is really doubtful. I, on the contrary, take meta-scepticism to be scepticism turned on itself, diffidence about the sceptic's conclusions.

7. O.E.D. (*The Compact Edition of the Oxford English Dictionary* [Oxford: Oxford University Press, 1971]): "Experience: The actual observation of facts or events, considered as a source of knowledge."

8. I here, and occasionally hereafter, use "deductive" in our sense, not in the eighteenth-century sense. Samuel Johnson gives, as his first sense of "deduce," "to draw in a regular connected series, from one time to another," quoting Pope: "O goddess, say shall I deduce my rimes From the dire nation in its earlies times?" Other listed senses leave out the requirement that the series be temporal, but no sense of "deduce" or "deduction" that Johnson gives is equivalent to the operation that Hume, Locke and Descartes call "demonstration." Johnson defines "demonstrate" as "to prove with the highest degree of certainty, to prove in such a manner as reduces the contrary position to evident absurdity."

9. Samuel Johnson cites Harvey, "Vomits infer some small detriment to the lungs," to show the earliest English sense of "infer," in which it means simply to bring on, or induce.

10. Jonathan Bennett, in *Locke, Berkeley, Hume* (Oxford: Clarendon Press, 1971), p. 302, charges Hume with wrongly denying us reasons for our predictions, ignoring Section XV which seems to tell us when we have good reasons both for predictions and for retrodictions.

11. See Antoine Arnauld and Pierre Nicole, *The Act of Thinking: The Port Royal Logic,* tr. Thomas Spencer Baynes (London, 1851), p. 301. John P. Wright quotes this passage in his discussion of Hume's scepticism in *The Sceptical Realism of David Hume* (Minneapolis: University of Minnesota Press, 1983), p. 28.

12. There may be no such class as "sceptics in general," so various are their many sects. For an account of the variety of ancient Greek sceptics, see James Allen, "The Skepticism of Sextus Empiricus," in *Aufstieg und Niedergang der Römische Welt,* II, 36, 4 (Berlin: De Gruyter, 1990); and C. L. Stough, *Greek Scepticism: A Study in Epistemology* (Berkeley: University of California Press, 1989).

13. There is no agreement about what label should be applied to Hume's own position. "Attenuated deism" is the choice of J. C. A. Gaskin, in *Hume's Philosophy of Religion* (Atlantic Highlands, N.J.: Humanities Press, 1988), p. 223. Gaskin grants that Hume would not have welcomed this characterization of his view, and notes that "it *is* atheism as far as the Christian God is concerned" (p. 222).

14. Fogelin, *Hume's Skepticism in the Treatise of Human Nature,* p. 62.

15. Those, like Bennett and Fogelin, who find, in Book One as a whole, and not just in its fourth and final part, "skeptical arguments aimed, in turn, at the

understanding, reason, and the *senses*" (Fogelin, p. 2) tend to play down Section XV of Part III. Part III as a whole has to be treated as expressing unsmiling scepticism about the causal reasoning it is examining. Louis Loeb, in *From Descartes to Hume: Continental Metaphysics and the Development of Modern Philosophy* (Ithaca: Cornell University Press, 1981), takes the "philosophical theory about causation, which he stated at the beginning of Section XV" (p. 355) to be that only observed constant conjunctions enable us to determine whether or not causal relations do obtain between specified objects. This ignores the detail of the eight rules. Simon Blackburn, in *Spreading the Word* (Oxford: Clarendon Press, 1984), says that "we are more subtle than Hume suggests: we take more into account than regular succession of similar events" (p. 211), then in a note refers us to Section XV, conceding that "Hume is more careful than often realized." Among those who discuss the rules, or at least the first four, is Nicholas Capaldi, in *David Hume: The Newtonian Philosopher* (Boston: Twayne, 1975).

16. John Passmore, *Hume's Intentions* (New York: Cambridge University Press, 1952), p. 2; Fogelin, *Hume's Skepticism in the Treatise of Human Nature,* p. 1.

17. Dorothy L. Grover, Joseph L. Camp, Jr., and Nuel D. Belnap, Jr., "A Prosentential Theory of Truth," *Philosophical Studies* 27 (1975), 73–125.

18. Fogelin, *Hume's Skepticism in the Treatise of Human Nature,* p. 46.

19. Norman Kemp Smith, *The Philosophy of David Hume* (London: Macmillan, 1941), p. 91. See also Fogelin, *Hume's Skepticism in the Treatise of Human Nature,* pp. 39–40; H. H. Price, "The Permanent Significance of Hume's Philosophy," *Philosophy* 15 (1940), 16–17; and Tom Beauchamp and Alexander Rosenberg, *Hume and the Problem of Causation* (New York: Oxford University Press, 1981).

20. Fogelin, *Hume's Skepticism in the Treatise of Human Nature,* p. 47.

21. Fogelin writes that the "reversal" he finds within Section VI is one that Hume is "systematically free" to make; since "Hume has abandoned the idea of grounding our causal inference in the idea of a necessary connection, *there is nothing wrong now* in giving an account of our idea of necessary connection through the use of transparently causal notions" (Fogelin, *Hume's Skepticism in the Treatise of Human Nature,* p. 47, my emphasis). But Hume has been doing this, and telling us that he is doing this, at least three sections earlier.

22. Fogelin, *Hume's Skepticism in the Treatise of Human Nature,* p. 56.

23. See Chapter 4 for more on determination and causal determination.

24. Fogelin, *Hume's Skepticism in the Treatise of Human Nature,* p. 45, finds that the point is made "with more clarity" in the *Enquiry,* where Hume uses only the rationalists' own terms, and so speaks of circular "proofs" and of taking for granted the very point that is in question (E. 35–36), rather than repeating his *Treatise* talk of a given principle being taken both to cause and to be caused by some one other principle. It suits Fogelin's interpretation to have Hume using the rationalist's language, rather than the causal theorist's language, so at this point he switches to the *Enquiry*'s "sceptical doubts," framed in the language of

that sceptic who is a parasite on the reason he attacks. But in the *Treatise*, Hume speaks his own true sceptic's causal language.

25. My interpretation so far agrees with that of Beauchamp and Rosenberg, who also raise this question. (*Hume and the Problem of Causation*, pp. 49ff.)

26. Locke's brief chapter on "Degrees of Assent," *Essay Concerning Human Understanding*, Book IV, Chapter XVI, is a fairly evident progenitor of Hume's account of degrees of vivacity.

4. Necessity, Nature, Norms

1. In the O.E.D. (*The Compact Edition of the Oxford English Dictionary* [Oxford: Oxford University Press, 1971]) one finds, "Perception: The receiving or partaking of the Eucharist or sacred elements. *Obs.*"

2. See Patrick Maher, "Probability in Hume's Science of Man," *Hume Studies* 7 (November 1981), 137–153; Ian Hacking, "Hume's Species of Probability," *Philosophical Studies* 33 (1978), 21–27; idem, *The Emergence of Probability* (New York: Cambridge University Press, 1975), ch. 9. For Hume's virtually Bayesian approach in the *Dialogues* see Wesley Salmon, "Religion and Science: A New Look at Hume's *Dialogues*," *Philosophical Studies* 33 (1978), 143–176.

3. Hume's earlier reference to the mind's "native situation of indifference" (T. 125) appears to conflict with his more usual attribution to us of a presumption favoring generality, a native expectation that nature will have her habits, and show them to us.

4. See John Passmore, *Hume's Intentions* (Cambridge: Cambridge University Press, 1952), p. 76.

5. Tom L. Beauchamp and Alexander Rosenberg, in *Hume and the Problem of Causation* (New York: Oxford University Press, 1981), give their own version of how the two alternate definitions can be seen to provide a unified theory, and give a good survey of interpretations that neglect half of Hume's double definition.

6. Beauchamp and Rosenberg, in *Hume and the Problem of Causation*, emphasize the importance of the fact that Hume does endorse these rules, but do not note that they have in fact been all carefully observed in Hume's causal reasoning leading up to his endorsement of them. W. V. Quine, according to Michael Palulak's notes on Quine's 1946 lectures on Hume (*Journal of the History of Philosophy* 27 [1989], 445–460), took the presence of these rules seriously and claimed that they had themselves been inductively arrived at, but as far as I know he did not claim that the induction by which they were arrived at satisfied their own demands.

7. See Antony Flew, *Hume's Philosophy of Belief* (New York: Humanities Press, 1961), p. 123; and Tom L. Beauchamp and Alexander Rosenberg's discussion of Flew's charge, in *Hume and the Problem of Causation*, pp. 11–12.

8. My efforts to arrive at this restatement have been assisted by James van Aken and by Ronald Jensen, who commented helpfully on earlier formulations

that aimed to attribute a recursive definition to Hume. They are, however, in no way to blame for this more modestly abstruse restatement.

9. There Hume also throws out a similar (equally contrived) account of how passions that vary in intensity must, "properly speaking" be said to be compounded out of smaller passion-parts: "Thus a man, who desires a thousand pound, has in reality a thousand or more desires, which uniting together, seem to make only one passion; tho' the composition evidently betrays itself upon every alteration of the object, by the preference he gives to the larger number, if superior only by an unite" (T. 141).

10. Perfection, for Hume, seems to be Spinozistic self-containment, avoidance of causal spillover. See his reference to "perfect ideas" at T. 8.

11. See Jonathan Bennett, *Locke, Berkeley, Hume: Central Themes* (Oxford: Clarendon Press, 1971), p. 300.

12. Norman Kemp Smith emphasizes the fact that Hume set himself to give a causal account of our belief in causes, and notes that the causal term "determines" occurs in Hume's definition of cause as a natural relation, making that definition "in the main ostensive" (*The Philosophy of David Hume* [London: Macmillan, 1941], p. 401). My own interpretation up to a point agrees with that of Kemp Smith, but I think we need the whole of Hume's definition to see how causal dependency is ostended, as distinct from merely referred to. For a critical discussion of Kemp Smith's views on Hume's definition, see Wade L. Robison, "Hume's Causal Scepticism," in *David Hume: Bicentenary Papers* (Edinburgh: Edinburgh University Press, 1977), pp. 156–166.

13. This term is also used by Yves Michaud to characterize Hume's reasoning about cause. *Hume et la fin de la philosophie* (Paris: Presses Universitaires de France, 1983), p. 163.

14. I advanced this interpretation of Hume's definitions and their relation to what precedes and follows them in "Real Humean Causes," in *Central Themes in Early Modern Philosophy: Essays Presented to Jonathan Bennett,* ed. J. A. Cover and M. A. Kulstad (Indianapolis: Hackett, 1990).

5. The Simple Supposition of Continued Existence

1. James Beattie, in his attack on Hume in *An Essay on the Nature and Immutability of Truth, in Opposition to Sophistry and Scepticism,* 10th ed. (London: Lackington, Allen & Co., 1810), exclaims "Alas! What is to become of the magnificence of external nature!" (p. 180). He forgives Berkeley more readily than Hume for seeming to turn God's creation into (in Berkeley's words) "a false imaginary glare," since Berkeley "was indeed a most excellent person" (p. 201), but Beattie is not at all confident that Hume is. His irreverent treatment of the magnificence of external nature is seen to go along with a similar deconstruction of "the wonders of intellectual energy, the immortal beauties of truth and virtue, and the triumphs of a good conscience!" (p. 180).

2. For a contrary view see Terence Penelhum, *Hume* (London: Macmillan,

and New York: St. Martin's, 1975), chs. 3 and 4. Penelhum takes Hume's claim that identity is a "fiction" to be tantamount to the claim that ascription of identity is "mistaken," whenever there is either interruption in our observation of the supposedly identical thing, or observed change in it. Hume surely does claim that there are some discoverable mistakes involved in our attributions of identity, and at T. 209 he says that the fiction of continued existence is "really false," but the label "fiction" does not itself attribute any mistake to those who use the fiction of continued existence, or even believe in fiction. In the nature of the case, their belief is not falsifiable.

3. It is discussed in Terence Penelhum, _Hume,_ ch. 3; Barry Stroud, _Hume_ (London: Routledge and Kegan Paul, 1977), ch. 5; John P. Wright, _The Sceptical Realism of David Hume_ (Minneapolis: University of Minnesota Press, 1983), ch. 2; Robert J. Fogelin, _Hume's Scepticism in the Treatise of Human Nature_ (London: Routledge and Kegan Paul, 1985), ch. 6. H. H. Price's book, _Hume's Theory of the External World_ (Oxford: Clarendon Press, 1940), is devoted entirely to it.

4. Fogelin, _Hume's Scepticism in the Treatise of Human Nature,_ p. 64.

5. This fact seems to me to count against John Wright's suggestion that constancy, unlike coherence, is found in the data of our _uninterrupted_ viewings. (_The Sceptical Realism of David Hume,_ pp. 62ff.)

6. Kant in the Second Analogy, _Critique of Pure Reason_ (A192–193 / B237–238), contrasts the reversible succession of our "representations" as we view a house before us with the irreversible succession of "representations" we have of a boat moving upstream.

7. Páll S. Árdal, _Passion and Value in Hume's Treatise_ (Edinburgh: Edinburgh University Press, 1966), p. 18, notes that this is the use that is involved when Hume, in Book Two, speaks of the objects of the indirect passions.

8. See Jonathan Bennett's discussion in _Locke, Berkeley, Hume: Central Themes_ (Oxford: Clarendon Press, 1971), ch. 4.

9. For a contrary view see Stroud, _Hume,_ pp. 129–130. Stroud attributes some features of Hume's account to his "penchant for talking about other people, not himself."

10. This paradox in Hume's treatment has inspired much of the huge secondary literature about this section, and about the worries concerning it that Hume expressed enigmatically in the "Appendix." See, for example, S. C. Patten, "Hume's Bundles, Self-Consciousness and Kant," _Hume Studies_ 2 (1976), 59–75; Jane L. McIntyre, "Is Hume's Self Consistent?" in _McGill Hume Studies,_ ed. David Fate Norton, Nicholas Capaldi, and Wade L. Robison (San Diego: Austin Hill Press, 1979), pp. 79–88; idem, "Further Remarks on the Consistency of Hume's Account of the Self," _Hume Studies_ 5 (1979), 55–61; Wade L. Robison, "In Defense of Hume's _Appendix,_" _McGill Hume Studies,_ pp. 89–99; David Pears, "Hume's Account of Personal Identity," in Pears, _Questions in the Philosophy of Mind_ (New York: Barnes and Noble, 1975), pp. 207–223; idem, "Naturalism in Book One of Hume's _Treatise of Human Nature,_" Dawes Hicks Lecture (London: British Academy, 1976); R. P. Wolff, "Hume's Theory of Mental Activity,"

Hume: Critical Essays, ed. V. C. Chappell (New York: Anchor Books, 1966), pp. 99–128; Fred Wilson, "Hume's Theory of Mental Activity," *McGill Hume Studies,* pp. 101–120; Stroud, *Hume,* ch. 6; Penelhum, *Hume,* ch. 4; idem, "Hume's Theory of the Self Revisited," *Dialogue* 14 (1975), 389–409; John Bricke, *Hume's Philosophy of Mind* (Princeton: Princeton University Press, 1980), ch. 5; Fogelin, *Hume's Skepticism in the Treatise of Human Nature,* ch. 8.

11. No consistency is to be found in the suggestions of Hume's commentators, such as those listed in the previous note, concerning exactly what inconsistency Hume found. In several talks on this topic, I have in the past suggested that the inconsistency lies in the combination of the claims he gives at T. 636 with his fairly confident supposition, mentioned at T. 634, that physical death "entirely destroys this self". The causal connection between a single person's present perceptions, and their vivacity, and her earlier perceptions is not, according to Hume's official Book One account, so close that it would be inconceivable or even unlikely that when say, a mother died in childbirth, her newborn child's first perceptions might be causally influenced by the mother's last perceptions, and so the child would have to count as a "continuer" of the mother, who would then turn out not to have been entirely destroyed by death. Hume, I think, would not welcome this consequence. Unlike Derek Parfit, he supposes a person's series of perceptions to have fairly definite temporal boundaries. I now find my own earlier suggestion fanciful, overly influenced by current discussions of personal identity, and good only to add another entry to the competition to "complete Hume's incomplete inconsistent triad, in the 'Appendix'."

6. Persons and the Wheel of Their Passions

1. Lorraine Code, while discussing Kant's claim that unless "I think" accompanies all my representations they are nothing to me, notes that Hume's version of the self as a bundle of perceptions shows that "the subject as person all too easily disappears from philosophical view" (*Epistemic Responsibility* [Hanover, N.H.: University Press of New England, 1987], p. 111n). Had Code looked at Hume's supplementation and completion of his account in Books Two and Three, she would have found the emphasis that she herself wants on "the primacy of practical action, for human beings" (p. 111).

2. Jane McIntyre, in "Personal Identity and the Passions," *Journal of the History of Philosophy* 27 (1989), 545–557, writes: "Somewhat paradoxically, then, self-concern is a product of the fact that we are social beings" (p. 557).

3. Here I agree with Terence Penelhum, "The Self in Hume's Philosophy," in *David Hume, Many-Sided Genius,* ed. Kenneth R. Merrill and Robert W. Shahan (Norman: University of Oklahoma Press, 1976), pp. 9–23; idem, "Self-Identity and Self Regard," in *The Identities of Persons,* ed. Amelie O. Rorty (Berkeley: University of California Press, 1976) pp. 253–280; and McIntyre, "Personal Identity and the Passions." See also Nicholas Capaldi, *David Hume: Newtonian Philosopher* (Boston: Twayne, 1975), ch. 6; idem, "The Historical and Philosophical

Significance of Hume's Theory of the Self," in A. J. Holland, ed., *Philosophy, Its History and Historiography* (Dordrecht, Holland: D. Reidel, 1985), pp. 271–285; and Michel Malherbe, *La Philosophie empiriste de David Hume* (Paris: Vrin, 1984), pp. 166ff. For my own earlier discussion of this question see "Hume on Heaps and Bundles," *American Philosophical Quarterly* 16 (1979), 285–295.

4. For a somewhat abstruse restatement of Hume's account of the intentionality of pride, see my essay "Hume's Analysis of Pride," *Journal of Philosophy* 75 (1978), 27–40.

5. See Patrick Maher, "Probability in Hume's Science of Man," *Hume Studies* 7 (1981), 146ff. See also T. 31, where Hume seems to treat infinite divisibility of time as entailing "an infinite number of co-existent moments," and so an impossibility. There he equates variety over time with variety at a time.

6. David Hume, *A Dissertation of the Passions*, II, 1. This was published by Hume in 1757 in *Four Dissertations*, along with *The Natural History of Religion, Of Tragedy*, and *Of the Standard of Taste*.

7. Ernest Campbell Mossner quotes this review in *The Life of David Hume* (Oxford: Clarendon Press, 1980), p. 122.

8. See Chapter 8, including notes 7 and 8, for a fuller discussion of "characters."

9. See Chapter 8 for more on this topic.

10. This constitutes a disagreement with Páll S. Árdal's claim that Humean approval and disapproval are indirect passions, but not with his weaker claim that there is a "close relation between the moral sense and the indirect passions." *Passion and Value in Hume's Treatise* (Edinburgh: Edinburgh University Press, 1966), p. 111.

11. My use of "me" rather than "I" in this list conforms to Nicholas Capaldi's convention of using "me" for the surveyable self, the one of which we can form an idea. (See "The Historical and Philosophical Significance of Hume's Theory of the Self," p. 279.) It conforms only by chance, since Capaldi's essay came to my attention after this chapter was written. I do not, in general, observe his convention.

12. See note 11 to Chapter 5.

13. The "difficulties" are apparent exceptions to the very claims that he has just so proudly corroborated by his experiments, and they include not just those concerning "service," and in particular concerning unintentional disservice, that are discussed in this section, but also the apparently "uncaused" love discussed in "Of the Love of Relations," and the selfless love of the rich and the powerful.

14. For a contrary interpretation see Philip Mercer, *Sympathy and Ethics: A Study of the Relationship between Sympathy and Morality with Special Reference to Hume's Treatise* (Oxford: Clarendon Press, 1972), pp. 32ff.

7. The Direction of Our Conduct

1. For a careful attempt to answer this question see Nicholas L. Sturgeon, "Hume on Reason and Passion," unpublished. For an earlier careful but incom-

plete account, see Rachael M. Kydd, *Reason and Conduct in Hume's Treatise* (London: Oxford University Press, 1946). See also W. D. Falk, "Hume on Practical Reason," *Philosophical Studies* 27 (1975), 1–18, reprinted in Falk, *Ought, Reasons and Morality* (Ithaca, N.Y.: Cornell University Press, 1986), pp. 143–162; Barry Stroud, *Hume* (London: Routledge and Kegan Paul, 1977), ch. 7; J. L. Mackie, *Hume's Moral Theory* (London: Routledge and Kegan Paul, 1980), ch. 3; Robert J. Fogelin, *Hume's Skepticism in the Treatise of Human Nature* (London: Routledge and Kegan Paul, 1985), ch. 9; and John Robertson, "Hume on Practical Reason," *Proceedings of the Aristotelian Society* 90 (1989–1990), 267–282. For an account that draws richly on Hume's writings beyond as well as within the *Treatise,* see Alasdair MacIntyre, *Whose Justice? Which Rationality?* (Notre Dame: Notre Dame University Press, 1988), ch. 16.

2. Richard Rorty writes that Hume's "pragmatical reconciliation of freedom and determinism, like his reconciliation of armchair skepticism with theoretical curiosity and practical benevolence, is an invitation to take the mechanization of the mind lightly—as no more than an intriguing intellectual exercise, the sort of thing that a young person might do in order to become famous". See Rorty, "Freud and Moral Reflection," in *Pragmatism's Freud: The Moral Disposition of Psychoanalysis,* ed. Joseph H. Smith and William Kerrigan, Psychiatry and the Humanities series, vol. 9 (Baltimore: Johns Hopkins University Press, 1986), p. 3.

3. Stroud, who criticises Hume for giving us insufficient "relief from uneasiness" about the compatibility of determinism with human responsibility, correctly notes that Hume at least avoids the non sequiturs of later compatibilists who try to give sense to "could have done otherwise" (*Hume,* p. 150–151).

4. It is neglected by Rachael Kydd when she raises the question of whether Hume thought that passions could be prompted not just by factual beliefs, such as "that fruit is ripe," but also by what she calls "practical judgments" (*Reason and Conduct in Hume's Treatise,* pp. 129ff.). R. David Broiles, in *The Moral Philosophy of David Hume* (The Hague: M. Nijhoff, 1964), although expressing himself, grudgingly, as willing to "jump around" (p. 25) in the *Treatise* to determine Hume's views on the role of reason in practical matters, is apparently willing only to jump back from Book Three (which he retitles *Treatise of Morals*) to Book Two, and so does not consider "Of the Influence of Belief." David Fate Norton, in *David Hume: Common Sense Moralist, Sceptical Metaphysician* (Princeton: Princeton University Press, 1982), p. 96, writes that "Hume's views on the relationship of reason and sentiment are first presented in *Treatise* II, 3, 3," thus also ignoring the earlier treatment in Book One. J. L. Mackie, who cites, as an objection against Hume's account, the occurrence of unconscious rationalization when desire leads us to suppress inconvenient beliefs (*Hume's Moral Theory,* p. 49), also neglects this section, where Hume discusses the effect of passions on belief, as well as of beliefs and thoughts upon passions (T. 120). Nicholas Sturgeon, who writes that he has not found any commentators who explicitly note how masterful the reason at work at T. 416, to which our passions "yield . . .

without any opposition," appears to be, himself does not note that this role for our belief-forming capacity was attributed in Book One.

5. See letter of March or April 1751 to Gilbert Elliot, in *The Letters of David Hume,* ed. J. Y. T. Greig (Oxford: Clarendon Press, 1969), I, 158.

6. Hume's *Enquiry Concerning Human Understanding* first appeared as *Philosophical Essays Concerning Human Understanding,* and some features distinguishing it from the *Treatise* treatment of the same topics depend upon this essay form.

7. Alasdair MacIntyre, in *Whose Justice? Which Rationality?* (ch. 16), discusses misunderstandings of Hume's views about passions, and writes that Hume "understands the objects of particular passions on particular occasions as internal to those passions in just the way that intentionality requires" (p. 303). See also Marcia Lind, "Hume and Moral Emotions," in *Psychology, Character and Morality,* ed. O. Flanagan and A. Rorty (Cambridge, Mass.: MIT Press, forthcoming).

8. See letter referred to in note 5.

9. O.E.D. (*The Compact Edition of the Oxford English Dictionary* [Oxford: Oxford University Press, 1971]): "Emotion: A moving, stirring, agitation, perturbation (in a physical sense). *Obs.*" Examples of this now obsolete sense are given from Locke ("When exercise has left any Emotion in his Blood or Pulse") and from Shelley ("the winds of heaven mix forever with a sweet emotion"). The earliest cited case of our modern sense, of "emotion" as feeling, is from 1808.

10. Thomas Nagel, referring to this passage, writes that this would-be world-destroyer "may not be involved in a contradiction or in any false expectations, but there is something the matter with him nonetheless, and anyone else not in the grip of an overnarrow conception of what reasoning is would regard his preference as objectively wrong." *The View from Nowhere* (Oxford: Oxford University Press, 1986), p. 155. Hume can, however, agree that the preference is wrong, since his "overnarrow" conception of reason, in this section, implies that the preference is not irrational, but not that it is not wrong.

11. Norman Kemp Smith, *The Philosophy of David Hume* (London: Macmillan, 1941), p. 198.

12. Those who have written about "Of the influencing motives of the will" have neglected "Of the influence of the imagination on the passions" almost as much as they have neglected "Of the influence of belief." But as Gilles Deleuze rightly says, the fixing of "les rapports" between passion and imagination is what constitutes the originality of Hume's theory of the passions. See Deleuze, *Empirisme et subjectivité: Essai sur la nature humaine selon Hume* (Paris: Presses Universitaires de France, 1953), p. 57.

8. The Contemplation of Character

1. Antony Flew, *David Hume: Philosopher of Moral Science* (Oxford: Basil Blackwell, 1986), pp. 144–145.

2. Here I agree with Alasdair MacIntyre, "Hume on 'Is' and 'Ought,'" *Philosophical Review* 68 (1959), 451–468.

3. I discuss this in "Natural Virtues, Natural Vices," forthcoming in *Social Philosophy and Policy* 8, no. 1 (1990). See also W. D. Falk, "Hume on Is and Ought," *Canadian Journal of Philosophy* 6 (1976), 359–378, reprinted in Falk, *Ought, Reasons, and Morality* (Ithaca, N.Y.: Cornell University Press, 1988), pp. 123–142; and D. D. Raphael, "Hume's Critique of Ethical Rationalism," in *Hume and the Enlightenment: Essays Presented to Ernest Campbell Mossner,* ed. William B. Todd (Edinburgh and Austin: Universities of Edinburgh and Texas, 1974), pp. 14–29.

4. Hume might even be said, in the eighteenth-century sense, to "deduce" these moral conclusions. Samuel Johnson concludes his long and delightful preface to his *Dictionary of the English Language* (London: W. Strahan, 1755; and New York: Arno Press, 1979), in which he gives extended samples of English from earlier writers, "Thus I have deduced the English language from the age of Alfred to that of Elizabeth . . ." (See Chapter 3, note 4.)

5. See Páll S. Árdal, "Convention and Value," in *David Hume: Bicentenary Papers,* ed. G. P. Morice (Austin: University of Texas Press, 1976; Edinburgh: Edinburgh University Press, 1977), pp. 51–68.

6. John L. Mackie, *Hume's Moral Theory* (London: Routledge and Kegan Paul, 1980), p. 129.

7. Thomas Reid, *Essays on the Active Powers of the Human Mind,* introduction by Baruch A. Brody (Cambridge, Mass.: MIT Press, 1969), essay 5, ch. 7, p. 474.

8. T. H. Green and T. H. Grose, *The Philosophical Works of David Hume,* 4 vols. (London: Longman, Green, 1875) II, 57.

9. Alasdair MacIntyre, in *Whose Justice? Which Rationality?* (Notre Dame: Notre Dame University Press, 1988), p. 302, writes: "Passions are on Hume's view preconceptual and prelinguistic. This is what enables him to speak of 'the correspondence of *passions* in men and animals (*Treatise* II, i, 12)'." This is not quite right, since Humean passions, such as Hume's own ruling passion for literary fame, can certainly also be post-conceptual and essentially post-linguistic.

10. Peter Jones, *Hume's Sentiments: Their Ciceronian and French Context* (Edinburgh: Edinburgh University Press, 1982), p. 98.

11. Ibid.

12. Ibid.

13. See Thomas Nagel, *The View from Nowhere* (London: Oxford University Press, 1986).

14. Allan Gibbard, in *Wise Choices, Apt Feelings: A Theory of Normative Judgment* (Cambridge, Mass.: Harvard University Press, 1990), agrees with Hume that our moral judgment expresses some special feeling. Gibbard takes it that two forms of anger—guilt and resentment or indignation—are the relevant feelings, whereas Hume gives these feelings no special place, except in his account of our sense of justice and injustice. Whereas Hume takes approbation and disapprobation to be higher-level forms of pleasure and pain, Gibbard takes disapprobation to be primary, and takes it to be a form of anger. "Moral inquiry develops

norms for guilt and anger" (p. 291). The norms for anger may involve appeal to other feelings such as benevolence, respect for persons, and a sense of fairness, but the main moral question is taken by Gibbard to be that of when guilt or indignation is appropriately felt. He grants that some cultures may have no concept equivalent to our "guilt," and he mentions the ancestors of my compatriots, the Maori, as such people—at least until they were "converted" by Christian missionaries. Gibbard is willing to say that such people, because they lack a concept of guilt, lack morality, and so cannot "ruminate" with us about moral norms. My own moral ruminations are affected by Maori influence, and thus in excluding them Gibbard also excludes me. For all his wit, wisdom and Humean expressivism, Gibbard aligns himself with those of Hume's enemies who dress morality very dismally, and focus on the feelings that a patriarchal religion has bequeathed to us. Regretfully, then, I judge that Hume would judge Gibbard to be, as a moral philosopher, basically a divine disguised as a fellow expressivist. (See E. 322.)

15. Carol Kay notes, "Hume's moral theory accounts for moral feelings in relation to moral judgments, but it has little to say about the experience of moral action." See Kay, *Political Constructions: Defoe, Richardson and Sterne in Relation to Hobbes, Hume, and Burke* (Ithaca, N.Y.: Cornell University Press, 1988), p. 278. But as Kay herself emphasizes, language can be potent.

16. Páll S. Árdal, *Passion and Value in Hume's Treatise* (Edinburgh: Edinburgh University Press, 1966), pp. 112ff.

17. McGill University Library possesses a volume of Theophrastus bearing Hume's bookplate.

18. The O.E.D. (*The Compact Edition of the Oxford English Dictionary* [Oxford: Oxford University Press, 1971]) lists fourteen senses of "character," many of the literal senses having to do with printing and what is imprinted. Among the metaphorical senses is one, common in the eighteenth century, in which a character is a testimonial. Another is a sense (found in Sterne but now obsolete) in which it is "the face or features as betokening moral qualities."

19. The O.E.D. cites R. L. Stevenson's reference to "the leading characters of Edward Hyde." In *The Strange Case of Dr. Jekyll and Mr. Hyde,* then, within one human being there were two personae or persons, Jekyll and Hyde, each with several "characters."

20. See David Hume, *The History of England, from the Invasion of Julius Caesar to the Revolution in 1688,* 8 vols. (Dublin: James Williams, 1780), IV, 279–280. Hume's *History* came and comes in many editions, with varying numbers of volumes. This discussion of Henry the Eighth's character occurs in the thirty-third chapter.

21. See David Fate Norton, *Hume: Common Sense Moralist, Sceptical Metaphysician* (Princeton: Princeton University Press, 1982), p. 113. Norton believes that this fact, along with the role given to reason in correcting our moral sentiment, makes Hume a "moral realist."

22. See ibid., pp. 108–120; Mackie, *Hume's Moral Theory,* pp. 71ff.; and Simon

Blackburn, "Truth, Realism, and the Regulation of Theory," in *Midwest Studies in Philosophy*, vol. 5: *Studies in Epistemology*, ed. Peter A. French, Theodore E. Uehling, Jr., and Howard K. Wettstein (Minneapolis: University of Minnesota Press, 1980), pp. 357–358.

23. Mackie cites this passage as evidence for attributing to Hume his own "error theory," that "objectification" is a fiction built into our moral language. See *Hume's Moral Theory*, p. 72.

24. See J. L. Mackie, *Ethics Inventing Right and Wrong* (New York: Penguin, 1977), pp. 48ff.; and idem, *Hume's Moral Theory*, pp 51ff., 71ff.

25. See Hume's reference to *De Finibus*, Book IV, in his letter of September 17, 1739, to Francis Hutcheson (*The Letters of David Hume*, ed. J. Y. T. Greig [Oxford: Clarendon Press, 1969], I, 35).

26. Christine Korsgaard, in "Normativity as Reflexivity" (a paper given at the sixteenth meeting of the Hume Society in Lancaster, England, August 1989), relates this feature of Hume's moral theory to what she sees as Kant's parallel demand that a maxim not offend against its own requirement. See also Chapter 12, note 7.

9. A Catalogue of Virtues

1. Hume uses this word at E. 174. William Davie americanized and reused it in his essay "Hume's Catalog of Virtue and Vice," in *David Hume, Many-Sided Genius*, ed. Kenneth R. Merrill and Robert W. Shahan (Norman: University of Oklahoma Press, 1976), pp. 45–57.

2. John B. Stewart, in *The Moral and Political Philosophy of David Hume* (New York: Columbia University Press, 1963) p. 83, complains in ch. 5 that while the title of Book Three, "Of Morals," would lead a casual reader to expect a discussion restricted to morality, Hume in fact discusses all good human qualities.

3. James Beattie, in *An Essay on the Nature and Immutability of Truth, in Opposition to Sophistry and Scepticism*, 10th ed. (London: Lackington, Allen & Co., 1810), pp. 290ff., summarizes what Hume writes in Sections IV and V of Part III, and waxes righteously indignant, more or less accusing Hume of "debauchery" (p. 295) and defective feelings (p. 290). After quoting Hume's claim (T. 609) that we are as jealous of our character in regard to sense as to our character for honour, Beattie comments that, in the "fashionable life" that Hume has sunk to, "the term *honour* is of dubious import. According to the notions of these times, a man may blaspheme God, sell his country . . . and employ his whole life in seducing others to vice and perdition, and yet be accounted a man of honour; provided he be accustomed to speak certain words, wear certain cloaths, and haunt certain company" (p. 294). Beattie here delivers not merely the usual charge of apostasy from the faith of the fathers, but also the Aberdonian's revenge on the Francophile!

4. The O.E.D. (*The Compact Edition of the Oxford English Dictionary* [Oxford: Oxford University Press, 1971]) says, "There is much that is obscure in the his-

tory of this word." The earliest use it cites is that in which an interest is a "legal concern *in* a thing; esp. right or title to property." Another very early sense is that in which it is "money paid for the use of money lent." Hume's use in the above passage is probably that which the O.E.D. lists as "5: Regard to one's own profit or advantage; selfish pursuit of one's own welfare."

5. Alasdair MacIntyre, *Whose Justice? Which Rationality?* (Notre Dame: University of Notre Dame Press, 1988), ch. 15.

6. John Laird, *Hume's Philosophy of Human Nature* (London: Methuen, 1932; Hamden, Conn.: Archon, 1967), p. 218.

7. Hume, at E. 242, explains Lucian's "spleen and irony" when writing about virtue as due to disgust at the "perpetual cant of the *Stoics* and *Cynics* concerning *virtue,* their magnificient professions and slender performances" (E. 242). He characterizes Lucian as one "who, though licentious with regard to pleasure, is yet in other respects a very moral writer."

8. Cicero, by contrast, seems to think that razing and plundering cities can be done with careful thought and humanity. See *De Officiis,* I, 82.

9. Sallust, "The War with Catiline," in *Sallust,* tr. J. C. Rolfe (London: W. Heinemann, and New York: G. P. Putnam's Sons, 1931), p. 113.

10. See Stephen Darwall, "Hume in Transition (or Approbation De-moralized en Route to Utilitarianism)," paper given at the sixteenth meeting the Hume Society, Lancaster, England, August 1989. Darwall takes Hume's reference to the "narrow circle" in which a person moves (T. 602) to specify the range of sympathy needed for *any* moral evaluation, not just for judging whether a person has the particular virtues Hume classifies as "good" rather than "great."

11. For an eloquent account of Hume's treatment, in his later works, of the degeneracy that he saw religion introduce into the human mind, see Donald T. Siebert, *The Moral Animus of David Hume* (Newark: University of Delaware Press, 1990), ch. 2, "Religion and 'the Peace of Society'."

12. *The Letters of David Hume,* ed. J. Y. T. Greig (Oxford: Clarendon Press, 1969), I, 34. See also E. 319, note. *The Whole Duty of Man* is a Calvinist tract, which had been given to Hume as a child to guide his soul searching. Its companion piece, *The Ladies Calling,* taught the somewhat different but equally joyless whole duty of woman, and doubtless Hume's sister Katty was directed to it.

13. "O Praecularum munus aetatis, si quidem id aufert a nobis, quod est in adulescentia vitiosissimum!" Cicero, *Cato Maior (De Senectute),* XII, 39. William Armistead Falconer, in his translation of *De Senectute, De Amicitia, De Divinatione,* Loeb Classical Library (Cambridge, Mass.: Harvard University Press, 1959), p. 49, gives this translation: "O glorious boon of age, if it does indeed free us from youth's most vicious fault!"

14. Theophrastus, *Characters,* tr. J. M. Edmonds (London: W. Heinemann), and New York: (G. P. Putnam's Sons, 1929). I have substituted "servant" for Edmonds' very British "butler," in this sentence.

15. James Beattie attributes "The Degeneracy of Moral Science" in his and Hume's time partly to the fact (as Strabo reports) that Theophrastus' heirs buried

his and Aristotle's writings in a hole in the ground, to prevent their being seized for the library at Pergamum. There they "suffered much from worms and dampness" (p. 281), and later editors filled in what the worms had eaten. But nothing that survives of what Theophrastus wrote can have struck Beattie as anything other than degenerate.

10. The Laws of Nature

1. See A. O. Hirschman, *The Passions and the Interests: Political Arguments for Capitalism before Its Triumph* (Princeton: Princeton University Press, 1977), pp. 32ff. See also Chapter 9, note 4.

2. "This type of justice, then, is complete virtue, not complete virtue unconditionally, but complete virtue in relation to another." Aristotle, *Nicomachean Ethics,* 1129b26–30, as translated by Terence Irwin (Indianapolis: Hackett, 1985), p. 119.

3. See David Gauthier, *Morals by Agreement* (Oxford: Clarendon Press, 1986).

4. Gauthier disowns any intention that his moral theory "require capitalist acts among consenting adults" (ibid., p. 341). It does, however, require everyone to obey rules making the social world commodious for capitalists, or at least for hucksters.

5. See, e.g., David Lewis, *Convention* (Cambridge, Mass.: Harvard University Press, 1969), pp. 3–4; and Russell Hardin, *Morality within the Limits of Reason* (Chicago: University of Chicago Press, 1988), ch. 2. Robert Cooter, who favors the game-theoretical approach to law, reported in conversation how, when his colleague Jeremy Waldron put these parts of the *Treatise* into his hands for the first time, he read and was "astonished" at the sophistication.

6. For a helpful account of Stair's *Institutions of the Law of Scotland,* and its relation to the works of Justinian, Grotius, Pufendorf, and others, see David M. Walker, *Scottish Jurists* (Edinburgh: Edinburgh University Press, 1985), pp. 131ff. Walker praises the creativity and beautifully logical structure of Stair's work, and Stair himself hoped that he had achieved more than had the mere compilers of cases from which he worked, the tedium of whose writings could "nauseate" delicate readers. I myself browsed in Spottiswoodes' *Practicks,* one of these compilations of Scots law from which Stair made his abstractions and generalities, and confess that I found them no more nauseating than what Stair "created" from them. As Walker writes, Stair's thought is "conservative and traditional" (p. 137). For an appreciation of its conservative beauties and its avoidance of any anglicizing subversion, see Alasdair MacIntyre, *Whose Justice? Which Rationality?* (Notre Dame: Notre Dame University Press, 1988), pp. 226ff. MacIntyre (p. 227) writes that "no English legal commentator is ever mentioned, nor is any English statute or case," but as Walker notes (*Scottish Jurists,* p. 154, note 44), Stair does refer, for purposes of comparison, to John Cowell's commentary on English law. Walker refers the interested reader to W. D. H. Sellar, "English Law

as a Source," in *Stair Tercentary Studies,* ed. D. M. Walker (Stair Society, Edinburgh, 1981).

7. According to David Fate Norton's reconstruction of the contents of Hume's library, given to me in private correspondence, it contained Stair's *Institutions of the Law of Scotland* (but only in an edition of 1759), Grotius' *De Jure Belli ac Pacis,* and Voet's *Compendium,* but no known copies of Pufendorf or of Vinnius.

8. An earlier attempt of mine to get the measure of it is "Hume's Account of Social Artifice—its Origins and Originality," *Ethics* 98 (1988), 757–778.

9. Duncan Forbes, *Hume's Philosophical Politics* (New York: Cambridge University Press, 1975); Jonathan Harrison, *Hume's Theory of Justice* (Oxford: Clarendon Press, 1981); and J. L. Mackie, *Hume's Moral Theory* (London: Routledge and Kegan Paul, 1980), ch. 6. See also Frederick G. Whelan, *Order and Artifice in Hume's Political Philosophy* (Princeton: Princeton University Press, 1985), chs. 4 and 5; Knud Haakonssen, *The Science of the Legislator: The Natural Jurisprudence of David Hume and Adam Smith* (New York: Cambridge University Press, 1981); Nicholas Phillipson, *Hume* (London: Weidenfeld and Nicolson, 1989); and Howard Sobel, *Walls and Vaults of Happiness: David Hume's Science of Morals* (forthcoming). For a recent excellent account of Hume's version of justice, see Gerald J. Postema, *Bentham and the Common Law Tradition* (Oxford: Clarendon Press, 1986), chs. 3 and 4. Postema there says he was influenced by earlier drafts of this chapter, then entitled "Hume on Fixing and Adjusting in Nature and Artifice," so my evaluation of his account is slightly biased.

10. Dorothy Brandenburg suggested to me that both Hume and Rousseau could have been influenced by reading Lucretius' *De Rerum Natura,* where Lucretius discusses the origin of language, and of singing (Book V).

11. Jonathan Harrison, in *Hume's Theory of Justice* (Oxford: Clarendon Press, 1981), p. 118, wonders why Hume did not discuss buying and selling as cases of "transfer by consent". But Hume reserves for contractual exchange all cases where what is transferred is *"absent or general"* (p. 520), and so since money counts as "general," sales presumably count as contracts. Hume's later essay "Of Money" defines money as "nothing but the representation of labour and commodities, and serves only as a method of rating or estimating them" (*Essays,* p. 285).

12. O.E.D. (*The Compact Edition of the Oxford English Dictionary* [Oxford: Oxford University Press, 1971]): "Transgress: to go beyond the bounds or limits prescribed (by a law, command, etc.); to break, violate, infringe, contravene, trespass against." There is no implication that such laws must be enforced by penalty. The association between the two notions is one for which we must thank (or blame) the Bible.

13. Edna Ullmann-Margalit describes the "prisoners dilemma" thus: "Two guilty prisoners, against whom there is not enough incriminating evidence, are interrogated separately. Each faces two alternative ways of acting: to confess the crime, or to keep silent. They both know that if neither confesses, they will be

convicted of some minor offence, concerning which there is sufficient evidence against them, and will be sentenced to a year in prison. If both confess, each will be sentenced to five years in prison. However, if only one confesses, he thereby turns king's evidence and is thus set free, whereas the other receives a heavy term of ten years." (*The Emergence of Norms* [Oxford: Clarendon Press, 1977], p. 18.) Ullmann-Margalit generalizes the structure of this situation in the following way (pp. 25–26):

> A generalized PD-structured situation is any situation involving at least two persons each of whom is repeatedly facing a decision as to whether to do A or non-A, such that
>
> (i) If, in any occurrence of the dilemma among them, most of them do A the outcome is (and is known to them to be) mutually harmful;
>
> (ii) If, in any occurrence of the dilemma among them, most of them do non-A, the outcome is (and is known to them to be) mutually beneficial—or at any rate better than the outcome produced when most of them do A;
>
> (iii) Each of the persons involved obtains, at least in some occurrences of the dilemma among them, the highest possible pay-off in the situation when he himself does A while most of the others do non-A;
>
> (iv) If, in any occurrence of the dilemma among them, some do A, the outcome to the non-A doers is less beneficial than it would have been had everyone done non-A.

In the "assurance game," discussed by Amartya K. Sen in "Isolation, Assurance and the Social Rate of Discount," *Quarterly Journal of Economics* 81 (1967), 112–124, (iii) is not the case—each prefers doing non-A provided others do, to doing A while others do non-A, but each needs the assurance that others will conform (do non-A), in order to be able to act so as to get this first preference. See also Amartya K. Sen, "Rational Fools: A Critique of the Behavioral Foundations of Economic Theory," *Philosophy and Public Affairs* 6 (1977), 317–344.

14. Rob Shaver pointed out to me that with given persons one may be fairly sure that one's interaction will be of some fixed duration, and so endgame problems may threaten. But how certain is certain enough? We teachers all know how students whom one thought one had seen the last of, after the last grades one gave them, can reappear in one's life in unexpected guises.

15. See Ullmann-Margalit, *The Emergence of Norms*, ch. 3, for a discussion of coordination problems. See William C. Charron, "Convention, Games of Strategy, and Hume's Philosophy of Law and Government," *American Philosophical Quarterly* 17 (1980), 327–334, for the case for seeing Humean conventions as coordination norms. See also Hardin, *Morality within the Limits of Reason*, ch. 2.

16. See above, note 11.

17. I have discussed the details of Hume's account of promises and contracts in "Promises, Promises, Promises," *Postures of the Mind* (Minneapolis: University of Minnesota Press, 1985), pp. 174–206.

18. Hume's example is "ten bushels of corn, or five hogsheads of wine". He

comments, "These are only general terms, and have no direct relation to any particular heap of corn, or barrels of wine" (T. 520). He might also have given, as an instance "five guineas' worth of corn".

19. Charles Fried, *Contract as Promise* (Cambridge, Mass.: Harvard University Press, 1981), p. 15, goes so far as to say that Hume's account of promissory obligation "is more like an argument *against* my keeping the promise, for it tells me how any feelings of obligation that I may harbor have come to lodge in my psyche and thus is the first step towards ridding me of such inconvenient prejudices."

20. See Sobel, *Walls and Vaults of Happiness: David Hume's Science of Morals.* See also Derek Parfit, *Reasons and Persons* (Oxford: Clarendon Press, 1984), ch. 2; Ullmann-Margalit, *The Emergence of Norms,* chs. 2 and 3; Jean Hampton, *Hobbes and the Social Contract Tradition* (New York: Cambridge University Press, 1986), ch. 6.

21. See Sheldon S. Wolin, "Hume and Conservatism," *American Political Science Review* 48 (1954), 999–1016, reprinted in *Hume: A Re-evaluation,* ed. Donald W. Livingston and James T. King (New York: Fordham University Press, 1976), pp. 239–256. Wolin writes that Hume sees society as "an accumulated set of responses to human needs and drives: to the 'natural appetite betwixt the sexes,' and to man's oscillation between altruism—which diminishes in force as it is extended through the concentric circles of self, family, friends, and strangers— and selfishness—which increases as societal demands become more abstract and remote" (*Hume: A Reevaluation,* p. 245).

22. See David Gauthier, "David Hume, Contractarian," *Philosophical Review* 89 (1979), 3–38; Sobel, *Walls and Vaults of Happiness: Hume's Science of Morals;* and Steven Darwall, "Hume in Transition (or Approbation De-Moralized en Route to Utilitarianism)," talk given at meeting of the Hume Society, Lancaster, England, 1989.

23. See Jerome Christensen, *Practicing Enlightenment: Hume and the Formation of a Literary Career* (Madison: University of Wisconsin Press, 1987). In his "non-mimetic" biographical exercise (p. 4), Christensen writes: "The *Treatise* is that text where we can all but see Hume taking the responsibility for saying what goes without saying" (p. 86). I here follow Hume's example.

24. Thomas Hobbes, *Leviathan,* ed. C. B. Macpherson (Harmondsworth: Penguin, 1968), ch. 15, p. 202.

25. At points in *Hobbes and the Social Contract Tradition* where Hampton finds Hobbes's argument to be in great difficulties, we get chapters headed with quotations from Hume (chapters 6 and 8). Hume's role in the book is to provide the solution to outstanding problems in Hobbes's account, even if the solution is "conversion" to a Humean psychology (p. 208). See also Jean Hampton, "Two Faces of Contractrian Thought," in *Contractarianism and Rational Choice,* ed. Peter Vallentyne (New York: Cambridge University Press, 1990), where Hume is again assimilated to the contractarian tradition at its most enlightened. There she even refers to "the . . . rebellious overtones of the contract argument welcomed

by Hume and Locke in a political context," despite Hume's explicit disavowal, in that context, of being a contractarian. In this she follows Gauthier, in "David Hume, Contractarian."

26. Hume discusses the sensible knave in the second *Enquiry* (E. 282–283), not in the *Treatise*. For a discussion of Hume's attitude to the knave, see David Gauthier, "Three against Justice: The Foole, the Knave, and the Lydian Shepherd," in Gauthier, *Moral Dealing: Contract, Ethics and Reason* (Ithaca: Cornell University Press, 1990), pp. 129–149; and Gerald Postema, "Hume's Reply to the Sensible Knave," *History of Philosophy Quarterly* 5 (1988), 23–40.

27. Hobbes, *Leviathan,* ch. 15, p. 205.

11. The Shelter of Governors

1. Lucy Ashton of Walter Scott's *The Bride of Lammermoor* was founded, Scott wrote in the introduction to the novel, on Janet Dalrymple, the eldest daughter of James Dalrymple, Viscount Stair, author of *Institutions of the Laws of Scotland.* She was ordered by her father to marry David Dunbar, although she had already pledged herself to Lord Rutherford. She reluctantly obeyed her father, then knifed the bridegroom on the bridal night, lost her reason and died three weeks later. So Stair knew first hand about the noisome rights of fathers to their daughters' obedience, and the weight they apparently carried in relation to other rights. (See Chapter 10, note 6, for more about Stair.)

2. In section 52 of the *Second Treatise of Civil Government,* ed. C. B. Macpherson (Indianapolis: Hackett, 1980), Locke writes that mothers have an "equal title" with fathers to parental authority over their children while they are minors. But in section 82 he argues that in conjugal society "the last determination, *i.e.* the rule, should be placed somewhere; it naturally falls to the man's share, as the abler and the stronger." Locke also endorses the duty of slaves, taken as captives in just wars, to obey their masters (section 85).

3. *Letters of David Hume,* ed. J. Y. T. Greig (Oxford: Clarendon Press, 1969), I, 168.

4. O.E.D. (*The Compact Edition of the Oxford English Dictionary* [Oxford: Oxford University Press, 1971]): "Fraud: The quality or disposition of being deceitful; faithlessness, insincerity. Now *rare.*" (But found in Edmund Burke, *Reflections on the French Revolution,* 1790.)

5. Russell Hardin, in "From Power to Order, from Hobbes to Hume," a talk given at the seventeenth meeting of the Hume Society, Canberra, Australia, June 28, 1990, noted: "We find that we cannot act collectively to accomplish our collective purposes when our numbers are too large. Hume himself is one of the earliest to recognize this problematic logic of collective action in his example of the difficulty a thousand neighbours would have in draining a marshy meadow. Unfortunately the class of important actions that fall under this . . . problem includes the task of creating government itself."

6. David Miller, *Philosophy and Ideology in Hume's Political Thought* Oxford: Clarendon Press, 1981), p. 82.

7. Thomas Hobbes, *Leviathan,* ed. C. B. Macpherson (Harmondsworth: Penguin, 1968), p. 239 (end of ch. 18). "For all men are by nature provided of notable multiplying glasses, (that is their Passions and Self-love,) through which, every little payment appeareth a great grievance; but are destitute of those prospective glasses (namely Morall and Civill Science,) to see a farre off the miseries that hang over them, and cannot without such payments be avoyded."

8. Friedrich Nietzsche, *On the Genealogy of Morals,* II. 10.

9. Hume's influence on James Madison, especially in the tenth of the *Federalist Papers* (New York: Modern Library, 1941), is generally recognized. Thomas Jefferson valued Hume's *History of England* enough to replace it after his library burned in 1770, but later came to regard it as a dangerously counterrevolutionary work, especially in some of its later footnotes, so that he banned it from the library of the University of Virginia, and tried instead to promote a peculiar "cleaned up" version of it, published in 1796 by John Baxter. See Douglass Adair, "'That Politics May Be Reduced to a Science:' David Hume, James Madison, and the Tenth *Federalist,*" in *Hume: A Reevaluation,* ed. Donald W. Livingston and James T. King (New York: Fordham University Press, 1976), pp. 404–417; and Craig Walton, "Hume and Jefferson on the Uses of History," ibid., pp. 389–403. See also Donald W. Livingston, *Hume's Philosophy of Common Life* (Chicago: Chicago University Press, 1984), p. 264; and Frederick Whelan, *Order and Artifice in Hume's Political Philosophy* (Princeton: Princeton University Press, 1985), pp. 342–343. My authority for the claim that Jefferson actually banned Hume's *History* from the University of Virginia, as distinct from promoting Baxter's in its place, is D. C. Yalden-Thomson, "Recent Work on Hume: A Survey of Hume Literature, 1969–1979," *American Philosophical Quarterly* 20 (1983), 4.

10. I am assuming that the resort to arms of the Jacobites in 1745, and that of the Irish and Northern Irish during this century, are the main rebellions that interrupted the peace within Great Britain from Hume's time till the present.

11. Douglass Adair, in "'That Politics May Be Reduced to a Science' . . . ," pp. 408ff., claims that James Madison was deeply influenced by "The Idea of a Perfect Commonwealth," in his proposals for the American Constitution.

12. For a helpful discussion of this and related essays by Hume, and their social and political background, see John Robertson, "The Scottish Enlightenment at the Limits of the Civic Tradition," in *Wealth and Virtue: The Shaping of Political Economy in the Scottish Enlightenment,* ed. Istvan Hont and Michael Ignatieff (Cambridge: Cambridge University Press, 1983), pp. 137–178.

13. Some laws could of course, if accepted as "higher," give us permission to break other "lower" laws, in specified conditions. Such disobedience would then be not merely permissible but constitutionally protected.

14. Duncan Forbes, *Hume's Philosophical Politics* (Cambridge: Cambridge University Press, 1975), p. 100.

15. Whelan, in *Order and Artifice in Hume's Political Philosophy,* speaks of

Hume's attitude to revolution as "ambivalent" (p. 320), and takes him to have a "conservative outlook that . . . is firmly grounded in his philosophical skepticism," which in turn "is quite consistent with reasoned positions on practical matters" (p. 322).

16. For a contrary view see Whelan, *Order and Artifice in Hume's Political Philosophy*, pp. 358ff.

17. In his *History of England*, chapter XVIII, Hume notes that Henry IV's authority, derived originally from consent of the governed, was soon seen to rest on other grounds, both by him and by his subjects. It suited neither to be tied down by some specific agreement. "The idea too of choice seemed always to imply that of conditions, and a liberty of recalling the consent upon any supposed violation of them; an idea which was not naturally agreeable to a sovereign, and might in England be dangerous to the subjects who . . . had ever paid but imperfect obedience even to their hereditary princes." See David Hume, *The History of England, from the Invasion of Julius Caesar to the Revolution in 1688*, 8 vols. (Dublin: James Williams, 1780), III, 64.

18. Miller, *Philosophy and Ideology in Hume's Political Thought*, p. 180.

19. I have discussed Hume's relations with women, and his views on sexual equality, in "Hume on Women's Complexion," *The Science of Man in the Scottish Enlightenment*, ed. Peter Jones (Edinburgh: Edinburgh University Press, 1990), pp. 33–53.

20. J. L. Mackie, *Hume's Moral Theory* (London: Routledge and Kegan Paul, 1980), p. 115.

21. "The government, which, in common appellation, receives the appellation of free, is that which admits of a partition of power among several members, whose united authority is no less, or is commonly greater than that of any monarch; but who, in the usual course of administration, must act by general and equal laws, that are previously known to all the members and to all their subjects. In this sense; it must be owned, that liberty is the perfection of civil society, but still authority must be acknowledged essential to its very existence" (*Essays*, pp. 40–41).

12. Reason and Reflection

1. See Páll S. Árdal, "The Implications of the Virtue of Reasonableness in Hume's *Treatise*," in *Hume: A Reevaluation*, ed. Donald W. Livingston and James T. King (New York: Fordham University Press, 1976), pp. 91–106.

2. At the seventeenth meeting of the Hume Society in Canberra, Australia, June 1990, Tito Magri gave a paper titled "The Evolution of Reason in Hume's *Treatise*" which treated Humean rationality as "an artificial capacity," and suggested that "reason as artifice and the natural mind can be reconciled if the former is seen as evolving from the latter". My own views are in substantial agreement with Magri's, and I look forward to the publication of his important paper.

3. David Miller emphasizes this fact in *Philosophy and Ideology in Hume's Political Thought* (Oxford: Clarendon Press, 1981), p. 59.

4. Hume regarded Elizabeth I of England as one of the more tyrannical of British monarchs. See Appendix III of *The History of England, from the Invasion of Julius Caesar to the Revolution in 1688,* 8 vols. (Dublin: James Williams, 1780), V, 446ff.

5. *The Letters of David Hume,* ed. J. Y. T. Greig (Oxford: Clarendon Press, 1969), II, 303.

6. Ibid., p. 258. It is therefore a cruel irony that Thomas Jefferson, whom surely Hume would have admired as a statesman, had Hume's *History of England* banned from the library of the University of Virginia. See Chapter 11, note 7.

7. Hume's implied account of truth then becomes not so very different from Descartes'. Most readers find what Descartes said about truth as puzzling as they find Hume's virtual silence on the matter. A true idea, for Descartes, has "objective reality," such that once the intellect perceives that reality, the will irresistibly affirms or perhaps reaffirms the idea's truth. For something to be "objectively real" in an idea is for it to be reliably presented there, presented in a way that agrees with its "formal reality," what it is in itself. A person's self-presentation to her friend (say, as one who keeps confidences) will have what by an extension of Descartes' usage we could call "objective reality," so long as she really does intend to keep confidences, and her intentions will themselves have "objective reality" if she does in fact keep them. Once it is clear that she has done so, she will be proved to have been a true friend, and will usually be reaffirmed as such.

8. "Reason first appears in possession of the throne, prescribing laws, and imposing maxims, with an absolute sway and authority. Her enemy, therefore, is oblig'd to take shelter under her protection, and by making use of rational arguments to prove the fallaciousness and imbecility of reason, produces, in a manner, a patent under her hand and seal" (T. 186).

9. One could see the final Humean version of reason as Ciceronian. Cicero takes reason to be basically the ability to discern a causally connected series of events. Derivatively it is the willingness to cooperate with others in a speech community, to try to create good conditions of life for one's descendants, to track down the truth on specific matters, and to value sincerity and veracity. (*De Officiis,* I, 11–13).

10. *The Letters of David Hume,* ed. J. Y. T. Greig (Oxford: Clarendon Press, 1969), I, 29.

11. A most helpful account of the initial response to Hume's *Treatise,* and his reaction to that response, especially in his manner of writing in the *Essays* and *Enquiries,* is to be found in M. A. Box, *The Suasive Art of David Hume* (Princeton; University Press, 1990).

12. "A work which the Author had projected before he left the College, and which he wrote and published not long after. But not finding it successful, he was sensible of his error of going to the press too early, and he cast the whole anew in the following pieces, where some negligences in his former reasoning

Notes to Page 288 323

and more in the expression, are, he hopes corrected." ("Advertisement" to the 1777 edition of the *Essays* and *Treatises,* prepared by Hume in 1775.)

13. The only query that this admirer would raise is one that Hume himself raises in the conclusion, when he notes that his demonstration that reason should serve calm corrected passions has itself been somewhat cold and passionless. It would take another work, he says, to *express* those warm passions with which he judges that sociable reason should concur. And only then, only when passions are expressed and appealed to, as well as analyzed, would morality really reflect on itself. Not until then could we really say "not only virtue must be approv'd of, but also the sense of virtue: And not only that sense, but also the principles, from whence it is deriv'd. So that nothing is presented on any side, but what is laudable and good" (T. 619). In the *Treatise* Hume makes this claim only hypothetically, for "such reflexions require a work a-part, very different from the genius of the present" (T. 620), where he claims to have employed nothing "but solid argument" (T. 619). Once, in the second *Enquiry,* he softens the arguments, gives more historical examples, and allows himself more self-consciously passionate self-expression, and he becomes, I believe, a better spokesman for our reflective moral passions. But to make that claim persuasive would itself require a work apart.

Index

Ability: as virtue, 198, 214–215; increase of, 227, 253; reflective affirmation of, 288

Absence. *See* Interruption

Actions, 152–173

Adair, D., 320nn9,11

Aggression, 221–224

Agreement: in moral evaluation, 178, 182–183, 196; private, 243; with self, 277; and reason, 278; and truth, 286. *See also* Convention

Alembert, J. d', 293

Allen, J., 302n12

Anger, 161–163; and moral sense, 311n14

Animals: instincts of, 79, 94; human superiority over, 227, 281; reason of, 278

Annandale, G., Marquess of, 292

"Appendix" (Hume): worries about personal identity in, 126–127, 137–139, 140–142

Approbation, 22, 187, 198–202. *See also* Evaluation, moral

Approval. *See* Approbation

Árdal, P., 185, 295n1, 306n7, 308n10, 311n5, 312n16, 321n1

Aristides, 170

Aristotle, 218, 221, 232, 285, 314n15, 315n2

Armies, 256, 261–262, 268

Arnauld, A.: and P. Nicole, 57, 302n11

Artifice, 175–179, 184, 188, 199, 246, 265, 278–279; and nature, 175–176

Association, 28–53, 66–76; of persons, 29–30, 52, 128; by cause, 39, 69–76; by contiguity, 39, 69, 81; of passions, 39–45; by resemblance, 39–43, 40–45, 69,

81; unconscious, 41–43, 300n11; of ideas, 52; of impressions, 52; constrained versus free, 81. *See also* Relations, natural

Assurance, 233–234, 317n13

Atoms, 8

Authority, 256–257, 277–279

Avidity, 222, 272. *See also* Self, interested affection of

Baier, A., 296n5, 300n12, 305n14, 308nn3,4, 311n3, 316n8, 317n17, 321n19

Barter, 240–241, 251

Baxter, J., 320n9

Baynes, T. S., 302n11

Beattie, J., 200, 299n3, 305n1, 313n3, 314n15

Beauchamp, T.: and A. Rosenberg, 301n5, 303n19, 304nn25,5,6,7

Beauty, 140, 200, 202, 208

Becket, T., 216

Belief, 69–70, 87–88; as proportioned to evidence, 82–85; influence on action, 158–159

Belnap, N. D., Jr., 303n17

Benevolence, 199, 213–214; towards the virtuous, 185

Bennett, J., 302nn10,15, 305n11, 306n8

Bentham, J., 148, 204, 205

Berkeley, G., 100, 305n1

Blackburn, S., 303n15, 313n22

Bodies, 101–121; mind-independent existence of, 4–6; continuous existence of, 4–6; human, 130–131, 136–140, 200–202

Boghossian, P. A., 300n10

Boufflers-Rouverel, H., Comtesse de, 293
Box, M. A., 322n11
Boyle, R., 117
Brains, 108
Brandenburg, D., 316n10
Bricke, J., 307n10
Brody, B. A., 311n7
Broiles, R. D., 309n4
Buffon, G.-L., Comte de, 293
Burke, E., 317n4
Burkhardt, F.: and S. Smith, 298n19
Burnyeat, M., 297n12, 298n17

Caesar, 33, 87, 212, 213
Camp, J. L., Jr., 303n17
Capaldi, N., 295n1, 298n19, 303n15, 307n3, 308n11
Capitalism, 151, 221
Carelessness: and carefreeness, 1
Cartesians. *See* Descartes, R., and Cartesians
Cato, 212, 213
Causal inference: rules of, 56, 93–96, 281
Causation, 4, 7–8, 112–114, 296n6, 299n3; as a natural relation, 59, 88–99; mutual, 68–69; definition of, 79; double definition of, 88–99; as a philosophical relation, 88–99; of later mental states by earlier ones, 126
Causes: secret, 11, 108; why always necessary, 64, 85; partial, 81–82; of action, 153–157. *See also* Causation
Change, 102–104
Chappell, V. C., 306n10
Character, 134, 174, 183, 188–191, 312n18; of the moral evaluator, 193; of the scientist of human nature, 193
Charles I of England, 273
Charm, 202–203, 204
Charron, W. C., 317n15
Chastity, 273–275
Children: flexibility of character of, 186. *See also* Love, parental
Christensen, J., 318n23
Churchland, P., 300n10
Cicero, M., 196, 218, 220, 314nn8,13, 322n9
Clarke, S., 13, 22
Code, L., 307n1

Coercion, 244–248; and promise, 244–246
Coherence, 102–103, 109–114
Colors, 38–39, 109; and virtues, 194–195
Community: of observers, 120–122; of moral evaluators, 195
Comparison, 146–149, 207–209
Competition, 148–151
Completion: of union of ideas, 74; of causes, 81–82; of the round of passions, 143
Concern, 143–151
Conflict, 97, 228. *See also* Contradiction
Connexion. *See* Necessity
Consent, 230–231, 251–252; transfer by, 240–241, 243; age of, 264; and international commerce, 275; and reason, 278
Constancy, 73; in what is sensed, 109–115
Constant conjunctions, 79, 97–98; limited verification of, 112–114
Contiguity, 142; of passions, 299n9
Contract, 231, 247–248, 247–250; trust in, 258; and magistrates, 263
Contractarianism, 248–253, 264, 318n25
Contradiction, 3, 6–20, 97, 277
Contrariety: of passions, 131–134, 145, 151
Convention, 100, 176–177, 182, 225, 243–244, 250–254; progression in, 243–244; to create contract, 248–250; and reason, 278
Cooperation, 148–151, 221, 224–225, 228–236, 248–250; pleasure in, 279; and truth, 287
Coordination, 234
Cooter, R., 315n5
Courage, 210–212
Cover, J. A.,: and M. A. Kulstad, 305n14
Cowell, J., 315n6
Credulity, 104
Custom, 32; and pleasure, 169–170; reflective affirmation of, 288

Dalrymple, J., Earl of Stair, 225, 256, 315n6, 316n7, 319n1
Darwall, S., 314n10, 318n22
Darwin, C., 25, 26, 93, 99 298n19

Davie, W., 313n1

Deleuze, G., 298n16, 310n12

Deliberation, 153, 171

Demonstration, 78–79, 279, 302n7

Demosthenes, 211

Deontologists, 184–185, 271–272; and moral realism, 195

Descartes, R., and Cartesians, 3, 13, 16, 30, 33, 106, 116, 299n9, 302n8, 322n7

Desires, 153–173; instinctive, 155–156, 167

Desmaizeaux, P., 288

Determination, 73, 79–85

Dialectic, 2, 173, 248, 295n3

Dicaearchus, 205

Diderot, D., 293

Dilemma, prisoner's, 233–234, 247–248, 316n13

Dionysius of Syracuse, 271

Disguise: of variation of mind state, 124–125; of pleasure, 203; of sentiments, 228

Displeasure: in vice, 278

Dispute, 3, 236–237, 240

Doubt, 172. *See also* Scepticism

Drummond, C., 291

Dubos, J.-B., 180

Duration, 102

Duty, 169, 186, 232

Edmonds, J. M., 314n14

Education, 76

Elizabeth I of England, 322n4

Eloquence, 171

Emotion, 161, 164, 167, 180, 310n9; in the spirits, 168

Emotivism, 179–181, 191

Empiricism, 34

Envy, 146–147

Epictetus, 213, 223, 259

Equality, 260

Equity, 199, 217, 223, 259–261, 276; in property rights, 239

Error, 4, 153

Eucharist, 117

Evaluation: moral, 174, 179–182, 189–191, 193–196; of trustworthiness of persons, 244

Experience, 1, 66–77, 79

Experiment, 25

Expression, 17, 33–34, 162, 189, 218–219, 229–230; of passion, 136; of moral sentiments, 323n13

External objects. *See* Bodies

Falconer, K., 291. *See also* Home, K.

Falconer, W. A., 314n13

Falk, W. D., 309n1, 311n3

Fallibilism, 27

Fame. *See* Reputation

Fancy, 31. *See also* Imagination

Feeling, 20–27

Ferguson, A., 225

Fictions, 12, 102–103

Fidelity, 286; of printers, 87

Filmer, R., 256

Fixity: and looseness, 73. *See also* Determination

Flattery, 144–145

Flew, A., 92, 304n7, 310n1

Flux, 124–125

Fogelin, R., 54, 55, 56, 57, 58, 59, 60, 62, 65, 108, 295n1, 297nn9,15, 299n7, 301n4, 302nn14,15, 303nn18–22,24, 306nn3,4, 307n10, 309n1

Forbes, D., 269, 316n9, 320n14

Force, 29, 71

Foucault, M., 25

Franklin, B., 284

Fraud, 223

Free-riders, 247, 250, 253–254

French, P. A.: coauthor with T. E. Uehling, Jr., and H. K. Wettstein, 312n22

Freud, S., 25, 299n9, 300n11

Fried, C., 318n19

Friendship, 221–222, 228; threatened by contract, 247; and truth, 286–287

Gain, 259; love of, 221, 257–258. *See also* Self, interested affection of

Galbraith, A., 292

Gaskin, C. A., 300n13

Gauthier, D., 315nn3,4, 318n22, 319n26

Generation, love of. *See* Lust

Generosity, 199, 221, 251; of Caesar, 212; limits of, 221, 226

Gibbard, A., 311n14

Gift, 240–241, 251

Goodman, N., 301n3

Goodness, 181–182, 190, 201; of Caesar, 212–213; as distinct from greatness, 212–215

Government, 37–38; of colonies, 284. *See also* Magistrates

Greatness, 181–182, 190, 201, 210–211; of Cato, 212–213

Green, T. H., 180; and T. H. Grose, 311n8

Gregory, J., 291

Greig, J. Y. T., 310n5, 313n25, 314n12, 319n3, 322nn5,10

Grose, T. H., 311n8

Grotius, H., 220, 225, 226, 316n7

Grover, D. L.: coauthor with J. L. Camp, Jr., and N. D. Belnap, Jr., 303n17

Guilt, 311n14

Haakonssen, K., 316n9

Habit, 15, 79–86; imperfection of, 84; and government, 273. *See also* Custom

Hacking, I., 297n10, 304n2

Hampton, J., 253, 318nn20,25

Happiness, 187, 219. *See also* Pleasure

Hardin, R., 315n5, 317n15, 319n5

Harrington, J., 22, 267

Harrison, J., 316nn9,11

Hatred, 155–156; of those we have harmed, 149

Helvetius, G.-A., 293

Henry IV of France, 205, 321n17

Henry VIII of England, 190

Herodotus, 211

Hirschman, A. O., 315n1

Hobbes, T., 52, 80, 220, 222, 223, 225, 226, 228, 253, 256, 268, 271, 318nn24,25, 319n27, 320n7

Holbach, P. H., Baron de, 293

Holland, A. J., 308n3

Home, H., Lord Kames, 116, 283

Home, J., 184, 291

Home, K., 292. *See also* Falconer, K.

Hont, I.: and M. Ignatieff, 320n12

Hood, R., 282

Hooker, R., 256

Humility, 206, 215–216. *See also* Pride

Hurley, S. L., 295n2

Hutcheson, F., 22, 218, 225, 256, 313n25

Huxley, T. H., 298n19

Ideas: abstract and general, 31–32, 100; abstract, 38–39; confounding of, 42

Identity, 102–128, 114–115; of persons, 3, 122–127, 129–139, 140–143

Ignatieff, M., 320n12

Illusion, 8–20; sensory, 118–120

Imagination, 4, 7–15, 40, 283, 296n4; and inference, 72; and memory, 72; effect of, on passions, 171; role of, in fixing property rights, 237; failure of, 257–258; and right to rule, 272

Impenetrability. *See* Solidity

Imperfection. *See* Perfection

Impressions: of sense, 109; of reflexion, 160–161

Incest, 199, 224

Indoctrination, 76

Induction, 54–56, 62–69, 278; in *Enquiry*, 301n3

Inequity. *See* Equity

Inertia: of the mind, 113; mental, 124

Inference, 302n8; causal, 7–12, 53–77, 96–99, 106, 108–113

Influence, 81–82

Injustice, 223–224

Instincts: animal, 79; epistemic, 79, 97; human and animal, 94; social, 227

Integrity, 254, 259–260

Intellect, 1

Intellectualism, 3, 285

Intention, 154–157; and convention, 229–231; mutual adjustment of, 278

Interest, 205, 220–221, 234, 250, 313n4; common, 228–229; public, 241–243; and promises, 249; short-term and long-term, 255–256; and need for government, 257–258; of magistrates, 259; interested restraint of, 272

Interruption: in our observation of particular bodies, 113–121

Intimates, 33

Irwin, T., 315n2

James, W., 25

Jefferson, T., 320n9, 322n6

Jensen, R., 304n8

Johnson, S., 80, 302nn8,9, 311n4

Jones, P., 180, 181, 311nn10,11,12, 321n19

Judgment, 281–283; moral, 179–180,

216–217. *See also* Evaluation, moral
Justice, 176, 205, 220–254, 272, 275–276; retributive, 245, 254; and magistrates, 260–261; and judges, 265

Kames. *See* Home, H., Lord Kames
Kant, I., and Kantians, 7, 11, 12, 14, 50, 103, 111, 217, 279, 295n3, 306n6, 307n1
Kay, C., 312n15
Kemp Smith, N., 64, 165, 295n1, 296n6, 303n19, 305n12, 306n6, 310n11
Kerrigan, W., 309n2
King, J. T., 302n6, 318n21, 320n9, 321n1
Klibansky, R.: and E. C. Mossner, 296n8
Knowledge, 60, 63. *See also* Demonstration; Scepticism
Korsgaard, C., 313n26
Kuehn, M., 295n3
Kulstad, M. A., 305n14
Kydd, R. M., 309nn1,4

Laird, J., 203, 213, 295n1, 297n9, 314n6
Langland, W., 54
Language, 31–32, 100, 209, 229–231; of moral evaluation, 191, 193–194; of the scientist of human nature, 192–193; as used in promising, 244, 248–249; and reason, 282; and passions, 311n9
Law, W., 291
Law: Hume's study of, 225–226, 291; Scottish, 315n6; higher and lower, 320n13
Laws: moral, 195; of nature, 225, 245, 250
Leibniz, G., 83
Lentulus, P., 213
Lewis, D., 315n5
Liberty, 267, 271–272, 273, 276; of the will, 154–155; of the press, 276. *See also* Necessity
Life, 30; love of, 167, 224. *See also* Vivacity
Lind, M., 310n7
Liveliness. *See* Vivacity
Livingston, D., 31, 299n2, 320n9; and J. T. King, 302n6, 318n21, 320n9, 321n1
Loan, 240, 279
Locke, J., and Lockeans, 22, 29, 47, 48,

54, 76, 114, 117, 127, 221, 225, 226, 237, 252, 253, 256, 257, 262, 266, 273, 299nn1,4,5, 302n8, 304n26, 319n2
Loeb, L., 303n15
Looseness, 81
Love, 130, 139–140; parental, 47, 184, 199, 214–215; causes of, 146–147; of those we have benefited, 149; of gain, 176; for the virtuous, 185
Lucretius, 316n10
Lust, 140; as original principle of human society, 227

MacIntyre, A., 203, 309n1, 310nn7,2, 314n5, 315n6
McIntyre, J. L., 306n10, 307n2
Mackie, J. L., 178, 179, 309nn1,4, 311nn6,9, 312n22, 313nn23,24, 316n9, 321n20
Macpherson, C. B., 318n24, 319n2, 320n7
Madison, J., 320nn9,11
Magistrates, 245, 255–273; as punishers, 155–156
Magri, T., 321n2
Maher, P., 304n2, 308n5
Malebranche, N., 299n8, 300n11
Malherbe, M., 308n3
Malice, 146–147
Mandeville, B., de, 225, 274
Marriage, 300n13; tyranny in, 257
Memory, 1, 46–47; value of, 280
Men, 300n13; and chastity, 273–275
Mercer, P., 308n14
Merrill, K. R.: and R. W. Shahan, 307n3, 313n1
Metaphysics, 22–23
Michaud, Y., 301n2, 305n13
Miller, D., 258, 273, 320n6, 321n18, 322n3
Miller, M., 292
Mirroring: of minds in each other, 136
Monteiro, J.-P., 298n19
Morality, 169; its content, 184–185; its form, 184–185; its motivating power, 184–188; its source, 184–185; puritan, 203, 205–206, 215–218; religious, 215–219
Morice, G. P., 311n5
Mossner, E., 226, 296n8, 298n16, 308n7

Motivation, 152–173; natural, moral
    approval of, 191
Motives. *See* Motivation
Murder, 199, 221, 224
Music, 170, 190

Nagel, T., 310n10, 311n13
Name. *See* Reputation
Names. *See* Language
Naturalism, 28, 65–67
Nature, 90, 93, 97–98, 108; uniformity
    of, 62–68; and artifice, 175–176; state
    of, 235–236. *See also* Laws, of nature
Necessity, 7–8, 78–100, 88–92, 154–156;
    causal, 78; normative, 78;
    psychological, 78; logical and
    mathematical, 78–79; and liberty, 81–
    82; logical, 100; imposed by natural
    appetites, 227–228
Negation, 82
Nero, 164, 271
Newton, I., 13, 25
Nicole, P., 57, 302n11
Nidditch, P. H., 299n1
Nietzsche, F., 320n8
Noon, J., 292
Normativity: as reflexivity, 99–100
Norms, 16, 57, 177. *See also* Rules
Norton, D. F., 309n4, 312nn21,22,
    316n7; coauthor with N. Capaldi and
    W. L. Robison, 298n19
Noxon, J., 298n20

Obedience, 256–257; and allegiance, 273;
    and reason, 278; to fathers, 319n1; to
    parents, 319n2
Objects, 116–119; external, 3; of
    thought, 125; of passions, 131–133,
    161–163
Obligations, 195, 232; natural and moral,
    241–243
Obliqueness: in workings of causal
    inference, 11
Oedipus, 164
Orde, N., 293
Orthodoxy, 18, 21

Palulak, M., 304n6
Parasites, 253, 259. *See also* Free-riders

Parenthood, 30, 221–224, 228. *See also*
    Love, parental
Parfit, D., 307n11, 318n20
Parricide, 199, 224
Passions, 1, 20–27, 34–37, 39–45, 220;
    circle of, 39; and time, 48–51;
    coherence of, 109–110; direct and
    indirect, 133–135; amorous, 139–140,
    205; as cause of action, 159–165; calm
    and violent, 167–171; strength of, 168–
    171; violent and calm, 258; and reason,
    279–280; reflective affirmation of, 288;
    and their parts, 303n9
Passmore, J., 60, 298n1, 299n6, 303n16,
    304n4, 306n10
Patten, S. C., 306n10
Peace, 276
Pears, D., 306n10
Penalty, 232–234, 251–254; for promise-
    breaking, 244–247, 249–250; for
    disobedience to magistrates, 263
Penelhum, T., 295n1, 305n2, 306n3,
    307n3
Perception, 80, 115–119; scepticism
    concerning, 300n10
Perfection: of habit, 83–86; of causes, 174
Persons, 4, 33, 47–53, 102–105
Philip of Macedon, 211
Philip II of Spain, 271
Phillipson, N., 316n9
Philosophers: as lovers of wisdom, 14–
    15; and non-philosophers, 24–25;
    reformed, 26–27; inventive, 277
Philosophy, 1–2; carefree, 1–2, alteration
    in, 2; obsessive theorizing in, 2;
    modern, 5, 115, 117, 194; saved by
    unphilosophical probability, 58, 87;
    moral, 157; genius of, 283. *See also*
    Philosophers
Physical objects. *See* Bodies
Plato, 132, 220
Pleasure, 36–37; and desire, 163; passive,
    169–170; active, 169–170, 173; in good
    character, 175, 181, 199–202;
    reflexivity of, 196; as a good, 203–205
Point of view: moral, 149, 177–179, 182–
    183, 190–193, 216–219, 241–243; of
    spectator to action, 152–155; general,
    178, 183, 190–192; of the scientist of
    human nature, 192–193

Polybius, 205
Postema, G. J., 316n9, 319n26
Power, 224; increase of, 227, 253; division of, 283
Prejudices, 86
Price, H. H., 303n19, 306n3
Pride, 36, 129–132, 161, 300n14; in virtue, 185; as a virtue, 203, 206–210
Pringle, J., 291
Probability, 10–12, 61, 278; as contrasted with knowledge, 60–65; in narrow sense, 63, 82–88, 132; unphilosophical, 86–88
Projection: of inertial thought onto the thought-about, 125
Projectivism: in ethics, 194–195
Promise, 240, 243–248; trust in, 258; and obedience to magistrates, 263; and alliances between states, 275; and allegiance, 278; and obedience, 279
Property, 221–224, 228–229, 248; rules for determining, 236–239; transfer of, 239–241, 243, 251–252; as insensible, 241; and war over territory, 275
Pufendorf, S., 225, 226, 256, 274, 316n7
Punishment, 154–156, 199, 214, 258; reform of, 187

Qualities, primary and secondary, 5, 109, 115, 119; mind-dependence of, 110; compared with virtues, 194
Quine, W. V. O., 304n6

Ramsay, M., 298n16
Raphael, D. D., 311n3
Rationalism, 2, 59, 87, 96; in ethics, 165, 176–177, 184–185; Hume's case against, 175–177
Realism: moral, 194–195
Reason, 8–15, 60–61, 79, 172, 258, 264, 277–278, 279–280, 282–283, 284–288; influence of, on action, 157–160; no combat with passion, 158–159; and action, 164–167; animal, 278; and motivation, 309n4; and artifice, 321n2
Rebellion, 261, 264–267, 269–272, 276, 320n10
Reference: of passions, 161–164
Reflection, 2, 55, 105–106, 173, 196–197,

277, 284–288; impressions of, 44. *See also* Reflexivity
Reflexion, 30. *See also* reflection
Reflexivity, 88–89, 91, 97–100, 134, 215–218; in convention, 243–244; of promise and contract, 263–264
Reid, T., 179, 180, 311n7
Relations: philosophical, 28; natural, 28, 48; social, 29; of blood, 29, 47–49, 140–141, 144–145; double, of impressions and ideas, 37, 39; dependent versus independent, 40; double sense of term, 47–49, 71. *See also* Space; Time
Religion, 23, 296n8; mummeries of, 69; celebrated argument against, 87; Christian, 215, 226–227, 241; ceremonies of, 246
Rents, 117
Repetition, 66–76. *See also* Experience
Representation, 46–47, 118
Republic: identity of, 126
Reputation, 139, 209–210; for trustworthiness, 244–245, 257
Resemblance: of passions, 39–45; of cause and effect, 73–74
Resentment, 238, 254
Resistance: right to, 265–272. *See also* Rebellion
Revenge, 155–156
Reward, 185. *See also* Punishment
Rights, 176–177
Robertson, J., 309n1, 320n12
Robison, W. L., 298n19, 302n6, 305n12, 306n10
Rolfe, J. C., 314n9
Rorty, A. O., 307n3
Rorty, R., 309n2
Rosenberg, A., 301n5, 303n19, 304nn25,5,6,7
Rousseau, J.-J., 52, 182, 183, 220, 222, 226, 230, 253, 293, 316n10
Rules, 15, 17; of causal inference, 56–59, 71–72; moral, 184–185; their limited usefulness, 281–282; for causal inference, 302n15

St. Clair, J., Lieutenant General, 293
Sallust, 212, 314n9
Salmon, W., 304n2

Scepticism, 57–59, 287, 297nn12,14,15, 298n17, 302n12; of reason, 87; of the senses, 100–122; concerning induction, 301n3

Schiffer, S., 300n10

Science, 13; of psychology, 25; of human nature, 25–26, 83

Science of man. *See* Science, of human nature

Scott, W., 291, 319n1

Seconding: of value judgements, 134, 143–145, 209–210

Security, 222–223; increase of, 227; in exchanges, 249

Self, 122; vivacity of idea of, 143; interested affection of, 178, 220–225, 259–260

Self-interest. *See* Interest; Self, interested affection of

Sellar, W. D. H., 315n6

Sen, A. K., 317n13

Sentiment, 1, 20–27, 33; moral, 134–135, 164, 179–182, 190–196; calmness of, 184; flexibility of, 200. *See also* Passions

Serenity, 189, 211

Sex, fair, 170

Shahan, R. W., 307n3, 313n1

Shaver, R., 317n14

Siebert, D. T., 314n11

Simplicity, 34–39; of the self, 114–115

Smith, A., 225, 294

Smith, J. H.: and W. Kerrigan, 309n2

Smith, S., 298n19

Sobel, H., 248, 298n19, 316n9, 318nn20,22

Socrates, 211

Solidity, 5, 115

Solipsism, 3, 32, 114, 141

Solipsists. *See* Solipsism

Solitude, 19, 284. *See also* Solipsism

Space, 49–51; location in, 35

Spenser, E., 211

Spinoza, B., 203

Spirits, animal, 108, 299n8

Stair, Earl of. *See* Dalrymple, J.

Stevenson, R. L., 312n19

Stewart, D., 225

Stewart, J. B., 313n2

Stewart, R., 291

Stich, S., 300n10

Stough, C. L., 300n12

Strabo, 314n15

Strawson, G., 300n1, 301n5

Strength, 206; of mind, 218

Strength of will. *See* Strength, of mind

Stroud, B., 295n1, 300n1, 306nn3,9, 307n10, 309nn1,3

Stupidity, 164, 214

Sturgeon, N., 301n4, 308n1

Substances: ideas of, 127–128

Sympathy, 143, 146–151, 166, 196, 217, 221, 250–251, 278, 279; of parts to their common end, 102; correction of, 179, 181–182; with public interest, 241–243

System: of memories and beliefs, 72; Hume's, 87–88; vulgar versus philosophical, 115–121

Tacitus, 211

Tat. *See* Tit

Taylor, C., 295n2

Temper, 204, 214

Testimony, 3, 283

Themistocles, 170

Theology, 87, 90

Theophrastus, 188, 193, 218, 219, 314nn14,15

Theorizing, 2

Threat, 247, 249; of law enforcement, 257–258

Thucydides, 211

Ties. *See* Relations

Time, 31, 48–51

Tit: for tat, 233–234, 247

Todd, W. B., 311n3

Trust, 228, 244, 249; in testimony, 87, 119; and distrust, 244–250; breakdown of, 258

Truth, 12, 22, 26–27, 62; love of, 172–173, 279–280, 285; as a virtue, 280, 286–287; and trust, 285–287

Tyranny, 276, 284; and right to resist, 270–272

Uehling, T. E., Jr., 313n22

Ullmann-Margalit, E., 316nn13,15, 318n20

Uncertainty, 83
Understanding, 8–9; limits of, 137
Union: completion of, 73; of attributes in a substance, 127
Utilitarianism, 250, 251
Utility, 198–199, 204–205, 221, 237, 250; of truths, 172

Vacillation, 107–108
Vallentyne, P., 318n25
Van Aken, J., 304n8
Veracity, 286
Vices. *See* Virtues
Vigour, 71, 200
Vinnius, 225, 316n7
Violence: causes of, in passions, 167–169; in desire for truth, 172–173
Virtues, 109, 188–195; natural versus artificial, 176–179; and vices, 195; natural, 198–219; expressive, 201–202, 218–219; puritan, 202–205; Christian, 203, 214; monkish, 207, 215–219; as abilities, 214. *See also* Artifice
Vivacity, 4, 29, 65, 88; communication of, 69–76; communication of, in sympathy, 143

Vocabulary. *See* Language
Voet, 225, 316n7
Von Gizcki, G., 298n19

Waldron, J., 315n5
Walker, D. M., 315n6
Walton, C., 320n9
War, 210–212, 223–224, 240, 275–276. *See also* Armies
Warburton, Rev. W., 13
Weakness: of mind, 165–166
Wettstein, H. K., 313n22
Whelan, F. G., 316n9, 320nn9,15,16
Wilbanks, J., 296n4
Will, 152–153; general, 183
Wilson, F., 307n10
Wit, 217
Wittgenstein, L., 2, 14, 295n2, 297n13
Wolf, R. P., 306n10
Wolin, S. S., 318n21
Women, 300n13; and property rights, 238; special obligations of, 273–275. *See also* Sex, fair
Wright, J. P., 299n8, 302n11, 306nn3,5

Yalden-Thomson, D. C., 320n9